Illustrated
Turbo C++

Wally Wang

and

Kenneth Bibb

Wordware Publishing, Inc.

Library of Congress Cataloging-in-Publication Data

Wang, Wally.
    Illustrated Turbo C++ / by Wally Wang and Kenneth Bibb.
       p.   cm.
  ISBN 1-55622-190-8
    1. C++ (Computer program language)   2. Turbo C++ (Computer program)
I. Bibb, Kenneth. II. Title.
QA76.73.C153W36   1990
005.265—dc20   90-12976
                                            CIP

Copyright © 1991, Wordware Publishing, Inc.

All Rights Reserved

1506 Capital Avenue
Plano, Texas 75074

No part of this book may be reproduced in any form or by any means
without permission in writing from Wordware Publishing, Inc.

Printed in the United States of America

ISBN 1-55622-190-8
10 9 8 7 6 5 4 3 2 1
9101

IBM, PC-DOS, and PC/XT are registered trademarks of International Business Machines Corporation.
MS DOS is a registered trademark of Microsoft Corporation.
Pascal and Turbo C++ are trademarks of Borland International.

All inquiries for volume purchases of this book should be addressed to Wordware Publishing, Inc., at the above address. Telephone inquiries may be made by calling:

(214) 423-0090

Contents

Module	Title	Page
1	About This Book	1
2	Turbo C Overview	6
3	A Sample Session with Turbo C	10

Turbo C++ Integrated Development Environment Menu Commands

Module	Title	Page
4	Compile Menu	16
5	Debug Menu	20
6	Edit Menu	27
7	File Menu	32
8	Help Menu	36
9	Options Menu	40
10	Project Menu	45
11	Run Menu	50
12	Search Menu	53
13	System Menu	58
14	Window Menu	60

Turbo C++ Language Commands

Module	Title	Page
15	# stringizing operator	67
16	## token pasting operator	69
17	#define and #undef	71
18	#error	75
19	#if, #elif, #else, #endif	77
20	#ifdef and #ifndef	81
21	#include	84
22	#line	88
23	#pragma	90
24	Advanced Data Types	96
25	Arithmetic Operators	102
26	Assembly Language	106
27	Assignment Operators	108
28	Basic Data Types	111
29	Break	116
30	Byte Operators	119
31	Class Operators	123
32	Classes	126
33	Comments	131
34	Continue	135
35	Do-while	138
36	For	140
37	Function Definition	143
38	Goto	149
39	Identifiers	154

Contents (Cont.)

Module	Title	Page
40	If-else	157
41	Inheritance	160
42	Logic Operators	163
43	Memory Models	169
44	Miscellaneous Operators	174
45	Overloading	179
46	Pointer Operators	182
47	printf( ) and scanf( )	187
48	References	193
49	Storage Class Specifiers	196
50	Streams	202
51	Switch	206
52	While	209

Turbo C++ Routines

Module	Title	Page
53	Classification Routines	211
54	Conversion Routines	214
55	Diagnostic Routines	221
56	Directory Control Routines	225
57	Graphics Routines	231
58	Input/Output Routines	255
59	Interface Routines	280
60	Manipulation Routines	299
61	Math Routines	303
62	Memory Allocation and Checking Routines	316
63	Miscellaneous Routines	325
64	Process Control Routines	329
65	Standard Routines	339
66	String Routines	344
67	Text Window Display Routines	355
68	Time and Date Routines	362
69	Variable Argument List Routines	370

Appendix A	Turbo C++ Function Key Commands	373
Appendix B	Using the Turbo C++ Command-Line Compiler	375
Appendix C	Customizing Turbo C++	379
Appendix D	ASCII Table	385
Appendix E	Operator Precedence Table	389
Appendix F	Keyboard Scan Code Table	391
Appendix G	Extended Key Code Table	393
Appendix H	Turbo C++ Exercises	395
Index		405

Recommended Learning Sequence

Sequence	Title	Module	Page
1	About This Book	1	1
2	Turbo C++ Overview	2	6
3	A Sample Session with Turbo C++	3	10
4	System Menu	13	58
5	File Menu	7	32
6	Edit Menu	6	27
7	Help Menu	8	36
8	Run Menu	11	50
9	Debug Menu	5	20
10	Search Menu	12	53
11	Window Menu	14	60
12	Options Menu	9	40
13	Compile Menu	4	16
14	Project Menu	10	45
15	Identifiers	39	154
16	Basic Data Types	28	111
17	printf( ) and scanf( )	47	187
18	#include	21	84
19	#define and #undef	17	71
20	#ifdef and #ifndef	20	81
21	Comments	33	131
22	Arithmetic Operators	25	102
23	Logic Operators	42	163
24	Byte Operators	30	119
25	Assignment Operators	27	108
26	While	52	209
27	Break	29	116
28	Continue	34	135
29	Do-while	35	138
30	For	36	140
31	If-else	40	157
32	Goto	38	149
33	Switch	51	206
34	Function Definition	37	143
35	Advanced Data Types	24	96
36	Pointer Operators	46	182
37	Streams	50	202

Recommended Learning Sequence (Cont.)

Sequence	Title	Module	Page
38	Storage Class Specifier	49	196
39	Miscellaneous Operators	44	179
40	References	48	193
41	Classes	32	126
42	Class Operators	31	123
43	Inheritance	41	160
44	Overloading	45	179
45	#if, #elif, #else, #endif	19	77
46	#error	18	75
47	#line	22	88
48	#pragma	23	90
49	# stringizing Operator	15	67
50	## token Pasting Operator	16	69
51	Classification Routines	53	211
52	Conversion Routines	54	214
53	Directory Control Routines	56	225
54	Diagnostic Routines	55	221
55	Graphics Routines	57	231
56	Input/Output Routines	58	255
57	Interface Routines	59	280
58	Manipulation Routines	60	299
59	Math Routines	61	303
60	Memory Allocation and Checking Routines	62	316
61	Miscellaneous Routines	63	325
62	Process Control Routines	64	329
63	Standard Routines	65	339
64	String Routines	66	344
65	Text Window Display Routines	67	355
66	Time and Date Routines	68	362
67	Variable Argument List Routines	69	370
68	Memory Models	43	169
69	Assembly Language	26	106

Module 1
ABOUT THIS BOOK

INTRODUCTION

This book describes how to program an IBM PC/XT/AT/386 computer or compatible using Borland International's Turbo C++ compiler. You will find Turbo C++ fast, easy, and powerful for any type of programming. Whether you are a beginner or an experienced programmer in any language, Turbo C++ can be versatile enough for any programming task.

Turbo C++ comes with four manuals describing its many program features. Since four manuals of information can be difficult to understand and use, *Illustrated Turbo C++* organizes this information into logical topics, such as graphics or data structures. While the Turbo C++ manuals explain what the Turbo C++ commands do, this book explains how and why to use them.

Illustrated Turbo C++ can appeal to a wide range of programmers. Beginners can use this book to learn about C programming using Turbo C++. More advanced programmers can use this book as a quick reference to specific Turbo C++ commands. Classroom instructors can use this book as a textbook for learning C++ programming in Turbo C++.

Turbo C++ contains many complex features that may intimidate inexperienced computer users or programmers unfamiliar with the C++ language. Don't worry. The recommended learning sequence will not only show you how to use Turbo C++, but will also show you how to create several small but useful programs using various Turbo C++ commands.

Since Turbo C++ contains over 400 different commands, this book only explains how to use the most common commands. Once you have mastered these commonly used Turbo C++ commands, you will be able to understand the more advanced Turbo C++ commands by reading the Turbo C++ manuals.

To get you started with Turbo C++, the sample session in Module 3 explains the steps for creating, editing, debugging, and compiling a complete Turbo C++ program. You can experiment with this sample program, and when you're ready, you can begin the recommended learning sequence.

Whether you're already familiar with C++ or another computer language, such as Pascal or BASIC, or just starting to learn a programming language for the first time, you will find Turbo C++ the perfect language to use and *Illustrated Turbo C++* the perfect book to help you learn Turbo C++.

WHY LEARN C?

Although you can choose from a variety of different programming languages, such as Pascal, BASIC, or FORTRAN, the C language continues to gain popularity because of its speed and power.

C has often been called "the portable assembler" because programs written in C run nearly as fast as programs written in assembly language. Because you can find a C compiler for nearly every computer, any program written in C can be run on any other computer with little or no modification.

For example, Lotus Development rewrote their famous Lotus 1-2-3 spreadsheet from assembly language to C. By doing this, Lotus could quickly develop versions of Lotus 1-2-3 that run on other computers besides the IBM PC.

By learning C, you will gain skill in a powerful programming language. Many companies develop programs in C, so your knowledge of the C language can translate into job opportunities for the future.

Since the C language has been used to develop everything from complete operating systems (similar to MS-DOS) to word processors, spreadsheets, and databases, you can use C to develop or modify your own applications.

No matter what your motives may be for learning C, you will find C popular, widespread, and powerful. By using Turbo C++, you will be using one of the most powerful C++ compilers available for the IBM PC.

But how did C become so popular in the first place? Like Pascal and BASIC, the C language began long before personal computers were available.

HISTORY OF C

The C language appeared in the early 1970s, about the same time as the UNIX operating system. When Kenneth Thompson designed the UNIX operating system, he also developed an experimental language called B.

Kenneth Thompson originally wrote the UNIX operating system in assembly language. When Kenneth Thompson and another programmer, Dennis Ritchie, created an advanced version of the B programming language, they called C, they decided to rewrite UNIX using the C language instead.

Thus the popularity of the UNIX operating system parallels the popularity of the C language. To provide the C language with more powerful object-oriented features, Bjarne Stroustrup of Bell Laboratories developed an extension to the C language that he called C++.

Originally, C++ was a preprocessor that converted object-oriented C++ code into normal C code which a C compiler would compile. Unlike other implementations of C++, Turbo C++ compiles code directly to machine code.

The C++ language offers object-oriented programming features. Essentially object-oriented programming makes writing programs easier. To do this, object-oriented programming offers three main features: encapsulation, inheritance, and polymorphism.

Encapsulation means you organize a program into logical parts, known as objects. Each object contains its own data and instructions for manipulating its data. By dividing a program into objects, you can better understand how each part works.

Inheritance lets you create new objects based on previously defined ones. Essentially, this means you can reuse large portions of an existing program and modify it to create an entirely new program.

Polymorphism means that you can manipulate different objects using the same command. This feature lets you concentrate on what you want your program to do and less on how to get it to work.

Although the idea of object-oriented programming has been around for years, C++ represents the latest implementation of the C programming language. Where early versions of C emphasized speed and portability between different computers, the latest versions of C also emphasize the ability to write complicated programs quickly and easily.

If you want to program different computers, C should be one of the first languages to learn. If you just want to program a computer as a hobby, learning the C language can be helpful because so many other people also program in C. By learning C, you can share tips with other programmers through the many books and magazines devoted to the C language. With the enhancement of C++, you can write powerful, complicated programs.

ADVANTAGES AND DISADVANTAGES OF C

Like all languages, the C language offers various advantages and disadvantages. Some of the main advantages include portability, efficiency, and flexibility.

Portability means you can write programs in C and run these same programs on other computers. For example, if you wrote a program in C using an IBM computer, you could copy the same program to a Cray, DEC, or Sun Workstation and the program should run with little or no modification.

Efficiency means that C programs translate into machine code much more efficiently than competing languages like Pascal or BASIC. As a result, programs written in C tend to run faster and be smaller than similar programs written in other languages.

Module 1

Flexibility means that the C language provides few restrictions, letting you perform different programming tricks not possible in other high-level languages like BASIC or Pascal.

Of course, C also has several disadvantages. The most common problem is that C was designed to be as sparse as possible. Thus C programs may tend to look cryptic and confusing.

Because C programs can be difficult to understand, they can be hard to modify as well. What's more, because C imposes few restrictions, bugs (errors) are much more likely to bury themselves in a C program than in other languages.

Despite these drawbacks, C continues to grow in popularity due in part to low-cost and powerful compilers such as Turbo C++.

ORGANIZATION

We organized *Illustrated Turbo C++* into small, easy-to-read modules to help readers learn the basics to writing C++ programs using Turbo C++. Each module lists several related commands together under headings, such as Graphics or Classification routines.

If you are learning to write C++ programs for the first time, the Recommended Learning Sequence lists modules from simple to complex. By following the Recommended Learning Sequence, you will learn to write your own Turbo C++ programs.

This module describes how to use this book, its organization, and its contents. Module 2 briefly describes the features of the Turbo C++ compiler.

Module 3 shows how to write, edit, debug, and compile a complete Turbo C++ program.

Modules 4 through 14 explain the different Turbo C++ integrated environment commands from loading a file to compiling a program and modifying the way the Programmer's Platform looks and works.

Modules 15 through 69 describe the different Turbo C++ commands as well as providing actual program examples. Each module describes what a particular command does, why you would use it, and how the command works.

Appendix A lists the commands assigned to each function key in the Turbo C integrated environment.

Appendix B explains how to use the Turbo C++ command-line compiler. The command-line compiler differs from the Turbo C++ integrated environment in that the command-line compiler does not provide an editor or debugging capabilities.

Appendix C explains how to customize the Turbo C++ integrated environment to your liking including colors, window size, and default directories.

Appendix D contains a more detailed and organized ASCII table than that provided by the Turbo C++ manuals.

Appendix E lists the operator precedence table.

Appendix F lists keyboard scan codes.

Appendix G lists the extended key codes.

Appendix H contains exercises for tracking your progress with Turbo C++. If you are learning by yourself, you can use these exercises to test what you've learned from each module. If you are a classroom instructor, you can use these exercises for student assignments. When you can answer the questions in each module, you are ready to move to the next module in the Recommended Learning Sequence.

HARDWARE REQUIREMENTS

Turbo C++ requires an IBM PC/XT/AT, PS/2, or compatible computer running DOS 2.0 or higher and at least 640K RAM. You must have at least one hard disk drive and one floppy drive to use Turbo C++.

Turbo C++ includes routines for using an 8087, 80287, or 80387 math co-processor. If your computer does not have a math co-processor, Turbo C++ contains emulation routines to make up for its absence. While not necessary, a math co-processor can make your Turbo C++ programs run faster, especially if they use numerical calculations extensively.

Other optional items include a mouse, such as the Microsoft or Logitech mouse, a color monitor, and a printer. Since programs may behave differently with other computer configurations, the following shows the equipment and software we used to write and test the program examples provided in this book:

Turbo C++ Version 1.0

Northgate 386/16	IBM PC/XT
MS-DOS 4.01	MS-DOS 3.30
65Mb hard disk	40Mb hard disk
VGA graphics monitor	EGA graphics monitor
Logitech mouse	Microsoft mouse
Panasonic 1080i	Epson FX-85

Leading Edge Model D/LT386SX
MS-DOS 3.30
40Mb hard disk
VGA graphics monitor

Module 2
PROGRAM OVERVIEW

INTRODUCTION

Turbo C++ is Borland International's latest C compiler. Turbo C++ includes an integrated editor, compiler, and debugger so you can write, compile, and test programs quickly and easily.

In addition, Turbo C++ supports multiple windows editing, mouse support, a hypertext help system, and the Borland Virtual Run-time Object-Oriented Memory Manager (VROOMM) that lets you run large programs in a limited amount of memory.

Multiple windows let you edit two or more programs at once or edit separate parts of the same program. Mouse support lets you quickly manipulate windows and select menu commands and text more conveniently than with the keyboard.

The hypertext help system helps you find information for any topic so you don't have to look through the Turbo C++ manuals. Because the hypertext help system includes program examples for each Turbo C++ function, you can copy these examples and use them in your own programs.

The VROOMM overlay portion of Turbo C++ lets you write programs that would normally be too big to fit into memory. But by using VROOMM, Turbo C++ lets you divide your program into segments. At any given time, only those segments necessary are stored in memory; the remaining program segments remain stored on disk. If this sounds confusing, don't worry. The Turbo C++ VROOMM features work automatically to make your programs run faster.

Turbo C++ offers something for everyone. If you want to learn C++ for the first time, program in C++ using Turbo C++'s speed, or use a fast C++ compiler, then Turbo C++ can meet all your needs.

USING TURBO C++ WITH A MOUSE AND A KEYBOARD

If you have a Microsoft, Logitech, IBM, or compatible mouse, you can use your mouse instead of the keyboard to choose commands from the Turbo C++ Programmer's Platform. The three most common ways to use a mouse include clicking, double-clicking, and dragging.

Clicking means pressing the mouse button once and releasing it. You can use clicking to highlight an item that appears on the screen.

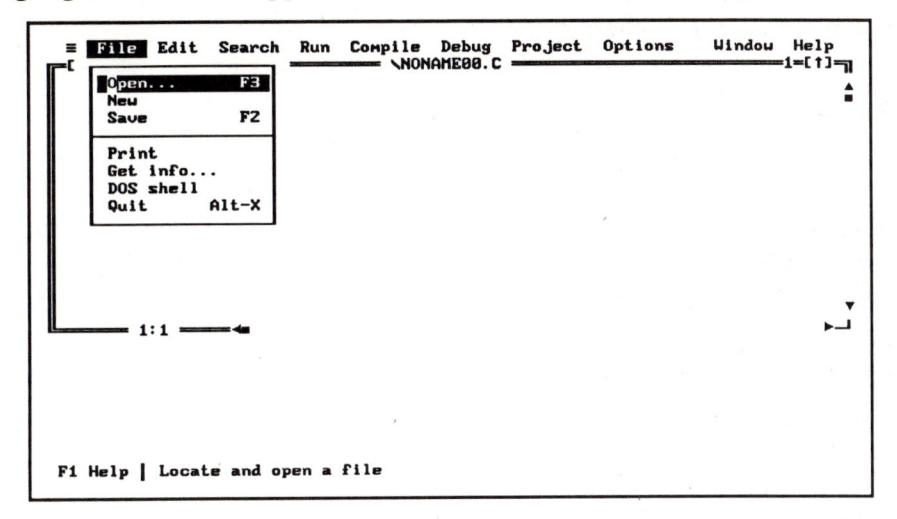

```
  ≡ File  Edit  Search  Run  Compile  Debug  Project  Options    Window  Help
┌─[ ─────────────────────── \NONAME00.C ═══════════════════════1=[↑]─┐
│ ┌──────────────┐                                                ▲ │
│ │ Open...   F3 │                                                ■ │
│ │ New          │                                                  │
│ │ Save      F2 │                                                  │
│ ├──────────────┤                                                  │
│ │ Print        │                                                  │
│ │ Get info...  │                                                  │
│ │ DOS shell    │                                                  │
│ │ Quit   Alt-X │                                                  │
│ └──────────────┘                                                  │
│                                                                   │
│                                                                 ▼ │
│══ 1:1 ══◀                                                       ►┘│
│                                                                   │
│ F1 Help │ Locate and open a file                                  │
└───────────────────────────────────────────────────────────────────┘
```

Double-clicking means pressing the mouse button twice in rapid succession. You can use double-clicking to highlight and choose a command or file.

Dragging means holding down the mouse button, moving the mouse, and releasing the mouse button. You can use dragging to highlight blocks of text for copying or deleting.

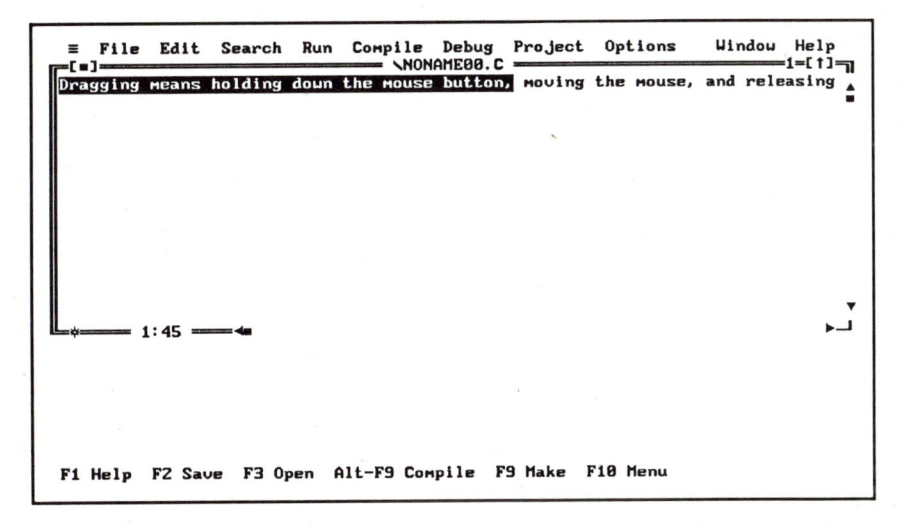

```
  ≡  File  Edit  Search  Run  Compile  Debug  Project  Options    Window  Help
┌─[■]═══════════════════════ \NONAME00.C ═══════════════════════1=[↑]─┐
│ Dragging means holding down the mouse button, moving the mouse, and releasing ▲│
│                                                                              ■ │
│                                                                                │
│                                                                                │
│                                                                                │
│                                                                                │
│                                                                              ▼ │
│─◆── 1:45 ══◀                                                                ►┘ │
│                                                                                │
│ F1 Help  F2 Save  F3 Open  Alt-F9 Compile  F9 Make  F10 Menu                   │
└────────────────────────────────────────────────────────────────────────────────┘
```

INSTALLING TURBO C++

Turbo C++ comes with an automatic installation program called INSTALL. To run the INSTALL program, follow these steps:

1. Insert Disk #1 of Turbo C++ in drive A of your computer.
2. Type **A:INSTALL** and press **Return**. Turbo C++ displays a welcome screen.
3. Press **Return**. Turbo C++ displays a message, asking you from which drive you will be installing Turbo C++. The default is A:\.
4. Press **Return** to accept the default drive. Another installation screen appears. The default drive and directory to install Turbo C++ is in a directory called TC.
5. Press the **Up/Down** arrow keys to highlight an option that you want to change. Otherwise, highlight **Start installation** and press **Return**.
6. Press **Return** after highlighting an option that you want to change.
7. Type the new directory where you want to store the Turbo C++ files and press **Return**.
8. Press **F9** to begin the installation, or highlight **Start installation** and press **Return**.

UNDERSTANDING THE TURBO C++ INTEGRATED ENVIRONMENT

The Turbo C++ integrated environment consists of a menu bar, windows, dialog boxes, and a status line. The menu bar contains commands organized into pull-down menus. You have three ways to display a pull-down menu:

- Click on the pull-down menu name with the mouse.
- Press F10 to highlight a pull-down menu. Use the arrow keys to highlight a specific menu category, or type the letter of the menu category you want to pull down. For example, to display the File menu, press F10 and then type F.
- Press Alt and press the highlighted letter of the menu name. For example, to display the File menu, press Alt and F.

The Turbo C++ integrated environment lets you display multiple windows on the screen. The four types of windows you can display are the editor window, the message window, the watch window, and the help window.

The editor window lets you write and edit your Turbo C++ programs. Turbo C++ lets you display two or more files in separate windows at the same time or display two or more parts of the same file in different windows. When you display the same file in separate windows, any changes you make in one window automatically changes the file displayed in other windows.

By using the Turbo C++ editor, you can quickly write programs and run them to see if they work. If you type a command wrong, the IDE will highlight the line containing the error. Once you have fixed the error, you can try running your program again.

Turbo C++ uses the message window to display error messages when you try to run your program. Scrolling through the error messages displayed in the message window lets Turbo C++ show you exactly which lines may be preventing your program from working.

You use the watch window to see how the values of any program variables change while the program runs. By watching how your program assigns different values to your variables, you can find how and where your program might be failing.

The help window lets you get additional information about different Turbo C++ commands. If you are learning to program in the C++ language, you can use the hypertext help system provided by the IDE. Pressing F1 lists the different Turbo C++ program commands and explains how to use them with actual program examples. By copying these examples, you can learn to write a C++ program with fewer chances of making mistakes.

Once you get your program to run, you still have to make sure it works correctly. Often you can write a program that seems to work perfectly, except when the user types the wrong key.

To prevent this from happening, the Turbo C++ integrated environment includes a debugger that lets you see how each line of your program works. By examining every line in your program, you can find the exact line that doesn't work.

If you're just getting started programming in C or using Turbo C++, you can selectively hide the more advanced features from the menus. That way you can concentrate on seeing only the commands you will likely use the most. Once you become familiar with Turbo C++, you can display the advanced commands on the pull-down menus.

Once you understand the parts of the Turbo C++ integrated environment and how to use it, you're ready to start writing your first Turbo C++ program.

Module 3
A SAMPLE SESSION WITH TURBO C++

INTRODUCTION

This module shows you how to write, compile, and debug a complete Turbo C++ program. In addition, this module also shows the typical structure of a C program.

The example program in this module is fairly simple but lets you experiment with some of the more commonly used Turbo C++ language commands. In the process, you also use the Turbo C++ integrated environment to create, edit, compile, and debug your Turbo C++ program.

THE TURBO C++ INTEGRATED ENVIRONMENT

The Turbo C++ integrated environment provides an editor, compiler, and debugger. The editor lets you create or modify your programs. The compiler converts your program into instructions that your computer can understand. The debugger helps you identify the parts of your program that don't work right.

The integrated environment consists of three parts:
- Windows
- Pull-down menus
- Status line

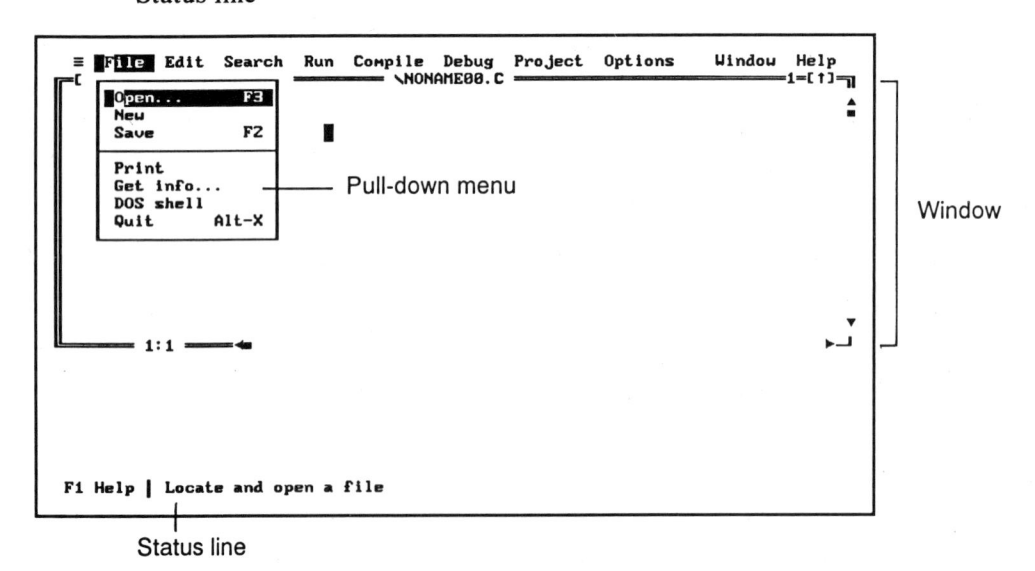

Windows let Turbo C++ display information on the screen. The pull-down menu provides commands for manipulating your programs. The status line shows your options.

WRITING PROGRAMS IN C

All C programs consist of one or more functions. Functions divide a program into parts. Think of functions as building blocks. Dividing a program into separate functions or parts offers two key advantages:

First, since programs rarely work correctly the first time you run them, dividing a program into parts lets you quickly isolate the part that doesn't work. This process of identifying which part of your program doesn't work is called "debugging."

Second, once the parts of your program work correctly, you can reuse these parts in other programs. In this way, you can create a collection or "library" of functions that you can use to write programs faster and free from errors or "bugs."

Every C program must have at least one function called *main*. All functions consist of two parts:
- A function header
- A function block

The function header identifies the name of the function. Every function in a C program must have a unique name.

The function block contains the instructions that the function performs. A function block may contain zero instructions, although such a function will not do anything useful.

A SAMPLE SESSION WITH TURBO C++

The following steps show you how to create, modify, and run a complete Turbo C++ program. Make sure you have installed Turbo C++ on your computer according to the steps in Module 2.

1. Type **TC** at the DOS prompt and press **Return**. The Turbo C++ integrated environment appears on the screen.

Module 3

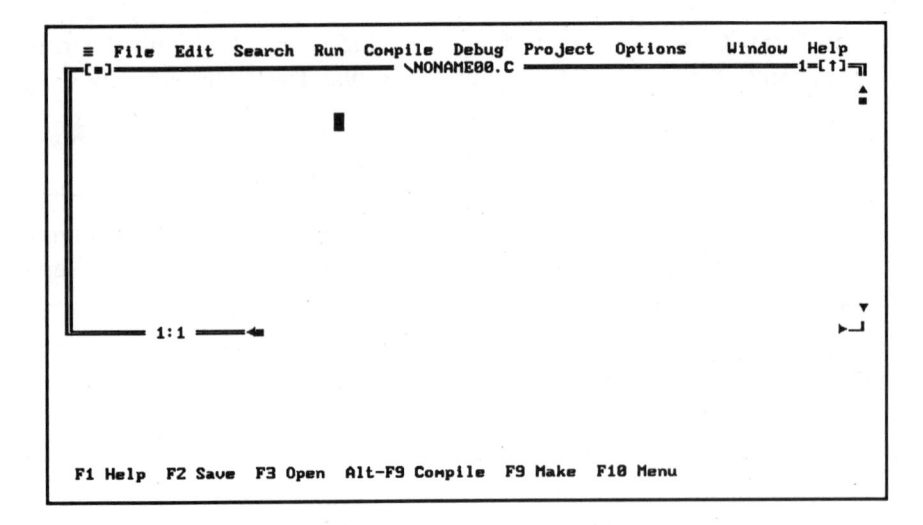

```
≡  File  Edit  Search  Run  Compile  Debug  Project  Options    Window  Help
┌─[■]────────────────────── \NONAME00.C ──────────────────────1=[↑]─┐
│                                                                    ▲│
│               ■                                                    ■│
│                                                                     │
│                                                                     │
│                                                                     │
│                                                                     │
│                                                                    ▼│
│   1:1  ──◄                                                         ┘│
│                                                                     │
│                                                                     │
│ F1 Help  F2 Save  F3 Open  Alt-F9 Compile  F9 Make  F10 Menu        │
```

2. Press **Alt-F**. The File menu appears.

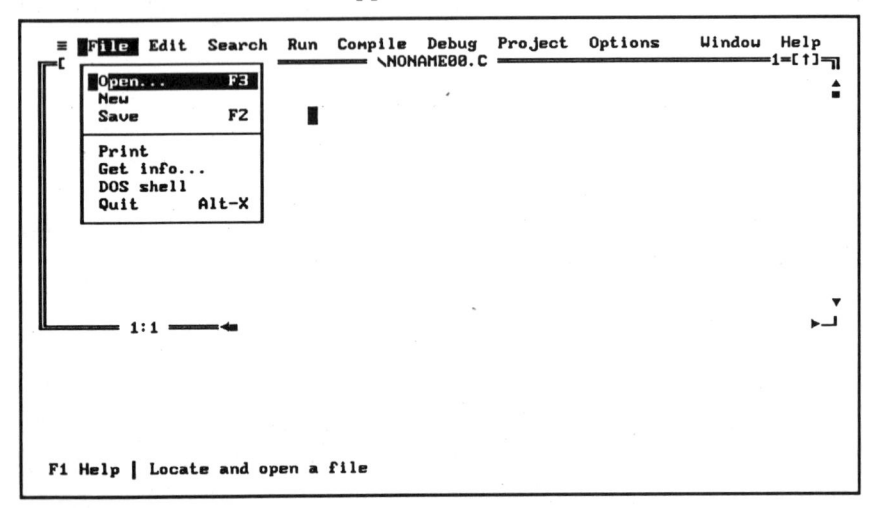

```
≡  File  Edit  Search  Run  Compile  Debug  Project  Options    Window  Help
┌─[                      \NONAME00.C ─────────────────────────1=[↑]─┐
│   ┌─────────────────┐                                              ▲│
│   │ Open...     F3  │                                              ■│
│   │ New             │                                               │
│   │ Save        F2  │  ■                                            │
│   ├─────────────────┤                                               │
│   │ Print           │                                               │
│   │ Get info...     │                                               │
│   │ DOS shell       │                                               │
│   │ Quit      Alt-X │                                               │
│   └─────────────────┘                                              ▼│
│   1:1  ──◄                                                         ┘│
│                                                                     │
│                                                                     │
│ F1 Help │ Locate and open a file                                    │
```

3. Choose **New** from the File menu in one of three ways:

    - Move the mouse pointer over **New** and click the left mouse button.
    - Press the **up** and **down** keys to highlight **New** and press **Return**.
    - Type **N**.

    Turbo C++ displays an empty file window.

4. Type the following:

    ```
    main ()
        {
        }
    ```

The above program is the simplest C program you can write; it only consists of one function header and block. In this case the function header is called "main."

5. Press **Ctrl-F9** to run this program. A dialog box appears to show you that Turbo C+ is compiling and linking your program. If you have typed this program correctly, you will see the screen momentarily flash.
6. Press **Alt-F5** to see the results of the program after it has run. Notice that the screen is blank. This happened because the function block did not contain any instructions. To make this program a bit more useful, add an instruction to print a message to the screen. Press **Alt-F5** to return to the integrated development environment.
7. Modify the program as follows:

```
main ()
    {
    printf ("This is my first Turbo C++ program.");
    }
```

8. Press **Ctrl-F9** to run your program. The screen momentarily flashes.
9. Press **Alt-F5** to see the results of your program.
10. Press **Alt-F5** to return to the integrated development environment.
11. Modify the program as follows:

```
#include <conio.h>

main ()
    {
    printf ("This is my first Turbo C++ program.");
    while (!kbhit());
    }
```

The addition of the last line, **while (!kbhit( ));**, displays the message on the screen until you press a key. The addition of the first line, **#include <conio.h>**, lets your program use functions stored in a separate file.

12. Press **Ctrl-F9** to run the program. This time instead of momentarily flashing, the message, "This is my first Turbo C++ program," remains on the screen. If you run this program several times, the same message will remain on the screen from the previous times you ran the program.
13. Press any key to return to the Turbo C++ integrated environment.
14. Modify the program as follows:

```
#include <conio.h>

main ()
    {
    clrscr ();
```

```
        window (20,10,60,20);

        printf ("This is my first Turbo C++ program.");
        while (!kbhit());
        }
```

15. Press **Ctrl-F9** to run the program. The addition of the line **clrscr ( );** clears the screen. The addition of the line **window (20,10,60,20);** defines an area on the screen where your program message will appear.

```
                This is my first Turbo C++ program.
```

16. Press any key to return to the Turbo C++ integrated environment.
17. Modify the program as follows to isolate part of your program into a function:

    ```
    #include <conio.h>

    void draw_box (void)
        {
        clrscr ();
        window (20,10,60,20);
        }

    main ()
        {
        void draw_box ();

        draw_box ();
        printf ("This is my first Turbo C++ program.");
        while (!kbhit());
        }
    ```

18. Press **Ctrl-F9** to run your program. Notice that the effect is still the same despite creating a function called draw_box.

A Sample Session with Turbo C++

19. Press any key to return to the Turbo C++ integrated environment.
20. Press **F7** to watch Turbo C++ run your program step-by-step. Notice that Turbo C++ highlights each instruction that your computer is currently following. Press **F7** several more times to watch the debugger step through each instruction.

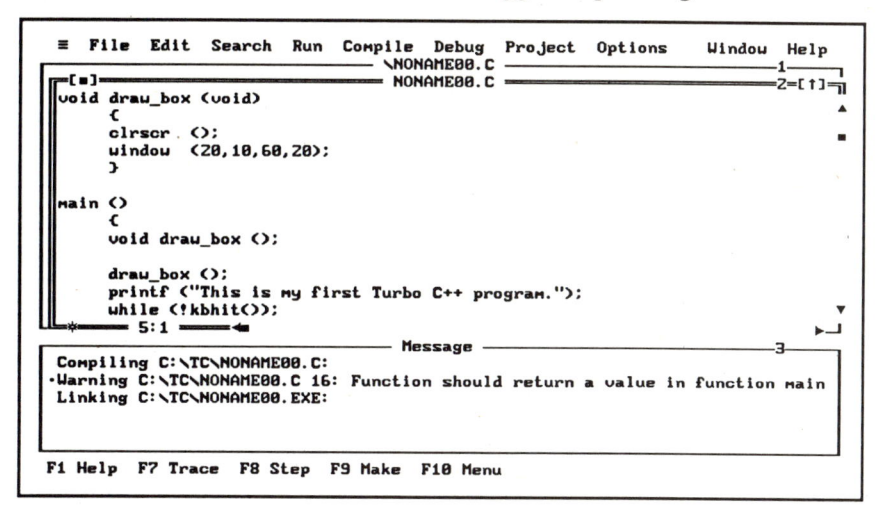

```
≡  File  Edit  Search  Run  Compile  Debug  Project  Options  Window  Help
                                  ╒══ \NONAME00.C ══════════════════1════╕
   ┌─[■]──────────────────────── NONAME00.C ═════════════════════2=[↑]═╗
   │void draw_box (void)                                                ▲
   │   {                                                                ■
   │   clrscr ();
   │   window (20,10,60,20);
   │   }
   │
   │main ()
   │   {
   │   void draw_box ();
   │
   │   draw_box ();
   │   printf ("This is my first Turbo C++ program.");
   │   while (!kbhit());                                                 ▼
   └──── 5:1 ════◄ ══════════════════════════════════════════════════►─┘
  ╒══════════════════════════ Message ═══════════════════════3══════╕
  │Compiling C:\TC\NONAME00.C:                                          │
  │•Warning C:\TC\NONAME00.C 16: Function should return a value in function main │
  │Linking C:\TC\NONAME00.EXE:                                          │
  │                                                                     │
  │                                                                     │
  └─────────────────────────────────────────────────────────────────────┘
 F1 Help   F7 Trace   F8 Step   F9 Make   F10 Menu
```

21. Press **Ctrl-F2** to stop the debugger. Notice that Turbo C++ no longer highlights any more instructions.
22. Press **F2** to save your file. A dialog box appears.

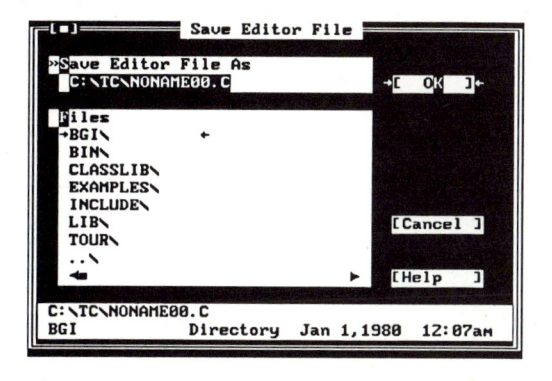

```
═[■]════════════════ Save Editor File ═══════════
  »Save Editor File As
    C:\TC\NONAME00.C                     ─[  OK  ]─
   ┌────────────┐
   │Files       │
   │→BGI\      ←│
   │ BIN\       │
   │ CLASSLIB\  │
   │ EXAMPLES\  │
   │ INCLUDE\   │
   │ LIB\       │         [Cancel  ]
   │ TOUR\      │
   │ ..\        │
   │ ←          │ ►       [Help    ]
   └────────────┘
  C:\TC\NONAME00.C
  BGI            Directory  Jan 1,1980  12:07am
```

23. Type **TEST** and press **Return**. This saves the current file, in the current directory, as TEST.C.
24. Press **Alt-X** when you are finished experimenting with the debugger and want to quit Turbo C++.
25. Turn to Module 13 to continue the learning sequence.

Module 4
COMPILE MENU

DESCRIPTION

The Compile menu contains commands for compiling your programs. When displayed with the Full menus option turned off, the Compile menu contains two commands:
- Make EXE file
- Build all

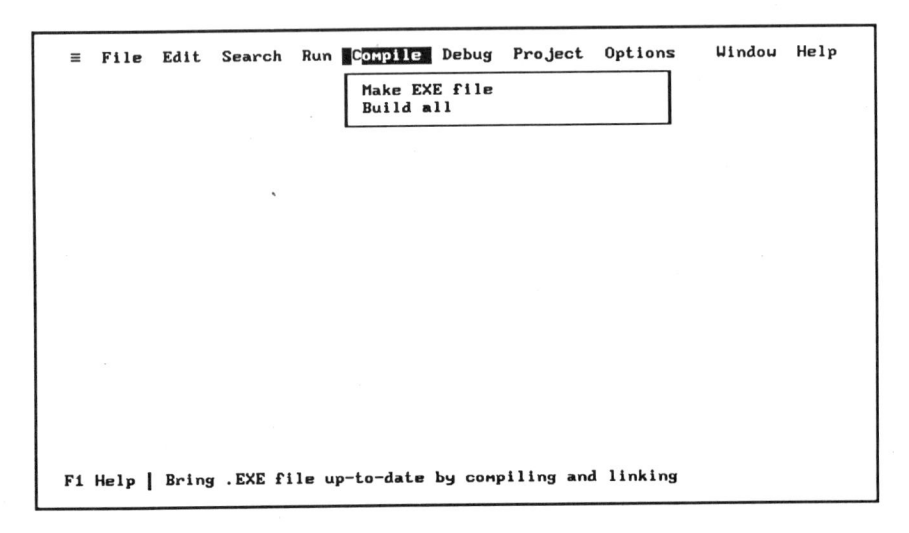

```
≡  File  Edit  Search  Run  Compile  Debug  Project  Options      Window  Help
                                Make EXE file
                                Build all










F1 Help | Bring .EXE file up-to-date by compiling and linking
```

When displayed with the Full menus option turned on, the Compile menu contains three additional commands:
- Compile to OBJ
- Link EXE file
- Remove messages

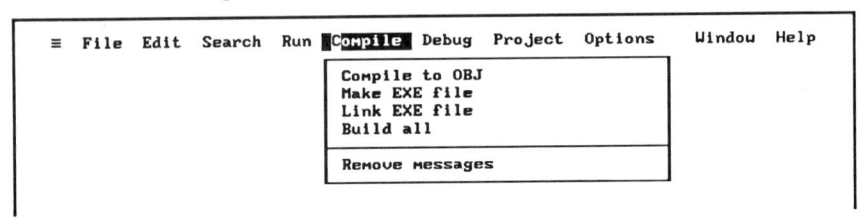

```
≡  File  Edit  Search  Run  Compile  Debug  Project  Options      Window  Help
                                Compile to OBJ
                                Make EXE file
                                Link EXE file
                                Build all
                                Remove messages
```

You can display the Compile menu in one of three ways:
- Click on the Compile menu with a mouse.
- Press Alt-C.
- Press F10 and use the arrow keys to highlight the Compile menu, then press Return.

APPLICATIONS

The Compile menu commands let you compile your Turbo C++ programs and projects. A project is simply a collection of related programs that work together.

Make EXE file creates an executable .EXE file, using the name of the current file or the name of the project file specified with the Project menu Open command. In the process of making an executable .EXE file, Turbo C++ will also create an .OBJ file.

Build all rebuilds all the files in your project regardless of their date.

Compile to OBJ creates an .OBJ object file. Once you have stored a program as an .OBJ file, you can link it together with .OBJ files created by other languages such as Pascal or assembly. You can also choose the Compile to OBJ command by pressing Alt-F9.

Link EXE file takes the current .OBJ or .LIB file and links them to produce an executable .EXE file.

Remove messages clears any messages in the Message window.

TYPICAL OPERATION

In this example, you practice using the different commands on the Compile menu. Begin from within Turbo C++ with no windows open.

1. Press **F3**. Turbo C++ displays the Load a File dialog box.
2. Type **C:\TC\EXAMPLES\HELLO.C** and press **Return**. (This assumes you have installed the Turbo C++ example programs in the C:\TC\EXAMPLES directory.) Turbo C++ displays the HELLO.C program in the edit window.
3. Press **Alt-C** and type **C**. Turbo C++ displays a Compiling dialog box.

Module 4

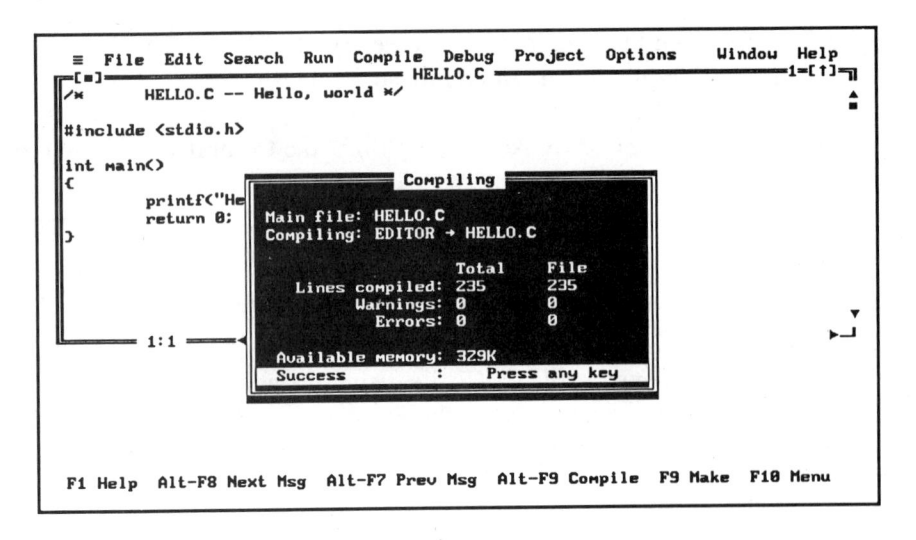

```
         ≡  File  Edit  Search  Run  Compile  Debug  Project  Options    Window  Help
┌─[■]─────────────────────────── HELLO.C ──────────────────────────1─[↑]─┐
│/*       HELLO.C -- Hello, world */                                     ▲│
│                                                                        ■│
│#include <stdio.h>                                                       │
│                                                                         │
│int main()                                                               │
│{                          ┌──────────── Compiling ────────────┐         │
│       printf("He          │ Main file: HELLO.C                │         │
│       return 0;           │ Compiling: EDITOR → HELLO.C       │         │
│}                          │                                   │         │
│                           │                    Total    File  │         │
│                           │  Lines compiled:   235      235   │         │
│                           │       Warnings:    0        0     │         │
│                           │         Errors:    0        0     │         ▼│
│     ── 1:1 ──◄            │                                   │        ┌┘│
│                           │ Available memory: 329K            │         │
│                           │ Success           :   Press any key│        │
│                           └───────────────────────────────────┘         │
│                                                                         │
│                                                                         │
│   F1 Help  Alt-F8 Next Msg  Alt-F7 Prev Msg  Alt-F9 Compile  F9 Make  F10 Menu
└─────────────────────────────────────────────────────────────────────────┘
```

4. Press **Return** to remove the dialog box.
5. Press **Alt-C** and type **L**. Turbo C++ creates an .EXE executable program from the .OBJ file you created in step 3. A Linking dialog box appears.

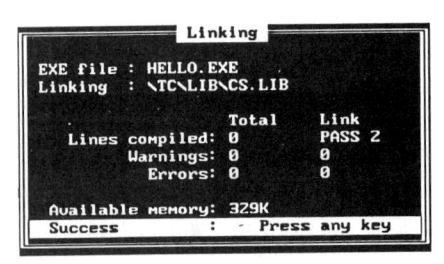

```
              ┌──────────── Linking ────────────┐
              │ EXE file : HELLO.EXE            │
              │ Linking  : \TC\LIB\CS.LIB       │
              │                                 │
              │                  Total    Link  │
              │ Lines compiled:  0        PASS 2│
              │      Warnings:   0        0     │
              │        Errors:   0        0     │
              │                                 │
              │ Available memory: 329K          │
              │ Success          :  - Press any key│
              └─────────────────────────────────┘
```

6. Press **Return**.
7. Press **Alt-F** and type **D** to display the DOS prompt.
8. Type **Hello** and press **Return**. Notice that the program displays the message "Hello, world."
9. Type **exit** and press **Return** to return to the Turbo C++ integrated development environment.
10. Change line 7 from printf ("Hello, world\n"); to

    printf ("Hello, everybody\n");

11. Press **Alt-C** and type **M**. Turbo C++ displays a Linking dialog box.
12. Press **Return**.
13. Press **Alt-F** and type **D** to display the DOS prompt.
14. Type **Hello** and press **Return**. Notice that now the HELLO.EXE program displays the message "Hello, everybody."

Compile Menu

15. Type **exit** and press **Return** to return to the Turbo C++ integrated development environment.
16. Type **N** in response to the dialog box warning you that HELLO.C is updated on disk. Reload?
17. Change line 7 from printf ("Hello, everybody\n"); to

    `printf ("Hello, Turbo C++\n");`
18. Press **Alt-C** and type **B**. Turbo C++ displays a Linking dialog box.
19. Press **Return**.
20. Press **Alt-F** and type **D**.
21. Type **Hello** and press **Return**. Notice that the HELLO.EXE program now displays the message "Hello, Turbo C++."
22. Type **exit** and press **Return**. Type **N** in response to the dialog box.
23. Press **Alt-W** and type **M**. Turbo C++ displays the Message window at the bottom of the screen.

```
   ≡ File  Edit  Search  Run  Compile  Debug  Project  Options     Window  Help
  ┌─────────────────────────── HELLO.C ──────────────────────────────1────┐
  │ /*       HELLO.C -- Hello, world */                                    │
  │                                                                        │
  │ #include <stdio.h>                                                     │
  │                                                                        │
  │ int main()                                                             │
  │ {                                                                      │
  │        printf("Hello, Turbo C++\n");                                   │
  │        return 0;                                                       │
  │ }                                                                      │
  │                                                                        │
  │                                                                        │
  │                                                                        │
  │ ──*─── 7:33 ─────                                                      │
  ┌─[■]──────────────────────── Message ═════════════════════════2=[↑]═┐
  │ Compiling C:\TC\EXAMPLES\HELLO.C:                                      │
  │ Linking C:\TC\EXAMPLES\HELLO.EXE:                                      │
  │                                                                        │
  │                                                                        │
  │ F1 Help  Space View source  ↵ Edit source  F10 Menu                    │
  └────────────────────────────────────────────────────────────────────────┘
```

24. Press **Alt-C** and type **R**. Notice that Turbo C++ clears the Message window.
25. Press **Alt-Spacebar** and type **C** to clear the desktop. Turbo C++ displays a Message dialog box asking if you want to save the modified HELLO.C program. Type **N**.
26. Turn to Module 10 to continue the learning sequence.

19

Module 5
DEBUG MENU

DESCRIPTION

The Debug menu contains six commands for using the integrated Turbo C++ debugger:
- Inspect
- Evaluate/modify
- Call stack
- Watches
- Toggle breakpoint
- Breakpoints

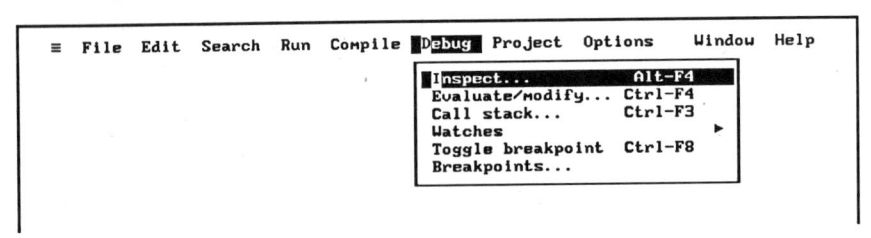

```
≡  File  Edit  Search  Run  Compile  Debug  Project  Options    Window   Help
                                     Inspect...         Alt-F4
                                     Evaluate/modify... Ctrl-F4
                                     Call stack...      Ctrl-F3
                                     Watches                   ▶
                                     Toggle breakpoint  Ctrl-F8
                                     Breakpoints...
```

You can display the Debug menu in one of three ways:
- Click on the Debug menu with a mouse.
- Press Alt-D.
- Press F10 and use the arrow keys to highlight the Debug menu, then press Return.

APPLICATIONS

The Debug menu commands let you debug your Turbo C++ programs.

Inspect lets you examine and modify the contents of a data element, such as a char, pointer, array, function, class, or structure. You can also choose this command by pressing Alt-F4.

Evaluate/modify lets you examine and modify the value of a variable. You can also choose this command by pressing Ctrl-F4.

Call stack lists the sequence of functions your program called. You can also choose this command by pressing Ctrl-F3.

Watches displays a pop-up menu of four watchpoint commands:
- Add Watch lets you examine the contents of a variable while running your program with the Turbo C++ integrated debugger.
- Delete Watch removes any displayed watchpoints created with the Add Watch command.
- Edit Watch lets you edit a watchpoint created with the Add Watch command.
- Remove All Watches deletes all watchpoints created with the Add Watch command.

Toggle breakpoint lets you set a breakpoint or remove an existing breakpoint. A breakpoint is a line in your program where your program stops running until you give the command to continue by pressing F7 (Trace into), F8 (Step over), or Ctrl-F9 (Run). You can also choose this command by pressing Ctrl-F8.

Breakpoints displays a list of all breakpoints, their line numbers, and their condition. This command lets you quickly view and delete any breakpoints you have set in your program.

TYPICAL OPERATION

In this example, you practice using the different commands on the Debug menu. Begin from within Turbo C++.

1. Press **Alt-Spacebar** and type **C** to clear the desktop.
2. Press **F3** to open a file. Turbo C++ displays the Load a File dialog box. Load the INTRO1.C file.

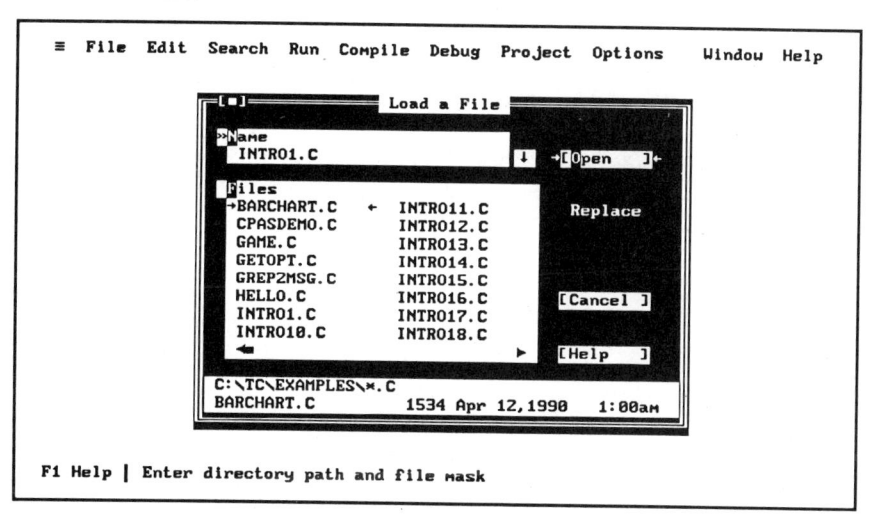

```
≡  File  Edit  Search  Run  Compile  Debug  Project  Options    Window  Help
                            ┌──────── Load a File ────────┐
                            │ Name                        │
                            │   INTRO1.C        ↓  →[Open]│
                            │ Files                       │
                            │ →BARCHART.C  ←  INTRO11.C   │
                            │   CPASDEMO.C    INTRO12.C   │  Replace
                            │   GAME.C        INTRO13.C   │
                            │   GETOPT.C      INTRO14.C   │
                            │   GREP2MSG.C    INTRO15.C   │
                            │   HELLO.C       INTRO16.C   │  [Cancel]
                            │   INTRO1.C      INTRO17.C   │
                            │   INTRO10.C     INTRO18.C   │
                            │   ←          ►              │  [Help]
                            │ C:\TC\EXAMPLES\*.C          │
                            │ BARCHART.C    1534 Apr 12,1990  1:00am │
                            └─────────────────────────────┘
 F1 Help │ Enter directory path and file mask
```

3. Press **Ctrl-Q F**. Turbo C++ displays a Find dialog box.
4. Type **rate = dollars / bushels;** and press **Return**.

Module 5

5. Press **Ctrl-F8** or press **Alt-D** and type **T**. Turbo C++ highlights this line as a breakpoint.

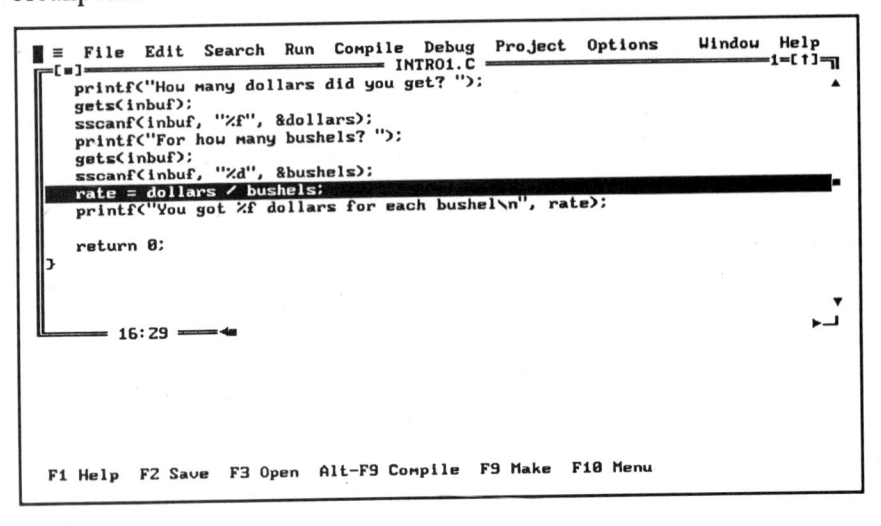

```
 ≡ File  Edit  Search  Run  Compile  Debug  Project  Options     Window   Help
[■]                               INTRO1.C                              1=[↑]
   printf("How many dollars did you get? ");
   gets(inbuf);
   sscanf(inbuf, "%f", &dollars);
   printf("For how many bushels? ");
   gets(inbuf);
   sscanf(inbuf, "%d", &bushels);
   rate = dollars / bushels;
   printf("You got %f dollars for each bushel\n", rate);

   return 0;
 }



     16:29

 F1 Help  F2 Save  F3 Open  Alt-F9 Compile  F9 Make  F10 Menu
```

6. Move the cursor under **dollars**.
7. Press **Ctrl-F7** or press **Alt-D**, type **W**, and type **A** to choose the Add watch... command. The Add Watch dialog box appears.

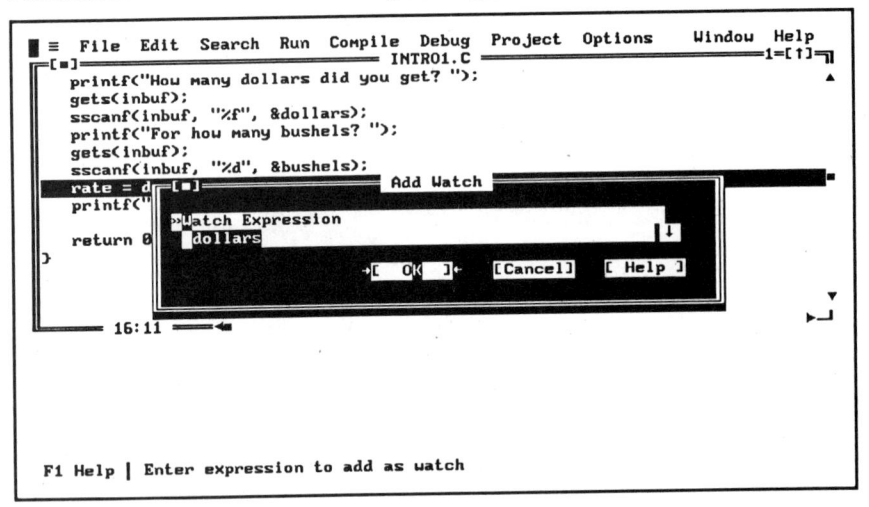

```
 ≡ File  Edit  Search  Run  Compile  Debug  Project  Options     Window   Help
[■]                               INTRO1.C                              1=[↑]
   printf("How many dollars did you get? ");
   gets(inbuf);
   sscanf(inbuf, "%f", &dollars);
   printf("For how many bushels? ");
   gets(inbuf);
   sscanf(inbuf, "%d", &bushels);
   rate = d ┌─[■]──────────── Add Watch ─────────────────┐
   printf(  │ ►Watch Expression                          │
   return 0 │  dollars                                 ↓ │
 }          │           ─[ OK ]─   [Cancel]   [ Help ]   │
            └────────────────────────────────────────────┘

     16:11

 F1 Help │ Enter expression to add as watch
```

8. Press **Return**. Turbo C++ displays a Watch window at the bottom of the screen.

Debug Menu

```
≡ File  Edit  Search  Run  Compile  Debug  Project  Options     Window  Help
┌─────────────────────────────── INTRO1.C ──────────────────────────1─┐
│   printf("How many dollars did you get? ");                         │
│   gets(inbuf);                                                      │
│   sscanf(inbuf, "%f", &dollars);                                    │
│   printf("For how many bushels? ");                                 │
│   gets(inbuf);                                                      │
│   sscanf(inbuf, "%d", &bushels);                                    │
│   rate = dollars / bushels;                                         │
│   printf("You got %f dollars for each bushel\n", rate);             │
│                                                                     │
│   return 0;                                                         │
│ }                                                                   │
│           ■                                                         │
│                                                                     │
│── 16:11 ──                                                          │
├[■]─────────────────────────── Watch ──────────────────────────2=[↑]─┤
│ dollars: Undefined symbol 'dollars'                                 │
│                                                                   ▲ │
│                                                                     │
│                                                                   ▼ │
│ ◄                                                                 ► │
│ F1 Help  F7 Trace  F8 Step  ↵ Edit  Ins Add  Del Delete  F10 Menu   │
└─────────────────────────────────────────────────────────────────────┘
```

9. Press **F6** to switch to the editor.
10. Move the cursor under **bushels**.
11. Press **Ctrl-F7** and press **Return**. Turbo C++ displays the variable bushels in the Watch window.
12. Press **Ctrl-F9** to run the INTRO1.C program. The program displays the message "How many dollars did you get?"
13. Type **300** and press **Return**. The next message asks "For how many bushels?"
14. Type **15** and press **Return**. Notice that Turbo C++ displays these values in the Watch window.

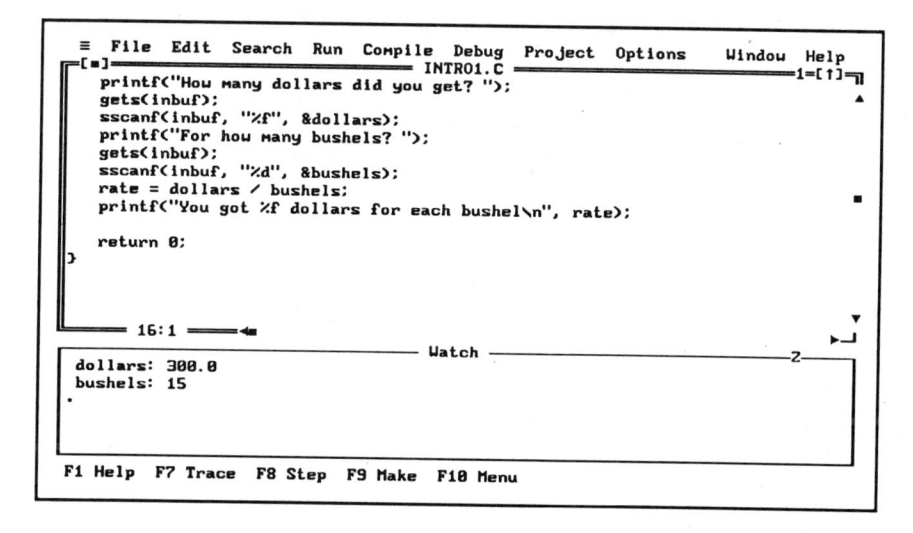

```
≡ File  Edit  Search  Run  Compile  Debug  Project  Options     Window  Help
┌[■]──────────────────────────── INTRO1.C ─────────────────────────1=[↑]─┐
│   printf("How many dollars did you get? ");                            │
│   gets(inbuf);                                                       ▲ │
│   sscanf(inbuf, "%f", &dollars);                                       │
│   printf("For how many bushels? ");                                    │
│   gets(inbuf);                                                         │
│   sscanf(inbuf, "%d", &bushels);                                       │
│   rate = dollars / bushels;                                            │
│   printf("You got %f dollars for each bushel\n", rate);              ■ │
│                                                                        │
│   return 0;                                                            │
│ }                                                                      │
│                                                                        │
│                                                                      ▼ │
│── 16:1 ── ◄                                                          ► │
├──────────────────────────────── Watch ────────────────────────────2────┤
│ dollars: 300.0                                                         │
│ bushels: 15                                                            │
│ ■                                                                      │
│                                                                        │
│                                                                        │
│ F1 Help  F7 Trace  F8 Step  F9 Make  F10 Menu                          │
└────────────────────────────────────────────────────────────────────────┘
```

23

Module 5

15. Press **Alt-D** and type **B**. Turbo C++ shows a list of all the breakpoints in your program.

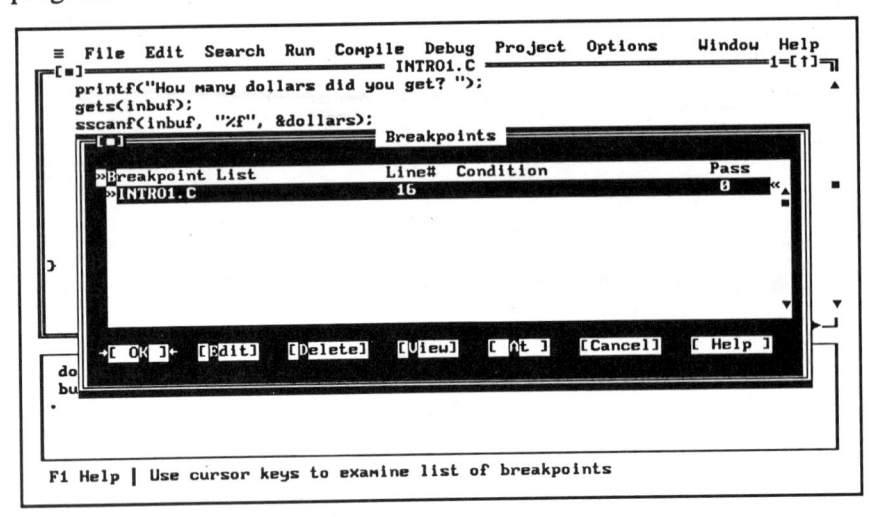

16. Press **Esc**.
17. Press **Alt-F4** or press **Alt-D** and type **I**. Turbo C++ displays a Data Inspect box.

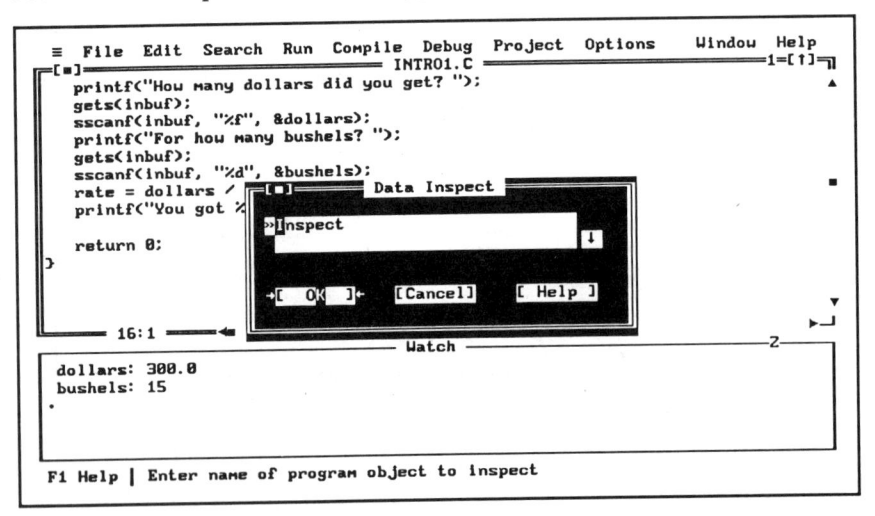

18. Type **dollars** and press **Return**. Turbo C++ displays the memory address of the variable, its type (float), and its value (300.0).

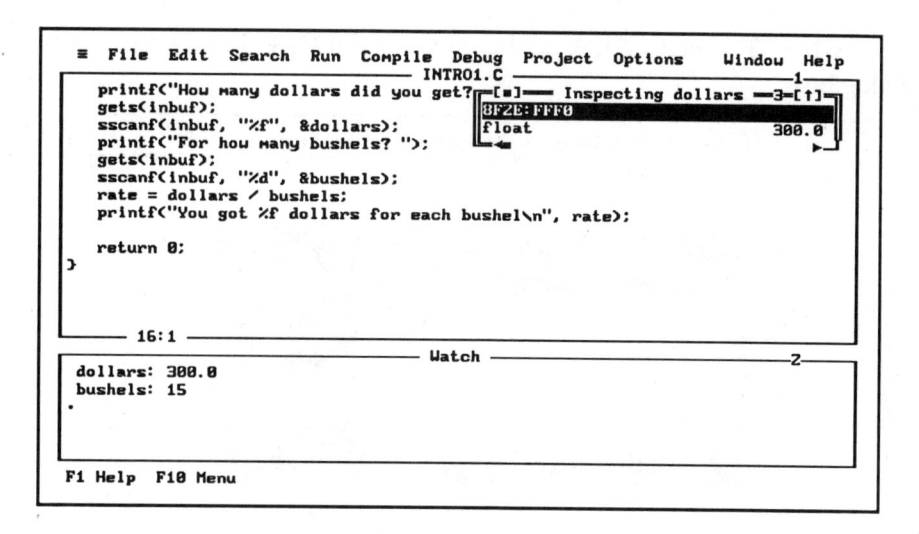

Debug Menu

```
≡ File  Edit  Search  Run  Compile  Debug  Project  Options    Window    Help
┌─────────────────────────── INTRO1.C ─────────────────────────1─┐
│  printf("How many dollars did you get?┌─[■]── Inspecting dollars ──3─[↑]─┐
│  gets(inbuf);                         │ 8FZE:FFF0                        │
│  sscanf(inbuf, "%f", &dollars);       │ float                      300.0 │
│  printf("For how many bushels? ");    └──────────────────────────────────┘
│  gets(inbuf);
│  sscanf(inbuf, "%d", &bushels);
│  rate = dollars / bushels;
│  printf("You got %f dollars for each bushel\n", rate);
│
│  return 0;
│ }
│
│
│──── 16:1 ────────────────
│                                    ─── Watch ──────────────────────2──
│  dollars: 300.0
│  bushels: 15
│  •
│
│
│ F1 Help  F10 Menu
└─────────────────────────────────────────────────────────────────┘
```

19. Press **Esc** to remove the Inspect window from view.
20. Press **Ctrl-F4** or press **Alt-D** and type **E**. Turbo C++ displays an Evaluate and Modify dialog box.

```
≡ File  Edit  Search  Run  Compile  Debug  Project  Options    Window    Help
┌─[■]──────────────────────── INTRO1.C ────────────────────────1=[↑]─┐
│  printf("How many dollars did you get? ");
│  gets(inbuf);
│  sscanf(inbuf, "%f", &dollars);
│  printf("┌─[■]═════════ Evaluate and Modify ═════════════════════┐
│  gets(inb│                                                       │
│  sscanf(i│  »Expression                                          │
│  rate = d│  ┌─────────────────────────────────────┐ ↓ •[Evaluate]│
│  printf(" │ └─────────────────────────────────────┘              │
│  return 0│   Result                                              │
│ }        │  ┌─────────────────────────────────────┐   [Modify ]  │
│          │  └─────────────────────────────────────┘              │
│          │   New Value                                           │
│          │  ┌─────────────────────────────────────┐              │
│──── 16:1 │  └─────────────────────────────────────┘ ↓ [Cancel ]  │
│  dollars:│                                              [Help  ] │
│  bushels:└───────────────────────────────────────────────────────┘
│  •
│
│ F1 Help │ Enter expression to evaluate
└──────────────────────────────────────────────────────────────────┘
```

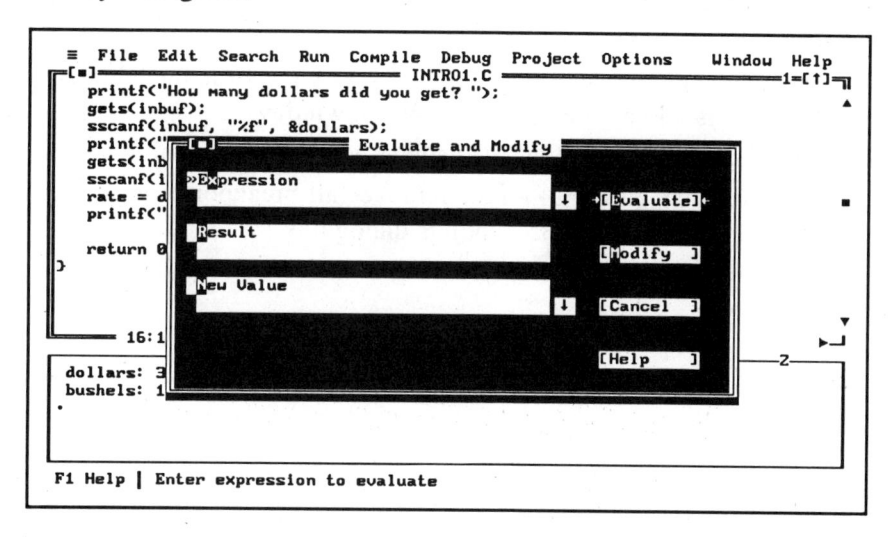

21. Type **dollars** in the Expression box and press **Return**. Turbo C++ displays the value of dollars (300.0) in the Result box.
22. Press **Tab** twice to move the cursor to the New Value box.
23. Type **500** and press **Return**. Notice that Turbo C++ displays the value of 500 in both the Result and New Value box.
24. Press **Esc** to remove the Evaluate and Modify dialog box. Notice that Turbo C++ displays the new value of 500.0 in the Watch window.

25

Module 5

25. Press **Ctrl-F3** or press **Alt-D** and type **C**. Turbo C++ displays the Call Stack dialog box.

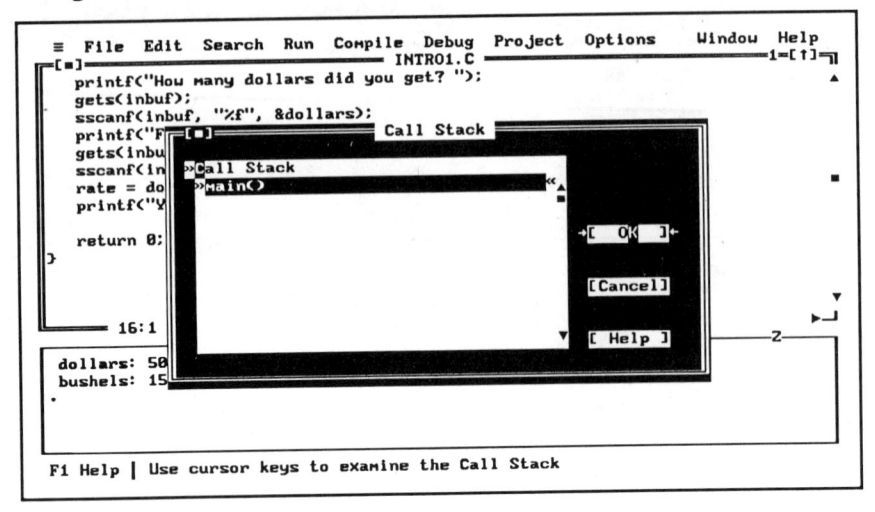

26. Press **Esc**.
27. Press **Ctrl-F2** to reset the program.
28. Press **Alt-D**, type **W**, and type **R** to remove all watches from the Watch window. Turbo C++ clears all variables from the Watch window.
29. Press **Alt-D** and type **B**. Turbo C++ displays a Breakpoints dialog box.
30. Type **D**. Notice that Turbo C++ now removes all breakpoints in the program. Press **Return** to remove the Breakpoints dialog box.
31. Turn to Module 12 to continue the learning sequence.

Module 6
EDIT MENU

DESCRIPTION

The Edit menu contains commands for editing files. When displayed with the Full menus option turned off, the Edit menu contains six commands.
- Restore line
- Cut
- Copy
- Paste
- Copy example
- Clear

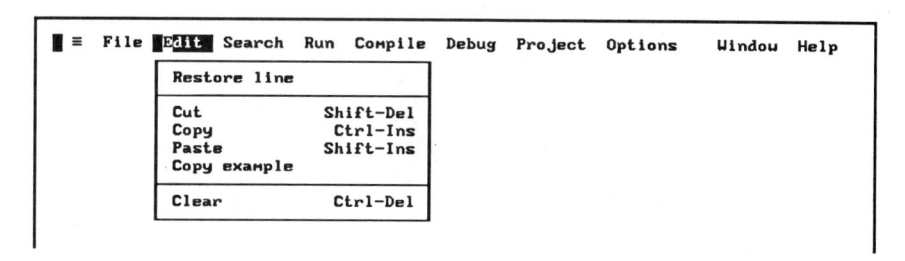

```
 ≡   File  Edit  Search  Run  Compile  Debug  Project  Options      Window  Help
           ┌─────────────────────────┐
           │ Restore line            │
           │                         │
           │ Cut           Shift-Del │
           │ Copy           Ctrl-Ins │
           │ Paste         Shift-Ins │
           │ Copy example            │
           │                         │
           │ Clear          Ctrl-Del │
           └─────────────────────────┘
```

When displayed with the Full menus option turned on, the Edit menu contains an additional command:
- Show clipboard

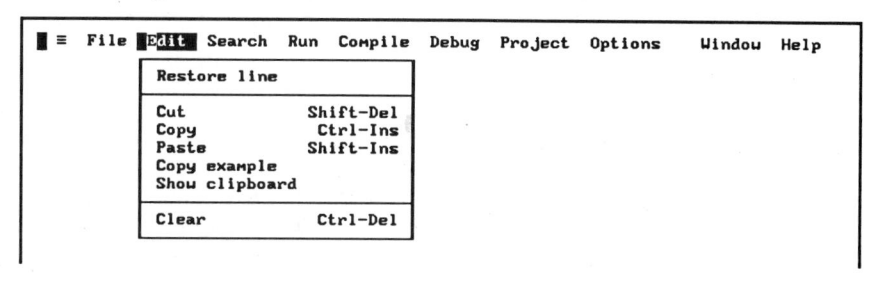

```
 ≡   File  Edit  Search  Run  Compile  Debug  Project  Options      Window  Help
           ┌─────────────────────────┐
           │ Restore line            │
           │                         │
           │ Cut           Shift-Del │
           │ Copy           Ctrl-Ins │
           │ Paste         Shift-Ins │
           │ Copy example            │
           │ Show clipboard          │
           │                         │
           │ Clear          Ctrl-Del │
           └─────────────────────────┘
```

You can display the Edit menu in one of three ways:
- Click on the Edit menu with a mouse.
- Press Alt-E.
- Press F10 and use the arrow keys to highlight the Edit menu, then press Return.

27

APPLICATIONS

The Edit menu commands let you cut, copy, and paste text within the same window or between different windows. Before you can use any commands on the Edit menu, you need to select text first.

You can select text in one of seven ways:

With the keyboard:
- Press Shift and an arrow key at the same time.
- Press Ctrl-K B to mark the start of a text block. Then move the cursor to the end of the text block and press Ctrl-K K.
- To select a single word, move the cursor to that word and press Ctrl-K T.
- To select an entire line, move the cursor to that line and press Ctrl-K L.

With a mouse:
- Drag the mouse over the text block you want to mark.
- To select an entire line, double-click anywhere on that line.
- To extend or reduce a selected text block, Shift-click (hold down the Shift key and press the mouse button)

Restore line restores the last line you modified or deleted. You can use this command to undo any changes you made to a line.

Cut removes a selected text block and puts it on the Clipboard. Once you have Cut a text block, you can use the Paste command to move the text somewhere else in the same or a different window. You can also choose this command by pressing Shift-Del.

Copy copies a selected text block and puts a copy on the Clipboard. Once you have Copied a text block, you can use the Paste command to copy the text somewhere else in the same or a different window. You can also choose this command from the Help window to copy program examples. You can also choose this command by pressing Ctrl-Ins.

Paste puts text from the Clipboard into a window. Before you can use the Paste command, you must first put text in the Clipboard using the Cut or Copy commands. You can also choose this command by pressing Shift-Ins.

Copy example copies preselected text blocks from the Help window to the Clipboard.

Show clipboard only appears if you have selected Full menus on. This command opens the Clipboard window so you can see the current Clipboard contents. The currently selected text block is the last text block copied or cut to the Clipboard.

Clear works like the Cut command except it does not place the selected text on the Clipboard. You can also choose this command by pressing Ctrl-Del.

TYPICAL OPERATION

In this example, you practice using the different commands on the Edit menu. Begin from within Turbo C++ with the HELLO.C program displayed in the edit window.

1. Press **Ctrl-Q R** to move the cursor to the top of the HELLO.C file.
2. Press **Ctrl-Y** to delete the top line.
3. Press **Alt-E** to display the Edit menu, and type **R** to choose the Restore line command. Notice that Turbo C++ restores the previously deleted line.
4. Press **Ctrl-K B** to mark the beginning of a text block.
5. Press **Ctrl-Q X** to move the cursor to the end of the file.
6. Press **Ctrl-K K** to mark the end of the text block.

```
 ≡  File  Edit  Search  Run  Compile  Debug  Project  Options    Window  Help
┌[■]════════════════════════════ HELLO.C ═══════════════════════════1=[↑]┐
│/*       HELLO.C -- Hello, world */                                      ▲│
│                                                                          │
│#include <stdio.h>                                                        │
│                                                                          │
│int main()                                                                │
│{                                                                         │
│        printf("Hello, world\n");                                         │
│        return 0;                                                         │
│}                                                                         │
│                                                                          │
│                                                                         ▼│
└──── 14:1 ═══◄                                                          ►┘

 F1 Help  F2 Save  F3 Open  Alt-F9 Compile  F9 Make  F10 Menu
```

7. Press **Alt-E** and type **T** to choose the Cut command, or press **Shift-Del**. Notice that the entire selected text block disappears.
8. Press **Alt-E** and type **S** to choose the Show clipboard command. Notice that the text you cut in step 7 now appears in the Clipboard window.

```
 ≡  File  Edit  Search  Run  Compile  Debug  Project  Options    Window  Help
                                    ══════ HELLO.C ═════════════════1══════
┌[■]════════════════════════════ Clipboard ═════════════════════════2=[↑]┐
│/*       HELLO.C -- Hello, world */                                      ▲│
│                                                                          │
│#include <stdio.h>                                                        │
│                                                                          │
│int main()                                                                │
│{                                                                         │
│        printf("Hello, world\n");                                         │
│        return 0;                                                         │
│}                                                                         │
│                                                                         ▼│
└──── 1:1 ═══◄                                                           ►┘
```

Module 6

9. Press **Alt-F3** to close the Clipboard window.
10. Press **Alt-E** and type **P** to choose the Paste command, or press **Shift-Ins**. Notice that the selected text appears in the edit window.
11. Press **Alt-E** and type **L** to choose the Clear command, or press **Ctrl-Del**. Notice that the selected text disappears.
12. Type **printf**.
13. Press **Ctrl-F1**. Turbo C++ displays a Help window, explaining how the printf command works.

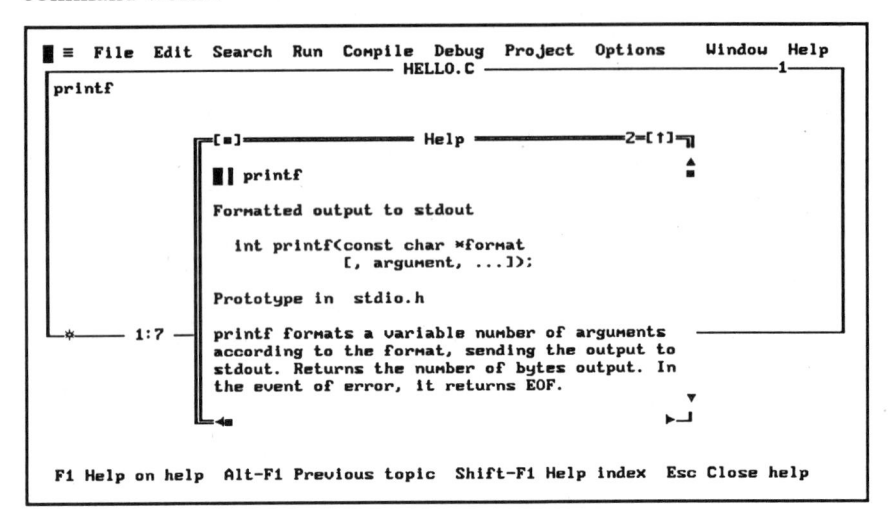

```
  ≡  File  Edit  Search  Run  Compile  Debug  Project  Options   Window   Help
 ─────────────────────────── HELLO.C ──────────────────────────1───
 printf

          ┌─[■]──────────────── Help ────────────────2=[↑]─┐
          │ ■│ printf                                       ▲ │
          │                                                   │
          │   Formatted output to stdout                      │
          │                                                   │
          │     int printf(const char *format                 │
          │                [, argument, ...]);                │
          │                                                   │
          │   Prototype in  stdio.h                           │
          │                                                   │
   ─*──  1:7 ─┤ printf formats a variable number of arguments  │
          │   according to the format, sending the output to  │
          │   stdout. Returns the number of bytes output. In  │
          │   the event of error, it returns EOF.             │
          │                                                 ▼ │
          │◄─                                             ►─┘ │
          │                                                   │
          │ F1 Help on help  Alt-F1 Previous topic  Shift-F1 Help index  Esc Close help │
          └───────────────────────────────────────────────────┘
```

14. Press **PgDn** and **PgUp** to scroll through the Help window.
15. Press **Alt-E** and type **E** to choose the Copy example command.
16. Press **Esc** to remove the Help window.
17. Press **Ctrl-Y** to remove the printf command you typed in step 12.
18. Press **Alt-E** and type **P** to choose the Paste command, or press **Shift-Ins**. Notice that Turbo C++ displays the printf example program that you copied from the Help window in step 15.
19. Press **Alt-F3** to close the edit window. A Message dialog box appears warning you that Hello.c is not saved.

30

Edit Menu

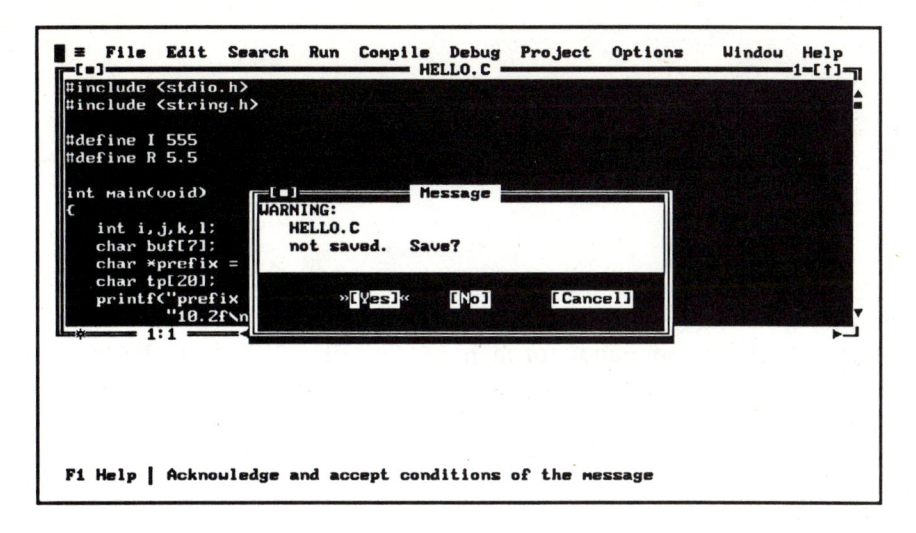

20. Type **N** to choose No.
21. Turn to Module 8 to continue the learning sequence.

Module 7
FILE MENU

DESCRIPTION

The File menu contains commands for manipulating files. When displayed with the Full menus option turned off, the File menu contains seven commands:
- Open
- New
- Save
- Print
- Get info
- DOS shell
- Quit

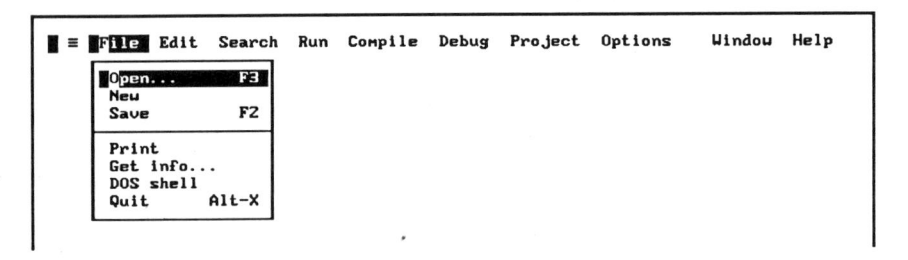

```
▌≡ █File█ Edit  Search  Run  Compile  Debug  Project  Options    Window  Help
    ┌─────────────────┐
    │ Open...    F3   │
    │ New             │
    │ Save       F2   │
    │─────────────────│
    │ Print           │
    │ Get info...     │
    │ DOS shell       │
    │ Quit      Alt-X │
    └─────────────────┘
```

When displayed with the Full menus option turned on, the File menu contains three additional commands:
- Save as
- Save all
- Change dir

```
▌≡ █File█ Edit  Search  Run  Compile  Debug  Project  Options    Window  Help
    ┌─────────────────┐
    │ Open...    F3   │
    │ New             │
    │ Save       F2   │
    │ Save as...      │
    │ Save all        │
    │─────────────────│
    │ Change dir...   │
    │ Print           │
    │ Get info...     │
    │ DOS shell       │
    │ Quit      Alt-X │
    └─────────────────┘
```

You can display the File menu in one of three ways:
- Click on the File menu with a mouse.
- Press Alt-F.
- Press F10 and use the arrow keys to highlight the File menu, then press Return.

APPLICATIONS

Open lets you load an existing file into an edit window. You can choose Open by pressing F3.

New opens a new edit window with the default name of NONAMExx.C where xx stands for a number between 00 to 99.

Save stores the file, in the active edit window, to disk. You can choose Save by pressing F2.

Save as lets you save the current file under a different filename, in a different directory, or on a different drive.

Save all saves the contents of all modified files, not just the current file in the active edit window.

Change dir lets you choose the current directory and drive.

Print sends the entire file, in the active edit window, to the printer. To print a portion of a file, mark the block you want to print using the Ctrl-K B and Ctrl-K K commands. After marking a block, use the Ctrl-K P command.

Get Info displays a box containing information about the current file.

DOS Shell temporarily exits Turbo C++ and displays the DOS prompt. To return from the DOS prompt back to Turbo C++, type exit and press Return.

Quit exits Turbo C++. You can choose Quit by pressing Alt-X.

TYPICAL OPERATION

In this example you practice using the different commands on the File menu. Begin from within Turbo C++ with no windows open.

1. Press **Alt-O** to display the Options menu.

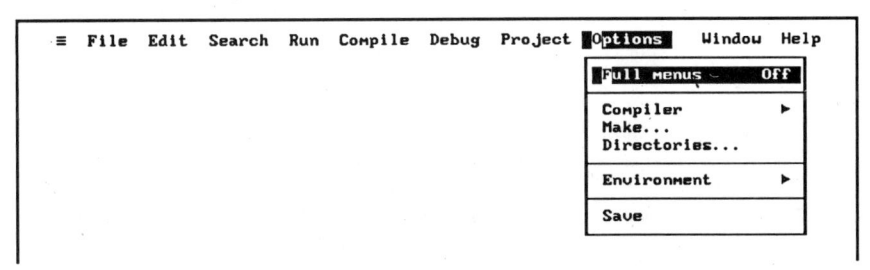

```
≡  File  Edit  Search  Run  Compile  Debug  Project  Options  Window  Help
                                                     ┌─────────────────────┐
                                                     │ Full menus      Off │
                                                     │ Compiler          ▶ │
                                                     │ Make...             │
                                                     │ Directories...      │
                                                     │ Environment       ▶ │
                                                     │ Save                │
                                                     └─────────────────────┘
```

Module 7

2. Type **F** to choose Full menus On.
3. Press **Alt-F** and type **C** to choose Change Dir. A dialog box appears, prompting you to specify a new drive or directory.

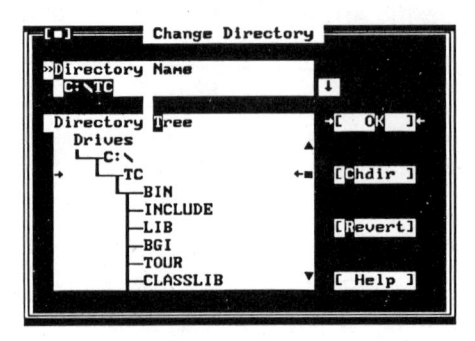

NOTE
Step 4 assumes you have installed Turbo C++ using the default installation values where Turbo C++ is on drive C in a directory called TC.

4. Type **C:\TC\EXAMPLES** and press **Return**.
5. Press **Alt-F** to display the File menu.
6. Choose Open or press **F3**. A dialog box appears, displaying a list of files to choose from.
7. Choose HELLO.C by typing **hello.c** and pressing **Return** or by clicking with the mouse. The HELLO.C program appears in an edit window on the screen.

8. Press **F2** to choose Save. Turbo C++ saves the HELLO.C file to disk.

File Menu

9. Press **Alt-F** and type **A** to choose Save as. A dialog box appears, prompting you to type a new name with an optional drive and directory.

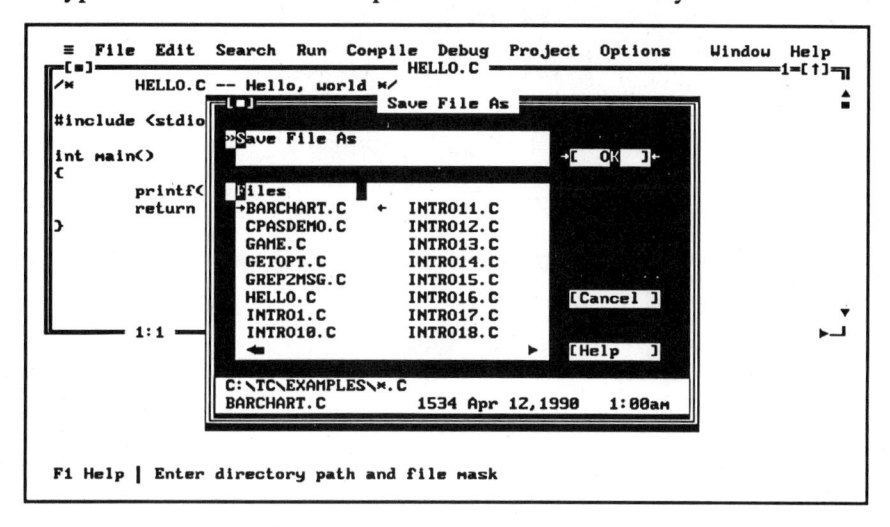

```
  ≡  File  Edit  Search  Run  Compile  Debug  Project  Options    Window  Help
┌─[■]─────────────────────────── HELLO.C ──────────────────────────────1─[↑]─┐
│/*       HELLO.C -- Hello, world */                                          │
│        ┌─[■]═════════════════ Save File As ═════════════════╗               │
│#include <stdio│                                                             │
│                │ ▶Save File As                                              │
│int main()      │                              ─┤ OK  ├─                     │
│{               │                                                             │
│       printf( │ ┌Files─────────────────────────┐                            │
│       return  │ │→BARCHART.C    ←   INTRO11.C  │                            │
│}               │ │ CPASDEMO.C        INTRO12.C │                            │
│                │ │ GAME.C            INTRO13.C │                            │
│                │ │ GETOPT.C          INTRO14.C │                            │
│                │ │ GREP2MSG.C        INTRO15.C │                            │
│                │ │ HELLO.C           INTRO16.C │  [Cancel]                  │
│                │ │ INTRO1.C          INTRO17.C │                            │
│    1:1         │ │ INTRO10.C         INTRO18.C │                            │
│                │ │ ←                       →   │  [Help]                    │
│                │ │                                                          │
│                │ C:\TC\EXAMPLES\*.C                                         │
│                │ BARCHART.C          1534 Apr 12,1990   1:00am              │
│                └─────────────────────────────────────────────┘               │
│                                                                              │
│                                                                              │
│ F1 Help | Enter directory path and file mask                                │
└──────────────────────────────────────────────────────────────────────────────┘
```

10. Press **Esc** to remove the Save File As dialog box, or click **Cancel** with a mouse. Make sure your printer is connected and ready.

11. Press **Alt-F** and type **P** to choose Print. Turbo C++ prints the HELLO.C file to your printer.

12. Press **Alt-F** and type **G** to choose Get Info. A dialog box appears, displaying information about the HELLO.C file.

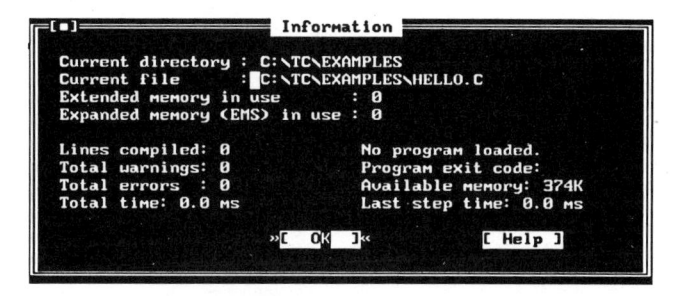

```
┌─[■]═══════════════════ Information ═══════════════════┐
│                                                        │
│ Current directory : C:\TC\EXAMPLES                     │
│ Current file      : C:\TC\EXAMPLES\HELLO.C             │
│ Extended memory in use       : 0                       │
│ Expanded memory (EMS) in use : 0                       │
│                                                        │
│ Lines compiled: 0         No program loaded.           │
│ Total warnings: 0         Program exit code:           │
│ Total errors  : 0         Available memory: 374K       │
│ Total time: 0.0 ms        Last step time: 0.0 ms       │
│                                                        │
│              »[  OK  ]«        [ Help ]                │
└────────────────────────────────────────────────────────┘
```

13. Press **Return** to remove the Information dialog box.
14. Press **Alt-F** and type **D** to choose DOS shell. The DOS prompt appears.
15. Type **exit** and press **Return**. Turbo C++ appears back on the screen.
16. Press **Alt-F** and type **Q**, or press **Alt-X** to choose Quit. Turbo C++ returns you to the DOS prompt.
17. Turn to Module 6 to continue the learning sequence.

Module 8
HELP MENU

DESCRIPTION

The Help menu displays five help options for using Turbo C++:
- Contents
- Index
- Topic search
- Previous topic
- Help on help

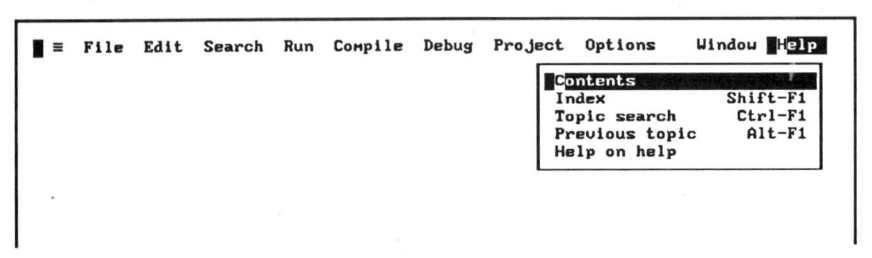

```
 ≡  File  Edit  Search  Run  Compile  Debug  Project  Options    Window  Help
                                                        Contents
                                                        Index           Shift-F1
                                                        Topic search    Ctrl-F1
                                                        Previous topic  Alt-F1
                                                        Help on help
```

You can display the Help menu in one of five ways:
- Press Alt-H.
- Click on the Help menu with a mouse.
- Press F1 to display the Turbo Help dialog box.
- Press Ctrl-F1 when the cursor is on a Turbo C++ command in a file, and Turbo C++ will display help on that particular C command.
- Press F10 and use the arrow keys to highlight the Help menu, then press Return.

APPLICATIONS

The Help menu lets you get more information about using the Turbo C++ integrated environment or in writing Turbo C++ programs.

Contents contains a complete list of topics available for more help.

Index lists keywords so you can get help on a specific topic or Turbo C++ command.

Topic search displays help on the C++ language. You can also choose this command by pressing Ctrl-F1.

Help Menu

Previous topic displays the last Help window you opened. You can back up through the last 20 help screens. To choose this command, you can also press Alt-F1.

Help on help explains how to use the Turbo C++ help system.

TYPICAL OPERATION

In this example, you practice using the different commands on the Help menu. Begin from within Turbo C++ with the HELLO.C program displayed in the edit window.

1. Press **F1**. Turbo C++ displays a Help window describing how to use the Turbo C++ editor.

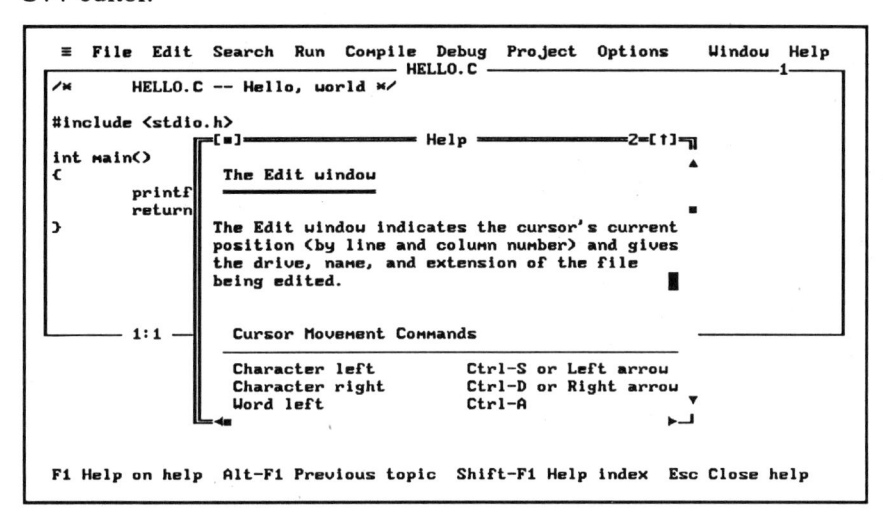

```
≡  File  Edit  Search  Run  Compile  Debug  Project  Options    Window  Help
┌─────────────────────────────── HELLO.C ──────────────────────────────1─┐
│/*       HELLO.C -- Hello, world */                                     │
│                                                                        │
│#include <stdio.h>                                                      │
│         ┌─[■]──────────────────── Help ═══════════════2=[↑]═╗          │
│int main()                                                   ▲          │
│{        │  The Edit window                                             │
│    printf│                                                             │
│    return│  The Edit window indicates the cursor's current  ■          │
│}        │  position (by line and column number) and gives             │
│         │  the drive, name, and extension of the file                 │
│         │  being edited.                                   ■          │
│         │                                                              │
│   1:1   │  Cursor Movement Commands                                    │
│         │                                                              │
│         │  Character left       Ctrl-S or Left arrow                  │
│         │  Character right      Ctrl-D or Right arrow    ▼            │
│         │  Word left            Ctrl-A                                │
│         └◄─                                               ►─┘         │
│                                                                        │
│ F1 Help on help  Alt-F1 Previous topic  Shift-F1 Help index  Esc Close help │
└────────────────────────────────────────────────────────────────────────┘
```

2. Press **PgDn** and **PgUp** to scroll through the Help window.
3. Press **Esc** to remove the Help window.
4. Move the cursor so it is on #include.
5. Press **Ctrl-F1** to get help on using the #include directive, or press **Alt-H** and type **T**.

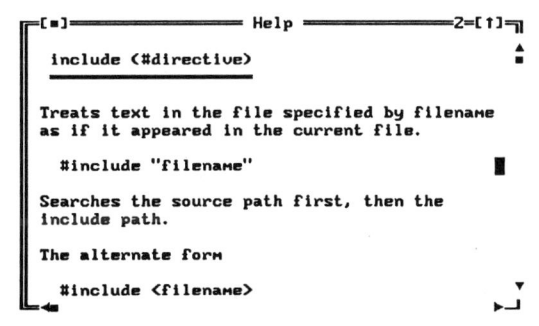

```
┌─[■]════════════════════ Help ═══════════════2=[↑]═╗
│  include (#directive)                             ▲
│                                                   
│  Treats text in the file specified by filename
│  as if it appeared in the current file.
│
│     #include "filename"                           ■
│
│  Searches the source path first, then the
│  include path.
│
│  The alternate form
│
│     #include <filename>                           ▼
└◄─                                               ►─┘
```

Module 8

6. Press **Esc** to remove the Help window.
7. Press **Alt-F1** to display the last Help window, or press **Alt-H** and type **P**.
8. Press **Esc** to remove the Help window.
9. Press **Shift-F1** to view the Turbo C++ Help Index, or press **Alt-H** and type **I**.

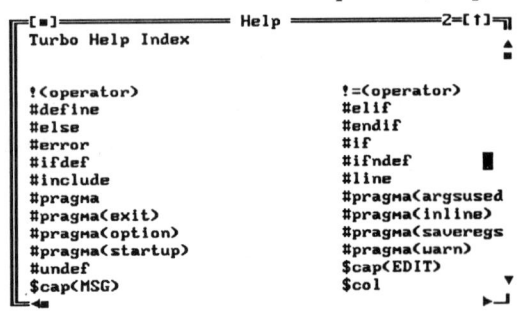

```
┌─[■]═══════════════════ Help ═══════════════2=[↑]─┐
│ Turbo Help Index                                 ▲│
│                                                  ■│
│ !<operator>              !=<operator>             │
│ #define                  #elif                    │
│ #else                    #endif                   │
│ #error                   #if                      │
│ #ifdef                   #ifndef      ■           │
│ #include                 #line                    │
│ #pragma                  #pragma<argsused>        │
│ #pragma<exit>            #pragma<inline>          │
│ #pragma<option>          #pragma<saveregs>        │
│ #pragma<startup>         #pragma<warn>            │
│ #undef                   $cap<EDIT>               │
│ $cap<MSG>                $col                    ▼│
└──◄■══════════════════════════════════════════►─┘
```

10. Highlight #define with the arrow keys and press **Return**. Turbo C++ displays help for using the #define directive.

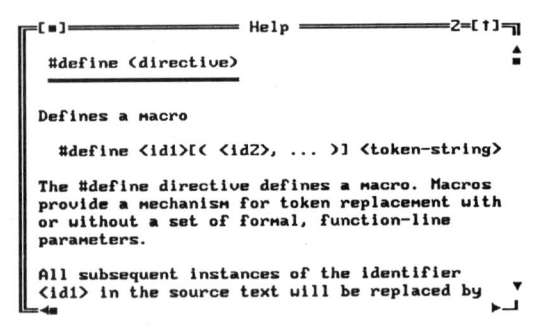

```
┌─[■]═══════════════════ Help ═══════════════2=[↑]─┐
│                                                  ▲│
│ #define <directive>                              ■│
│ ─────────────────                                 │
│                                                   │
│ Defines a macro                                   │
│                                                   │
│   #define <id1>[( <id2>, ... )] <token-string>    │
│                                                   │
│ The #define directive defines a macro. Macros     │
│ provide a mechanism for token replacement with    │
│ or without a set of formal, function-line         │
│ parameters.                                       │
│                                                   │
│ All subsequent instances of the identifier        │
│ <id1> in the source text will be replaced by    ▼ │
└──◄■══════════════════════════════════════════►─┘
```

11. Press **Esc** to remove the Help window.
12. Press **Alt-H** and type **C** to display the Turbo C++ Table of Contents.

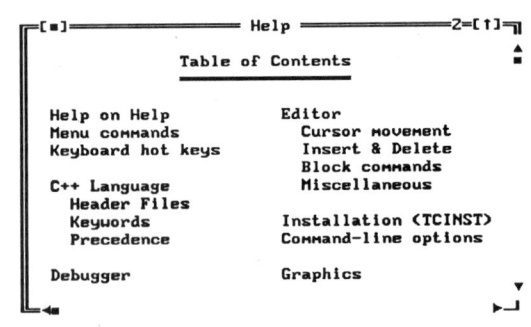

```
┌─[■]═══════════════════ Help ═══════════════2=[↑]─┐
│                                                  ▲│
│             Table of Contents                    ■│
│                                                   │
│  Help on Help          Editor                     │
│  Menu commands            Cursor movement         │
│  Keyboard hot keys        Insert & Delete         │
│                           Block commands          │
│  C++ Language             Miscellaneous           │
│     Header Files                                  │
│     Keywords           Installation (TCINST)      │
│     Precedence         Command-line options       │
│                                                   │
│  Debugger              Graphics                   │
│                                                  ▼│
└──◄■══════════════════════════════════════════►─┘
```

13. Highlight Menu commands with the arrow keys and press **Return**. Turbo C++ displays help for using the Turbo C++ menus.

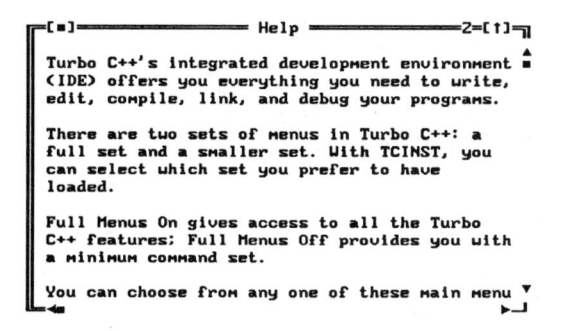

```
┌─[■]═══════════════ Help ═══════════════2=[↑]═┐
│ Turbo C++'s integrated development environment ▲
│ (IDE) offers you everything you need to write, ■
│ edit, compile, link, and debug your programs.
│
│ There are two sets of menus in Turbo C++: a
│ full set and a smaller set. With TCINST, you
│ can select which set you prefer to have
│ loaded.
│
│ Full Menus On gives access to all the Turbo
│ C++ features; Full Menus Off provides you with
│ a minimum command set.
│
│ You can choose from any one of these main menu ▼
└─◄■────────────────────────────────────────►─┘
```

14. Press **Esc** to remove the Help window.
15. Press **Alt-H** and type **H** to display a Help window describing how to use the Turbo C++ help system.

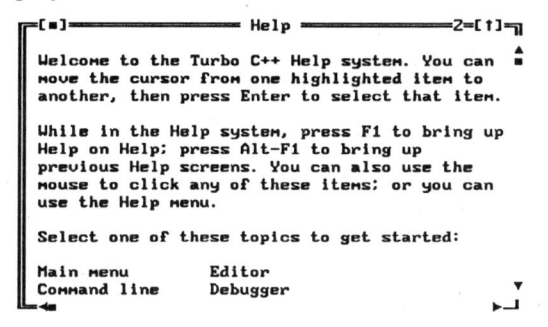

```
┌─[■]═══════════════ Help ═══════════════2=[↑]═┐
│ Welcome to the Turbo C++ Help system. You can ▲
│ move the cursor from one highlighted item to  ■
│ another, then press Enter to select that item.
│
│ While in the Help system, press F1 to bring up
│ Help on Help; press Alt-F1 to bring up
│ previous Help screens. You can also use the
│ mouse to click any of these items; or you can
│ use the Help menu.
│
│ Select one of these topics to get started:
│
│ Main menu          Editor
│ Command line       Debugger                    ▼
└─◄■────────────────────────────────────────►─┘
```

16. Press **PgDn**, highlight Graphics, and press **Return**. Turbo C++ displays help on using the Turbo C++ graphics routine.

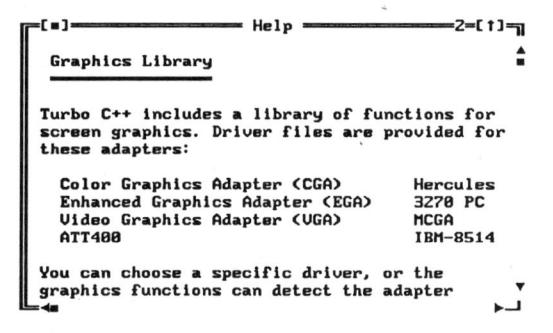

```
┌─[■]═══════════════ Help ═══════════════2=[↑]═┐
│ Graphics Library                              ▲
│                                               ■
│ Turbo C++ includes a library of functions for
│ screen graphics. Driver files are provided for
│ these adapters:
│
│   Color Graphics Adapter (CGA)     Hercules
│   Enhanced Graphics Adapter (EGA)  3270 PC
│   Video Graphics Adapter (VGA)     MCGA
│   ATT400                           IBM-8514
│
│ You can choose a specific driver, or the
│ graphics functions can detect the adapter     ▼
└─◄■────────────────────────────────────────►─┘
```

17. Press **Esc** to remove the Help window.
18. Turn to Module 11 to continue the learning sequence.

Module 9
OPTIONS MENU

DESCRIPTION

The Options menu contains commands for changing the settings of the Turbo C++ integrated development environment. When displayed with the Full menus option turned off, the Options menu contains six commands:
- Full menus
- Compiler
- Make
- Directories
- Environment
- Save

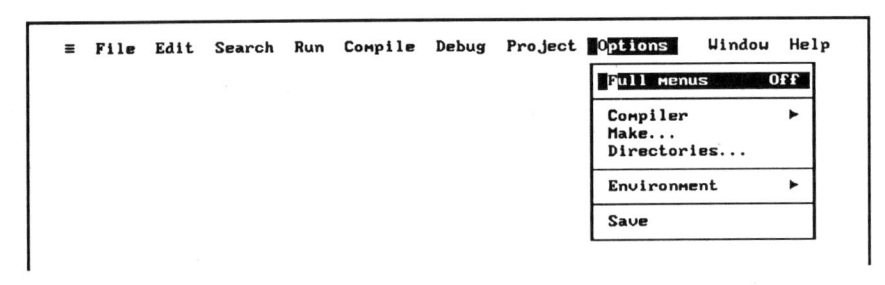

```
≡  File  Edit  Search  Run  Compile  Debug  Project  Options   Window  Help
                                                   ┌─────────────────┐
                                                   │ Full menus  Off │
                                                   ├─────────────────┤
                                                   │ Compiler      ▶ │
                                                   │ Make...         │
                                                   │ Directories...  │
                                                   ├─────────────────┤
                                                   │ Environment   ▶ │
                                                   ├─────────────────┤
                                                   │ Save            │
                                                   └─────────────────┘
```

When displayed with the Full menus option turned on, the Options menu contains three additional commands:
- Transfer
- Linker
- Debugger

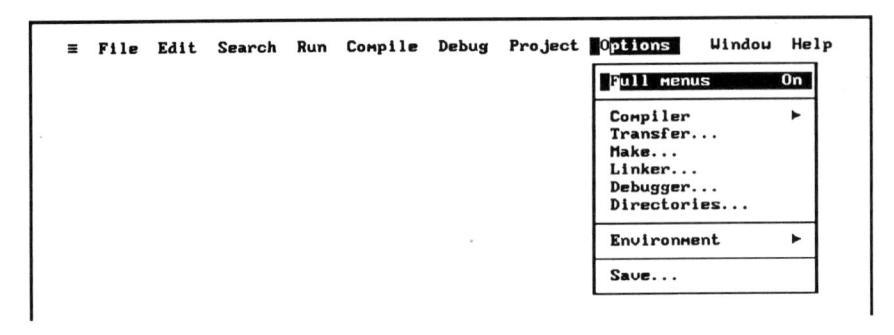

```
≡  File  Edit  Search  Run  Compile  Debug  Project  Options   Window  Help
                                                   ┌─────────────────┐
                                                   │ Full menus   On │
                                                   ├─────────────────┤
                                                   │ Compiler      ▶ │
                                                   │ Transfer...     │
                                                   │ Make...         │
                                                   │ Linker...       │
                                                   │ Debugger...     │
                                                   │ Directories...  │
                                                   ├─────────────────┤
                                                   │ Environment   ▶ │
                                                   ├─────────────────┤
                                                   │ Save...         │
                                                   └─────────────────┘
```

You can display the Options menu in one of three ways:
- Click on the Options menu with a mouse.
- Press Alt-O.
- Press F10 and use the arrow keys to highlight the Options menu, then press Return.

APPLICATIONS

The Options menu commands let you define the Turbo C++ integrated environment settings.

Full menus lets you display the complete Turbo C++ menus or only a partial set. Turning Full menus off makes the Turbo C++ menus easier to use. Turning Full menus on gives you more advanced commands for creating Turbo C++ programs.

Compiler displays a pop-up menu that lets you specify how Turbo C++ creates optimized code from your program. Until you are familiar with Turbo C++, you should use the default settings.

Make lets you specify conditions that will stop the making of a project file.

Directories specifies in which directories Turbo C++ can find include and library files. This command also lets you specify which directory to save program files.

Environment lets you specify the appearance of the Turbo C++ integrated environment, how the integrated debugger behaves, when Turbo C++ will automatically save your files, how the editor works, and how a mouse works with Turbo C++.

Save saves any options you set so Turbo C++ will automatically use them the next time you run Turbo C++.

Transfer lets you add or delete programs to the System menu.

Linker lets you define how Turbo C++ links your .OBJ files together.

Debugger lets you define how the integrated debugger works.

TYPICAL OPERATION

In this example, you practice using the different commands on the Options menu. Begin from within Turbo C++.

1. Press **Alt-Spacebar** and type **C** to clear the desktop.
2. Press **Alt-O** to display the Options menu. If Full menus is Off, type **F**. If Full menus is On, skip to step 4.
3. Press **Alt-O**.

Module 9

4. Type **C**. Turbo C++ displays a list of six options for customizing the Turbo C++ compiler: Code generation, C++ options, Optimizations, Source, Messages, and Names.

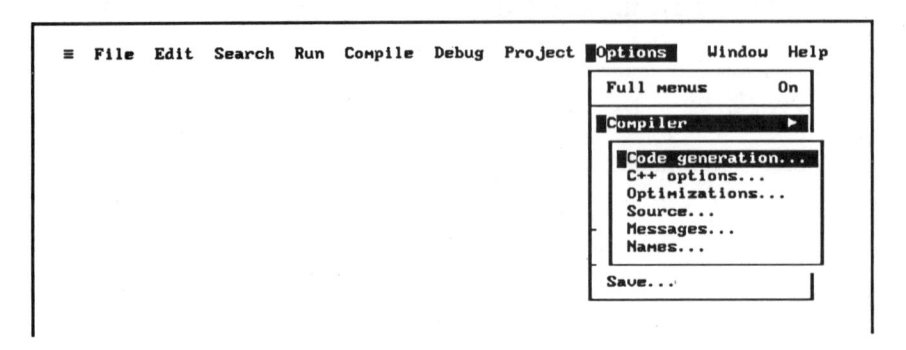

5. Press **Esc**.
6. Type **T** from the Options menu. Turbo C++ displays a Transfer dialog box, listing all the program titles that appear in the System menu.

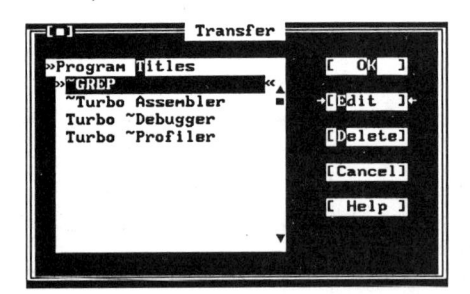

7. Press **Esc**.
8. Press **Alt-O** and type **M**. Turbo C++ displays a Make dialog box.

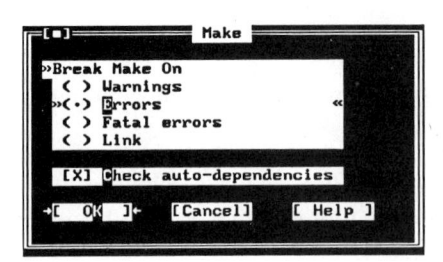

Options Menu

9. Press **Esc**.
10. Press **Alt-O** and type **L**. Turbo C++ displays a Linker dialog box.

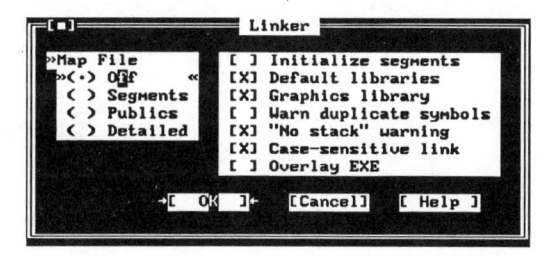

```
┌─[■]═══════════════════Linker═══════════════════┐
│ »Map File            [ ] Initialize segments   │
│  »(·) Off      «     [X] Default libraries     │
│   ( ) Segments       [X] Graphics library      │
│   ( ) Publics        [ ] Warn duplicate symbols│
│   ( ) Detailed       [X] "No stack" warning    │
│                      [X] Case-sensitive link   │
│                      [ ] Overlay EXE           │
│                                                │
│            →[ OK ]←    [Cancel]    [ Help ]    │
└────────────────────────────────────────────────┘
```

11. Press **Esc**.
12. Press **Alt-O** and type **B**. Turbo C++ displays a Debugger dialog box.

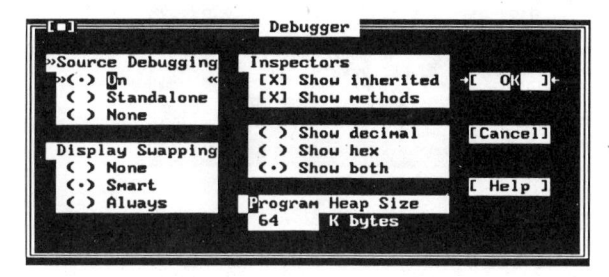

```
┌─[■]══════════════════Debugger══════════════════┐
│ »Source Debugging   Inspectors                 │
│  »(·) On       «    [X] Show inherited →[ OK ]←│
│   ( ) Standalone    [X] Show methods           │
│   ( ) None                                     │
│                     ( ) Show decimal  [Cancel] │
│  Display Swapping   ( ) Show hex               │
│   ( ) None          (·) Show both              │
│   (·) Smart                           [ Help ] │
│   ( ) Always        Program Heap Size          │
│                     64    K bytes              │
└────────────────────────────────────────────────┘
```

13. Press **Esc**.
14. Press **Alt-O** and type **D**. Turbo C++ displays a Directories dialog box.

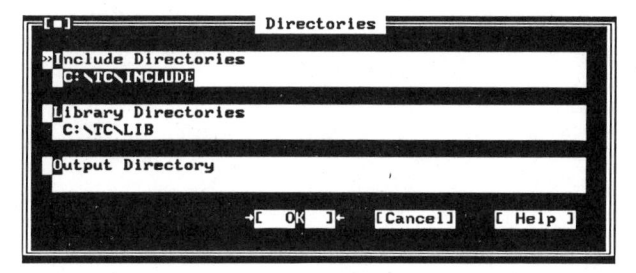

```
┌─[■]═════════════════Directories════════════════┐
│ »Include Directories                           │
│   C:\TC\INCLUDE                                │
│                                                │
│  Library Directories                           │
│   C:\TC\LIB                                    │
│                                                │
│  Output Directory                              │
│                                                │
│            →[ OK ]←    [Cancel]    [ Help ]    │
└────────────────────────────────────────────────┘
```

15. Press **Esc**.
16. Press **Alt-O** and type **E**. Turbo C++ displays a menu of three additional options: Preferences, Editor, and Mouse.

Module 9

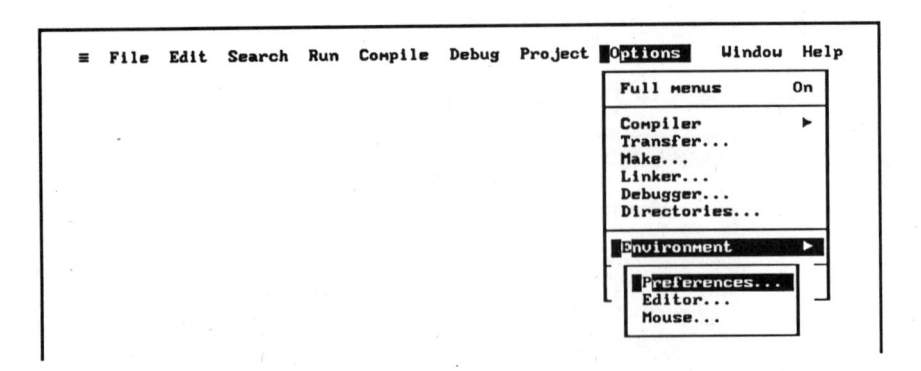

```
≡  File  Edit  Search  Run  Compile  Debug  Project  Options   Window  Help
                                                     Full menus      On
                                                     Compiler        ▶
                                                     Transfer...
                                                     Make...
                                                     Linker...
                                                     Debugger...
                                                     Directories...
                                                     Environment     ▶
                                                        Preferences...
                                                        Editor...
                                                        Mouse...
```

17. Press **Esc**.
18. Type **S**. Turbo C++ displays a Save Options dialog box.

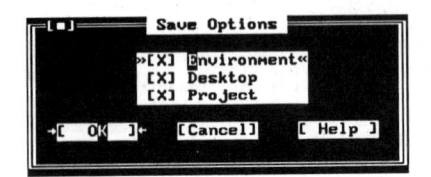

```
         Save Options
        »[X] Environment«
         [X] Desktop
         [X] Project
    →[  OK  ]   [Cancel]   [ Help ]
```

19. Press **Esc**.
20. Turn to Module 4 to continue the learning sequence.

Module 10
PROJECT MENU

DESCRIPTION

The Project menu contains six commands for managing projects:
- Open project
- Close project
- Add item
- Delete item
- Local options
- Include files

```
≡  File  Edit  Search  Run  Compile  Debug  Project  Options      Window  Help
                                            Open project...
                                            Close project

                                            Add item...
                                            Delete item
                                            Local options...
                                            Include files...
```

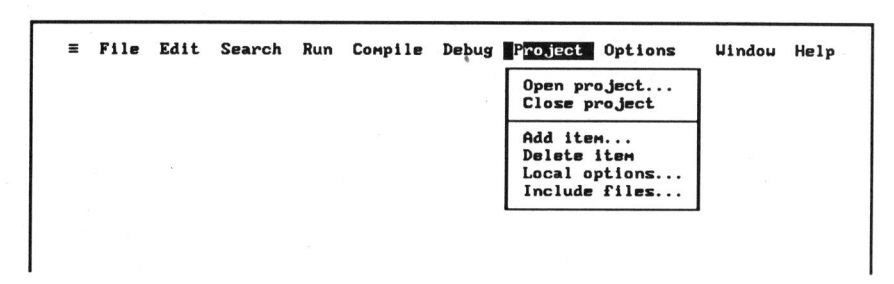

You can display the Project menu in one of three ways:
- Click on the Project menu with a mouse.
- Press Alt-P.
- Press F10 and use the arrow keys to highlight the Project menu, then press Return.

APPLICATIONS

The Project menu commands let you manage your Turbo C++ projects. A project is simply a collection of separate files that work together to create a single program.

Open project lets you create a new project or load an existing project. Project files contain information needed to create an executable .EXE program file.

Close project removes the current project.

Add item lets you add a file to a project.

Delete item lets you delete files from a project.

Module 10

Local options displays an Override Options dialog box that defines options for a project. The three available options are:
- Overlay this module makes selected project items as overlay files.
- Exclude debug information makes smaller .EXE programs at the expense of removing debugging information. Without debugging information, you cannot examine how a file works with the Turbo C++ integrated debugger.
- Exclude from link prevents a file from being linked to create an .EXE executable program file.

Include files lists the Include files the current project file uses.

TYPICAL OPERATION

In this example, you practice using the different commands on the Project menu. Begin from within Turbo C++ with no windows open.

1. Press **Alt-P** and type **O**. Turbo C++ displays a Load Project File dialog box.

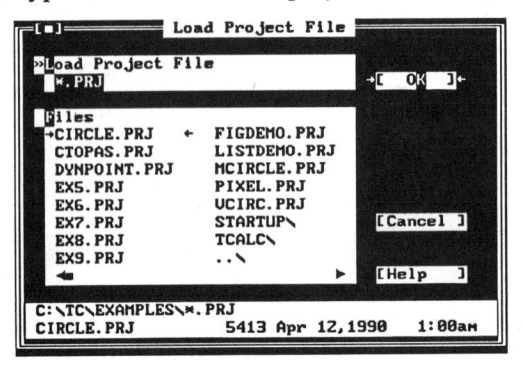

2. Type **C:\TC\EXAMPLES*.PRJ** and press **Return**. (This assumes you have stored the Turbo C++ example programs in the C:\TC\EXAMPLES directory.) Turbo C++ displays all the example .PRJ project files.

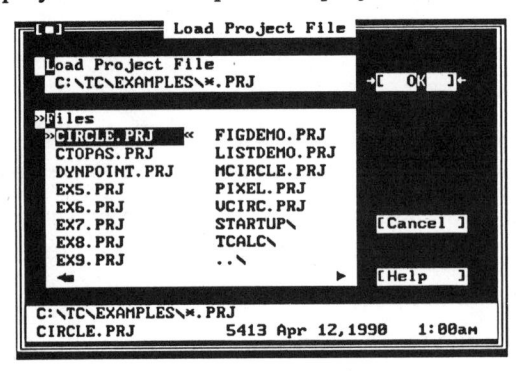

3. Choose CIRCLE.PRJ and press **Return**. Turbo C++ displays a Project window at the bottom of the screen. The Project window lists all the files in a project.

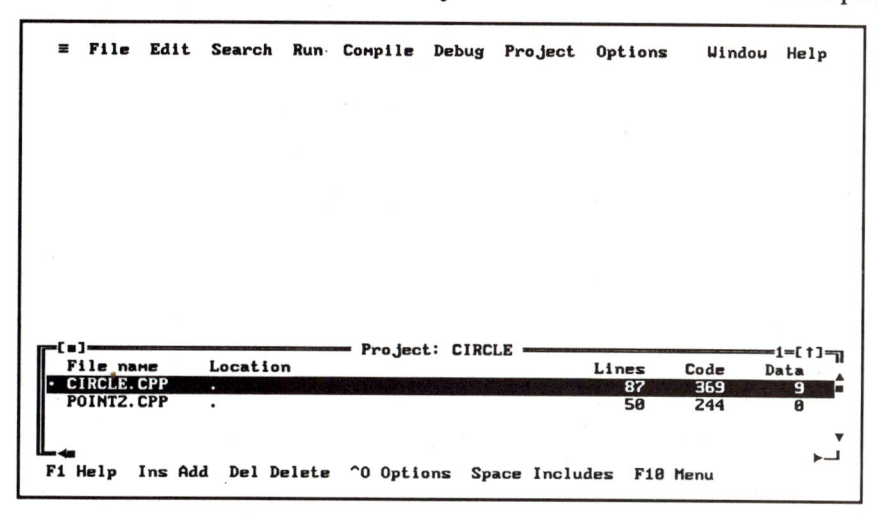

4. Press **Alt-P** and type **A**. Turbo C++ displays an Add Item to Project List dialog box.

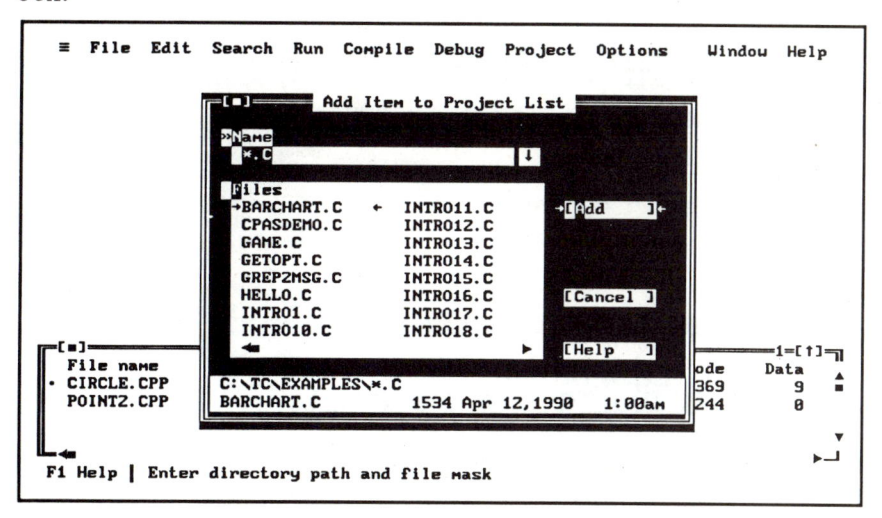

5. Choose BARCHART.C with the arrow keys and press **Return**. Turbo C++ keeps the Add Item to Project List dialog box on the screen so you can keep adding more files to a project.

6. Press **Esc**. Notice that Turbo C++ now displays the BARCHART.C file in the Project window.

Module 10

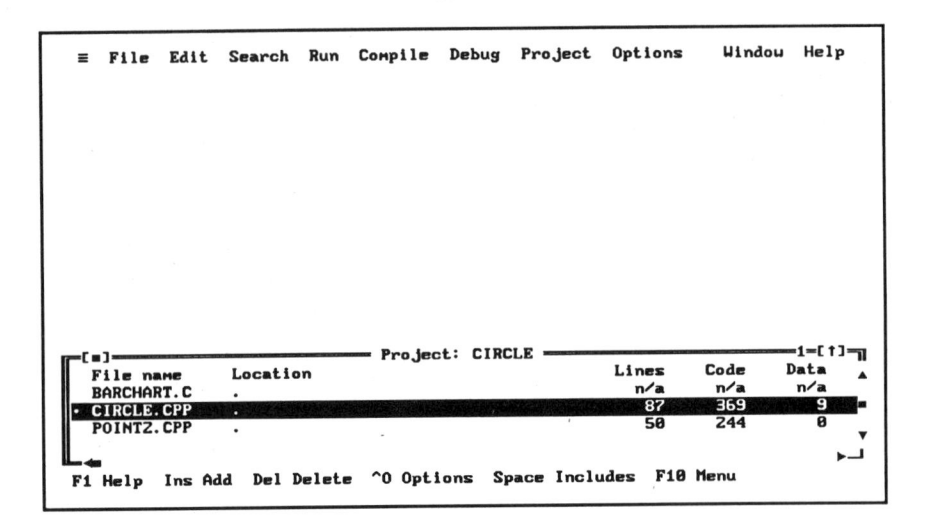

```
 ≡  File  Edit  Search  Run  Compile  Debug  Project  Options     Window  Help




















┌[■]──────────────────── Project: CIRCLE ──────────────────1=[↑]┐
│ File name      Location                        Lines    Code    Data  ▲
│ BARCHART.C     .                                n/a     n/a     n/a
│▶CIRCLE.CPP     .                                 87     369       9  ■
│ POINTZ.CPP     .                                 50     244       0
│                                                                       ▼
└←┘                                                                    ►┘
 F1 Help  Ins Add  Del Delete  ^O Options  Space Includes  F10 Menu
```

7. Highlight BARCHART.C in the Project window with the arrow keys.

8. Press **Alt-P** and type **D**. Turbo C++ deletes the BARCHART.C file from the Project window.

9. Press **Alt-P** and type **L**. Turbo C++ displays an Override Options dialog box.

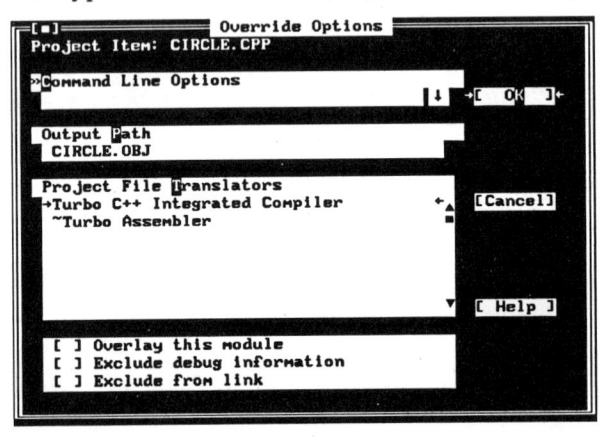

```
┌[■]═══════════════ Override Options ═══════════════┐
│ Project Item: CIRCLE.CPP                          │
│                                                   │
│ ▶Command Line Options                             │
│                                        │↓│ →[ OK ]←│
│                                                   │
│  Output Path                                      │
│   CIRCLE.OBJ                                      │
│                                                   │
│  Project File Translators                         │
│  →Turbo C++ Integrated Compiler         ▲ [Cancel]│
│   ~Turbo Assembler                      ■         │
│                                                   │
│                                                   │
│                                         ▼ [ Help ]│
│                                                   │
│  [ ] Overlay this module                          │
│  [ ] Exclude debug information                    │
│  [ ] Exclude from link                            │
└───────────────────────────────────────────────────┘
```

10. Press **Esc** to remove this dialog box from the screen.

11. Highlight CIRCLE.CPP with the arrow keys and press **Return**. Turbo C++ displays the CIRCLE.CPP file in the edit window.

12. Press **Alt-P** and type **I**. Turbo C++ displays an Include Files dialog box showing you which Include files the CIRCLE.CPP file uses.

Project Menu

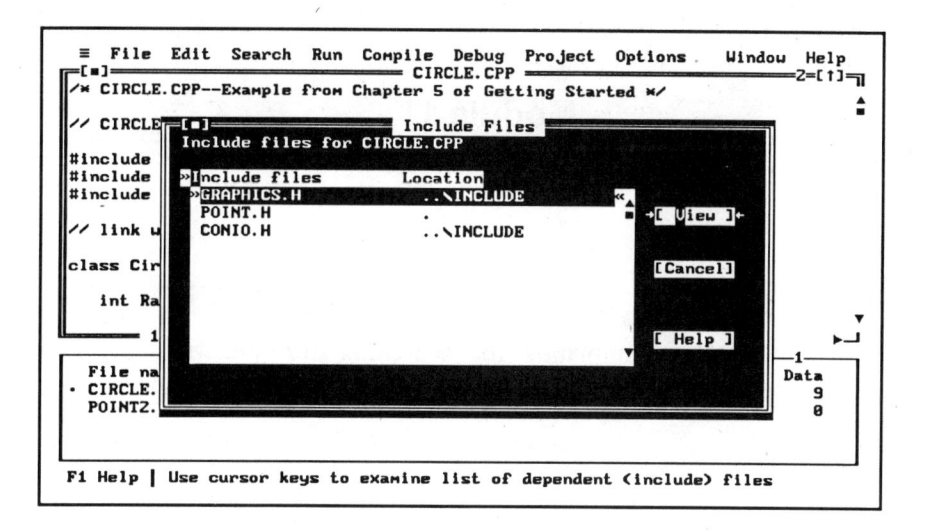

```
 ≡  File  Edit  Search  Run  Compile  Debug  Project  Options   Window  Help
┌[■]──────────────────────── CIRCLE.CPP ════════════════════════2=[↑]┐
│/* CIRCLE.CPP--Example from Chapter 5 of Getting Started */         ▲
│                                                                    ■
│// CIRCLE┌[■]═══════════════ Include Files ═══════════════┐
│         │ Include files for CIRCLE.CPP                   │
│#include │                                                │
│#include │ ▶Include files         Location                │
│#include │  ▷GRAPHICS.H          ..\INCLUDE       «▲      │
│         │   POINT.H              .               ■       │
│// link u│   CONIO.H             ..\INCLUDE        ─→[ View ]←
│         │                                                │
│class Cir│                                                │
│         │                                        [Cancel]│
│   int Ra│                                                │
│         │                                                │
│      1  │                                        [ Help ]│
│         │                                        ▼       ├─1─┐
│   File na└────────────────────────────────────────┘    Data  │
│ • CIRCLE.                                                 9  │
│   POINTZ.                                                 0  │
│                                                              │
└──────────────────────────────────────────────────────────────┘
 F1 Help │ Use cursor keys to examine list of dependent (include) files
```

13. Highlight the GRAPHICS.H file with the arrow keys and type **V**. Turbo C++ displays the GRAPHICS.H file in a second edit window.

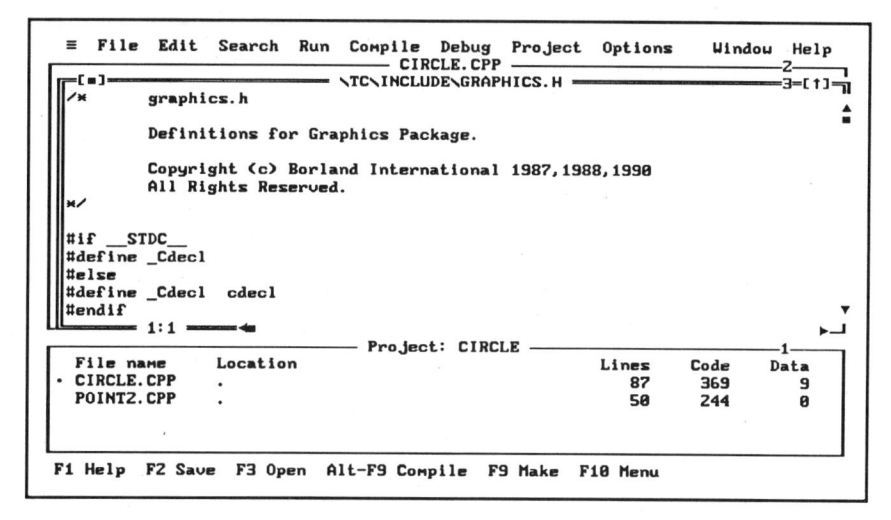

```
 ≡  File  Edit  Search  Run  Compile  Debug  Project  Options   Window  Help
┌──────────────────────────── CIRCLE.CPP ──────────────────────2─┐
┌[■]═══════════════════ \TC\INCLUDE\GRAPHICS.H ═══════════════3=[↑]┐
│/*       graphics.h                                             ▲
│                                                                ■
│         Definitions for Graphics Package.
│
│         Copyright (c) Borland International 1987,1988,1990
│         All Rights Reserved.
│*/
│
│#if __STDC__
│#define _Cdecl
│#else
│#define _Cdecl cdecl
│#endif                                                          ▼
│    1:1 ◀                                                      ─┘
├──────────────────── Project: CIRCLE ──────────────────────1─┐
│   File name   Location                    Lines   Code   Data
│ • CIRCLE.CPP    .                            87    369      9
│   POINTZ.CPP    .                            50    244      0
│
│
└────────────────────────────────────────────────────────────┘
 F1 Help  F2 Save  F3 Open  Alt-F9 Compile  F9 Make  F10 Menu
```

14. Press **Alt-P** and type **C**. Turbo C++ closes the CIRCLE.PRJ project.
15. Turn to Module 39 to continue the learning sequence.

49

Module 11
RUN MENU

DESCRIPTION

The Run menu contains commands for searching for specific text, function declarations, and errors in a file. The Run menu contains six commands.
- Run
- Program reset
- Go to cursor
- Trace into
- Step over
- Arguments

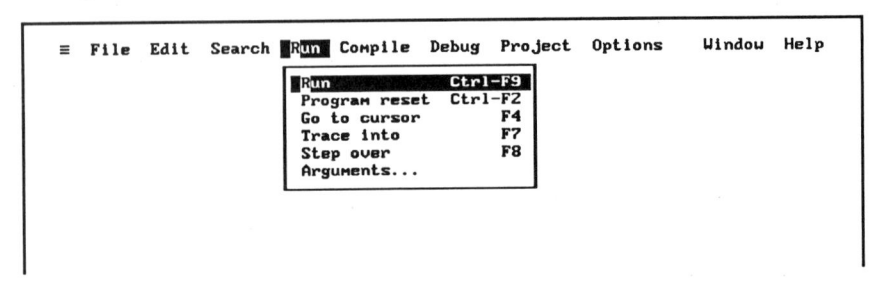

```
≡  File  Edit  Search  Run  Compile  Debug  Project  Options     Window  Help
                              Run              Ctrl-F9
                              Program reset   Ctrl-F2
                              Go to cursor    F4
                              Trace into      F7
                              Step over       F8
                              Arguments...
```

You can display the Run menu in one of three ways:
- Click on the Run menu with a mouse.
- Press Alt-R.
- Press F10 and use the arrow keys to highlight the Run menu, then press Return.

APPLICATIONS

The Run menu commands let you run a program that appears in the current window.

Run will compile, link, and run your program. You can also choose the Run command by pressing Ctrl-F9.

Program reset stops the program from continuing while you are using the Turbo C++ integrated debugger. You can also choose the Program reset command by pressing Ctrl-F2.

Go to cursor works while you are using the Turbo C++ integrated debugger. This command lets you run your program from the current highlighted line to the location of the cursor. You can also choose the Go to cursor command by pressing F4.

Trace into runs your program line-by-line. When the debugger reaches a function call, the debugger displays the lines of the called function. Upon exiting the function, the debugger displays the main program. You can also choose the Trace into command by pressing F7.

Step over runs your program line-by-line, like the Trace into command. The difference is when the debugger reaches a function call, it does not display the lines of the called function. You can also choose the Step over command by pressing F8.

Arguments lets you define any command-line arguments for your program to use as if you had typed them from the DOS command line.

TYPICAL OPERATION

In this example, you practice using the different commands on the Run menu. Begin from within Turbo C++ with the HELLO.C program displayed in the edit window.

1. Modify the HELLO.C program as follows:

   ```
   /* HELLO.C -- Hello, world */

   #include <stdio.h>

   void Hello (void);

   int main()
   {
       Hello ();
       return 0;
   }

   void Hello ()
       {
       printf ("Hello, world\n");
       }
   ```

2. Press **Ctrl-F9** or press **Alt-R** and type **R** to run the HELLO.C program in the edit window. The screen may flash momentarily as Turbo C++ prints the message "Hello, world" on the screen.
3. Press **Alt-F5** to see the "Hello, world" message as it would appear if you ran the HELLO.C program from the DOS command line.
4. Press **Alt-F5** to return to the Turbo C++ integrated development environment.
5. Press **F7** or press **Alt-R** and type **T** to choose the Trace into command. Turbo C++ highlights the first line of the HELLO.C program, int main( ).

Module 11

```
  ≡  File  Edit  Search  Run  Compile  Debug  Project  Options  Window  Help
┌─[■]─────────────────────── HELLO.C ───────────────────────1=[↑]─┐
│/*        HELLO.C -- Hello, world */                              ▲│
│                                                                   ■│
│#include <stdio.h>                                                  │
│                                                                    │
│void Hello (void);                                                  │
│                                                                    │
│int main()                                                          │
│{                                                                   │
│        Hello ();                                                   │
│        return 0;                                                   │
│}                                                                   │
│                                                                    │
│void Hello ()                                                       │
│        {                                                         ▼ │
├──*─── 7:1 ═══◄─────────────── Message ────────────────────── 2 ──┤
│•Compiling C:\TC\EXAMPLES\HELLO.C:                                  │
│ Linking C:\TC\EXAMPLES\HELLO.EXE:                                  │
│                                                                    │
│                                                                    │
└────────────────────────────────────────────────────────────────────┘
 F1 Help  F7 Trace  F8 Step  F9 Make  F10 Menu
```

6. Press **F7** again. Turbo C++ highlights the next line of the HELLO.C program, Hello ( ).
7. Press **F7**. Notice that Turbo C++ now highlights the void Hello ( ) line.
8. Press **F7** twice.
9. Press **Alt-F5** to see the result of the printf ("Hello, world\n"); statement.
10. Press **Alt-F5** to return to the Turbo C++ integrated development environment.
11. Press **Ctrl-F2** or press **Alt-R** and type **P** to reset the program and stop the Trace into command. Notice that Turbo C++ removes the highlighting from the HELLO.C program.
12. Press **F7** twice until Turbo C++ highlights the Hello ( ); line.
13. Press **F8** or press **Alt-R** and type **S**. Notice that Turbo C++ does not highlight the statements in the function Hello ( ) as it did in step 7.
14. Press **Ctrl-F2** or press **Alt-R** and type **P**.
15. Press **F7**. Turbo C++ highlights the first line of the HELLO.C program.
16. Move the cursor to the return 0 line by pressing the **Up/Down Arrow**.
17. Press **F4** or press **Alt-R** and type **G**. Notice that Turbo C++ runs all the statements between the previously highlighted line and the line where the cursor appears.
18. Press **Alt-F3** to close the edit window. Turbo C++ displays a message box, asking if you want to save the modified HELLO.C program. Type **N**.
19. Turn to Module 5 to continue the learning sequence.

52

Module 12
SEARCH MENU

DESCRIPTION

The Search menu contains commands for searching for specific text, function declarations, and errors in a file. The Search menu contains seven commands.
- Find
- Replace
- Search again
- Go to line number
- Previous error
- Next error
- Locate function

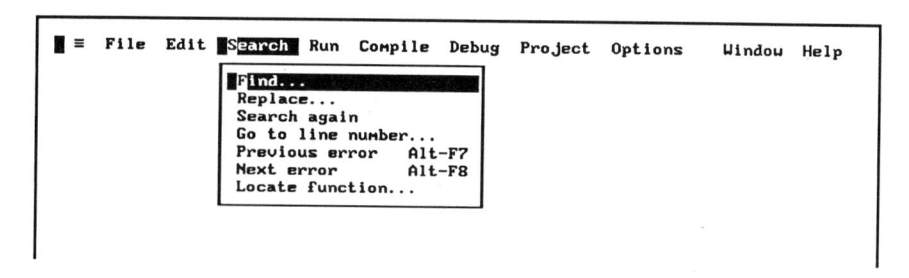

```
■ ≡  File  Edit  Search  Run  Compile  Debug  Project  Options    Window  Help
                    ┌─────────────────────────┐
                    │ Find...                 │
                    │ Replace...              │
                    │ Search again            │
                    │ Go to line number...    │
                    │ Previous error   Alt-F7 │
                    │ Next error       Alt-F8 │
                    │ Locate function...      │
                    └─────────────────────────┘
```

You can display the Search menu in one of three ways:
- Click on the Search menu with a mouse.
- Press Alt-S.
- Press F10 and use the arrow keys to highlight the Search menu, then press Return.

APPLICATIONS

The Search menu commands let you search for text within a file.

Find displays a dialog box that provides several search criteria:
- Case sensitive — Differentiates between uppercase and lowercase letters.
- Whole words only — Searches for strings separated by punctuation or spaces on both sides.
- Regular expression — Recognizes GREP-like wildcards in a search string: ^, $, ., *, +, [ ], and \.

53

Module 12

- Direction — Determines which direction for Turbo C++ to search, forward or backward, starting from the origin defined by the Origin option below.
- Scope — Determines whether to search selected text in a file or the entire file.
- Origin — Determines where searching begins, from the cursor or from the beginning or end of a file.

You can also choose the Find command by pressing Ctrl-Q F.

Replace displays a dialog box that lets you search and replace text within a file. This Replace dialog box contains the same options as the Find dialog box, with the addition of a Prompt to Replace option.

When Prompt to Replace is checked, Turbo C++ prompts you before replacing text. When Prompt to Replace is not checked, Turbo C++ automatically replaces text.

You can choose the Replace command by pressing Ctrl-Q A.

Search again repeats the last Find or Replace command, using any settings made in the last Find or Replace dialog box. You can also choose the Search again command by pressing Ctrl-L.

Go to line number displays a specific line number that you want to see.

Previous error displays the line in your program that contains the previous error or warning message. This command only works if the Message window contains messages. You can also choose this command by pressing Alt-F7.

Next error displays the line in your program that contains the next error or warning message. This command only works if the Message window contains messages. You can also choose this command by pressing Alt-F8.

Locate function lets you find the name of a function. This command is only available while using the integrated Turbo C++ debugger.

TYPICAL OPERATION

In this example, you practice using the different commands on the Search menu. Begin from within Turbo C++ with the INTRO1.C program in the edit window.

1. Press **Ctrl-Q** to move to the top of the program. Press **Alt-S** and type **F**. Turbo C++ displays a Find dialog box.

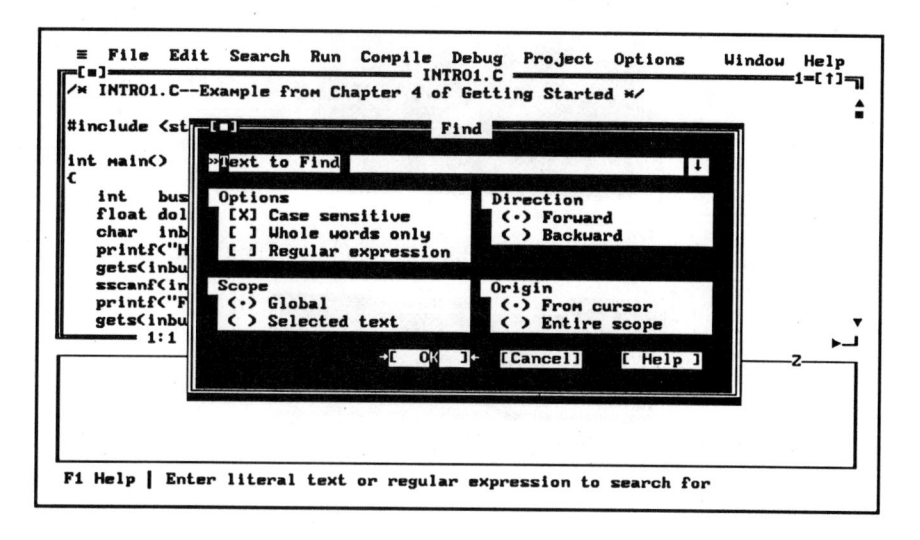

```
 ≡  File  Edit  Search  Run  Compile  Debug  Project  Options     Window  Help
┌─[■]─────────────────────── INTRO1.C ═══════════════════════════1═[↑]─┐
│ /* INTRO1.C--Example from Chapter 4 of Getting Started */            ▲
│                                                                      │
│ #include <st┌─[■]──────────────── Find ────────────────────┐         │
│             │ Text to Find                             ↓  │         │
│ int main()  │                                              │         │
│ {           │ ┌Options─────────────┐ ┌Direction──────────┐ │         │
│    int  bus │ │ [X] Case sensitive │ │ (•) Forward       │ │         │
│    float dol│ │ [ ] Whole words only│ │ ( ) Backward      │ │         │
│    char  inb│ │ [ ] Regular expression│ └───────────────┘ │         │
│    printf("H│ └─────────────────────┘                      │         │
│    gets(inbu│ ┌Scope───────────────┐ ┌Origin─────────────┐ │         │
│    sscanf(in│ │ (•) Global         │ │ (•) From cursor   │ │         │
│    printf("F│ │ ( ) Selected text  │ │ ( ) Entire scope  │ │         │
│    gets(inbu│ └────────────────────┘ └───────────────────┘ │         │
│ ──── 1:1 ───│         ─[ OK ]─  [Cancel]  [ Help ]         │    ▼    │
│             └──────────────────────────────────────────────┘    ►⌐   │
│                                                                  2   │
│                                                                      │
│                                                                      │
│                                                                      │
│                                                                      │
└──────────────────────────────────────────────────────────────────────┘
  F1 Help │ Enter literal text or regular expression to search for
```

2. Type **sscanf** and press **Tab** five times. Notice that each time you press Tab, Turbo C++ highlights a different option in the Find dialog box.

3. Press **Return**. Turbo C++ highlights the first occurrence of sscanf.

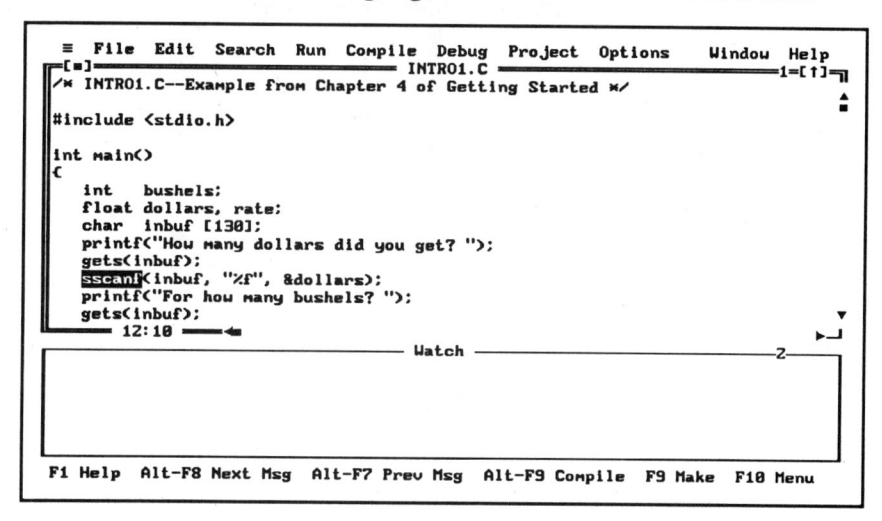

```
 ≡  File  Edit  Search  Run  Compile  Debug  Project  Options     Window  Help
┌─[■]─────────────────────── INTRO1.C ═══════════════════════════1═[↑]─┐
│ /* INTRO1.C--Example from Chapter 4 of Getting Started */            ▲
│                                                                      │
│ #include <stdio.h>                                                   │
│                                                                      │
│ int main()                                                           │
│ {                                                                    │
│    int    bushels;                                                   │
│    float  dollars, rate;                                             │
│    char   inbuf [130];                                               │
│    printf("How many dollars did you get? ");                         │
│    gets(inbuf);                                                      │
│    sscanf(inbuf, "%f", &dollars);                                    │
│    printf("For how many bushels? ");                                 │
│    gets(inbuf);                                                      │
│ ──── 12:10 ────                                                 ▼    │
│                                                                 ►⌐   │
├─────────────────────────────── Watch ──────────────────────────2─────┤
│                                                                      │
│                                                                      │
│                                                                      │
│                                                                      │
└──────────────────────────────────────────────────────────────────────┘
  F1 Help  Alt-F8 Next Msg  Alt-F7 Prev Msg  Alt-F9 Compile  F9 Make  F10 Menu
```

4. Press **Alt-S** and type **S** or press **Ctrl-L**. Turbo C++ highlights the next occurrence of sscanf.

5. Press **Alt-S** and type **S**. This time Turbo C++ displays an Error dialog box, meaning that there are no more occurrences of the sscanf string in the file.

Module 12

6. Press **Return**.
7. Press **Alt-S** and type **G**. Turbo C++ displays a Go to Line Number dialog box.

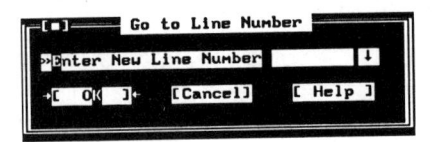

8. Type **1** and press **Return**. Turbo C++ moves the cursor to line 1 of the current file.
9. Press **Alt-S** and type **R**. Turbo C++ displays a Replace dialog box.

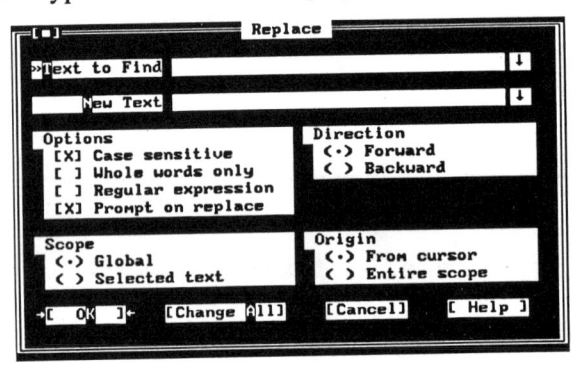

10. Type **printf** and press **Tab**.
11. Type **writeln** and press **Return**. Turbo C++ displays a Message dialog box, asking if you want to replace the currently highlighted printf string.

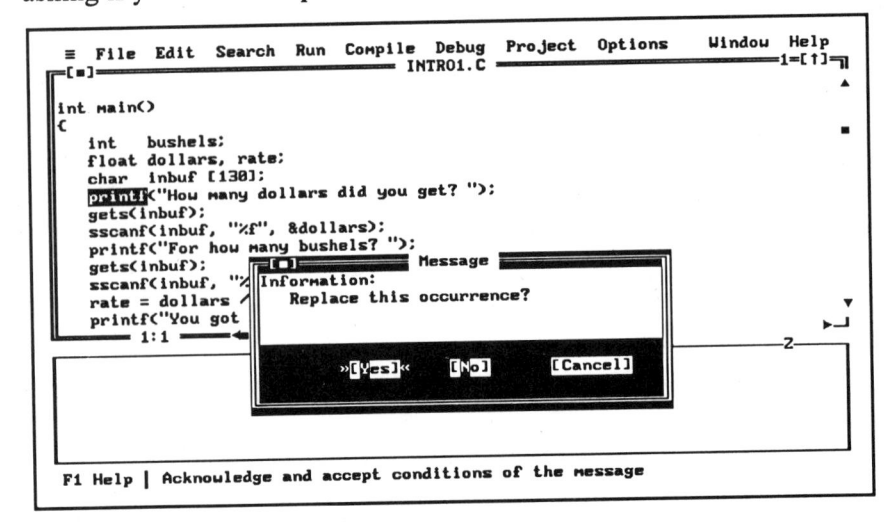

56

Search Menu

12. Press **Esc**.
13. Press **Alt-S** and type **G**. The Go to Line Number dialog box appears.
14. Type **10** and press **Return**. Turbo C++ moves the cursor to line 10.
15. Press **Ctrl-F8** to set a breakpoint at line 10.
16. Press **Ctrl-F9**. Turbo C++ highlights the breakpoint at line 10.
17. Press **Alt-S** and type **L**. Turbo C++ displays a Locate Function dialog box.

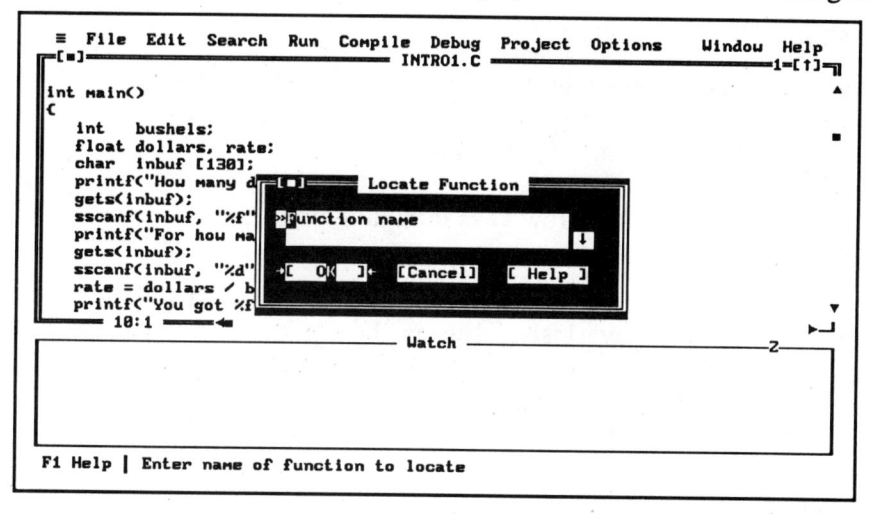

```
≡ File  Edit  Search  Run  Compile  Debug  ProJect  Options  Window  Help
┌─[■]───────────────────────── INTRO1.C ──────────────────────────1=[↑]─┐
│int main()                                                           ▲ │
│{                                                                      │
│   int    bushels;                                                   ■ │
│   float  dollars, rate;                                               │
│   char   inbuf [130];                                                 │
│   printf("How many d┌─[■]────── Locate Function ──────┐               │
│   gets(inbuf);      │                                 │               │
│   sscanf(inbuf, "%f"│ ▶Function name                  │               │
│   printf("For how ma│                              ↓  │               │
│   gets(inbuf);      │                                 │               │
│   sscanf(inbuf, "%d"│ →[  OK  ]←   [Cancel]   [ Help ]│               │
│   rate = dollars / b└─────────────────────────────────┘               │
│   printf("You got %f                                                ▼ │
│─── 10:1 ────◄────                                                   ►─┘
┌───────────────────────────── Watch ─────────────────────────────2─────┐
│                                                                       │
│                                                                       │
│                                                                       │
└───────────────────────────────────────────────────────────────────────┘
 F1 Help │ Enter name of function to locate
```

18. Type **main** and press **Return**. Notice that Turbo C++ moves the cursor to highlight the line containing the function named main.
19. Press **Ctrl-F2** to reset the program.
20. Press **Alt-D** and type **B**. Turbo C++ displays a Breakpoint dialog box.
21. Type **D** to delete the highlighted breakpoint from the program. Press **Return**.
22. Turn to Module 14 to continue the learning sequence.

Module 13
SYSTEM MENU

DESCRIPTION

The System menu appears at the far left of the menu bar. You can display the System menu in one of three ways:
- Click on the System menu with a mouse.
- Press Alt-Spacebar.
- Press F10 and use the arrow keys to highlight the System menu, then press Return.

The System menu contains four items: About, Clear desktop, Repaint desktop, and a list of any programs you have installed using the Options menu and the Transfer command. By default, the System menu contains three programs: Turbo Assembler, Turbo Debugger, and Turbo Profiler.

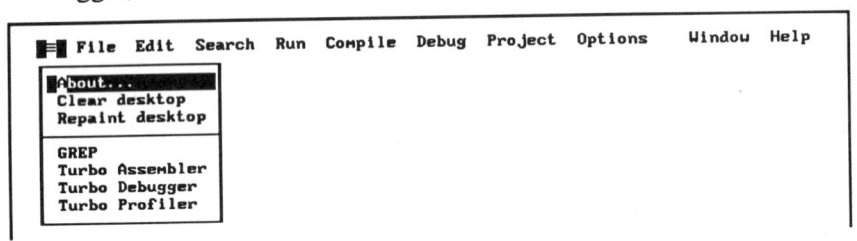

```
≡ File   Edit   Search   Run   Compile   Debug   Project   Options      Window   Help
  About...
  Clear desktop
  Repaint desktop
  
  GREP
  Turbo Assembler
  Turbo Debugger
  Turbo Profiler
```

APPLICATIONS

You use the System menu to control the display of the Turbo C++ Programmer's Platform. Anytime you want to clear all the windows from the screen quickly, use the Clear desktop command.

Sometimes, when you run a Turbo C++ program that doesn't work correctly, the program may display characters and symbols on the screen. To clear these characters and symbols from the screen without clearing away any windows, use the Repaint desktop command.

Finally, the System menu lets you install other programs that you may want to use with Turbo C++, such as Turbo Assembler and Turbo Debugger.

Note that not all programs that you install on the System menu may run within Turbo C++. This problem may occur because Turbo C++ temporarily stores itself in memory. When another program tries to run, there may not be enough memory.

TYPICAL OPERATION

In this example, you practice using the System menu commands. Begin at the DOS prompt.

1. Type **TC** and press **Return** to load Turbo C++.
2. Press **Alt-Spacebar** to display the System menu.
3. Type **A** to choose the About command. A dialog box appears, showing you the copyright and version number for your copy of Turbo C++.

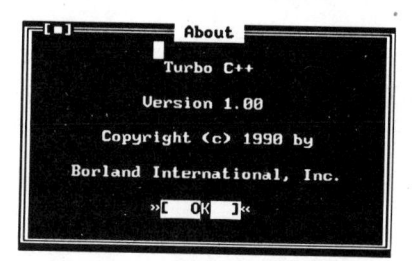

4. Press **Esc** to clear the dialog box from the screen.
5. Press **Shift-F1** to display the Turbo C++ help system.

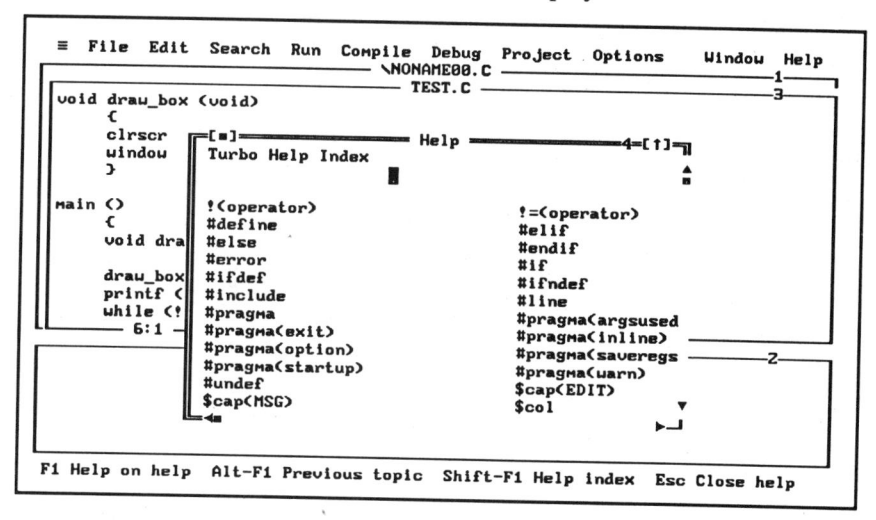

6. Press **Alt-Spacebar** to display the System menu.
7. Type **C** to choose Clear desktop. Notice that the help system window disappears.
8. Turn to Module 7 to continue the learning sequence.

Module 14
WINDOW MENU

DESCRIPTION

The Window menu contains commands for changing the appearance of the Turbo C++ integrated development environment windows. When displayed with the Full menus option turned off, the Window menu contains twelve commands:
- Size/Move
- Zoom
- Tile
- Cascade
- Next
- Close
- Message
- Output
- Watch
- User screen
- Project
- List

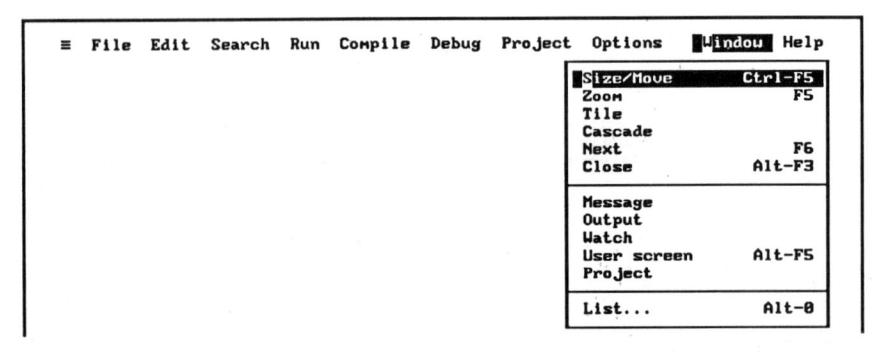

```
 ≡  File  Edit  Search  Run  Compile  Debug  Project  Options  Window  Help
                                                     ┌─────────────────────┐
                                                     │ Size/Move   Ctrl-F5 │
                                                     │ Zoom             F5 │
                                                     │ Tile                │
                                                     │ Cascade             │
                                                     │ Next             F6 │
                                                     │ Close        Alt-F3 │
                                                     ├─────────────────────┤
                                                     │ Message             │
                                                     │ Output              │
                                                     │ Watch               │
                                                     │ User screen  Alt-F5 │
                                                     │ Project             │
                                                     ├─────────────────────┤
                                                     │ List...       Alt-0 │
                                                     └─────────────────────┘
```

When displayed with the Full menus option turned on, the Window menu contains two additional commands:
- Register
- Project notes

Window Menu

```
≡  File  Edit  Search  Run  Compile  Debug  Project  Options  ▌Window▐  Help
                                                ┌─────────────────────────┐
                                                │ Size/Move      Ctrl-F5  │
                                                │ Zoom                F5  │
                                                │ Tile                    │
                                                │ Cascade                 │
                                                │ Next                F6  │
                                                │ Close           Alt-F3  │
                                                ├─────────────────────────┤
                                                │ Message                 │
                                                │ Output                  │
                                                │ Watch                   │
                                                │ User screen     Alt-F5  │
                                                │ Register                │
                                                │ Project                 │
                                                │ Project notes           │
                                                ├─────────────────────────┤
                                                │ ▌List...▐        Alt-0  │
                                                └─────────────────────────┘
```

You can display the Window menu in one of three ways:
- Click on the Window menu with a mouse.
- Press Alt-W.
- Press F10 and use the arrow keys to highlight the Window menu, then press Return.

APPLICATIONS

The Window menu commands let you define the appearance of the Turbo C++ integrated environment windows.

Size/Move lets you change the size and position of a window. You can also change the size of a window by pressing Shift and an arrow key. To choose this command, you can also press Ctrl-F5.

Zoom resizes the current window to fill the entire screen. Choosing this command again restores it to its original size. You can also choose this command by pressing F5.

Tile displays all windows so they fit on the screen. With tiled windows, no window will overlap another window.

Cascade displays windows so they may overlap one another.

Next makes another window active. You can also choose this command by pressing F6.

Close removes the active window from the screen. You can also choose this command by pressing Alt-F3.

Message opens the Message window. If a Message window already appears, this command will make the Message window the active window.

Output opens a window that shows the output of your program. For a larger view of your program's output, use the User screen command described below.

61

Watch opens a Watch window and makes it active. The Watch window displays variables and their values.

User screen displays a full screen of your program's output. For a smaller view, choose the Output command described above. You can also choose this command by pressing Alt-F5.

Project lists all the files in your current project.

Project notes lets you write ideas, lists, or notes to yourself about each project.

List displays all the files currently open. You can also choose this command by pressing Alt-O.

Register displays the CPU registers and their contents to help you debug your program.

TYPICAL OPERATION

In this example, you practice using the different commands on the Window menu. Begin from within Turbo C++ with the INTRO1.C program in the edit window.

1. Press **Alt-W** and type **T**. Notice that Turbo C++ resizes the windows so they all fit on the screen.

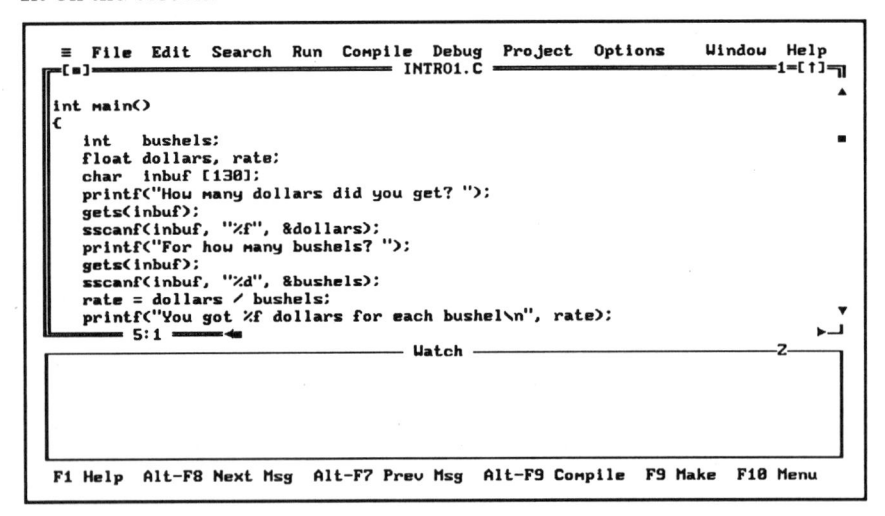

```
≡ File  Edit  Search  Run  Compile  Debug  Project  Options    Window  Help
┌─[■]──────────────────────── INTRO1.C ───────────────────────1=[↑]─┐
│int main()                                                         ▲
│{                                                                  
│    int    bushels;                                                ■
│    float  dollars, rate;                                          
│    char   inbuf [130];                                            
│    printf("How many dollars did you get? ");                      
│    gets(inbuf);                                                   
│    sscanf(inbuf, "%f", &dollars);                                 
│    printf("For how many bushels? ");                              
│    gets(inbuf);                                                   
│    sscanf(inbuf, "%d", &bushels);                                 
│    rate = dollars / bushels;                                      
│    printf("You got %f dollars for each bushel\n", rate);          ▼
│─── 5:1 ─────◄────────                                             ►┘
┌──────────────────────────── Watch ──────────────────────────2────┐
│                                                                  │
│                                                                  │
│                                                                  │
│                                                                  │
└──────────────────────────────────────────────────────────────────┘
  F1 Help  Alt-F8 Next Msg  Alt-F7 Prev Msg  Alt-F9 Compile  F9 Make  F10 Menu
```

2. Press **Alt-W** and type **Z,** or press **F5**. Turbo C++ zooms the current window to fill the entire screen.

```
     ≡  File  Edit  Search  Run  Compile  Debug  Project  Options     Window  Help
  ┌─[■]──────────────────────── INTRO1.C ────────────────────────1=[↕]─┐
  │int main()                                                         ▲│
  │{                                                                   │
  │    int    bushels;                                                 │
  │    float  dollars, rate;                                          ■│
  │    char   inbuf [130];                                             │
  │    printf("How many dollars did you get? ");                       │
  │    gets(inbuf);                                                    │
  │    sscanf(inbuf, "%f", &dollars);                                  │
  │    printf("For how many bushels? ");                               │
  │    gets(inbuf);                                                    │
  │    sscanf(inbuf, "%d", &bushels);                                  │
  │    rate = dollars / bushels;                                       │
  │    printf("You got %f dollars for each bushel\n", rate);           │
  │                                                                    │
  │    return 0;                                                       │
  │}                                                                   │
  │                                                                   ▼│
  │── 5:1 ───◄                                                       ►─│
  │ F1 Help  Alt-F8 Next Msg  Alt-F7 Prev Msg  Alt-F9 Compile  F9 Make  F10 Menu
  └────────────────────────────────────────────────────────────────────┘
```

3. Press **Alt-W** and type **R**. Turbo C++ displays the contents of the registers in the CPU window.

```
     ≡  File  Edit  Search  Run  Compile  Debug  Project  Options     Window  Help
  ┌──────────────────────────── INTRO1.C ────────────┌─[■]── CPU ──────3─┐
  │int main()                                        │AX FF00  DX 000C  │
  │{                                                 │BX 000C  CX 0000  │
  │    int    bushels;                               │CS 89D9  IP 0240  │
  │    float  dollars, rate;                         │DS 8F2E  SI 0000  │
  │    char   inbuf [130];                           │ES 89C1  DI 000C  │
  │    printf("How many dollars did you get? ");     │SS 8F2E  SP FF68  │
  │    gets(inbuf);                                  │BP FFF6           │
  │    sscanf(inbuf, "%f", &dollars);                │c=0 z=0 s=1 o=0   │
  │    printf("For how many bushels? ");             │p=0 i=1 a=1 d=0   │
  │    gets(inbuf);                                  └──────────────────┘
  │    sscanf(inbuf, "%d", &bushels);
  │    rate = dollars / bushels;
  │    printf("You got %f dollars for each bushel\n", rate);
  │
  │    return 0;
  │}
  │
  │── 5:1 ──
  │ F1 Help  Alt-F8 Next Msg  Alt-F7 Prev Msg  Alt-F9 Compile  F9 Make  F10 Menu
  └────────────────────────────────────────────────────────────────────┘
```

4. Press **Alt-W** and type **A**. Turbo C++ displays the Watch window overlapping the Message window.

Module 14

```
  ≡  File  Edit  Search  Run  Compile  Debug  Project  Options    Window    Help
  ─────────────────────── INTRO1.C ──────────────┌─[■]══ CPU ═══3─┐
                                                 │ AX FF00 DX 000C│
  int main()                                     │ BX 000C CX 0000│
  {                                              │ CS 89D9 IP 0240│
      int    bushels;                            │ DS 8F2E SI 0000│
      float dollars, rate;                       │ ES 89C1 DI 000C│
      char   inbuf [130];                        │ SS 8F2E SP FF68│
      printf("How many dollars did you get? ");  │ BP FFF6        │
      gets(inbuf);                               │ c=0 z=0 s=1 o=0│
      sscanf(inbuf, "%f", &dollars);             │ p=0 i=1 a=1 d=0│
      printf("For how many bushels? ");          └────────────────┘
      gets(inbuf);
      sscanf(inbuf, "%d", &bushels);
      rate = dollars / bushels;
      printf("You got %f dollars for each bushel\n", rate);
  ──── 5:1 ──────────────────────────────
  ─────────────────────── Watch ─────────────────────2──
  



  
  F1 Help  Alt-F8 Next Msg  Alt-F7 Prev Msg  Alt-F9 Compile  F9 Make  F10 Menu
```

5. Press **Alt-W** and type **C**, or press **Alt-F3** to close the CPU window.
6. Press **Alt-W** and type **M**. Turbo C++ makes the Message window active.

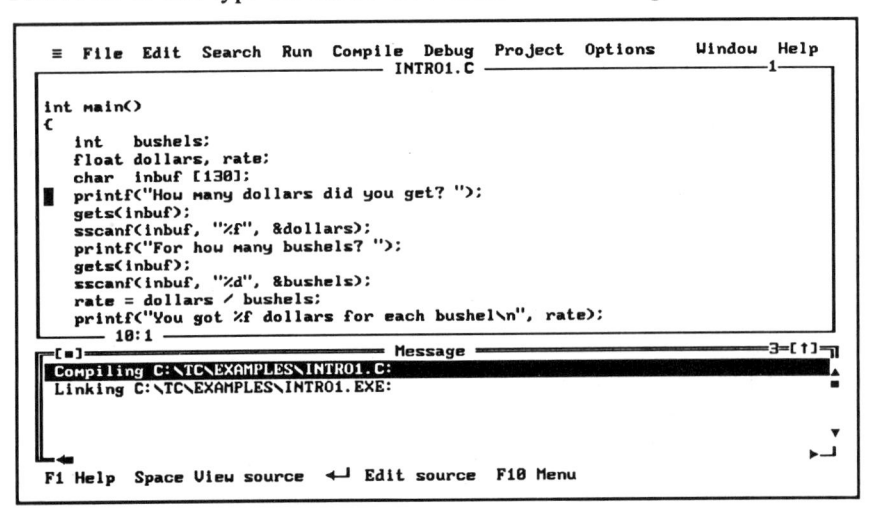

```
  ≡  File  Edit  Search  Run  Compile  Debug  Project  Options   Window   Help
  ─────────────────────── INTRO1.C ─────────────────────────────1─
  int main()
  {
      int    bushels;
      float dollars, rate;
      char   inbuf [130];
  ▌   printf("How many dollars did you get? ");
      gets(inbuf);
      sscanf(inbuf, "%f", &dollars);
      printf("For how many bushels? ");
      gets(inbuf);
      sscanf(inbuf, "%d", &bushels);
      rate = dollars / bushels;
      printf("You got %f dollars for each bushel\n", rate);
  ──── 10:1 ──────────────────────────────
  ┌─[■]──────────────────── Message ═══════════════════3═[↑]═┐
  │ Compiling C:\TC\EXAMPLES\INTRO1.C:                        ▲
  │ Linking   C:\TC\EXAMPLES\INTRO1.EXE:                      ■
  │                                                           ▼
  └───────────────────────────────────────────────────────────┘
  F1 Help  Space View source  ↵ Edit source  F10 Menu
```

7. Press **Alt-F3** to close the Message window.
8. Press **Alt-W** and type **W**. Turbo C++ makes the Watch window active.

```
  ≡  File  Edit  Search  Run  Compile  Debug  Project  Options   Window  Help
 ┌─────────────────────────── INTRO1.C ───────────────────────1───┐
 │ int main()                                                     │
 │ {                                                              │
 │    int    bushels;                                             │
 │    float dollars, rate;                                        │
 │    char   inbuf [130];                                         │
 │    printf("How many dollars did you get? ");                   │
 │    gets(inbuf);                                                │
 │    sscanf(inbuf, "%f", &dollars);                              │
 │    printf("For how many bushels? ");                           │
 │    gets(inbuf);                                                │
 │    sscanf(inbuf, "%d", &bushels);                              │
 │    rate = dollars / bushels;                                   │
 │    printf("You got %f dollars for each bushel\n", rate);       │
 │──  10:1                                                        │
 ┌─[■]─────────────────────── Watch ──────────────────────2=[↑]─┐
 │                                                              ▲│
 │                                                              ░│
 │                                                              ░│
 │                                                              ▼│
 └←┘────────────────────────────────────────────────────────────→┘
   F1 Help  F7 Trace  F8 Step  ←┘ Edit  Ins Add  Del Delete  F10 Menu
```

9. Press **Alt-W** and type **X** to make the edit window active.
10. Press **F6** to make the Watch window active.
11. Press **Alt-W** and type **C,** or press **Alt-F3** to close the Watch window.
12. Press **Alt-W** and type **L,** or press **Alt-0**. Turbo C++ displays a list of all the windows you have opened or closed in the past.
13. Press **Esc**.
14. Press **Ctrl-F9** to run the program. The program displays the message "How many dollars did you get?"
15. Type **250** and press **Return**. The next message asks, "For how many bushels?"
16. Type **60** and press **Return**. Turbo C++ momentarily displays the answer before returning to the integrated development environment.
17. Press **Alt-W** and type **U,** or press **Alt-F5**. Turbo C++ displays the program's output completely on the screen.

```
C:\TC>TC
How many dollars did you get? 250
For how many bushels? 60
You got 4.166667 dollars for each bushel
```

18. Press **Alt-F5** to return to the integrated development environment.

Module 14

19. Press **Alt-W** and type **O**. Notice that Turbo C++ now displays the program's output in a window.

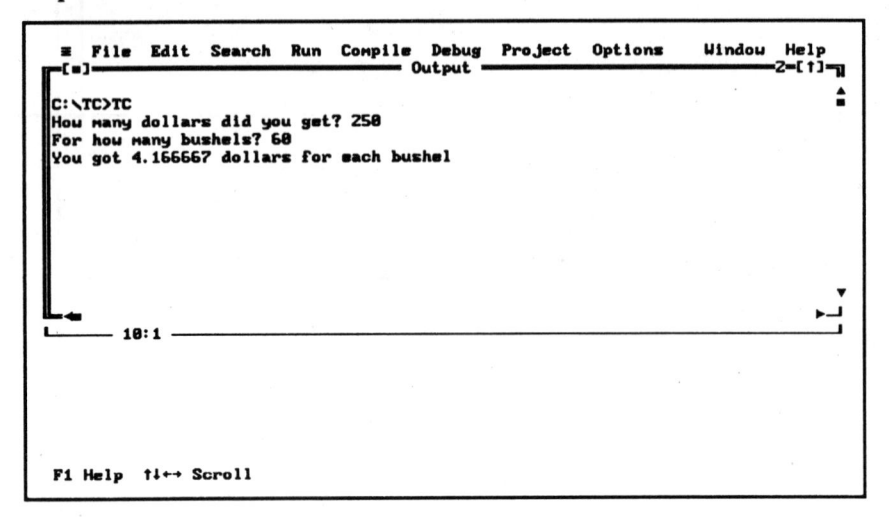

```
   File   Edit   Search   Run   Compile   Debug   Project   Options      Window   Help
┌─[■]────────────────────────────── Output ──────────────────────────2─[↑]─┐
│C:\TC>TC                                                                   │
│How many dollars did you get? 250                                          │
│For how many bushels? 60                                                   │
│You got 4.166667 dollars for each bushel                                   │
│                                                                           │
│                                                                           │
│                                                                           │
│                                                                           │
│                                                                           │
│                                                                           │
│└─ 10:1 ───────────────────────────────────────────────────────────────────┘
│                                                                           │
│                                                                           │
│  F1 Help  ↑↓↔ Scroll                                                      │
└───────────────────────────────────────────────────────────────────────────┘
```

20. Press **Alt-F3** to close the Output window.
21. Turn to Module 9 to continue the learning sequence.

Module 15
stringizing operator

DESCRIPTION

The stringizing operator (#) converts a preprocessor macro argument to a string. The syntax is:

    #define macro(arg)   #arg

APPLICATIONS

You can use the stringizing operator to store frequently used statements as strings. Once you have stored a statement as a string, you can quickly access that statement by calling the preprocessor macro name. An example of a stringized macro definition would be:

    #define stringize(arg)   #arg

If we have the following code in the program:

```
s = stringize(token);
s = stringize(int);
printf(stringize(The following will be concatenated) "to this" "\n");
printf(stringize(Print a " here, please\n) "\n");
```

The preprocessor expands into the following:

```
s = "token";
s = "int";
printf("The following will be concatenated to this \n");
printf("Print a \" here, please\\n\n");
```

TYPICAL OPERATION

In this program, you use the # stringizing operator to represent a statement as a preprocessor macro name. Begin from within Turbo C++ with no windows open.

1. Press **Alt-F** and type **N** to create a new file.
2. Type the following:

```
#define debug(s,t)    printf("x" #s "=%d, x" #t "=%s\n",x##s,x##t)

void main()
{
    int x1=1;
```

67

Module 15

```
    char *x2 = "Not another string!";

    debug(1,2);
// expands to:
//    printf("x1=%d, x2=%s\n",x1,x2);
}
```

3. Press **Ctrl-F9** to run the program.
4. Press **Alt-F5** to view the program results. Notice that the program expands the debug(s,t) macro into the statement, printf ("x1=%d, x2=%s\n",x1,x2);

    x1=1, x2=Not another string!

5. Press **Alt-F5** to return to the Turbo C++ editor.
6. Press **Alt-Spacebar** and type **C** and type **N** to clear the desktop.
7. Turn to Module 16 to continue the learning sequence.

Module 16
token pasting operator

DESCRIPTION

The token pasting preprocessor operator concatenates ("pastes") two tokens together. The syntax is:
```
token1 ## token2
```

The white space around the ## operator is optional.

This example expands to:
```
token1token2
```

APPLICATIONS

Token pasting concatenates tokens together during the preprocessor phase of compilation. This can be used to create variables with similar names. For example, if we have the following declarations:
```
#define    new_var(n)      var##n
```
and the following code fragment:
```
int        new_var(1), new_var(2);
```
it would expand into:
```
var1, var2;
```

TYPICAL OPERATION

In this program, you experiment with creating two variables using the token operator. Begin from within Turbo C++ with no windows open.

1. Press **Alt-F** and type **N** to create a new file.
2. Type the following:

```
#define new_var(n) var##n

void main ()
    {
    int new_var(1), new_var(2);
    /* Creates two variables: var1 and var2 */

    var1 = 4;
```

Module 16

```
        printf ("%d\n", var1);
        var2 = 5;

        printf ("%d\n", var2);
        }
```

3. Press **Ctrl-F9** to run the program. The program creates two variables called var1 and var2 and assigns them the values of 4 and 5.
4. Press **Alt-F5** to view the program results.

   4
   5

5. Press **Alt-F5** to return to the Turbo C++ editor.
6. Press **Alt-Spacebar** and type **C** and type **N** to clear the desktop.
7. Turn to Module 53 to continue the learning sequence.

Module 17
#define and #undef

DESCRIPTION

The #define command defines a macro, which is a text string represented by a name. Whenever the computer finds the macro name, it replaces the macro name with the text string it represents. The following sample macro consists of the macro name (PI) and the text string it represents (3.14159):

```
#define    PI    3.14159

int main()
    {
    printf ("%f", PI);
    return (0);
    }
```

The above program is equivalent to:

```
int main()
    {
    printf ("%f", 3.14159);
    return (0);
    }
```

Running the above program displays 3.141590 on the screen. If you omit the **#define PI 3.14159** statement, the program does not run because PI is undefined.

When defining macros with #define, be careful that the macro is a valid C++ text string. For example, many beginners make the mistake of ending the macro definition with a semicolon such as:

```
#define    PI    3.14159;
```

When Turbo C++ replaces the macro name with the macro text string, the semicolon is included:

```
int main()
    {
    printf ("%f", 3.14159;); /* Invalid C++ syntax */
    return (0);
    }
```

which is illegal.

The #undef command undefines a previously defined macro, such as:
```
#undef     PI
```
The following program will not run because PI is undefined:
```
#define    PI    3.14159

int main()
    {
    #undef     PI           /* Undefines PI */

    printf ("%f", PI);
    return (0);
    }
```

APPLICATIONS

You can use the #define command to assign a value to a variable, assign a text string to a macro name, or compile certain parts of your program (called conditional compilation) using the #ifdef command.

Assigning a value to a variable lets you quickly change the value of a variable that may appear in multiple locations in your program.

Assigning a text string to a macro name can simplify writing long statements. Rather than write the complete statement each time you need it, you can use a macro instead.

For example, to simplify writing ((x)*(x)), you could define a macro called square(x) such as:
```
#define square(x)     ((x)*(x))
```
When defining macros, be careful that the macro follows valid C++ syntax. Using the following #define,
```
#define square(x)     (x * x)
```
if we try to expand the statement
```
y = square(x+3);
```
we'll get
```
y = (x + 3 * x + 3);
```
which evaluates as
```
y = (x + (3 * x) + 3);
```
which calculates the incorrect answer. To correct this macro, we need parentheses around the variable as it appears in the expanded part of the macro definition.
```
#define square(x)     ((x) * (x))
```
Now if we expand the example we get
```
y = ((x + 3) * (x + 3));
```

which will give us the correct result.

You can also use #define with the #ifdef or #ifndef command to conditionally compile certain parts of your program. First you define a variable such as:

```
#define DEBUG 1
```

(You can assign any value to the macro name.)

Now you can compile certain parts of your program using #ifdef or #ifndef in a command such as:

```
#define DEBUG 1

int main()
    {
    #ifdef DEBUG
    /* Any statements here will compile */
    #endif

    #ifndef DEBUG
    /* Any statements here will NOT compile */
    #endif
    }
```

TYPICAL OPERATION

In this program, you experiment with the #define command. Begin from within Turbo C++ with no windows open.

1. Press **Alt-F** and type **N** to create a new file.
2. Type the following:

```
#define square(x)    ((x)*(x))
#define MESSAGE      printf ("Enter a number: ");

int main ()
    {
    int     num;

    MESSAGE
    scanf ("%d", &num);
    printf ("The square of %d is %d\n", num, square(num));
    return (0);
    }
```

3. Press **Ctrl-F9** to run the program. The program only displays the message:

```
Enter a number:
```

73

Module 17

4. Type **5** and press **Return**. The program briefly displays the message "The square of 5 is 25" before returning you to the Turbo C++ editor.
5. Modify the program as follows:

    ```
    int main ()
        {
        int    num;

        printf ("Enter a number: ");
        scanf ("%d", &num);
        printf ("The square of %d is %d\n", num,((num)*(num)));
        return (0);
        }
    ```

6. Press **Ctrl-F9** to run the program. Notice that this program behaves exactly as the program in step 2. The only difference is that macros would let you quickly reuse code without typing an entire program statement all over again.
7. Type **5** and press **Return**. Turbo C++ displays the editing window.
8. Press **Alt-Spacebar** and type **C** and type **N** to clear the desktop.
9. Turn to Module 20 to continue the learning sequence.

Module 18
#error

DESCRIPTION

The #error directive lets you put diagnostic messages into your preprocessor statements. It has a syntax of:

```
#error errmsg
```

APPLICATIONS

When working with conditional compilation (using #if, #ifdef, etc.), you may need to display error messages to inform the user to compile your program with specific compiler options.

You may have a value, X11, which must be a 0 or a 1. If the X11 preprocessor variable was not defined to be 0 or 1, the following code in your program:

```
#if (X11 != 0 && X11 != 1)
#error Please set the X11 preprocessor variable to 0 or 1 before compilation.
#endif
```

would display the message:

```
Please set the X11 preprocessor variable to 0 or 1 before compilation.
```

TYPICAL OPERATION

The #error preprocessor command lets you display messages during compilation. The following example will display error messages if the program is compiled on a machine that isn't using C++ and MS-DOS. Begin from within Turbo C++ with no windows open.

1. Press **Alt-F** and type **N** to create a new file.
2. Type the following:

```
#ifndef __MSDOS__      // is the operating system MS-DOS?
#error This program must be compiled on an MS-DOS machine
#endif

#ifndef __TURBOC__     // is the language Turbo C++?
#error This program must be compiled using C++
#endif
```

Module 18

```
void main()
{
}
```

3. Press **Ctrl-F9** to run the program. Since the program contains no instructions, the program does nothing.

4. Modify the program as follows:

   ```
   #ifdef __MSDOS__      // is the operating system MS-DOS?
   #error You cannot compile this program on an MS-DOS machine
   #endif

   #ifndef __TURBOC__    // is the language Turbo C++?
   #error This program must be compiled using C++
   #endif

   void main()
   {
   }
   ```

5. Press **Ctrl-F9** to run the program. Turbo C++ displays an error message.

6. Press **Return**. Turbo C++ displays the message "You cannot compile this program on an MS-DOS machine" in the Message window at the bottom of the screen.

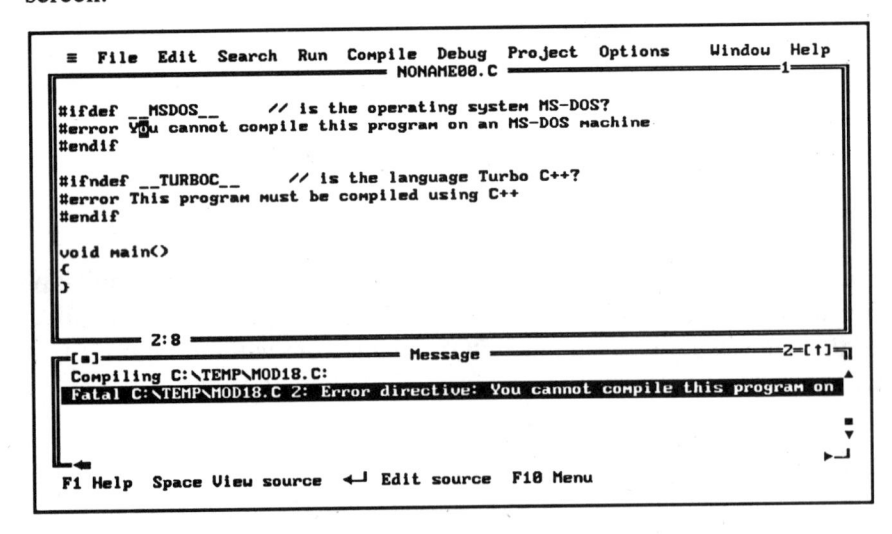

7. Press **Alt-Spacebar** and type **C** and type **N** to clear the desktop.
8. Turn to Module 22 to continue the learning sequence.

Module 19
#if, #elif, #else, #endif

DESCRIPTION

These preprocessor commands control which sections of your program Turbo C++ will compile, depending on the value of some condition. They are used in one of three ways:

```
#if condition
   code
#endif

#if condition
   code
#else
   code
#endif

#if condition1
   code
#elif condition2
   code
#endif

#if condition1
   code
#elif condition2
   code
#else
   code
#endif
```

APPLICATIONS

The #if preprocessor command and the related preprocessor commands #elif, #else, and #endif control which portions of your program are compiled. Known as conditional compilation, this feature lets you selectively compile certain parts of your program.

Since you can compile your Turbo C++ programs on other computers, you may want to make sure that MS-DOS-specific features are only compiled on computers using MS-DOS.

Suppose you have a program that uses a function available only in MS-DOS and Turbo C++. You could protect that function with the following:

```
#if defined(__MSDOS__) && defined(__cplusplus__)
void protected_function() {...}
#endif
```

The above commands translates to "If the computer is running MS-DOS and is using Turbo C++ (as opposed to a different C++ compiler) then compile the protected _function( ).

Note that you can use logical operators in the #if preprocessor command such as || (OR) or && (AND).

You can use the other logical operators (like <, >, <=, >=, ==, and !=) with preprocessor variables. To compile a program that uses specific functions if compiled in certain modes, and a generic function otherwise, you could do the following:

```
int main(int argc, char **argv)
    {
    #if TESTMODE == 0
      test1();
    #elif TESTMODE == 1
      test2();
    #else
      generic_test(argc,argv);
    #endif
    }
```

If you compiled this with:

```
tcc -DTESTMODE=1 test.c
```

the main( ) function would look like:

```
int main(int argc, char **argv)
    {
    test2();
    }
```

after being preprocessed. If you had compiled with TESTMODE=3, it would look like:

```
int main(int argc, char **argv)
    {
    generic_test(argc,argv);
    }
```

TYPICAL OPERATION

In this program, you use the #ifdef, #elif, #else, and #endif commands to identify the memory model currently defined. Begin from within Turbo C++ with no windows open.

#if, #elif, #else, #endif

1. Press **Alt-F** and type **N** to create a new file.
2. Type the following:
   ```
   void main()
      {
      #ifdef __COMPACT__
        printf ("Using compact memory model\n");
      #elif __HUGE__
        printf ("Using huge memory model\n");
      #elif __LARGE__
        printf ("Using large memory model\n");
      #elif __MEDIUM__
        printf ("Using medium memory model\n");
      #elif __SMALL__
        printf ("Using small memory model\n");
      #else
        printf ("Using tiny memory model\n");
      #endif
      }
   ```
3. Press **Alt-O** to pull down the Options menu.
4. Type **C** to choose the Compiler options, and type **C** again to choose the Code generation options. Turbo C++ displays a Code Generation dialog box.

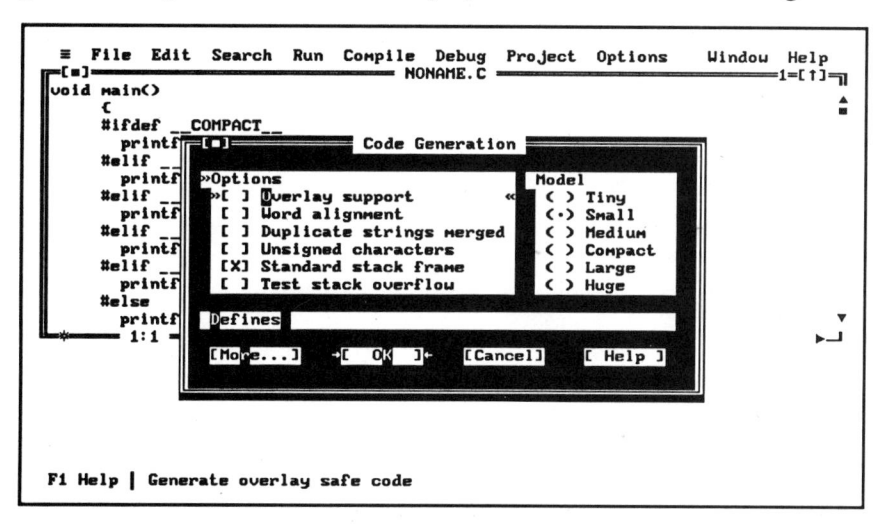

5. Press **Tab,** type **L** to choose the Large memory model, and press **Return**.
6. Press **Ctrl-F9** to run the program.
7. Press **Alt-F5** to view the program results. The program displays the message "Using large memory model."
8. Press **Alt-F5** to return to the Turbo C++ editor.

Module 19

9. Press **Alt-O** to pull down the Options menu.
10. Type **C** to choose the Compiler options, and type **C** again to choose the Code generation options. Turbo C++ displays a Code Generation dialog box.
11. Press **Tab**, type **S** to choose the Small memory model, and press **Return**.
12. Press **Alt-C** and type **B** to choose the Build all command. This will recompile your program using the new memory model you specified in step 11. After recompiling your program, Turbo C++ displays a Linking dialog box on the screen.
13. Press **Return**, then press **Ctrl-F9** to run the program.
14. Press **Alt-F5** to view the program results. The program displays the message "Using small memory model."
15. Press **Alt-F5** to return to the Turbo C++ editor.
16. Press **Alt-Spacebar**, type **C**, and type **N** to clear the desktop.
17. Turn to Module 18 to continue the learning sequence.

Module 20
#ifdef and #ifndef

DESCRIPTION

The #ifdef and #ifndef preprocessor directives let you conditionally compile a section of your program. The program will compile the statements between a #ifdef and its corresponding #elif, #else, or #endif if a variable exists.

If the variable does not exist, the program will compile code between a #ifndef and its corresponding #elif, #else, or #endif commands.

The following shows the correct syntax for using the #ifdef and #ifndef commands:

```
#ifdef CONDITION              #ifndef CONDITION
    statement;                    statement;
#endif                        #endif


#ifdef CONDITION              #ifndef CONDITION
    statement;                    statement;
#else                         #else
    statement;                    statement;
#endif                        #endif


#ifdef CONDITION              #ifndef CONDITION
    statement;                    statement;
#elif CONDITION2              #elif CONDITION2
    statement;                    statement;
#else                         #else
    statement;                    statement;
#endif                        #endif
```

APPLICATIONS

Use the #ifdef and #ifndef preprocessor directives to comment out sections of a program during testing. To do this, create a condition name (such as OLDSCR) that is not defined with the #define command, and surround the questionable piece of code with

```
#ifdef OLDSRC
    questionable code
#endif
```

81

Module 20

If you want to test the effects of alternate code, you can use

```
#ifdef OLDSRC
     questionable code
#else
     alternate code
#endif
```

Note that this is the same as

```
#ifndef OLDSRC
     alternate code
#else
     questionable code
#endif
```

If you are writing C++ programs for different operating systems, such as MS-DOS, UNIX, or Open Windows, you could include code like:

```
#ifdef MSDOS
     msdos code
#elif UNIX
     unix code
#elif OPEN_WINDOWS
     open windows code
#endif
```

In this way, you can write a program that will compile the correct program statements, depending on the type of operating system you are using.

TYPICAL OPERATION

In this program, you experiment with the #ifdef command. Begin from within Turbo C++ with no windows open.

1. Press **Alt-F** and type **N** to create a new file.
2. Type the following:

```
int main ()
    {
    int     num;

    #ifdef DEBUG
       printf ("Testing, testing, 1,2,3\n");
    #else
       printf ("No testing needed.\n");
    #endif
    }
```

3. Press **Ctrl-F9** to run the program. Notice that the program never prints the message "Testing, testing, 1,2,3." The program only displays the message:

No testing needed.

4. Modify the program as follows:

    #define DEBUG   1

    ```
    int main ()
        {
        int     num;

        #ifdef DEBUG
           printf ("Testing, testing, 1,2,3\n");
        #else
           printf ("No testing needed.\n");
        #endif
        }
    ```

5. Press **Ctrl-F9** to run the program. Notice that now the program prints the "Testing, testing, 1,2,3" message.
6. Press **Alt-Spacebar** and type **C** and type **N** to clear the desktop.
7. Turn to Module 33 to continue the learning sequence.

Module 21
#include

DESCRIPTION

Computer programs can be as short as a single line or as long as several pages. To make programs easier to read and understand, you can break a large program into several smaller parts. This is known as structured programming.

As an alternative, you can break a large program into one or more separate files. This is called modular programming.

Once you break a program into separate files, you need to connect the separate files together again. To do this, you use the #include directive.

The #include preprocessor directive is used as follows:

    #include "header_file"

or

    #include <header_file>

where header_file is a valid filename.

Generally when you use a header file provided by Turbo C++, you use the <header_file> method. When you use a header file that you have made yourself, use the "header_file" method.

By following this method, you can quickly identify which header files the original programmer created.

The following table lists the header files provided by Turbo C++:

Header file	Description
alloc.h	Memory management definitions
assert.h (ANSI)	assert( ) macro definition
bios.h	Bios access definitions
complex.h (C++)	Complex number definitions
conio.h	Console I/O definitions
ctype.h (ANSI)	Character classification definitions
dir.h	Directory and path name handling definitions
dos.h	MS-DOS, 80x86, and Port I/O definitions
errno.h (ANSI)	System Error handling definitions
fcntl.h	ope and sopen support definitions
float.h (ANSI)	Floating-point support and 80x87 definitions

float.h (ANSI)	Floating-point support and 80x87 definitions
graphics.h	Graphics package definitions
io.h	Low-level I/O definitions
limits.h (ANSI)	Data type limit definitions
locale.h (ANSI)	setlocale( ) support definitions
math.h (ANSI)	Floating-point math definitions
mem.h	Direct memory-manipulation definitions
process.h	Process control definitions
setjmp.h (ANSI)	setjmp/longjmp support definitions
share.h	File sharing (sopen( )) support definitions
signal.h (ANSI)	signal( ) support definitions
stdargs.h (ANSI)	Variable arg list handling definitions
stddef.h (ANSI)	Standard constant definitions
stdio.h (ANSI)	Stream I/O definitions (not C++ streams)
stdlib.h (ANSI)	Common function support and definitions
stream.h (C++)	C++ Streams support and definitions
string.h (ANSI)	String and direct memory-manipulation definitions
sys\stat.h	File status definitions
sys\timeb.h	ftime( ) support and definitions
sys\types.h	Time support definitions
time.h (ANSI)	Time function support and definitions
values.h	Common constants

APPLICATIONS

The #include directive reads a header file into the current program. Header files traditionally use a .h file extension such as math.h or bios.h.

By defining your own header files, you can store commonly used definitions or macros that you can use in other programs. Rather than type the same information into each program, you can type the information once in a header file.

TYPICAL OPERATION

In this program, you write a program that uses a Turbo C++ header file. Begin from within Turbo C++ with no windows open.

1. Press **Alt-F** and type **N** to create a new file.
2. Type the following:
   ```
   int        number;
   char       letter;
   ```
3. Press **F2**. Turbo C++ displays a Save Editor File dialog box.

Module 21

4. Type **a:myfile.h**. Make sure you have a blank, formatted floppy disk in drive A.
5. Press **Return**.
6. Press **Alt-F** and type **N** to create another new file.
7. Type the following:

   ```
   int main()
       {
       number = 5;
       letter = 'a';
       return (0);
       }
   ```

8. Press **Ctrl-F9** to run the program. Turbo C++ displays an error message in the Compiling dialog box.

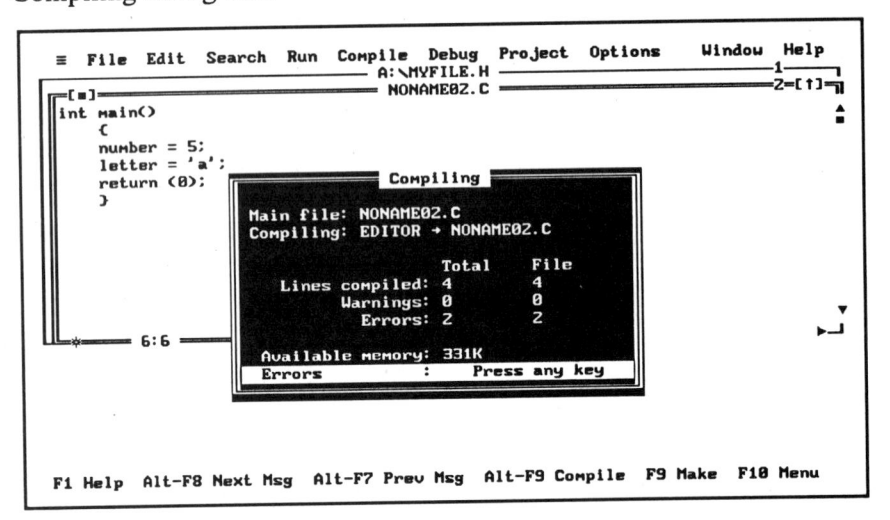

```
  ≡  File  Edit  Search  Run  Compile  Debug  Project  Options   Window  Help
                                 A:\MYFILE.H
 ─[■]─────────────────────────── NONAME02.C ══════════════════════════2=[↑]═╗
 int main()
     {
     number = 5;
     letter = 'a';
     return (0);
     }
                           ┌──────── Compiling ────────┐
                           │ Main file: NONAME02.C     │
                           │ Compiling: EDITOR → NONAME02.C │
                           │                Total   File│
                           │ Lines compiled:  4      4  │
                           │       Warnings:  0      0  │
                           │         Errors:  2      2  │
 ──── 6:6 ─────             │ Available memory: 331K    │
                           │ Errors         :  Press any key│
                           └──────────────────────────┘

  F1 Help  Alt-F8 Next Msg  Alt-F7 Prev Msg  Alt-F9 Compile  F9 Make  F10 Menu
```

9. Press **Return**. Turbo C++ displays two error messages in the Message window at the bottom of the screen. Notice that both error messages occur because the variables 'number' and 'letter' are not defined within the main program.
10. Press **F6** twice.
11. Add the following line to the program:

    ```
    #include "a:myfile.h"
    int main()
        {
        number = 5;
        letter = 'a';
        return (0);
        }
    ```

12. Press **Ctrl-F9** to run the program. Turbo C++ compiles the program with no errors because the declarations for 'number' and 'letter' are included in the main program through the myfile.h header file you created in step 4.
13. Press **Alt-Spacebar** and type **C** and type **N** to clear the desktop.
14. Turn to Module 17 to continue the learning sequence.

Module 22
#line

DESCRIPTION

The #line directive causes the compiler to treat the next lines in a program as if the source file is new_file_name and the line number of all lines begin at new_line_number. The syntax for the #line directive is:

```
#line new_line_number "new_file_name"
```

APPLICATIONS

The #line command is primarily used by programs that generate C code, and not by programs written by people. The main use for the #line command is to list line numbers in a program that uses code from several separate files.

By listing line numbers in a program, the #line command lets you quickly locate statements that are stored in separate files.

Program generators (programs that create C code) sometimes need line numbers to generate code. If you are using a program that generates C code, this will be the only reason to use the #line command.

TYPICAL OPERATION

In this program, you use the Turbo C++ preprocessor program (CPP.EXE) to experiment with the #line directive. Begin from within Turbo C++ with no windows open.

1. Press **Alt-F** and type **N** to create a new file.
2. Type the following:
   ```
   #line 100 "testit.c"
   int main(int argc, char **argv)
       {
       printf("Goodbye, World!\n");
       }
   ```
3. Press **F2**. Turbo C++ displays a dialog box, asking for a file name.
4. Type **Testit.c** and press **Return**.

#line

NOTE
The following step assumes you have installed Turbo C++ on drive C in the directories C:\TC\BIN.

5. Press **Alt-F** and type **D** to exit to MS-DOS.
6. Type **CPP testit.c** and press **Return**.
7. Type **DIR** and press **Return**. Notice that the Turbo C++ preprocessor program (CPP.EXE) has created a file called TESTIT.I.
8. Type **Type Testit.I** and press **Return**. The Testit.I file contains the following:

```
testit.c 1:
testit.c 100: int main(int argc, char **argv)
testit.c 101: {
testit.c 102: printf("Goodbye, World!\n");
testit.c 103: }
testit.c 104:
```

9. Type **Del Testit.*** and press **Return** to erase the testit.c and testit.I files.
10. Type **exit** and press **Return**. Turbo C++ displays the editing window.
11. Press **Alt-Spacebar** and type **C** to clear the desktop.
12. Turn to Module 23 to continue the learning sequence.

Module 23
#pragma

DESCRIPTION

The #pragma preprocessor directive lets you control features that may only exist in Turbo C++. A #pragma directive uses the following syntax:

```
#pragma directive_name
```

APPLICATIONS

Turbo C++ supports the following pragmas:

#pragma argsused	disable argument not used warning
#pragma exit	specify program exit function
#pragma inline	enable inline assembly language feature
#pragma option	include command line options in the program
#pragma saveregs	protect registers from corruption for asm or huge functions
#pragma startup	specify program startup function
#pragma warn	override default warning settings

#pragma argsused

You can only use the #pragma argsused between function definitions. This directive disables the warning message:

```
"Parameter name is never used in function func-name"
```

Place this directive before the function that produces the warning. If routine set_weights( ) was generating the error, we could turn it off in the following way:

```
void update_weights(float *weights,float *connections)
{ ... }

#pragma argsused

void set_weights(float *weights, float *in, float *out)
{ ... }
```

The #pragma argsused only affects the function that immediately follows it.

#pragma exit

If you want your program to run a function before terminating, use the #pragma exit directive. The #pragma exit has the following syntax:

    #pragma exit function-name priority

The function-name is any valid function name. The priority is an integer between 64 and 255 (inclusive). (Priorities 0 to 63 are used by the C libraries.)

#pragma inline

The #pragma inline directive lets you embed assembly code in your C programs. (Optionally, you can start the compiler with the -B option.) The following program fragment correctly sets up the program for embedded assembly language:

    // program description...
    #pragma inline
    // includes, etc.
    ...

#pragma option

The #pragma option lets you control which options the compiler uses. It has limitations, and it can be confusing to beginning C programmers, so you probably won't be using this unless you're an advanced programmer, a programmer working on a programming team, or if you're writing C code for publication and want to make sure that the required options are set.

Turbo C++ processes programs in two states: parse-only and coding. The parse-only state is on until a macro name or C declaration is encountered, then the compiler toggles into the coding state.

The following compiler options can be internally set using the #pragma option only if the compiler is in parsing mode. To be safe, you will probably want to include these #pragmas at the beginning of your program, before any #ifdefs, #ifs, etc. You can safely use them after #includes, #pragmas, and #defines.

-Efff	Assembly name string option
-f*	Any floating point option except -ff
-i#	Significant identifier chars option
-m*	Any memory model option
-nddd	Output directory option
-offf	Output filename option
-u	Use underscores with cdecl names option
-z*	Any segment name option

Module 23

The following compiler options can be internally set using the #pragma option in either state. They are divided into two sets: those that must be declared between functions or object declarations, and those that can be declared anywhere.

The compiler options which can be internally set between functions or object declarations are:

-1	Generate 80186 or 80286 real mode code option
-2	Generate 80286 protected mode code option
-a	Align to word-boundary option
-ff	Fast floating point option
-G	Optimize for speed option
-k	Use standard stack frames option
-N	Stack checking option
-O	Optimization option
-p	Pascal conventions option
-r	Use register variables option
-rd	Use declared register variables option
-v	Verbose debug information (Turbo Debugger) option
-y	Include line number debug information option

The compiler options which can be internally set anywhere are:

-A	ANSI-compatible option
-C	Nest comments option
-d	Merge duplicate strings option
-gn	Stop after n warnings option
-jn	Stop after n errors option
-K	Unsigned char option
-wxxx	Set warning message option (#pragma warn is more explicit)

Any of these options which can be toggled (like -a) can be restored to its original state by following the option with a . symbol. To set the -a option for one function only, you could use the following code:

```
#pragma option -a+
void needs_word() {...}
#pragma option -a.
```

Options that cannot be included in #pragma options include:

-B	Embedded assembly option
-c	Compile-only option
-dxxx	Define a macro option
-Dxxx=ccc	Set a macro to a value option
-efff	Name .exe file option
-ifff	Name include file option
-Lfff	Name library option

-lx	Set linker option
-M	Create a .map option
-o	Overlays option
-Q	EMS option
-S	Generate assembly code option
-Uxxx	Undefine macro option
-Y	Generate overlay-compatible code

#pragma saveregs

When working with huge functions or assembly language, you need to protect the registers from being overwritten by mistake. To protect the registers, you can use the #pragma saveregs. You don't want to always use #pragma saveregs, because the overhead created by saving registers will slow your programs down.

When you have a function that you want to protect, use the #pragma saveregs directive before the function as in the following example:

```
#pragma saveregs
huge *juggernaut()      {...}
```

#pragma startup

The startup pragma operates like the #pragma exit directive. It has the following syntax:

```
#pragma startup function-name priority
```

The function-name is any valid function name. The priority is an integer between 64 and 255 (inclusive). (Priorities 0 to 63 are used by the C libraries.)

Use the #pragma startup directive to set up certain conditions before program execution. For example, some window libraries require initialization before they work, and databases require data files to be opened before you can access them. You could use the following #pragmas after the corresponding function declarations to allow automatic initialization:

```
#pragma startup window_init 100    // window_conclude()
                                   //   already defined
#pragma startup datab_init 80      // datab_conclude()
                                   //   already defined
```

#pragma warn

This pragma lets you override the current settings for the various warning messages available with Turbo C++. You can force a warning on, off, or restore it to the condition it had at the beginning of compilation. It has the following syntax:

```
#pragma warn +xxx     // turn on warning xxx
#pragma warn -xxx     // turn off warning xxx
```

```
#pragma warn .xxx    // restore xxx to its original value
```

If you want to turn off the eff (Code has no effect) warning for a section of code, you could use the following code:

```
#pragma warn -eff
void suspect_function() {...}
#pragma warn .eff
```

Use . instead of + after the function that needs to have eff disabled. Since you don't know the initial state of the eff warning (whether it's off or on), the safest thing to do is restore it to its original value.

Similarly, to turn on the eff warning for a section of code, you could do it with the following code:

```
#pragma warn +eff
void suspect_function() {...}
#pragma warn .eff
```

This code turns the eff warning on for the suspect_function( ) and then restores it to its original value.

TYPICAL OPERATION

In this program you experiment with using the #pragma start and the #pragma exit directives. Begin from within Turbo C++ with no windows open.

1. Press **Alt-F** and type **N** to create a new file.
2. Type the following:

```
#include <stdio.h>

void start_function()
    {
    printf ("Initializing program\n");
    }

#pragma startup start_function

void exit_function()
    {
    printf ("End of program\n");
    }

#pragma exit exit_function

void main()
    {
    printf ("This is the main program\n");
    }
```

3. Press **Ctrl-F9** to run the program.
4. Press **Alt-F5** to view the program results. Notice that the program runs the start_function first and the exit_function last because of the #pragma startup and #pragma exit directives.

   ```
   Initializing program
   This is the main program
   End of program
   ```

5. Press **Alt-F5** to return to the Turbo C++ editor.
6. Press **Alt-Spacebar** and type **C** and type **N** to clear the desktop.
7. Turn to Module 15 to continue the learning sequence.

Module 24
ADVANCED DATA TYPES

DESCRIPTION

Turbo C++ provides five advanced data types:

Data type	Description
enum	ennumerated type
struct	structures
union	unions (a type of structure)
typedef	type definitions (often used with structs and unions)
class	classes

Enum

Enumerated types let you define sets. The format of an enumerated data type is:

```
enum enum_name {name1, name2..namen} var1, var2..varn
```

Examples of an enumerated data type are:

```
enum {red, white = 12, blue} flag_colors;
enum weekend {saturday, sunday} rest_days;
```

The first item in an enum data type gets assigned a value of 0. Each additional item gets assigned a value 1 greater than the previous item unless you specifically declare a different value. In the first example, red = 1, white = 12, and blue = 13.

Multiple items can have the same value. You can use the enum as a data type:

```
// define background and foreground color
flag_colors    back,fore;

back = blue;        // background is blue
fore = white;       // foreground is white
```

You can't use the names of enum members as names of other variables.

```
int blue;     // this would be flagged as an error
```

Another useful enum is:

```
enum Bool {FALSE,TRUE};    // FALSE=0, TRUE=1
```

The following table lists the characteristics of enumerated data types in C++:

Type	Range	Size (in bytes)
enum	0 to 65,353	2

Struct

Structures let you group related data types together. For example, a structure that creates a window on the screen might look like the following:

```
struct alertbox
{
    int startx;      // upper left x coordinate
    int starty;      // upper left y coordinate
    int endx;        // lower right x coordinate
    int endy;        // lower right y coordinate
    char *msg;       // alert message
};
```

The previous example defines an alertbox structure data type. Before you could use this data type, you would have to declare a variable of the alertbox data type. You could do this in one of two ways:

```
struct alertbox
{
    int startx;      // upper left x coordinate
    int starty;      // upper left y coordinate
    int endx;        // lower right x coordinate
    int endy;        // lower right y coordinate
    char *msg;       // alert message
} a1, a2, *a3;
```

The variables a1 and a2 are alertbox structures, but a3 is a pointer to an alertbox structure. These variables could also have been declared after the original definition later in the program:

```
struct alertbox     a1, a2, *a3;
```

Note that items in a structure can be other structures:

```
struct popup
{
    struct alertbox a;
};
```

To access items in a structure, you can use the . operator or the -> operator. If you have declared a variable to a structure, use the . operator. For example:

```
struct alertbox     a1;

a1.startx = 0;
// the upper left x coord of alertbox a1 is 0
```

If you had declared a pointer to a structure, use the -> operator instead:

```
struct alertbox     *a3;

a3->startx = 0;
// the upper left x coord of alertbox pointer a1 is 0
```

Union

Unions lets multiple structure or variable definitions share the same area of memory. For example, the Intel registers can be viewed as word or byte sized registers:

```
Word    Byte
AX      AL,AH       // AX uses the same memory as AL and AH
BX      BL,BH
CX      CL,CH
DX      DL,DH
```

Turbo C++ defines them in the <dos.h> header file as follows:

```
struct WORDREGS {
    unsigned int    ax, bx, cx, dx, si, di, cflag, flags;
};

struct BYTEREGS {
    unsigned char   al, ah, bl, bh, cl, ch, dl, dh;
};

union    REGS {
    struct      WORDREGS x;
    struct      BYTEREGS h;
};
```

Because REGS is defined as a union, you can access a REGS type data item using either view.

```
union REGS regs;

regs.x.ax = 0xFFFF;    // word view
regs.h.bl = 0x10;      // byte view
```

Typedef

The typedef specifier creates a new name that represents an existing or previously declared data type. For example, you can refer to "int" data types as "size_t" to make your program easier to read.

```
typedef    int    size_t;
```

You can then use this new data type declaration like any ordinary data type:

```
size_t    s, l;
```

The typedef specifier lets you create data types that describe the data that your program uses.

Class

Classes are part of Turbo C++'s object-oriented features. Module 32 discusses classes in more detail.

APPLICATIONS

Advanced data types can simplify the organization of your program and the data it uses.

Use enumerated data types for defining your own set of related variables. Properly used, enumerated data types can better represent how your program uses information while being easier to understand.

For example, suppose you wanted to represent the days of the week. Without enumerated data types, you might declare your variables like this:

```
int     sunday, monday, tuesday, wednesday, thursday,
        friday, saturday;
```

By using enumerated data types, you could organize your data like this:

```
enum weekdays {monday, tuesday, wednesday, thursday, friday}
enum weekends {saturday, sunday}
```

Note how enumerated data types make the structure of your data easier to recognize.

Use structures to group related data together. For example, suppose you wanted to keep a list of names and addresses. Without using structures, you might declare your variables like this:

```
char        name[80], street[80], city[40], state[2];
unsigned int        zip;
```

By using a structure, you could organize your data like this:

```
struct people
{
    char        name[80];
    char        street[80];
    char        city[40];
    char        state[2];
    unsigned int    zip;
}

    struct      people       people_list[100];
```

The above structure declaration declares a structure called "people" and an array called "people_list" that holds 100 names and addresses.

Use unions like structures, except when you need to view the same data in different ways.

Use the typedef specifier to create more descriptive data types. For example, suppose you wanted to declare two unsigned int data types that represent two different sets of variables called "unit_sales" and "part_num." You could declare both variables as unsigned int data types:

```
unsigned int        unit_sales, part_num;
```

Module 24

But to differentiate between part_num (that represents parts numbers in a catalog, a fixed number of digits) and unit_sales (that represents a variable number of digits), use a typedef specifier as follows:

```
typedef    unsigned int    sales;
typedef    unsigned int    five_digits;
```

Now you can declare other variables that best fit into these declarations such as:

```
sales          unit_sales;
five_digits    part_num, zipcode;
```

Classes are part of Turbo C++'s object-oriented features. Classes let you organize related data structures and algorithms together.

TYPICAL OPERATION

In this program, you experiment with using different Turbo C++ data types. Begin from within Turbo C++ with no windows open.

1. Press **Alt-F** and type **N** to create a new file.
2. Type the following:

```
typedef int    INTEGER;

struct date
    {
    INTEGER    month;
    INTEGER    day;
    INTEGER    year;
    };

struct names
    {
    char name[30];
    struct date birthdate;
    } people;

void main()
    {
    char reply;
    enum    boolean {false = 0, true = 1};
    enum    boolean    flag;

    flag = true;

    while (flag)
      {
      printf ("Type your name.\n");
      scanf("%s", people.name);
      printf ("What day were you born? (Type the day number)\n");
```

100

```
        scanf("%d", &people.birthdate.day);
        printf ("What month were you born? (Type the month number)\n");
        scanf ("%d", &people.birthdate.month);
        printf ("What year were you born?\n");
        scanf ("%d", &people.birthdate.year);

        printf ("\nYour name is %s\n", people.name);
        printf ("Your birthdate is %d-", people.birthdate.month);
        printf ("%d-", people.birthdate.day);
        printf ("%d\n", people.birthdate.year);

        printf ("Run again? (Y or N)\n");
        scanf ("%*c%c", &reply);
        if ((reply == 'n') || (reply == 'N'))
          flag = false;
      }
    }
```

3. Press **Ctrl-F9** to run the program. The program displays the message "Type your name."

4. Type **John** and press **Return**. The program displays the message "What day were you born? (Type the day number)."

5. Type **1** and press **Return**. The program displays the message "What month were you born? (Type the month number)."

6. Type **4** and press **Return**. The program displays the message "What year were you born?"

7. Type **1970** and press **Return**. The program displays the following:

    ```
    Your name is John
    Your birthdate is 4-1-1970
    Run again? (Y or N)
    ```

8. Type **N** and press **Return**.
9. Press **Alt-Spacebar** and type **C** and type **N** to clear the desktop.
10. Turn to Module 46 to continue the learning sequence.

Module 25
ARITHMETIC OPERATORS

DESCRIPTION

Turbo C++ provides the following arithmetic operators:

unary operators

    −   unary minus (negation)
    +   unary plus
    − −   decrement
    ++   increment

binary operators

    +   addition
    −   subtraction
    *   multiplication
    /   division
    %   modulo

The unary minus (−) makes a positive number into a negative number and a negative number into a positive number.

The unary plus (+) makes a negative number into a positive number.

The decrement and increment operators can be prefix (++a) or postfix (a++). Prefix means that Turbo C++ first increments or decrements the variable by 1.

Postfix means Turbo C++ uses the value of the variable and then increments or decrements the variable by 1. For example:

Statement	*Turbo C++ interpretation*
a++;	a = a + 1;
a− −;	a = a − 1;
a += 5;	a = a + 5;
b *= a;	b = b * a;
b = c + a++;	b = c + a;
	a = a + 1;
b = c + − −a;	a = a − 1;
	b = c + a;

Division operator (/)

If you use the division operator with two integer values, the result will also be an integer value. To correct this problem, you need to use float values or cast the integer values as a float data type such as:

    `result = 5 / 2;`   `// result is 2 not 2.5`

If you divide using floats, your result will be a float

    `result = 5.0 / 2.0;`   `// result is 2.5 as expected`

You can make the first example return a float value by casting the first operator into a float

    `result = (float)5 / 2;`   `// result is 2.5 because of cast`

Modulo operator (%)

The modulo operator (%), sometimes called the "remainder" operator, is useful when converting numeric bases. Modulo would be used to convert time from a 24-hour clock to a 12-hour by moduloing the time by 12.

    `time12 = time24 % 12;`

If time24 was 13 (1 PM), time12 would be 1.

Precedence

You can combine arithmetic operators into equations such as:

    `result = ((b*b) + (c/(a%4))) * 2.5)`

Use parentheses to clarify the evaluation of the equation. Turbo C++ evaluates operators in the deepest (most nested) level of parentheses first, followed by the next level, until all levels have been processed.

Turbo C++ evaluates arithmetic operators from highest to lowest precedence, from left to right. The following list shows the precedence of arithmetic operators:

++	increment (postfix)
--	decrement (postfix)
++	increment (prefix)
--	decrement (postfix)
+	unary plus
-	unary minus (negation)
* / %	multiplication, division, modulo
+ -	addition and subtraction

APPLICATIONS

When using the arithmetic operators, do not mix data types, such as integers with float, or the arithmetic operator may produce unexpected results.

If you need to increment or decrement a variable by 1, use the prefix or postfix increment or decrement operators instead of adding or subtracting by 1.

Most computer processors (8088, 80286, 80386, etc.) have special instructions for decrementing and incrementing numbers, which means your programs will run faster than using the addition operator (+) or subtraction operator (–).

Use	Instead of
a++	a = a + 1;
– –b	b = b – 1;

Use prefix to increment or decrement a variable first. Use postfix to increment or decrement a variable after evaluating the rest of the line.

Statement	Turbo C++ interpretation
a –= b – c / d;	a = a – (b – (c / d));
a /= – –b * c / d;	b = b – 1;
	a = a / ((b * c) / d);
a /= – –b * (c / d);	b = b – 1;
	a = a / (b * (c / d));

TYPICAL OPERATION

In this program, you experiment with the different Turbo C++ arithmetic operators. Begin from within the Turbo C++ with no windows open.

1. Press **Alt-F** and type **N** to create a new file.
2. Type the following:

```
void main()
    {
    int i=0;

    printf("1 + 2 = %d\n", 1+2);
    printf("1 - 2 = %d\n", 1-2);
    printf("1 * 2 = %d\n", 1*2);
    printf("1 / 2 = %d\n", 1/2);
    printf("1./2. = %d\n", 1./2.);
    printf("1 % 2 = %d\n", 1%2);
    printf("3 % 2 = %d\n", 3%2);

    printf("++i = %d\n",++i);
    printf("i++ = %d\n",i++);
    printf("--i = %d\n",--i);
    printf("i-- = %d\n",i--);
    }
```

3. Press **Ctrl-F9** to run the program.

Arithmetic Operators

4. Press **Alt-F5** to view the program results.

        1 + 2 = 3
        1 - 2 = -1
        1 * 2 = 2
        1 / 2 = 0
        1./2. = 0
        1 % 2 = %d
        3 % 2 = %d
        ++i = 1
        i++ = 1
        --i = 1
        i-- = 1

5. Press **Alt-F5** to return to the Turbo C++ editor.
6. Press **Alt-Spacebar** and type **C** and type **N** to clear the desktop.
7. Turn to Module 42 to continue the learning sequence.

105

Module 26
ASSEMBLY LANGUAGE

DESCRIPTION

The asm constructs let you embed assembly language in your C++ programs. There are two types of syntax:

```
asm opcode operand;          // single assembly opcode
```
or
```
asm
{
// block of assembly opcodes
}
```

APPLICATIONS

Assembly language produces compact and fast programs. Unfortunately, assembly language programming can be time-consuming and tedious, unless you already have an extensive library of routines at your fingertips.

Fortunately, most programs don't need to be completely written in assembly language to take advantage of assembly language's speed. You can incorporate assembly language functions into your C++ code, speeding up your program.

If you look at your Turbo C++ documentation, using assembly language with your C++ programs can look pretty intimidating. Fortunately, there is an easy way to do it.

When you need to use assembly language, embed it in one of the two following ways:

```
asm opcode operand;
```
or
```
asm
{
block of assembly language
}
```

The first method is for a single line of assembly language that you want to use. The second method is for multiple lines of assembly language.

```
int getxych(int x,int y)
{
#define SET_CURSOR     2
asm     mov ah,SET_CURSOR;     /* sample of single line */
asm                            /* sample of group asm */
```

106

```
    {
    mov bh,0
    mov dh,y
    mov dl,x
    int 10h

    mov ah,8
    mov bh,0
    int 10h
    }
return(_AL);
}
```

TYPICAL OPERATION

To use assembly language within your Turbo C++ programs, you must own a copy of Turbo Assembler (TASM). Then you need to follow these steps:

1. Enable the inline assembly option of Turbo C++ by including the following line in your program:

   `#pragma inline`

   When mixing assembly language with Turbo C++ programs, the Turbo C++ compiler will create an assembly language source code file with the .ASM file extension.
2. Run Turbo Assembler (TASM.EXE) to create an .OBJ object file.
3. Run Turbo Linker (TLINK.EXE) to create an .EXE executable file from the .OBJ object file.

You have now finished the learning sequence for *Illustrated Turbo C++*. At this point you should have enough programming experience with Turbo C++ to begin reading the Turbo C++ User's Guide and the Programmer's Guide.

Module 27
ASSIGNMENT OPERATORS

DESCRIPTION

There are two categories of assignment operator: simple assignment and compound assignment. Assignment operators assign a variable the value of a constant, another variable, or an expression.

Simple

    =   simple assignment

Compound

    +=   addition assignment
    −=   subtraction assignment
    *=   multiplication assignment
    /=   division assignment
    %=   modulo assignment
    <<=   left shift assignment
    >>=   right shift assignment
    &=   bitwise AND assignment
    |=   bitwise OR assignment
    ^=   bitwise XOR assignment

Simple assignment

The = operator assigns a value to a variable. The variable must be of the same type as the value such as int, float, or char. For example:

```
int   n;
n = 0;
```

After this statement executes, n will have a value of 0. You can evaluate expressions the same way:

```
float n;
n = tan(sqrt((sin(n) * 3.) + (sin(n) * 2.)));
```

Compound assignments

Compound assignments provide shorthand notation for using an arithmetic or logic operator. The following compound assignments show their translations into simple assignment statements on the right:

n += 2;	n = n + 2;
n -= 2;	n = n - 2;
n *= 2;	n = n * 2;
n /= 2;	n = n / 2;
n %= 2;	n = n % 2;
n <<= 2;	n = n << 2;
n >>= 2;	n = n >> 2;
n &= 2;	n = n & 2;
n |= 2;	n = n	2;
n ^= 2;	n = n ^ 2;

APPLICATIONS

You use the simple assignment statement to assign a value to a variable. The value can be a constant, another variable, a function call, or a mathematical expression.

```
number = 5;              /* constant */

number = a;              /* another variable */

number = sqrt(5);        /* function call */

number = a + (b * 3) - (sqrt(a + 4));      /* mathematical expression */
```

You use compound assignments as a shorthand way to use arithmetic or logic operators. Compound assignments have the advantage of making your program smaller, but they have the disadvantage of making the program harder to read, especially to people unfamiliar with the C++ language.

TYPICAL OPERATION

In this program, you experiment with compound assignments. Begin from within Turbo C++ with no windows open.

1. Press **Alt-F** and type **N** to create a new file.

2. Type the following:

```
void main()
    {
    float f = 1.;
    int n = 1,o=0;

    printf("This evals to %f\n",tan(sqrt((sin(f) * 3.) + (sin(f) * 2.))));
    o = n; printf("(%d += 2) = %d\n",o,n += 2);// n = n + 2;
    o = n; printf("(%d -= 2) = %d\n",o,n -= 2);// n = n - 2;
    o = n; printf("(%d *= 2) = %d\n",o,n *= 2);// n = n * 2;
    o = n; printf("(%d /= 2) = %d\n",o,n /= 2);// n = n / 2;
```

Module 27

```
        o = n; printf("(%d \%= 2) = %d\n",o,n %= 2);// n = n % 2;
        o = n; printf("(%d <<= 2) = %d\n",o,n <<= 2);// n = n << 2;
        o = n; printf("(%d >>= 2) = %d\n",o,n >>= 2);// n = n >> 2;
        o = n; printf("(%d &= 2) = %d\n",o,n &= 2);// n = n & 2;
        o = n; printf("(%d |= 2) = %d\n",o,n |= 2);// n = n | 2;
        o = n; printf("(%d ^= 2) = %d\n",o,n ^= 2);// n = n ^ 2;
        }
```

3. Press **Ctrl-F9** to run the program.
4. Press **Alt-F5** to view the program results on the screen.

```
        This evals to 0.000000
        (1 += 2) => 3
        (3 -= 2) => 1
        (1 *= 2) => 2
        (2 /= 2) => 1
        (1 %= 2) => %d
        (1 <<= 2) => 4
        (4 >>= 2) => 1
        (1 &= 2) => 0
        (0 |= 2) => 2
        (2 ^= 2) => 0
```

5. Press **Alt-F5** to return to the Turbo C++ editor.
6. Press **Alt-Spacebar** and type **C** and type **N** to clear the desktop.
7. Turn to Module 52 to continue the learning sequence.

Module 28
BASIC DATA TYPES

DESCRIPTION

Any computer program consists of two parts: algorithms and data. Algorithms are instructions that tell the computer what to do, and data is the information that the computer uses to perform specific tasks.

C++ uses four data types: integer, floating point, character, and enumeration. Unlike languages like Pascal, C++ does not provide Boolean data types (TRUE and FALSE). Instead, C++ uses any nonzero value to mean TRUE and a zero value to mean FALSE.

Integer

Integers consist of whole numbers. Usually C++ uses integers in decimal (base 10) but you can specify octal (base 8) or hexadecimal (base 16).

Decimal numbers range from the set [0..9]. Octal numbers range from the set [0..7]. Hexadecimal numbers range from the set [0..9, A..F].

The following table lists the integer types provided in C++:

Type	Range	Size (in bytes)
unsigned int (unsigned)	0 to 65,535	2
short int (short)	−32,768 to 32,767	2
int	−32,768 to 32,767	2
long	−2,147,483,648 to 2,147,483,647	4
unsigned long	0 to 4,294,967,295	4

Floating point

Floating point numbers consist of one or more of the following parts: digits, a decimal point, digits, and an exponential part according to the following format:

    [+ or -] [digits] [.digits] [e or E] [+ or -] [digits]

Examples of floating point numbers are:
```
3.14
-15.6
1.09E-4   (0.000109)
```

111

Module 28

The following table lists the floating point types for C++:

Type	Range	Size (in bytes)
float	3.4E–38 to 3.4E+38	4
double	1.7E–308 to 1.7E+308	8
long double	3.4E–4932 to 1.1E+4932	10

Character

Characters consist of the numeric value defined by the standard ASCII table (see Appendix D). ASCII characters are either alphanumeric or nonprintable characters.

Alphanumeric characters are those characters you see on your keyboard such as 'a,' '7,' and '*.'

Nonprintable characters are those keys that do not print anything on the screen such as a carriage return, tab, or backspace.

Since you cannot type a nonprintable character, C++ provides a way to represent the characters. The following table lists some of the more common keys and their equivalent representation:

Character	Represented as
Backspace	'\b'
Carriage return	'\r'
Tab	'\t'

The following table lists the characteristics of character data types in C++:

Type	Range	Size (in bytes)
char	–128 to 127	1
unsigned char	0 to 255	1

APPLICATIONS

Before you can use a variable, you must assign it to a data type such as:

```
int     count;
char    letter;
double  dollars;
```

Whenever possible, use integer instead of floating point data types. Integer types are smaller in size and thus use less memory.

For further program efficiency, use the data type with the appropriate range you will need. If you know that a certain variable will always be positive (such as a variable for counting), use an unsigned data type.

Basic Data Types

For example, if you use a variable to count, use a short int data type rather than an int data type. The short data type only uses 2 bytes of space but an int data type uses 4 bytes of space.

Sometimes you may need to convert a variable from one data type to another, such as from int to float. To do this, Turbo C++ provides type casting.

Type casting has the following syntax:

```
(type name) variable
```

Consider the following program that type casts a variable of type int to type float:

```
void main()
    {
    int     whole_number;
    float   real_number;

    whole_number = 8;
    real_number = (float) whole_number;
    }
```

The following table shows the proper statement to use when type casting variables:

Variable type	Change to	Statement to use
float	int	(int) variable
int	float	(float) variable

TYPICAL OPERATION

In this program, you experiment with using different Turbo C++ data types. Begin from within Turbo C++ with no windows open.

1. Press **Alt-F** and type **N** to create a new file.
2. Type the following:

```
void main()
    {
    int  number1;

    number1 = 5;
    number2 = number1;
    }
```

3. Press **Ctrl-F9** to run the program. Notice that Turbo C++ displays an error message.

Module 28

```
≡ File  Edit  Search  Run  Compile  Debug  Project  Options     Window  Help
┌[■]─────────────────────── NONAME03.C ─────────────────────1=[↑]─┐
│void main()                                                      ▲
│ {                                                               ■
│   int      number1;
│
│   number1 = 5;
│   number2 = num┌──────────── Compiling ────────────┐
│   }           │                                    │
│               │ Main file: NONAME03.C              │
│               │ Compiling: EDITOR → NONAME03.C     │
│               │                                    │
│               │                      Total   File  │
│               │    Lines compiled:   7       7     │
│               │         Warnings:    1       1     │
│               │           Errors:    1       1     │
│               │                                    │ ▼
│──── 7:7 ──────│ Available memory:  330K            │ ►┘
│               │ Errors          :  Press any key   │
│               └────────────────────────────────────┘
│
│ F1 Help  Alt-F8 Next Msg  Alt-F7 Prev Msg  Alt-F9 Compile  F9 Make  F10 Menu
└─────────────────────────────────────────────────────────────────┘
```

4. Press **Return**. Turbo C++ highlights the statement "number2 = number1;" and displays an error message in the Message window. This occurs because your program does not declare the variable "number2" as a specific data type.

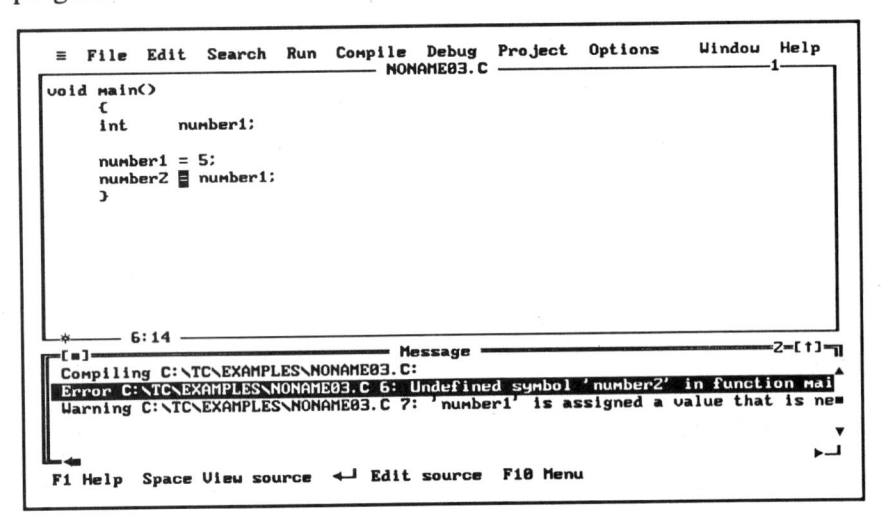

```
≡ File  Edit  Search  Run  Compile  Debug  Project  Options     Window  Help
┌──────────────────────────── NONAME03.C ─────────────────────1───┐
│void main()
│ {
│   int      number1;
│
│   number1 = 5;
│   number2 ▌ number1;
│   }
│
│
│
│
│──── 6:14 ────
├[■]───────────────────────── Message ────────────────────────2=[↑]─┐
│ Compiling C:\TC\EXAMPLES\NONAME03.C:                              ▲
│ Error C:\TC\EXAMPLES\NONAME03.C 6: Undefined symbol 'number2' in function mai│
│ Warning C:\TC\EXAMPLES\NONAME03.C 7: 'number1' is assigned a value that is ne■
│                                                                   ▼
│                                                                   ►┘
│ F1 Help  Space View source  ↵ Edit source  F10 Menu
└───────────────────────────────────────────────────────────────────┘
```

5. Press **F6** to make the editing window active.
6. Add the following to the program:

    ```
    void main()
        {
        int    number1, number2;
        char   letter1;

        number1 = 5;
    ```

```
        number2 = number1;
        letter1 = 'A';
        printf ("%c\n", letter1);
        printf ("%d", letter1);
        }
```

7. Press **Ctrl-F9** to run the program. Turbo C++ displays the following. Notice that Turbo C++ can treat character variables as characters and as the corresponding ASCII number.

    A
    65

8. Press **Alt-Spacebar,** type **C** and type **N** to clear the desktop without saving the program.
9. Turn to Module 47 to continue the learning sequence.

Module 29
BREAK

DESCRIPTION

The break statement transfers control out of a do-while, for, switch, or while statement. You can also use the break statement to separate case labels in switch statements.

```
break;
```

APPLICATIONS

You use the break statement with a conditional statement. Depending on the value of the conditional statement (True or False), the break statement exits a do-while, for, switch, or while loop.

The break statement acts like a limited GOTO statement found in other languages like BASIC and Pascal. Unlike a GOTO statement, the break statement exits out of the current loop (do-while, for, switch, or while) and transfers control to the statement immediately following the control structure, effectively prematurely exiting a loop.

```
void main()
   {
   int i;
   i = 1;
   while (i > 0)
     {
     printf ("count = %d\n", i++);
     /* Breaks out of the while statement when i > 5 */
     if (i > 5) break;
     }
   printf ("End of program");
   }
```

Running this program creates the following output:

```
count = 1
count = 2
count = 3
count = 4
count = 5
End of program
```

The while loop first checks if i is equal to 5. Since i equals 1, the program prints the message "count = 1" and increments the value of i by 1.

When i equals 5, the break statement transfers control out of the while statement and to the printf statement that prints the message "End of program."

When used with the switch statement, use the break statement between each case label to prevent executing statements in the case labels immediately following.

```
switch(key)
    {
    case 'A': printf ("You pressed the 'A' key.");
              break;
    case 'B': printf ("You pressed the 'B' key.");
    case 'C': printf ("You pressed the 'C' key.");
              break;
    }
```

If key is equal to 'A,' the program prints the following:
```
You pressed the 'A' key.
```

If key is equal to 'B,' the program prints the following:
```
You pressed the 'B' key.
You pressed the 'C' key.
```

Notice that the program prints both messages because there is no break statement between the case 'B' and the case 'C' labels.

If key is equal to 'C,' the program prints the following:
```
You pressed the 'C' key.
```

TYPICAL OPERATION

In this program, you use a break statement to break out of a loop and switch statement. Begin from within Turbo C++ with no windows open.

1. Press **Alt-F** and type **N** to create a new file.
2. Type the following:

```
void main ()
    {
    int i;
    i = 1;
    while (i > 0)
      {
      printf ("count = %d\n", i++);
      /* Breaks out of the while statement when i > 5 */
      if (i > 5) break;
      }
    printf ("End of program");
    }
```

Module 29

3. Press **Ctrl-F9** to run the program.
4. Press **Alt-F5** to see the following program results on the screen.
   ```
   count = 1
   count = 2
   count = 3
   count = 4
   count = 5
   End of program
   ```
5. Press **Alt-F5** to return to the Turbo C++ editor.
6. Press **Alt-F** and type **N** to create a new file.
7. Type the following:
   ```
   void main ()
       {
       char key;
       for (;;)
          {
          key = toupper(getchar());
          switch (key)
             {
             case 'A': printf ("You pressed the 'A' key.\n");
                       break;
             case 'B': printf ("You pressed the 'B' key.\n");
             case 'C': printf ("You pressed the 'C' key.\n");
                       break;
             default : break;
             }
          if (key == 'X') break;
          }
       }
   ```
8. Press **Ctrl-F9** to run the program.
9. Type **a** and press **Return**. Turbo C++ displays the following message:
   ```
   You pressed the 'A' key.
   ```
10. Type **b** and press **Return**. Notice that Turbo C++ displays the following message because there is not a break statement immediately following the case 'B': statement:
    ```
    You pressed the 'B' key.
    You pressed the 'C' key.
    ```
11. Type **c** and press **Return**. Turbo C++ displays the following message:
    ```
    You pressed the 'C' key.
    ```
12. Type **x** and press **Return**. Turbo C++ returns you to the Turbo C++ editor.
13. Press **Alt-Spacebar** and type **C** and type **N** twice to clear the desktop.
14. Turn to Module 34 to continue the learning sequence.

Module 30
BYTE OPERATORS

DESCRIPTION

The byte operators provide low-level operators that manipulate data at a bit level, a byte at a time.

unary operators
    ~   bitwise negation

binary operators
    <<   left shift
    >>   right shift
    &   bitwise AND
    | bitwise OR
    ^   bitwise XOR

The ~ operator

Bitwise negation requires one operand. The ~ operator changes all 1 bits to 0 and all 0 bits to 1. If you had an 11 in variable n:

```
n = 12;        // binary: 00001100
~n;            // binary: 11110011
```

this could be rewritten as:

```
~(n=12);       // results with n = binary: 11110011
```

Note that the ~ operator affects signed and unsigned decimal integers differently. The bitwise negation of an unsigned integer will always be positive. The bitwise negation of a signed integer may be positive or negative.

For example, the bitwise negation of a signed and unsigned variable gives two different results, even if the variable is assigned the same value.

	Original		*Result*	
Data type	Decimal	Binary	Binary	Decimal
unsigned	12	00001100	11110011	65523
signed	12	00001100	11110011	−13

Module 30

The << and >> shift operators

The right and left shift operators take the contents of a register or variable and shifts them a specified number of bits. A single left shift is a fast way of multiplying by 2 and a single right shift is a fast way of dividing by 2.

The &, |, and ^ operators

The & operator performs a bitwise AND between two operands. The | operator performs a bitwise OR between two operands. The ^ operator performs a bitwise XOR between two operands.

& (AND) Boolean table	| (OR) Boolean table	^ (XOR) Boolean table
0 & 0 = 0	0 | 0 = 0	0 ^ 0 = 0
0 & 1 = 0	0 | 1 = 1	0 ^ 1 = 1
1 & 0 = 0	1 | 0 = 1	1 ^ 0 = 1
1 & 1 = 1	1 | 1 = 1	1 ^ 1 = 0

APPLICATIONS

Byte operators let you do low-level processing of data for graphics, hardware control, data compression, and many other low-level, speed intensive applications. Beginners can safely ignore using byte operators until they become more familiar with the C++ language.

The ~ operator, bitwise negation, can be used for inverting an image on the screen.

You can use the << and >> shift operators to perform faster multiplication and division by 2. The shift operators work faster than multiplying or dividing a value using the * or / operators. By using the shift operators whenever possible, you can make your programs run faster.

Multiplication	*Equivalent to*
n<<1	n * 2
n<<2	n * 4
n<<3	n * 8
n<<4	n * 16

Division	*Equivalent to*
n>>1	n / 2
n>>2	n / 4
n>>3	n / 8
n>>4	n / 16

You can use the bitwise & operator (AND) to "mask" a bit to see if it is set or quickly set variables to zero. You can use the bitwise | operator (OR) and ^ operator (XOR) to set bits for performing low-level advanced programming.

TYPICAL OPERATION

In this program, you experiment with using the byte operators. Begin from within Turbo C++ with no windows open.

1. Press **Alt-F** and type **N** to create a new file.
2. Type the following:

```
void main()
{
    unsigned int      u = 12;
    int               s = 12;

    printf ("Unsigned int: the bitwise negation of %u is %u\n",u,~u);
    printf ("Signed int   : the bitwise negation of %d is %d\n\n",s,~s);

    printf ("Left shift (multiply by 2) of %u is %u\n", u, (u<<1));
    printf ("Left shift (multiply by 4) of %d is %d\n\n", s, (s<<2));

    printf ("Right shift (divide by 2) of %u is %u\n", u, (u>>1));
    printf ("Right shift (divide by 4) of %d is %d\n\n", s, (s>>2));

    u = 12;              // binary: 00001100
    if((u & 8) != 0)     // binary: 00001000 = 00001100 & 00001000
        printf("The bit is set\n");
    else
        printf("The bit is not set\n");

    u = 12;              // binary: 00001100
    s = u;               // binary: 10111100 = 00001100 | 10110000
        printf("%x = %x | 0xB0\n", u = u | 0xB0,s);

    u = 12;              // binary: 00001100
    s = u;               // binary: 00001011 = 00001100 ^ 00000111
        printf("%x = %x ^ 0x07\n",u = u ^ 0x07,s);
}
```

3. Press **Ctrl-F9** to run the program.
4. Press **Alt-F5** to view the program results. The program displays the following:

```
Unsigned int: the bitwise negation of 12 is 65523
Signed int   : the bitwise negation of 12 is -13

Left shift (multiply by 2) of 12 is 24
Left shift (multiply by 4) of 12 is 48

Right shift (divide by 2) of 12 is 6
Right shift (divide by 4) of 12 is 3
```

Module 30

```
The bit is set
bc = c | 0xB0
b = c ^ 0x07
```

5. Press **Alt-F5** to return to the Turbo C++ editor.
6. Press **Alt-Spacebar** and type **C** and type **N** to clear the desktop.
7. Turn to Module 27 to continue the learning sequence.

Module 31
CLASS OPERATORS

DESCRIPTION

The class operators are:
new   constructor operator
delete   destructor operator
::   scope access operator

The new constructor operator allocates memory for an object (like declaring a variable).

The delete destructor operator removes an object, previously created with the new constructor, from memory.

The :: operator lets you access a global variable even if a local variable uses the same name. Local variables can only be accessed within the function that declares them. Global variables can be accessed by any function in a program.

APPLICATIONS

The new constructor operator and the delete destructor operator simplify initializing variables of a class. If you have declared several variables of a class type, the new constructor operator lets you initialize all these variables quickly and easily.

You would use the :: scope access operator to override a local variable name. For example, the following program declares a global and local variable with the name "sybil":

```
#include <iostream.h>

int     sybil;

void main()
  {
  void subfunction();

  sybil = 2;

  // Prints the value of 2
  cout << "This is the global variable = " << sybil << "\n";
  subfunction();
  }
```

123

Module 31

```
void subfunction()
  {
  int sybil;

  sybil = 1;
  ::sybil++;       // Increments the global variable sybil

  // Prints the value of 1
  cout << "This is the local variable  = " << sybil << "\n";

  // Prints the value of 3
  cout << "This is the global variable = " << ::sybil;
  }
```

Running this program would give the following program results:

```
This is the global variable = 2
This is the local variable  = 1
This is the global variable = 3
```

TYPICAL OPERATION

In this program, you modify the OBJECT.CPP file you created in Module 32. Begin from within Turbo C++ with no windows open.

1. Press **F3**. Turbo C++ displays a Load a File dialog box.
2. Type **OBJECT.CPP** and press **Return**. Turbo C++ loads the OBJECT.CPP file you created in Module 32.
3. Modify the program as follows:

   ```
   #include <iostream.h>

   class location
       {
       int x;
       int y;
   public:
       void initlocation(int NewX, int NewY);
       };

   void location::initlocation (int NewX, int NewY)
       {
       x = NewX;
       y = NewY;
       cout << "X-coordinate = " << x << "\n";
       cout << "Y-coordinate = " << y << "\n";
       }
   ```

```
void main()
    {
    location mylocation, yourlocation;

    mylocation.initlocation(4, 45);
    yourlocation.initlocation(75, 20);
    }
```

4. Press **F2** to save your program.
5. Press **Ctrl-F9** to run the program.
6. Press **Alt-F5** to view the program results.

```
X-coordinate = 4
Y-coordinate = 45
X-coordinate = 75
Y-coordinate = 20
```

Notice that this version of the OBJECT.CPP program lets you initialize variables by stating the values when you call the member function.

Also notice that this program can also initialize variables of two class variables (mylocation and yourlocation) easily as well.

7. Press **Alt-F5** to return to the Turbo C++ editor.
8. Press **Alt-Spacebar** and type **C** to clear the desktop.
9. Turn to Module 41 to continue the learning sequence.

Module 32
CLASSES

DESCRIPTION

Classes are a special data type that forms the basis of object-oriented programming. Essentially, a class organizes related data structures and algorithms (instructions that tell the computer what to do). Data structures and algorithms in a class are called members (data structures are called data members and algorithms are called member functions).

A class acts like an independent program that logically organizes data and algorithms together. A collection of classes makes up a larger program. Classes offer three levels of accessibility: private, protected, and public.

Private

Private accessibility means that members within a class can only be accessed by that class.

Protected

Protected accessibility means that members within a class can be accessed by member functions declared by that class and any classes "inherited" from that class. (See Module 41 for more information about "inheritance.")

Public

Public accessibility means that members within a class can be accessed by any part of a program. Classes declared as public are essentially the same as ordinary data structures and algorithms in the normal C language. (In other words, public classes don't take advantage of the C++ language.)

APPLICATIONS

In C++, you can define a class using the keywords: struct, union, or class.

Struct declaration

The struct keyword defines a class where all members are public by default, unless you specifically change them using the private or protected keywords.

```
    struct Point          // Example class declaration
```

```
        {
        int x;          // Public by default, can be changed
        int y;          // to private or protected
        }

    Point Cursor;       // Declares Cursor of type Point
```

Union declaration

The union keyword defines a class where all members are always public by default. (You cannot change the class accessibility.)

```
    union Point         // Example class declaration
        {
        int x;          // Public by default, cannot be
        int y;          // changed
        }

    Point Cursor;       // Declares Cursor of type Point
```

Class declaration

The class keyword defines a class where all members are private by default, unless you specifically change them using the public or protected keywords. Because class declarations are private by default, you should use them for creating most of your C++ objects.

```
    class Point         // Example class declaration
        {
        int x;          // Private by default, can be changed
        int y;          // to public or protected
        }

    Point Cursor;       // Declares Cursor of type Point
```

To change the accessibility of members within a class, use the private, protected, or public keywords such as:

```
    class Point         // Example class declaration
        {
        int x;          // This is private by default
    public:
        int y;          // This is now public
        }
```

Member functions

The above examples show objects that contain data. Objects can also contain functions (called member functions) that operate on that data.

You can define a member function in two ways: define it within the class declaration or declare it inside the class (like a function prototype) and define it outside the class.

To define a function within a class, simply add the function directly to the class.

```
class Point            // Example class declaration
    {
    int x;             // Private by default, can be changed
    int y;             // to public or protected
    int Position()
        {
        return X;
        }
    }
```

This method works for short functions. For longer functions, declare the function inside the class but define it outside.

```
class Point            // Example class declaration
    {
    int x;             // Private by default, can be changed
    int y;             // to public or protected
    int Position();
    }

int Point::Position()  // Tells the compiler which class
    {                  // this function belongs to
    return X;
    }
```

To call a class function, you need to specify the function plus the name of the object that function works with. For example, to use the above function, you would type the following:

```
Point.Position();
```

The syntax for object declarations in C++ is:

```
[declaration] [class name]
    {
    [accessibility type]
        [data members]
        [member functions]
    }
```

where   [declaration] = struct, union, or class
        [class name] = any valid C++ identifier
        [accessibility type] = public, private, or protected
        [data member] = any data type declarations
        [member functions] = any function definitions or declarations

Classes let you reuse portions of a program for other programs. Unlike structured languages, object-oriented languages let you modify existing code without having to understand how the original code actually works. Classes isolate the details so you can focus on making your program work and not on understanding how it's going to work.

TYPICAL OPERATION

In this program, you create a simple object-oriented program. Begin from within Turbo C++ with no windows open.

1. Press **Alt-F** and type **N** to create a new file.
2. Type the following:

```
#include <iostream.h>

class location
    {
    int x;
    int y;
public:
    void initlocation()
        {
        cout << "Enter X-coordinate: ";
        cin >> x;

        cout << "Enter Y-coordinate: ";
        cin >> y;

        cout << "MyLocation.X = " << x << "\n";
        cout << "MyLocation.Y = " << y << "\n";
        }
    };

void main()
    {
    location mylocation;

    mylocation.initlocation();
    }
```

Notice how the class called "location" contains data members (int x, int y) and a member function (void initlocation( )). The main program never accesses the data members directly; only the member function can access the data members. This feature of C++ prevents other functions from accidentally modifying data.

3. Press **F2** to save the file. Turbo C++ displays a Save Editor File dialog box.
4. Type **object.cpp** and press **Return**.
5. Press **Ctrl-F9** to run the program. The program displays the message "Enter X-coordinate:."

Module 32

6. Type **4** and press **Return**.
7. Type **45** and press **Return**.
8. Press **Alt-F5** to view the program results.

   ```
   Enter X-coordinate: 4
   Enter Y-coordinate: 45
   MyLocation.X = 4
   MyLocation.Y = 45
   ```

9. Press **Alt-F5** to return to the Turbo C++ editor.
10. Press **Alt-Spacebar** and type **C** to clear the desktop.
11. Turn to Module 31 to continue the learning sequence.

Module 33
COMMENTS

DESCRIPTION

Comments let you leave notes to yourself (or to those who may follow you) that explain how parts of your program work. Typical comments explain the purpose of a function, the purpose and names of its variables, and how the program works.

You can use three kinds of comments: traditional C comments, C++ comments, and preprocessor comments.

Traditional C comments surround the comment using /* and */ such as:

```
/* This is a comment on a single line */
```

or

```
/* This is a comment on
 * multiple lines
 */
```

C++ comments use // before the line you want to comment such as:

```
// This is a comment
```

Preprocessor comments surround the comment using #ifdef and #endif such as:

```
#ifdef CONDITION_NAME
code to be commented out
#endif
```

APPLICATIONS

When programming, there are two main reasons to use comments:

1) To remind yourself what a section of code does and how it works. Often times, a program you have written will look unfamiliar several weeks or days later. By leaving comments, you or any other programmer can quickly understand how a program works.

2) To temporarily remove a section of code while debugging. Many times your program may not work correctly. To help isolate the problem, you can comment out sections of your program. That way if the program still fails to work right, you know that the fault doesn't lie with the portion of code you commented out.

To comment out a single line of your program, use the // Turbo C++ comment such as:

```
main()
    {
    // This is a comment.
    }
```

To comment out multiple lines of your program, use the traditional /* and */ comments such as:

```
main()
    {
    /*
    printf("The program ignores the following 3 lines.\n");
    printf("Will not print.\n");
    printf("Also will not print.\n");
    */
    }
```

To comment out multiple lines simultaneously, use the #ifdef and #endif comments such as:

```
#define COMMENT
main()
    {
    #ifdef COMMENT
    printf("Will not print if COMMENT is defined.\n");
    #endif

    #ifdef COMMENT
    printf("Also will not print if COMMENT is defined.\n");
    #endif
    }
```

You can put comments anywhere, but for easy recognition, put them to the side or on separate lines so you can see them. For example:

```
/* This is a multiline description
 * of what the following function is doing.
 */

void function(int args)
{
int c;                  // the current character
int count;              // number of read characters

#ifdef NOT_NOW
function2(c,count);     // an old comment
#endif
exit();                 /* leave, activating the destructor */
}
```

This program fragment starts with a multiline description of the function. Some programmers prefer starting each line with //, but the traditional comment of asterisks can be more eye-catching.

The two declarations use the C++ comment to describe the variables "c" and "count." If the preprocessor variable NOT_NOW has been defined as True, then the first section of code will be included in the compilation. If it has not been set, then the second declaration will be used.

The exit( ) function call is an example of the traditional comment (/* and */) at the end of a line. The C++ comment (//) can be more convenient, because you don't have to worry about the closing comment characters.

You can't nest traditional style comments because the first */ that the compiler finds after the initial /* will be considered the end of the comment and the compiler will try to compile the rest of the comment. For example:

```
/* this is a new comment
statement1;
statement2;     /* an old comment */
   the compiler starts compiling again starting with this line
   because of the previous */
*/
```

If you want to comment out sections of a program which already contains comments, use #ifdef instead.

```
#ifdef NEW_COMMENT_AREA
statement1;
statement2;     /* an old comment */
statement3;     // the compiler will not compile this
#endif
```

TYPICAL OPERATION

In this example, you experiment with using different Turbo C++ comments. Begin from within Turbo C++ with no windows open.

1. Press **Alt-F** and type **N** to create a new file.
2. Type the following:

```
main()
{
printf("This line will appear on the screen.\n");

/*
printf("This line will NOT appear on the screen.\n");
*/

// printf("Neither will this line.\n");
```

Module 33

```
        #ifdef COMMENT
        printf("Or this line.\n");
        #endif

        return 0;
        }
```

3. Press **Ctrl-F9** to run the program.
4. Press **Alt-F5** to view the program results.

    ```
    This line will appear on the screen.
    ```

5. Press **Alt-F5** to return to the Turbo C++ editor. Modify the program as follows:

```
#define COMMENT
main()
    {
    printf("This line will appear on the screen.\n");

    printf("This line will NOT appear on the screen.\n");

    printf("Neither will this line.\n");

    #ifdef COMMENT
    printf("Or this line.\n");
    #endif

    return 0;
    }
```

6. Press **Ctrl-F9** to run the program.
7. Press **Alt-F5** to view the program results. Notice that the previously commented lines now appear on the screen.

    ```
    This line will appear on the screen.
    This line will NOT appear on the screen.
    Neither will this line.
    Or this line.
    ```

8. Press **Alt-Spacebar** and type **C** and type **N** to clear the desktop.
9. Turn to Module 25 to continue the learning sequence.

Module 34
CONTINUE

DESCRIPTION

The continue statement works with a loop control statement (do-while, for, while). A continue statement skips the remaining statements in a loop and begins the next iteration of the loop. If you need to exit a loop, use the break statement instead (see Module 29).

APPLICATIONS

Use the continue statement whenever you need to execute the next iteration of a loop but need to skip certain statements in the loop.

TYPICAL OPERATION

In this program, you create a program that totals the sum of five nonzero numbers that you enter from the keyboard. Begin from within Turbo C++ with no windows open.

1. Press **Alt-F** and type **N** to create a new file.
2. Type the following:

```
void main()
    {
    char  keyread;
    int   count, total;

    count = 0;
    total = 0;

    do
      {
      printf ("Type a number\n");
      scanf ("%d", &keyread);
      if (keyread == 0)
         continue;
      total = total + keyread;
      printf ("Sum total = %d\n", total);
      count++;
      }
    while (count < 5);
    }
```

Module 34

3. Press **F5** to zoom the editing window to the full screen.
4. Move the cursor to the "continue" statement.
5. Press **Ctrl-F8** to place a breakpoint on that statement. Turbo C++ highlights the breakpoint.

```
 ≡  File  Edit  Search  Run  Compile  Debug  Project  Options  Window  Help
─[■]──────────────────────── NONAME.C ──────────────────────1=[↕]─┐
void main()
{
  char     keyread;
  int      count, total;

  count = 0;
  total = 0;

  do
   {
    printf ("Type a number\n");
    scanf ("%d", &keyread);
    if (keyread == 0)
       continue;
    total = total + keyread;
    printf ("Sum total = %d\n", total);
    count++;
   }
  while (count < 5);
 }

──── 14:10 ────
 F1 Help  F2 Save  F3 Open  Alt-F9 Compile  F9 Make  F10 Menu
```

6. Press **Ctrl-F9** to run the program. The program displays the message "Type a number" on the screen.
7. Type **5** and press **Return**. The program displays the "Type a number" message.
8. Type **0** and press **Return**. Turbo C++ highlights the "continue" statement in bold.

```
 ≡  File  Edit  Search  Run  Compile  Debug  Project  Options  Window  Help
─[■]──────────────────────── NONAME.C ──────────────────────1=[↕]─┐
void main()
{
  char     keyread;
  int      count, total;

  count = 0;
  total = 0;

  do
   {
    printf ("Type a number\n");
    scanf ("%d", &keyread);
    if (keyread == 0)
       continue;
    total = total + keyread;
    printf ("Sum total = %d\n", total);
    count++;
   }
  while (count < 5);
 }

──── 14:1 ────
 F1 Help  F7 Trace  F8 Step  F9 Make  F10 Menu
```

9. Press **F7**. Notice on your screen that Turbo C++ skips over the remaining statements in the do-while loop and bold highlights the while condition.

```
≡  File  Edit  Search  Run  Compile  Debug  Project  Options    Window  Help
┌─[■]─────────────────────── NONAME.C ─────────────────────────1=[↕]─┐
│ void main()                                                        ▲│
│ {                                                                  ■│
│     char      keyread;                                              │
│     int       count, total;                                         │
│                                                                     │
│     count = 0;                                                      │
│     total = 0;                                                      │
│                                                                     │
│     do                                                              │
│     {                                                               │
│       printf ("Type a number\n");                                   │
│       scanf ("%d", &keyread);                                       │
│       if (keyread == 0)                                             │
│         continue;                                                   │
│       total = total + keyread;                                      │
│       printf ("Sum total = %d\n", total);                           │
│       count++;                                                      │
│     }                                                               │
│     while (count < 5);                                              │
│ }                                                                  ▼│
│──*── 19:1 ──◄─                                                    ►─┘
  F1 Help  F7 Trace  F8 Step  F9 Make  F10 Menu
```

10. Press **Ctrl-F2** to reset the program.
11. Press **Alt-Spacebar** and type **C** and type **N** to clear the desktop.
12. Turn to Module 35 to continue the learning sequence.

Module 35
DO-WHILE

DESCRIPTION

The do control structure provides the do-while loop, one of the three ways of looping in structured programming (the other two are while and the for loop). A do-while loop always executes at least once. (This differs from a while loop which may never execute at all.)

The syntax of a do-while loop is:
```
do
  {
  statement1;
  }
while(condition);
statement2;
```

The do-while loop first executes any statements enclosed within the do-while loop. In the above example, statement1 represents one or more statements.

After executing the statements once, the program tests the condition by the while statement. If condition is true, the statements execute again. When condition is false, control transfers to any statements directly following the do-while loop. In the above example, statement2 represents one or more statements outside the do-while loop.

To avoid an endless loop (when the condition always remains true), make sure that the statements within the do-while loop change the condition. Otherwise your program will go into an endless loop and not work correctly.

APPLICATIONS

Use the do-while loop to repeat a statement (or block of statements) at least once. The do-while is not seen as often as the while loop, since it is often possible to replace the do-while with a while loop that executes a function.

For example, when reading a file, you need to read a character from the file at least once. If the character is an EOF, then you can stop processing. If the character is not an EOF, you may process it. In this case, you need to use a do-while loop to make sure your program checks for a character at least once.

TYPICAL OPERATION

In this program, you use a do-while loop that performs the same function as the while-do loop you created in Module 56. Begin from within Turbo C++ with no windows open.

1. Press **Alt-F** and type **N** to create a new file.
2. Type the following:

   ```
   #include <stdio.h>

   main()
       {
       int i, loop;

       i = 0;
       printf ("How many times do you want to loop?\n");
       scanf ("%d", &loop);

       do
         {
         printf ("Loop %d\n", i);
         }
       while (i++ < loop);
       }
   ```

3. Press **Ctrl-F9** to run the program. The program will display the message:

   ```
   How many times do you want to loop?
   ```

4. Type **5** and press **Return**.
5. Press **Alt-F5** to see the program results on the screen. Notice that the program prints "Loop 0" on the screen. This occurs because the do-while loop executes the loop at least once before checking the condition to stop or continue.

   ```
   How many times do you want to loop?
   5
   Loop 0
   Loop 1
   Loop 2
   Loop 3
   Loop 4
   Loop 5
   ```

6. Press **Alt-F5** to return to the Turbo C++ editor.
7. Press **Alt-Spacebar** and type **C** and type **N** to clear the desktop.
8. Turn to Module 36 to continue the learning sequence.

Module 36
FOR

DESCRIPTION

The for loop repeats one or more statements a specific number of times. To do this, the for statement uses an initial statement, a condition, and a modifying statement (which changes something in the condition unless the condition is self-modifying). The for loop can be particularly useful for processing arrays.

The syntax of the for loop is:

```
for(initial,condition,modify)
   statement(s);
```

The following example prints the message "Hello, world!" five times across the screen:

```
void main()
    {
    int     i;
    for(i=0; i<5; i++)
       {
       printf ("Hello, world!\n");
       }
    }
```

To prevent an endless loop (when the loop executes forever and "hangs" your computer), make sure that the modify statement of the for loop changes the condition.

You can replace a for loop with a while loop such as:

```
initial;
while(condition)
    {
    statement(s);
    modify;
    }
```

```
void main()
    {
    int     i;
    i = 0;  /* initial */
    while (i < 5)
       {
       printf ("Hello, world!\n");
```

```
        i++;
      }
}
```

APPLICATIONS

Use the for loop to repeat a command a specified number of times. The limit can be specified using either constants (if you know the limit when you write the program) or variables (if you can determine a limit when the program is running).

For situations where you can't determine a limit (reading a file, for example), use a while loop instead (see Module 52).

TYPICAL OPERATION

In this program, you use two nested for loops to draw a 7x7 board with references around the edges as in the following diagram:

```
    A B C D E F G
1   . . . . . . .
2   . . . . . . .
3   . . . . . . .
4   . . . . . . .
5   . . . . . . .
6   . . . . . . .
7   . . . . . . .
```

Begin from within Turbo C++ with no windows open.

1. Press **Alt-F** and type **N** to create a new file.
2. Type the following:

   ```
   void main()
       {
       int i,j;

       printf ("  A B C D E F G\n");
       for (i=0; i<7; i++)
         {
         printf ("%1.1d", i+1);
         for (j=0; j<7; j++)
           printf (" .");
         printf("\n");
         }
       }
   ```

3. Press **Ctrl-F9** to run the program.

141

Module 36

4. Press **Alt-F5** to see the program results on the screen.

   ```
     A B C D E F G
   1 . . . . . . .
   2 . . . . . . .
   3 . . . . . . .
   4 . . . . . . .
   5 . . . . . . .
   6 . . . . . . .
   7 . . . . . . .
   ```

5. Press **Alt-F5** to return to the Turbo C++ editor.
6. Press **Alt-Spacebar** and type **C** and type **N** to clear the desktop.
7. Turn to Module 40 to continue the learning sequence.

Module 37
FUNCTION DEFINITION

DESCRIPTION

Every C++ program consists of one main function and zero or more additional functions. The main function has a structure that looks like this:

```
[data type] main()
    {
    statements;
    return (value);  /* Not needed if "void" data type */
    }
```

Any additional functions you define have a structure that looks like the following:

```
[data type] function_name (parameter list)
    {
    statements;
    return (value);  /* Not needed if "void" data type */
    }
```

The data type can be an integer, floating point, character, or enumerated value. If a function does not return a value, the data type should be "void." Functions of type "void" do not need a return statement.

For example, examine the following two functions:

```
int square (int ii)
    {
    return (ii * ii);
    }

void message ()
    {
    printf ("Enter a number to square: ");
    }
```

The first function returns a value of type int (integer). The second function does not return a value, so it is declared as type void and does not use a return statement.

Functions must have unique names. The main function must always be called "main." You can name other functions any name you want.

Following each function name is a set of parentheses ( ). The parentheses allow a function to accept data from another function. This is called the parameter list.

Module 37

If a function does not require data from another function, the parameter list will be blank ( ). If the function requires data, the parameter list contains the data type followed by the variables such as:

```
int square (int ii)
```

The { (left curly bracket) marks the start of the program and the } (right curly bracket) marks the end of the program. Between the brackets would be the actual program statements that make the computer do something useful such as:

```
void main()
    {
    printf ("Hello, world!");
    }
```

A complete C++ program consists of several functions within the main function such as the following:

```
void hello_function();
void world_function();

main()
    {
    hello_function();
    world_function();
    return (0);
    }

hello_function()
    {
    printf ("Hello, ");
    }

world_function()
    {
    printf ("world!");
    }
```

To make your programs easier to understand, Turbo C++ lets you declare function prototypes. A function prototype contains the data type, function name, and parameter list of a function and usually appears at the top of the program for easy identification.

In the above example, the two function prototypes are:

```
void hello_function();
void world_function();
```

Notice that the function prototypes end with a semicolon but the function declaration does not. Beginners often omit the semicolon in the function prototype or place a semicolon in a function declaration.

APPLICATIONS

You use functions to divide a large program into several smaller, more manageable pieces. To make your programs easier to read, try to divide your programs into functions that perform one specific task. That way if your program does not work correctly, you can quickly isolate the faulty function.

Use function prototypes to help you identify the names of all the functions in a program. In addition, function prototypes tell you what type of data each function expects and what type if returns.

TYPICAL OPERATION

In this program, you write a program that uses two types of functions. One function returns a value to the main function and the second function simply performs a specific task. Begin from within Turbo C++ with no windows open.

1. Press **Alt-F** and type **N** to create a new file.
2. Type the following:

```
#include <stdio.h>

void message ();
int square (int ii);

void main()
    {
    int     i, sq;

    message();
    scanf ("%d", &i);
    sq = square (i);
    printf ("\nThe value entered was %d\n", i);
    printf ("The value squared is %d\n", sq);
    }

void message ()
    {
    printf ("Enter a number to square: ");
    }

int square (int ii)
    {
    return (ii*ii);
    }
```

3. Press **F5** to zoom the editor window to a full screen.

Module 37

4. Move the cursor to the line that contains the "message( );" statement and press **Ctrl-F8** to set a breakpoint.

```
≡ File  Edit  Search  Run  Compile  Debug  Project  Options  Window  Help
[■]=========================== \TEMP\MOD37. ===========================1=[‡]
#include <stdio.h>

void message ();
int square (int i1);

void main()
{
    int     i, sq;

    message();
    scanf ("%d", &i);
    sq = square (i);
    printf ("\nThe value entered was %d\n", i);
    printf ("The value squared is %d\n", sq);
}

void message ()
{
    printf ("Enter a number to square: ");
}

───── 10:6 ─────
F1 Help  F2 Save  F3 Open  Alt-F9 Compile  F9 Make  F10 Menu
```

5. Move the cursor to the line that contains the "sq = square (i)" statement and press **Ctrl-F8** to set a breakpoint.

```
≡ File  Edit  Search  Run  Compile  Debug  Project  Options  Window  Help
[■]=========================== \TEMP\MOD37. ===========================1=[‡]
#include <stdio.h>

void message ();
int square (int i1);

void main()
{
    int     i, sq;

    message();
    scanf ("%d", &i);
    sq = square (i);
    printf ("\nThe value entered was %d\n", i);
    printf ("The value squared is %d\n", sq);
}

void message ()
{
    printf ("Enter a number to square: ");
}

───── 12:6 ─────
F1 Help  F2 Save  F3 Open  Alt-F9 Compile  F9 Make  F10 Menu
```

6. Press **Ctrl-F9** to run the program. Turbo C++ displays the cursor on the "message( );" statement in the editing window.

Function Definition

7. Press **F7**. Notice that Turbo C++ now highlights in bold the "void message( )" function.

```
  File   Edit   Search   Run   Compile   Debug   Project   Options   Window   Help
[■]═════════════════════════ \TEMP\MOD37. ═══════════════════════════1=[‡]═┐
#include <stdio.h>

void message ();
int square (int ii);

void main()
   {
   int    i, sq;

   message();
   scanf ("%d", &i);
   sq = square (i);
   printf ("\nThe value entered was %d\n", i);
   printf ("The value squared is %d\n", sq);
   }

void message ()
   {
      printf ("Enter a number to square: ");
   }

──── 17:1 ────
F1 Help  F7 Trace  F8 Step  F9 Make  F10 Menu
```

8. Press **Ctrl-F9** to continue running the program. The program displays the message "Enter a number to square:" on the screen.

9. Type **5** and press **Return**. Turbo C++ highlights in bold the "sq = square (i)" statement.

```
  File   Edit   Search   Run   Compile   Debug   Project   Options   Window   Help
[■]═════════════════════════ \TEMP\MOD37. ═══════════════════════════1=[‡]═┐
#include <stdio.h>

void message ();
int square (int ii);

void main()
   {
   int    i, sq;

   message();
   scanf ("%d", &i);
   sq = square (i);
   printf ("\nThe value entered was %d\n", i);
   printf ("The value squared is %d\n", sq);
   }

void message ()
   {
      printf ("Enter a number to square: ");
   }

──── 12:1 ────
F1 Help  F7 Trace  F8 Step  F9 Make  F10 Menu
```

10. Press **F7**. Notice on your screen that Turbo C++ now highlights the "int square (int ii)" function.

Module 37

```
  ≡  File  Edit  Search  Run  Compile  Debug  Project  Options    Window  Help
┌─[■]──────────────────────── \TEMP\MOD37. ══════════════════════════1═[↕]═╗
│       sq = square (i);                                                  ▲
│       printf ("\nThe value entered was %d\n", i);
│       printf ("The value squared is %d\n", sq);
│   }
│
│  void message ()
│   {
│       printf ("Enter a number to square: ");
│   }                                                                     ■
│
│  int square (int ii)
│   {
│       return (ii*ii);
│   }
│
│
│
│                                                                         ▼
│──── 22:1 ────◄                                                         ►┘
   F1 Help  F7 Trace  F8 Step  F9 Make  F10 Menu
```

11. Press **F7**. Turbo C++ highlights the "return (ii * ii);" statement in the square function.
12. Press **F7** twice. Turbo C++ now highlights the next statement in the main function, following the "sq = square (i);" function call.
13. Press **Ctrl-F2** to reset the program.
14. Press **Alt-Spacebar** and type **C** and type **N** to clear the desktop.
15. Turn to Module 24 to continue the learning sequence.

Module 38
GOTO

DESCRIPTION

The goto command lets you force execution to another part of the program. You can usually replace a goto statement with a break or continue statement, or by restructuring your program.

The syntax for the goto statement is:
```
goto label;
    .
    .
    .
label:
```

Where label is any valid C++ name. For example:
```
goto JUMP
    .
    .
    .
JUMP: printf ("Jumped to GOTO statement.");
```

APPLICATIONS

Use the goto statement as a last-resort command to transfer control to another part of your program. Because goto statements transfer control to a specific statement located somewhere else in the program, you cannot always clearly see how the program works, making it difficult to understand.

Since you can usually replace a goto statement with a break or continue statement instead, you should generally avoid using goto statements. If you insist on using a goto statement, make sure you clearly identify the goto label such as:
```
void main()
    {
    goto END;
    printf ("This line will never print.\n");
    END: printf ("End of program.\n");
    }
```

The goto statement has three main limitations. First, you cannot use a goto statement to transfer control in or out of a function such as:

Module 38

```
    void main()
        {
        goto RESULT;   /* Illegal */
        }
square (int ii);
        {
        RESULT: return (ii*ii);
        }
```

Second, you cannot have a goto label as the last statement in a function, such as:

   label:

   end: // this is illegal

If you need to put a goto label as the last statement, put a null statement (;) immediately after it such as:

   label:

   end: ;   // this is legal

Finally, you cannot use a goto to jump over an explicitly or implicitly initialized variable definition unless the definition occurs in a block and you jump over the block.

```
    int main(int argc, char **argv)
    {
        goto end;          // this is illegal
        String errmsg(1);
        end: ;
    }

    int main(int argc, char **argv)
    {
        goto end;          // this is legal
        if(!done)
          {
            String errmsg(1);
                .
                .
                .
          }
        end: ;
    }
```

TYPICAL OPERATION

In this program, you experiment with the goto statement. Begin from within Turbo C++ with no windows open.

1. Press **Alt-F** and type **N** to create a new file.
2. Type the following:

```c
#include <stdio.h>
#define TAB     '\t'
#define RETURN  '\r'
#define ESC     0x1B

void main()
    {
    int c;

    while ((c = getch()) != EOF)
       {
       if (c == TAB)
          goto TAB_label;

       if (c == RETURN)
          goto RETURN_label;

       if (c == 'A')
          goto A_label;

       if (c == 'a')
          goto a_label;

       if (c == ESC)
          exit (0);
       else
          printf ("%c", c);
       return (0);

       TAB_label:
          {
          printf ("You pressed a TAB\n");
          continue;
          }

       RETURN_label:
          {
          printf ("\n");
          continue;
          }

       A_label:
          {
          printf ("\nYou've hit A\n");
          continue;
          }

       a_label:
          {
```

Module 38

```
            printf ("Not another a\n");
            continue;
        }
    }
}
```

3. Press **F5** to expand the editing window to the full screen.
4. Move the cursor to the "goto TAB_label;" statement and press **Ctrl-F8** to place a breakpoint.

```
≡ File  Edit  Search  Run  Compile  Debug  Project  Options  Window  Help
┌[■]━━━━━━━━━━━━━━━━━━━━━━ \TEMP\MOD38. ━━━━━━━━━━━━━━━1=[↕]┐
#include <stdio.h>
#define TAB      '\t'
#define RETURN   '\r'
#define ESC      0x1B

void main()
{
    int c;

    while ((c = getch()) != EOF)
    {
        if (c == TAB)
            goto TAB_label;

        if (c == RETURN)
            goto RETURN_label;

        if (c == 'A')
            goto A_label;

        if (c == 'a')
     13:11
 F1 Help  F2 Save  F3 Open  Alt-F9 Compile  F9 Make  F10 Menu
```

5. Press **Ctrl-F9** to run the program.
6. Press **Tab**. Notice that Turbo C++ highlights in bold the breakpoint in your program.

```
≡ File  Edit  Search  Run  Compile  Debug  Project  Options  Window  Help
┌[■]━━━━━━━━━━━━━━━━━━━━━━ \TEMP\MOD38. ━━━━━━━━━━━━━━━1=[↕]┐
#include <stdio.h>
#define TAB      '\t'
#define RETURN   '\r'
#define ESC      0x1B

void main()
{
    int c;

    while ((c = getch()) != EOF)
    {
        if (c == TAB)
            goto TAB_label;

        if (c == RETURN)
            goto RETURN_label;

        if (c == 'A')
            goto A_label;

        if (c == 'a')
     13:1
 F1 Help  F7 Trace  F8 Step  F9 Make  F10 Menu
```

7. Press **F7**. Notice that Turbo C++ jumps to printf ("You pressed a TAB\n"); in your program.
8. Press **Ctrl-F9** to run the rest of the program. The program prints the following message:
   ```
   You pressed a TAB
   ```
9. Type **a**. The program prints the following message:
   ```
   Not another a
   ```
10. Type **A**. Notice that program prints a blank line and then the following message:
    ```
    You've hit A
    ```
11. Press **Return**. The program prints a blank line.
12. Press **Esc**. The program returns you to the Turbo C++ editor.
13. Press **Alt-Spacebar** and type **C** and type **N** to clear the desktop.
14. Turn to Module 51 to continue the learning sequence.

Module 39
IDENTIFIERS

DESCRIPTION

An identifier is a name of a variable, function, class, etc. in a C++ program. All identifiers must follow these conventions:

1. The first letter must be a letter or an underscore (_).
2. The identifier can only contain the following:

Letters
   A B C D E F G H I J K L M N O P Q R S T U V W X Y Z
   a b c d e f g h i j k l m n o p q r s t u v w x y z

Digits
   0 1 2 3 4 5 6 7 8 9

Underscore
   _

You can create identifiers of any length, but Turbo C++ only considers the first 32 characters as "significant." In other words, Turbo C++ would treat the following two identifiers as the same since Turbo C++ only recognizes the first 32 characters:

   this_is_an_extremely_long_variable

and

   this_is_an_extremely_long_variable_too

In C++, identifiers are case sensitive. This means that lowercase letters are not the same as uppercase. Turbo C++ considers the following variables as four distinct variables:

   TEST   test   Test   tesT

You cannot use Turbo C++ reserved words as identifiers. If you do, the Turbo C++ compiler will display an error message. The following table lists Turbo C++ reserved words:

Turbo C++ Reserved Words

asm	auto	break	case	cdecl
char	class	const	continue	default
delete	do	double	else	enum
_export	extern	far	float	for
friend	goto	huge	if	inline

154

Identifiers

int	interrupt	_loadds	long	near
new	operator	pascal	private	protected
public	register	return	_saveregs	_seg
short	signed	sizeof	static	struct
switch	template	this	typedef	union
unsigned	virtual	void	volatile	while

The following are unique and valid variable identifiers:

    c   C   c1   _c   _c1   c_1   c1_

The following are invalid identifiers:

    1c   (doesn't start with a letter or an underscore)
    c$ (uses a character which is not a letter, digit, or _)
    c 1   (uses a character which is not a letter, digit, or _)

APPLICATIONS

You use identifiers for naming functions, variables, and classes. By using descriptive identifiers, you can clearly show what type of information the identifier represents. For example, compare the following statements:

    x = 0.10 * y;   commission = 0.10 * sales;

Although the above two statements represent the same equation, the second statement uses complete words to describe the variable, thus making it easier to understand.

For long identifiers, use capital letters or underscores to emphasize separate words. For example:

    Taxrate   TaxRate   Tax_Rate

TYPICAL OPERATION

In this example, you examine how Turbo C++ treats illegal identifier names. Begin from within Turbo C++ with no windows open.

1. Press **Alt-F** and type **N** to create a new file.
2. Type the following:

```
void main()
    {
    int     number1, 1number;

    number1 = 1;
    1number = 2;
    printf ("number1 = %d\n", number1);
    printf ("1number = %d\n", 1number);
    }
```

3. Press **Ctrl-F9** to run the program. Turbo C++ displays an error message.

Module 39

4. Press **Return**. Turbo C++ highlights the line containing the illegal identifier, "1number."

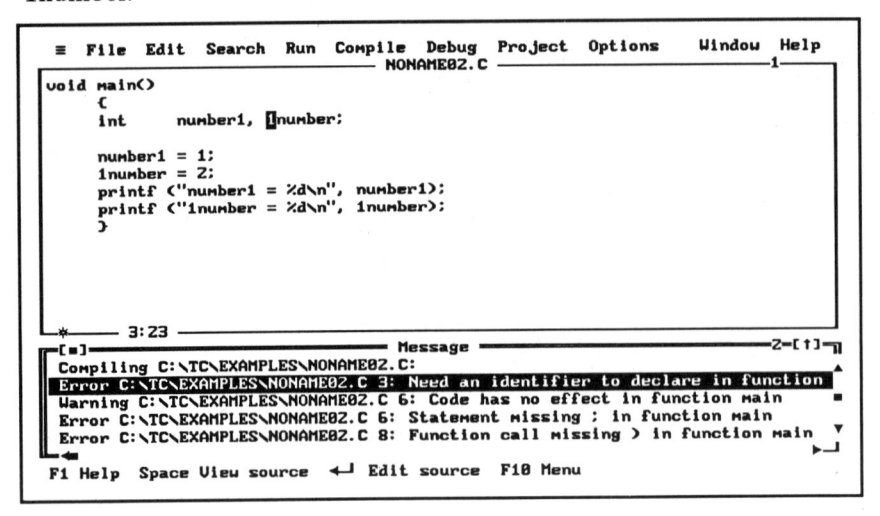

```
≡ File  Edit  Search  Run  Compile  Debug  Project  Options    Window   Help
┌─────────────────────────── NONAME02.C ─────────────────────────1──┐
│void main()                                                         │
│   {                                                                │
│   int      number1, 1number;                                       │
│                                                                    │
│   number1 = 1;                                                     │
│   1number = 2;                                                     │
│   printf ("number1 = %d\n", number1);                              │
│   printf ("1number = %d\n", 1number);                              │
│   }                                                                │
│                                                                    │
│                                                                    │
│──*─── 3:23 ────────────────────────────────────────────────────────│
┌─[■]──────────────────────── Message ───────────────────────2=[↑]──┐
│ Compiling C:\TC\EXAMPLES\NONAME02.C:                               │
│ Error C:\TC\EXAMPLES\NONAME02.C 3: Need an identifier to declare in function │
│ Warning C:\TC\EXAMPLES\NONAME02.C 6: Code has no effect in function main │
│ Error C:\TC\EXAMPLES\NONAME02.C 6: Statement missing ; in function main │
│ Error C:\TC\EXAMPLES\NONAME02.C 8: Function call missing ) in function main │
└────────────────────────────────────────────────────────────────────┘
  F1 Help  Space View source  ↵ Edit source  F10 Menu
```

5. Press **F6** to edit the program.
6. Press **Ctrl-Q A**. Turbo C++ displays a Replace dialog box.
7. Type **1number** and press **Tab**.
8. Type **Number1** and press **Tab**.
9. Press **Down Arrow** three times to highlight the Prompt on replace option.
10. Press **Spacebar** and type **A** to choose the Change All option. Turbo C++ replaces all occurrences of 1number with Number1.
11. Press **Ctrl-F9** to run the program. Turbo C++ briefly displays the program results on the screen, then returns you to the Turbo C++ editing window.
12. Press **Alt-F5** to see the program results on the screen. Notice that your program has assigned separate values to the variables "number1" and "Number1."

    number1 = 1
    Number1 = 2

13. Press **Alt-F5** to return to the Turbo C++ editor.
14. Press **Alt-Spacebar** and type **C** and type **N** to clear the desktop.
15. Turn to Module 28 to continue the learning sequence.

Module 40
IF-ELSE

DESCRIPTION

Like all programming languages, C++ gives you a way of having your program make decisions. In C++, decisions are made with the if-else statement. There are three main variants:

```
if(condition)                /* variant #1 */
    if_statements;

if(condition)                /* variant #2 */
    if_statements;
else
    else_statements;

if(condition1)               /* variant #3 */
    if_1_statements;
else if(condition2)
    if_2_statements;
else
    else_statements;
```

Variant #1 uses a single if condition, followed by one or more if_statements. If the condition is true, the program executes the if_statements. Otherwise, it ignores the if_statements.

Variant #2 uses an if condition followed by an else condition. If the condition is true, the program executes the if_statements, then execution continues with the first statement after the if-else structure.

If the condition is false, the program executes the else_statements, then execution continues with the first statement after the if-else structure.

Variant #3 uses two or more if conditions and an else condition. If the first condition is true, the program executes the if_statements followed by the first statement after the if-else structure.

If the first condition is false, the program tests if condition2 is true. If it is true, the program executes the if_2_statements. Otherwise, any following conditions are tested until an else is encountered. If none of the conditions have been met, the program executes the else_statements.

Conditions must evaluate to a single numeric value. If it evaluates to 0, it is considered FALSE; any other value is TRUE.

Conditions can consist of relationships, variables, or routines.

When you compare two values together, they can be related to each other in the following ways:

Binary Boolean Relations

a < b	a is less than b
a > b	a is greater than b
a <= b	a is less than or equal to b
a >= b	a is greater than or equal to b
a == b	a is equal to b
a != b	a is not equal to b

Beginners often make the mistake in using a single = sign to compare two values. For example, the following two statements perform completely different functions:

a = b	This sets the value of 'a' equal to the value of 'b'
a == b	This compares the value of 'a' to the value of 'b'

You can join multiple relations together using the following operators:

Binary Boolean Operators

!a	not a
&&	and
||	or

APPLICATIONS

The if-else statement is one of the basic control structures for programming. Although you usually use the Boolean relations and operators for checking a condition, you can also use a function or expression instead (to check for the end of a string, for example). If you were writing a game program, you might use:

```
if(validmove(move))
     place(move);
else
     invalidmove();
```

TYPICAL OPERATION

In this program, you use multiple if-else statements to read characters from the keyboard. Begin from within Turbo C++ with no windows open.

1. Press **Alt-F** and type **N** to create a new file.
2. Type the following:

If-Else

```c
#include <stdio.h>
#define TAB     '\t'
#define RETURN  '\r'
#define ESC     0x1B

void main()
    {
    int c;

    while ((c=getch()) != EOF)
      if (c == TAB)
        printf ("You pressed a TAB\n");
      else if (c== RETURN)
        printf ("\n");
          else if (c == 'A')
            printf ("\nYou've hit A\n");
              else if (c=='a')
                printf ("Not another a\n");
                  else if (c == ESC)
                    exit(0);
                      else printf ("%c",c);

    }
```

3. Press **Ctrl-F9** to run the program.
4. Press **Tab**. The program prints the following message:

    You pressed a TAB

5. Type **a**. The program prints the following message:

    Not another a

6. Type **A**. Notice that the program prints the message:

    You've hit A

7. Press **Return**. The program advances the screen display by a line.
8. Press **Esc**. The program returns you to the Turbo C++ editor.
9. Press **Alt-Spacebar** and type **C** and type **N** to clear the desktop.
10. Turn to Module 38 to continue the learning sequence.

Module 41
INHERITANCE

DESCRIPTION

The C++ languages uses classes to organize related data and functions together. Once you have defined a class, you can define other classes that consist of similar features.

Rather than define a completely separate class with similar features, C++ lets you "inherit" features from an existing class. Through inheritance, you can create a library of base classes and derive additional classes with a minimum amount of work.

Classes can inherit features from a single class, or a class can inherit features from two or more different classes (called multiple inheritance).

Inheritance only works with classes declared with the class or struct keyword. You can never inherit features from a class declared with the union keyword.

APPLICATIONS

Inheritance lets you create new classes from existing classes. Rather than "reinvent the wheel," inheritance lets you borrow features from existing code and extend it for your own use.

For example, you could declare a structure that consists of an X and Y coordinate such as:

```
struct location
    {
    int x;
    int y;
    }
```

Now if you wanted to declare a data structure to represent a point on the screen, its structure might look like this:

```
enum Boolean {false, true};

struct point
    {
    int x;
    int y;
    Boolean visible;
    }
```

Notice that the structures of "location" and "point" are essentially the same, yet the traditional C languages forces us to declare the same data twice. With C++, we can use classes to inherit features such as:

```
enum Boolean {false, true};

class location
    {
protected:
    int x;
    int y;
    }

class point : public location
    {
protected:
    Boolean visible;
    }
```

Notice how much simpler the point structure looks now without the repetition of data type declarations. Inheritance lets you quickly write programs that are also easier for others to understand.

TYPICAL OPERATION

In this program, you modify the OBJECT.CPP file you created in Module 32. Begin from within Turbo C++ with no windows open.

1. Press **F3**. Turbo C++ displays a Load a File dialog box.
2. Type **OBJECT.CPP** and press **Return**. Turbo C++ loads the OBJECT.CPP file you created in Module 32.
3. Modify the program as follows:

```
#include <iostream.h>

enum Boolean {false, true};

class location
    {
protected:
    int x;
    int y;
public:
    void initlocation(int NewX, int NewY);
    };

void location::initlocation (int NewX, int NewY)
    {
    x = NewX;
```

161

Module 41

```
        y = NewY;
        cout << "X-coordinate = " << x << "\n";
        cout << "Y-coordinate = " << y << "\n";
        }
// This class inherits features from the location class
class point : public location
        {
protected:
        Boolean visible;
public:
        void initlocation (int NewX, int NewY, Boolean Newvisible);
        };

void point::initlocation (int NewX, int NewY, Boolean Newvisible)
        {
        x = NewX;
        y = NewY;
        visible = Newvisible;
        cout << "X-coordinate = " << x << "\n";
        cout << "Y-coordinate = " << y << "\n";
        cout << "Visible      = " << visible << "\n";
        }

void main()
        {
        location mylocation;
        point pixel;

        mylocation.initlocation(4, 45);
        pixel.initlocation(75, 20, true);
        }
```

4. Press **F2** to save your program.
5. Press **Ctrl-F9** to run the program.
6. Press **Alt-F5** to view the program results.

```
        X-coordinate = 4
        Y-coordinate = 45
        X-coordinate = 75
        Y-coordinate = 20
        Visible      = 1
```

Notice that the point class inherits data members (int x and int y) from the location class.

7. Press **Alt-F5** to return to the Turbo C++ editor.
8. Press **Alt-Spacebar** and type **C** to clear the desktop.
9. Turn to Module 45 to continue the learning sequence.

Module 42
LOGIC OPERATORS

DESCRIPTION

Logic operators test or compare a condition between two operands. Turbo C++ provides relational operators, equality operators, logical operators, and the condition operator.

Relational operators

Relational operators include <, >, <=, and >=.

The < operator produces a nonzero value (true) if the left operand is less than the right operand. Otherwise it produces a zero (false).

Expression	Result
3 < 8	1 (true)
8 < 3	0 (false)

The > operator produces a nonzero value (true) if the left operand is greater than the right operand. Otherwise it produces a zero (false).

Expression	Result
3 > 8	0 (false)
8 > 3	1 (true)

The >= operator produces a nonzero value (true) if the left operand is greater than or equal to the right operand. Otherwise it produces a zero (false).

Expression	Result
3 >= 8	0 (false)
8 >= 3	1 (true)
8 >= (3 * 2)	1 (true)
8 >= (4 * 2)	1 (true)
8 >= (5 * 2)	0 (false)

The <= operator produces a nonzero value (true) if the left operand is less than or equal to the right operand. Otherwise it produces a zero (false).

Expression	Result
3 <= 8	1 (true)
8 <= 3	0 (false)
8 <= (3 * 2)	0 (false)
8 <= (4 * 2)	1 (true)

Equality operators

Equality operators include == and !=.

The == operator produces a nonzero value (true) if the left operand is equal to the right operand. Otherwise it produces a zero (false).

Expression	Result
6 == 4	0 (false)
6 == (2 * 3)	1 (true)

The != operator produces a nonzero value (true) if the left operand is not equal to the right operand. Otherwise it produces a zero (false).

Expression	Result
6 != 4	1 (true)
6 != (2 * 3)	0 (false)

Logic operators

Logic operators include &&, ||, and !.

The && operator is the C++ logical AND operator. If two operands are nonzero (true), then the entire expression is nonzero (true). Otherwise the expression is zero (false).

Expression	Result
True && True	True
True && False	False
False && True	False
False && False	False

The || operator is the C++ logical OR operator. If two operands are zero (false), then the entire expression is zero (false). Otherwise the expression is nonzero (true).

Expression	Result
True || True	True
True || False	True
False || True	True
False || False	False

The ! operator is the C++ logical NOT operator. If the operand is nonzero (true), the expression is zero (false). If the operand is zero (false), the expression is nonzero (true).

Expression	Result
!True	False
!False	True

Condition operator

The condition operator looks like:
```
expression1 ? expression2 : expression3
```

If expression1 is nonzero (true), the value of the entire expression is the value of expression2. If expression1 is zero (false), the value of the entire expression is the value of expression3.

Examine the following program:

```
void main()
    {
    int a, b, c;

    a = 5;
    b = 4;
    c = (a > b ? 3 : 10);       /* c = 3  */
    c = (a == b ? 14 : 0);      /* c = 0  */
    c = (a <= b ? 25 : 12);     /* c = 12 */
    }
```

The following table shows the number of operands needed for each type of operator:

unary
    !   (logical NOT)

binary
    && (logical AND)
    || (logical OR)
    <   (less than)
    >   (greater than)
    <= (less than or equal)
    >= (greater than or equal)
    == (equal)
    != (not equal)

tertiary
    ? : (condition)

APPLICATIONS

Logical operators are usually used to test a condition for an if-else, while-do, or do-while loop.

The ! (logical NOT) operator gets the opposite of a value. If a value is true, ! makes it false. If a value is false, ! makes it true.

```
if(!isodd(n))
    printf("It must be even.\n");
```

This statement checks to see if n is odd. If it is not, the ! operator prints the message "It must be even."

Module 42

The && (logical AND) operator returns true only if both conditions are true:
```
if(isfemale(subject) && residesin(subject,"California"))
    printf("%s already has a boyfriend\n",subject);
```

The || (logical OR) operator returns true if either of the conditions are true (or if both of them are true).
```
if(stolen(car) || smashed_by_idiot(car))
    new_raised_rate = call_insurance();
```

The < (less than) relation checks if the first operand is less than the second operand.
```
if(a < b)
    statement;
```

You will often use this as the terminating condition of a loop, especially when incrementing is involved.

The > (greater than) relation checks if the first operand is greater than the second operand.
```
if(a > b)
    statement;
```

This is often used in determining the terminating condition of a loop, especially if decrementing is involved.

The <= (less than or equal) relation checks if the first operand is less than or equal to the second operand.
```
if(a <= b)
    statement;
```

You will usually find <= used in determining the terminating condition of a loop, especially if incrementing is involved. (But when incrementing, it is often better to change the condition to use a < since < is faster than <=.)

The >= (greater than or equal) relation checks if the first operand is greater than or equal to the second operand.
```
if(a >= b)
    statement;
```

This is commonly used in loops to determine the terminating condition, especially if you are decrementing a value. (But when decrementing, it is often better to change the condition so it uses a > since > is faster than >=.)

The == (equal) relation checks if two operands are equal.
```
if(a == b)
    statement;
```

A common error beginners often make is using the = (simple assignment) operator when they meant to use == (equal).

```
a = 2
b = 3
if(a = b)
    statement;
```

At the end of this example, a would be equal to 3 and statement would execute (a=b will evaluate to a nonzero, therefore, it is considered TRUE).

The != (not equal) relation checks if two operands are not equal.

```
if(a != b)
    statement;
```

Not equal is often used in while loops, since you usually want the loop to continue until an event occurs. For example,

```
while((c=fgetc(infile) != EOF)
    .
    .
    .
```

checks each incoming character to see if it is the end of file (EOF) mark. If an end of file is encountered, the loop stops processing.

The ?: (condition) operator lets your code be more compressed. If you wanted to determine if a number were odd or even, you could use a program like

```
if(isodd(n))
    printf("%d is odd\n",n);
else
    printf("%d is even\n",n);
```

or you could use the condition operator

```
printf("%d is %s\n",n,(isodd(n)) ? "odd" : "even");
```

and condense the code into something more terse.

The condition operator evaluates as

```
condition ? true : false
```

If the condition evaluates to a nonzero, the true part executes, otherwise the false part executes.

TYPICAL OPERATION

In this program, you experiment with using different logic operators. Begin from within Turbo C++ with no windows open.

1. Press **Alt-F** and type **N** to create a new file.
2. Type the following:

Module 42

```c
#include <stdio.h>

main()
    {
    int i=1,j;

    j = i;
    printf("%d !=%d\n",!i,j);
    if('a' < 'b')
        printf("a < b\n");
    if('b' > 'a')
        printf("b > a\n");
    if(('a' < 'b') && ('b' > 'a'))
        printf("a < b && b > a\n");
    if(('a' < 'b') || ('b' > 'a'))
        printf("a < b || b > a\n");
    if('a' <= 'b')
        printf("a <= b\n");
    if('b' >= 'a')
        printf("b >= a\n");
    if('a' == 'a')
        printf("a == a\n");
    if('a' != 'b')
        printf("a != b\n");
    printf("(a == b) is %s\n",('a'=='b')?"True":"False");
    }
```

3. Press **Ctrl-F9** to run the program.
4. Press **Alt-F5** to view the program results. Notice that Turbo C++ treats the character 'a' as less than the character 'b.'

   ```
   0 != 1
   a < b
   b > a
   a < b && b > a
   a < b || b > a
   a <= b
   b >= a
   a == a
   a != b
   (a == b) is False
   ```

5. Press **Alt-F5** to return to the Turbo C++ editor.
6. Press **Alt-Spacebar** and type **C** and type **N** to clear the desktop.
7. Turn to Module 30 to continue the learning sequence.

Module 43
MEMORY MODELS

DESCRIPTION

The family of 8086/80186/80286/80386/80486 microprocessors used in IBM and compatible computers creates the need for memory models. Essentially, memory models define how your program addresses your computer's memory. The six available memory models with Turbo C++ are:

    tiny
    small
    medium
    compact
    large
    huge

You also need to be aware of the following pointer modifiers:

    near
    far
    huge

You should only change memory models if you are familiar with the Intel 8086 microprocessor architecture and how these microprocessors use registers. Beginning programmers should avoid changing memory models.

APPLICATIONS

The different size memory models let you choose the optimum model for your program. The default memory model for Turbo C++ is Small.

You can change the memory model through the Options menu or by using command-line options when using the command-line version of Turbo C++.

Memory model	Command-line option
Tiny	-mt or -mt!
Small	-ms or -ms!
Medium	-mm or -mm!
Compact	-mc
Large	-ml
Huge	-mh

Tiny
The tiny model is used for programs that are smaller than 64K (including data, code, and stack space). Tiny model programs can easily be turned into .COM files by using the /t option when using the TLINK linker.

Small
The small model is the most commonly used memory model. If you plan on working with less than 64K of data and 64K of code, this is a good model to use. But when you need to have more than 64K of either data or code, you'll have to move up to one of the following models.

Medium
The medium model is used for large programs which don't manipulate a lot of data. The data (both stack and heap) are limited to 64K and the code is limited to 1M.

Compact
The compact model is used for small programs that work with less than a megabyte of data (it's the opposite of medium). The data (both stack and heap) are limited to 1M and the code is limited to 64K.

Large
The large model is used for very large programs that don't have individual items (like arrays) which are larger than 64K in size. Data and Code are limited to 1M in size each.

Huge
The huge model is used for very large programs that have individual items larger than 64K. This is useful when working with great quantities of data in an array.

Memory Model	Code Size	Data Size	Comments
Tiny	<64K n,cs	<64K n,ds	(code+data <= 64K)
Small	64K n,cs	64K n,ds	
Medium	1M f	64K n,ds	
Compact	64K n,cs	1M f	(@item must be <=64K)
Large	1M f	1M f	(@item must be <=64K)
Huge	1M f	1M f	(@item can be >64K)

The letters after code and data size describe the type of pointers that are available to you in that model:

    cs   The _cs modifier is used (code segment)
    ds   The _ds modifier is used (data segment)
    f   Far pointers are used
    n   Near pointers are used

Pointer Modifiers

If you need to access a single huge array or if you're working with the large model and there are a couple of small arrays that you'd like to speed up access to, you can mix models by explicitly declaring a pointer to be a size other than the default size.

When working with pointer modifiers, you should use function prototypes so the compiler will catch any conversion errors which might occur (it's easier to do than you think).

You can modify functions or data with the pointer modifiers. For example, you are working in the huge model and you want to create a fast string processing routine called strprocess( ):

```
char *strprocess(const char *s)    {...}
```

If you declared it like this, the char * will be a far pointer (which is slow compared to near pointers). You can explicitly tell Turbo C++ to use near pointers with this function by saying:

```
char near *strprocess(const char *s) {...}
```

Your function doesn't need to return to take advantage of the speed up:

```
int near strlen(const char *s) {...}
```

defines a function which would use the near model to define how the function will return its return type.

To change the model of a data type is similar to changing the model of a function. If you have a struct box_item * array which is larger than 64K, you could access it from a nonhuge model program using the following:

```
struct box_item huge *b1[NUM_BOX_IN_WIN1];
```

You can't use the model modifiers to change a nonpointer data item.

Near

Near pointers are the smallest pointers used in Turbo C++, so they're the fastest pointers to use. When working with near pointers, the addresses don't have to be as large as far or huge addresses.

The limitation to working with near pointers is that you can't access items which don't lie in the current data segment (to access other segments you have to use a far or huge pointer).

You can declare a near by using the following syntax:

```
return-type near function_declaration(args) {...}
```

or

```
data_type near *variable;
```

Examples of these two different ways of declaring near:
```
char near *strcpy(const char *a, const char *b) {...};

char near *name;
```

Far
The far pointer is used when you have more than 64K of data that you want to access or if you need to access an item which is being stored in another data segment (if you want to access video memory, you'll need to either implicitly or explicitly use far pointers since video memory is kept in a segment different from your data).

You can declare a far by using the following syntax:
```
return-type far function_declaration(args) {...}
```
or
```
data_type far variable;
```
Some examples of far declarations are:
```
char far *strprocess(const char *a) {...}

char far *videomem = VIDEO;
```

Huge
Huge pointers are used when you have an array or single data item which is greater than 64K in size. When working with classes or data types which you've created, you might come across situations where you need to access a single item of this size (like in editors, database applications, compilers, or other large, commercial application-size projects).

You can declare a huge pointer by using the following syntax:
```
data_type huge variable;
```
For example:
```
struct popup_window huge *popwin[NUM_POP_WINS];
```

TYPICAL OPERATION

In this module, you learn how to change memory models within the Turbo C++ integrated development environment. Begin from within Turbo C++ with no windows open.

1. Press **Alt-O** to pull down the Options menu.
2. Type **C** to choose the Compiler command. Turbo C++ displays a pop-up menu.
3. Type **C** to choose the Code generation command. Turbo C++ displays a Code Generation dialog box.

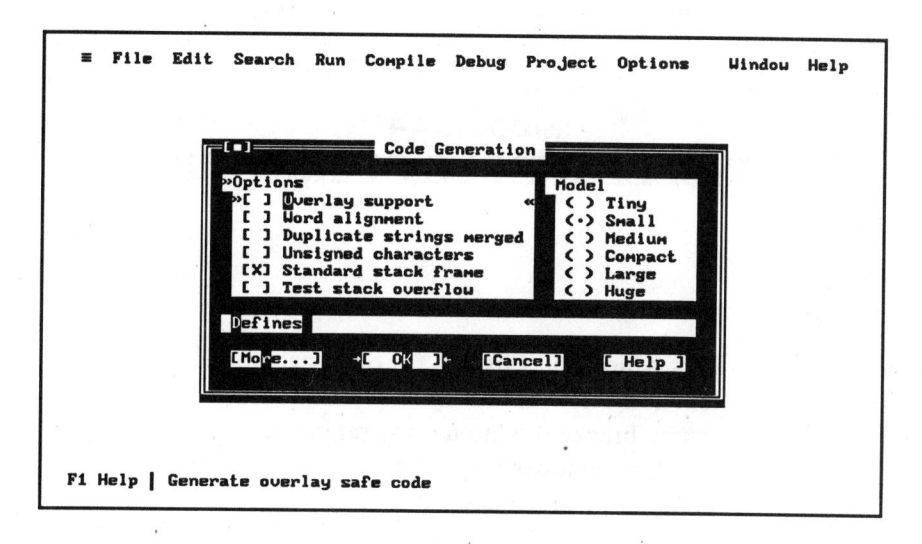

4. Press **Tab**. The cursor moves under the Model options of Tiny, Small, Medium, Compact, Large, and Huge.
5. Type **H**. Notice that the Huge option is now checked.
6. Press **Up Arrow** twice. Notice that the Compact option is now checked.
7. Type **S**. Notice that the Small option is now checked.
8. Press **Return**.
9. Turn to Module 26 to continue the learning sequence.

Module 44
MISCELLANEOUS OPERATORS

DESCRIPTION
There are a few operators which don't fit into the other categories:

( )	function call
[ ]	square bracket notation array reference
.	structure member reference
.*	structure member selector
(type)	cast
sizeof(object)	size of object in bytes
,	sequential evaluator
::	scope access operator
<<	stream output operator
>>	stream input operator
X(X&)	x of x ref operator

APPLICATIONS

The ( ) operator
The ( ) (function call) operator calls predefined functions or functions that you define yourself. To call the sqrt function, you use
```
n = sqrt(4);
```
Functions can call other functions
```
n = abs(pow(-4,37));
```
and some functions can even call themselves (that is called recursion).

The [ ] operator
The [ ] square bracket notation lets you access arrays. (As a faster alternative, you can access array elements by using pointers.)

To use the square bracket notation to access element i,j of array board:
```
n = board[i][j];
```
when converting between square bracket notation and * notation, you can think of each * and [ ] as being interchangeable;
```
**argv
*argv[]
```

```
argv[][]
```
are all different declarations for the same array.

The . operator
The . structure member reference operator lets you access a member of a structure. (For more information about structures, see Module 24.)
```
n = window.background_color;
```

The .* operator
The .* structure member selector lets you access a pointer to a member of a class. If you have a class defined as follows:
```
class K
{
    public:
    int a;
};

int K::*p = &K::a;
```
you can access the member with the following:
```
K kitem;

kitem.*p = 801;
```
Pointers to members cannot point to static members of a class.

The sizeof( ) operator
The sizeof( ) operator returns the size of an object in bytes. For example,
```
n = sizeof(struct window);
```
returns the size of a window structure in bytes. The sizeof( ) operator is useful in determining memory allocation requirements. For example,
```
n = malloc(sizeof(struct window));
```
will allocate enough memory to store a window structure.

The type casting operator
Casting changes the data type of a variable, such as casting an int to a float to force the result to be float:
```
result = (float)5/2;
```
Beware of casting ints into chars and chars into ints
```
i = 48;
c = (char)i;    // c has the char '0', not 48!
c = '0';
i = (int)c;     // i has the value 48, not '0'!
```

There are times that you'll really want to do this, but most of the time C++ programmers are trying to convert from an integer to a char (or vice versa).

```
i = 48;
s = itoa(i);    // c has the value "48"
s = "0";
i = atoi(s):    // i has the value 0
```

The , operator

The , operator forces everything to the left of the , to be evaluated.

```
for(i=0, j=43; i < n; ++i, --j)
    .
    .
    .
```

This example first sets the value of i to 0, then sets the value of j to 43 before beginning the loop. The , operator is often used to initialize loop variables.

The :: operator

When used as a unary operator, the :: scope access operator lets you access a global variable that has the same name as a local variable.

```
int i=0;

void main()
    {
    int i=10000;

    printf("local  i = %d\n",i);
    printf("global i = %d\n",::i);
    }
```

When used as a binary operator, the :: operator lets you access a member of a class by putting the class before the :: operator.

```
class::member
```

The binary use of :: is described in Module 31 on Class Operators.

The << operator

The << operator is used in C++ language to print out different variables without specifying the data type of each variable.

```
char s[] = "of multiple types of output";
int i=1;
cout << "This is" << i << " example " << s << '\n';
```

will produce the line

```
This is 1 example of multiple types of output
```

The >> operator

The >> operator is used in the C++ language to accept different variables without specifying the data type of each variable.

```
cin >> newstring;
```

The X(X&) operator

The x of x ref operator (X(X&)) is a copy constructor: when used with an overloaded = operator it ensures correct initialization of a copy and correct semantic use of the class X.

If we wanted to copy two items of the Album class as follows:

```
Album a,b;

a = b;
```

we would need to have the following two lines in the public portion of our Album class:

```
Album(Album&);
Album& operator =(Album&);
```

The use of references is important. You cannot use X(X): it must be X(X&).

TYPICAL OPERATION

In this program, you experiment with the C++ << and >> operators. Begin from within Turbo C++ with no windows open.

1. Press **Alt-F** and type **N** to create a new file.
2. Type the following:

```
#include <iostream.h>

void main()
    {
    void readme();

    readme();
    }

void readme()
    {
    char newstring;
    char s[] = "of multiple types of output";
    int i = 1;

    cout << "Type any key" << '\n';
    cin >> newstring;
```

Module 44

```
        cout << "You typed " << newstring << '\n';
        cout << "This is " << i << " example " << s << '\n';
    }
```

3. Press **F2** to save the file. Turbo C++ displays a Save Editor File dialog box.
4. Type **MISC.CPP** and press **Return**. The .CPP file extension tells the Turbo C++ compiler to compile the program using C++ features.
5. Press **Ctrl-F9** to run the program. The program displays the message "Type any key."
6. Type **3** and press **Return**.
7. Press **Alt-F5** to view the program results on the screen.

   ```
   Type any key
   3
   You typed 3
   This is 1 example of multiple types of output
   ```

8. Press **Alt-F5** to return to the Turbo C++ editor.
9. Press **Alt-Spacebar** and type **C** to clear the desktop.
10. Turn to Module 48 to continue the learning sequence.

Module 45
OVERLOADING

DESCRIPTION

Overloading lets you use the same operators and functions on different data types. For example, you could create a function called copy, which would work with char, int, and File data types.

```
char* copy(char*);
int   copy(int);
File& copy(File&);
```

These three functions use the same name but work with different data types. In ordinary C, you would have to use different function names. In C++, you can use the same name, thus reducing the number of function names in your program.

You can overload operators (such as the + operator) or functions. You can think of the + operator as a built-in overloaded operator because it works with both int and float data types.

APPLICATIONS

You can use overloading to create intuitive commands for your programs. For example, you might create a + operator to operate on a class object called String where

```
AString = "The Quick Brown Fox"
BString = " jumps over Bill"
CString = AString + BString;
```

The result would set CString = "The Quick Brown Fox jumps over Bill."

There are only a few operators that you can't modify:

.	member access
.*	dereferenced member access
::	scope access
::*	dereferenced scope access
?:	if else operator
#	stringizing operator
##	tokenpasting operator

You can modify any of the other operators. The syntax of operator is:

```
return_type operator op(arguments) { body };
```

179

Module 45

where	return_type	= the data type the operator works on
	operator	= Turbo C++ keyword
	op(arguments)	= any arguments the operator expects
	{ body }	= operator statements

Function overloading is simpler than operator overloading. To do function overloading, you reuse the name that you want, making sure that either the return type or argument list is different from the existing copies of the function.

When working with inherited functions, you can reuse the name of the function, but the return type must be the same. This isn't really function overloading, it is really function overwriting. To access the overwritten function, you can use the scope access operator ::.

To overload the abs( ) function, you could have the following:

```
int abs(int i) {return(abs(i));}
long abs(long l) {return(labs(l));}
double abs(double d) {return(fabs(d));}
```

When working with numbers you can invoke abs( ) and not have to worry about whether you need to use fabs( ), labs( ), or abs( ).

```
int i,j;
long l,m;
double d,e;
     .
     .
     .
i = abs(j);
l = abs(m);
d = abs(e);
```

TYPICAL OPERATION

In this program, you examine how Turbo C++ overloads the + operator. Begin from within Turbo C++ with no windows open.

1. Press **F3**. Turbo C++ displays a Load a File dialog box.

NOTE
The following step assumes you have stored the Turbo C++ example programs in the directory C:\TC\EXAMPLES.

2. Type **C:\TC\EXAMPLES\XSTRING.CPP** and press **Return**.
3. Press **Ctrl-F9** to run the program.
4. Press **Alt-F5** to view the program results.

```
The Quick Brown fox
The Quick Brown fox jumps over Bill
```

Notice that the program displays two messages. The first string, "The Quick Brown fox," is assigned to the string AString. The second string, " jumps over Bill," is assigned to the string BString.

Using the overloaded operator +, CString adds AString and BString together to create the new string, "The Quick Brown fox jumps over Bill."

5. Press **Alt-F5** to return to the Turbo C++ editor.
6. Press **Alt-Spacebar** and type **C** to clear the desktop.
7. Turn to Module 19 to continue the learning sequence.

Module 46
POINTER OPERATORS

DESCRIPTION

The C++ programming language uses pointers extensively. Unlike variables that correspond to specific data, pointers correspond to the machine address of the data.

To declare a pointer, place an asterisk in front of the variable name.

```
char     *ptr1, name;     /* ptr1 is a pointer to char */
int      *ptr2, whole;    /* ptr2 is a pointer to int */
float    *ptr3, real;     /* number is a pointer to float */
```

Pointer variables store the address of a variable. To retrieve the address of a variable, use the address of (&) operator.

```
ptr_to_char  = &name;
ptr_to_int   = &whole;
ptr_to_float = &real;

name = "John";
whole = 93;
real = 3.14159;
```

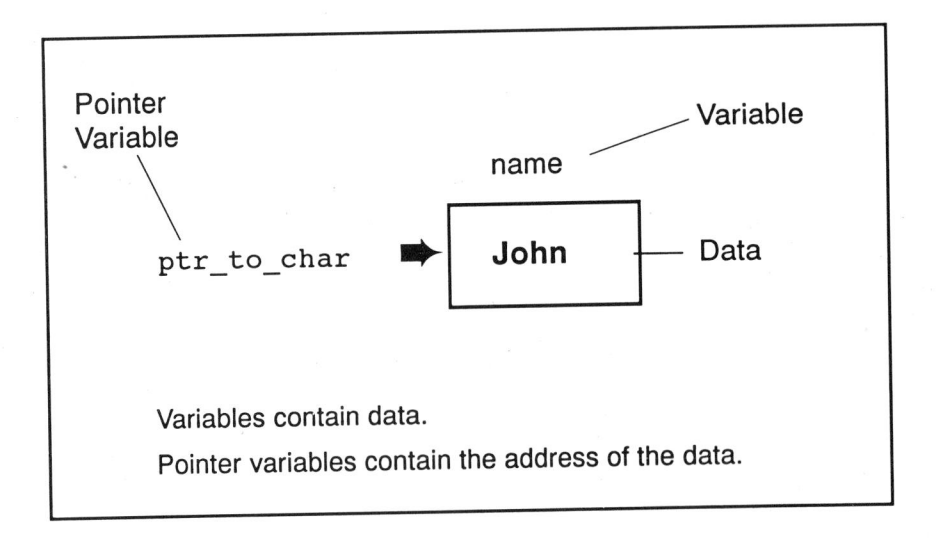

```
Pointer
Variable                          Variable
                         name
                       ┌────────┐
ptr_to_char    ──►     │  John  │  ── Data
                       └────────┘

Variables contain data.
Pointer variables contain the address of the data.
```

APPLICATIONS

The following lists pointer operators available in Turbo C++:

*	pointer reference
&	address of
[ ]	array of
->	pointer to a structure member reference
->*	pointer to a structure member pointer reference

You use pointers to work with arrays, strings (C++ treats strings as an array of characters), structures, and unions.

Arrays

Arrays consist of a fixed number of items of the same data type. Array declarations look like the following:

```
int   numbers[10];        /* numbers is an array of 10 integers */
char  string[20];         /* string is an array of 20 characters */
float real[12];           /* real is an array of 12 float */
```

To create multidimensional arrays, you could declare the following:

```
int   numbers[10][20];    /* 10 x 20 array */
char  string[5][20];      /* 5 x 20 array */
float real[12][3];        /* 12 x 3 array */
```

You can use the [ ] array of operator to define explicit or implicit arrays:

```
char wally[15] = "Wallace E. Wang";    // explicit declaration
char ken[] = "Kenneth W. Bibb";        // implicit declaration
```

The first example shows an explicit array declaration that defines the exact length of the array. In this case, wally[ ] is declared as an array of 15 chars.

The second example shows an implicit array declaration. In this case, the ken[ ] can hold a string of any length.

To access an array, you can assign a variable of the same data type as the elements in the array. For example:

```
char    c;
char    wally[15] = "Wallace E. Wang"
char    ken[] = "Kenneth W. Bibb"
```

You can access an the first element from the array by using:

```
c = ken[0];
```

or the seventh element with:

```
c = wally[6];
```

Notice that the array index starts at 0. As an alternative, you can also access arrays using pointers.

Module 46

```
char *wp = wally;      // wp points to the address of wally[0]
c = *wp;               // c = wally[0];
c = *(wp+6);           // c = wally[6];
```

Strings

The C++ language does not have a string data type as other languages do, such as Pascal. Instead, you have to create an array of characters.

```
#define ARRAY 12
char s[ARRAY] = "First String";
```

This string can be represented as the array:

```
s[0]  = 'F';
s[1]  = 'i';
s[2]  = 'r';
s[3]  = 's';
s[4]  = 't';
s[5]  = ' ';
s[6]  = 'S';
s[7]  = 't';
s[8]  = 'r';
s[9]  = 'i';
s[10] = 'n';
s[11] = 'g';
s[12] = 0;             // NULL, 0x00, 0, EOS,...
```

The address of this string can be described using:

```
address = s;           // These are all the same
address = &s;
address = &s[0];
```

You can assign a pointer, p, to s by saying

```
char *p;               // this var will hold the address of a char

p = &s;                // put the address of s into p
```

You can then manipulate the information inside of the array by using addresses:

```
for (p = &s[0]; p < &s[ARRAY]; p++)
    putchar (*p);
```

This loop displays the character pointed at by p, then increments p to the next character in the string. (The * on variable p dereferences p — p no longer looks at the address of p but at the contents of p. The increment operator operates on the address of p, not on the value of p, which is why this example will print the entire string.)

Structures

The -> operator points to a member of a structure pointer. We create an instance of a structure:

```
struct GoBoard goban;
    {
    int     x;
    int     y;
    }
```

To access x and y we would use:
```
goban.x = 13;
goban.y = 13;
```

If we define goban as:
```
struct GoBoard *goban;
// goban is a pointer to a GoBoard structure
```

we would access it using pointers:
```
goban->x = 13;
goban->y = 13;
```

The following are equivalent:
```
goban->x = 13;
(*goban).x = 13;
goban[0].x = 13;
```

The ->* operator is a special form of -> that accesses references through pointers to members of structures. For example:

```
class X              // example class
{
    int x;
};

X *p = new X;    // declares a pointer to an X and initializes it

int y;

x = &X::x;       // x is a reference to X::x
y = p->*x;       // y accesses p->x
```

TYPICAL OPERATION

In this program, you experiment with using pointers to access an array. Begin from within Turbo C++ with no windows open.

1. Press **Alt-F** and type **N** to create a new file.
2. Type the following:

```
#define    ARRAY 12

void main ()
    {
    char s[ARRAY] = "First String";
```

```c
    char *p;
    int  i;

    /* Using a pointer to access an array */
    for (p = &s[0]; p < &s[ARRAY]; p++)
      putchar (*p);

    printf ("\n");

    /* An array name is actually a pointer to the first */
    /* element in the array */
    for (i = 0; i < ARRAY; i++)
      putchar (s[i]);
}
```

3. Press **Ctrl-F9** to run the program.
4. Press **Alt-F5** to view the program results. Notice that your program stored a string, "First String," into an array of characters called s[ARRAY]. First the program used a separate pointer to access the array contents. Then the program used the array name (which is a pointer to the array) to access the array contents.

   First String
   First String

5. Press **Alt-F5** to return to the Turbo C++ editor.
6. Press **Alt-Spacebar** and type **C** and type **N** to clear the desktop.
7. Turn to Module 50 to continue the learning sequence.

Module 47
printf( ) and scanf( )

DESCRIPTION

The printf( ) function displays data, usually on the screen. The following program would print the message "Hello, world!" on the screen:

```
void main()
    {
    printf ("Hello, world!");
    }
```

The syntax for the printf( ) function is:

```
%[flags][width][.precision][modifier]type
```

The flags, width, precision, and modifier fields are all optional. The flags field can consist of the following:

Flags Field

Flags	Meaning
−	Left justification, pads on the right with blanks.
+	Right justification, pads on the left with blanks.
blank	If value is nonnegative, pads with a single blank. If negative, prints the minus (−) sign.

The width field specifies the size of the print zone. The default width is the total width of the value to display. If you declare a width smaller than the total width of the value, Turbo C++ automatically extends the print zone; it will never truncate the value to fit within the print zone.

The width field can consist of a digit that represents the print zone width. The precision field consists of a decimal point (.) followed by a digit, which defines the number of decimal points to display.

The modifier field gives the size of the data represented by type.

Modifier Field

Modifier	Data type
h	short int
l	long
L	long double
F	far pointer
N	near pointer

The type field defines the data type to display. The most common data types are:

Numbers

Type	Data type
d or i	signed decimal int
o	unsigned octal int
u	unsigned decimal int
x	unsigned hexadecimal int (a,b,c,d,e,f)
X	unsigned hexadecimal int (A,B,C,D,E,F)
f	floating-point
e or E	exponential floating-point
g or G	floating-point in fixed decimal format or exponential format, whichever is smaller

Characters

c	char
s	string
%	prints the % character

Character escapes

\a	Sounds a beep
\b	Backspace
\f	Formfeed, starts a new screen or page
\n	Newline, moves to beginning of next line
\r	Carriage return, moves to beginning of current line
\t	Horizontal tab, moves to next tab position
\v	Vertical tab, moves down a fixed amount
\\	Prints the backslash character \
\'	Prints the single quote character '
\"	Prints the double quote character "
\?	Prints the question mark
\OOO	Prints the character represented by the ASCII code as an octal value
\xHHH	Prints the character represented by the ASCII code as a hexadecimal value

The scanf( ) function reads data, usually from the keyboard. The syntax for the scanf( ) function is:

```
%[*][width][pointer size][argument type]type
```

The following program accepts a letter you type from the keyboard:

```
void main()
    {
    char     letter;
    printf ("Type a letter: ");
    scanf ("%c", &letter);
    printf ("You typed the letter %c", letter);
    }
```

NOTE

Notice that you must use the & symbol in front of any variable listed in the scanf( ) function. If you omit the & symbol, Turbo C++ displays an error message.

The asterisk (*) is a suppression character. On each call, the scanf( ) function reads two characters, storing the first character in the variable and ignoring the second character.

The width field defines how many characters to read. The pointer size field defines either N (near pointer) or F (far pointer).

The argument type field defines the address argument:

    h   short int
    l   long int (if the type character specifies an integer conversion)
    l   double (if the type character specifies a floating-point conversion)
    L   long double

The type field defines the data type to read. The most common data types are:

Numbers

Type	*Data type*
d or i	decimal int
o	octal int
u	unsigned decimal int
x or X	hexadecimal int
f,e,E,g,G	floating-point

Characters

c	char
s	string
%	the % character

APPLICATIONS

You use the printf( ) function to display and format your data. The most common character escape you will use is the new line \n character escape. The following two examples produce the same result:

Module 47

```
void main()                     void main()
{                               {
    printf ("Hello, ");             printf ("Hello, world!");
    printf ("world!");          }
}
```

In both programs, the result is the message:

    Hello, world!

To display data on a new line, you must use the \n character escape such as:

```
void main()
{
    printf ("Hello, \n");
    printf "world!");
}
```

The result of this program is:

    Hello,
    world!

When using the scanf( ) function, always include the & symbol. If you are reading a character with the scanf( ) function, you may want to suppress nonprintable characters such as the carriage return.

For example, the following program echoes back any letter you type. After you type a letter, you need to press the Return key. If you did not use the suppression character with the scanf( ) function, the scanf( ) function would mistakenly read the carriage return as a valid character and prematurely end the program.

```
void main()
{
    char    letter = 'a';

    printf ("Type a letter\n");
    printf ("Press any nonletter key to quit\n");
    while ((letter <= 'z' && letter >= 'a') ||
           (letter <= 'Z' && letter >= 'A'))
      {
      printf ("Type a key and press Return\n");
      scanf ("%c%*c", &letter);
      printf ("Letter is %c\n", letter);
      }
}
```

TYPICAL OPERATION

In this program, you experiment with the printf( ) and scanf( ) functions to enter numbers and letters. Begin from within Turbo C++ with no windows open.

1. Press **Alt-F** and type **N** to create a new file.

2. Type the following:

```
void main()
    {
    int     number;
    char    letter;

    printf ("Hello, world!\n");
    printf ("Hello, ");
    printf ("world!\n");
    printf ("\n");

    printf ("Enter a letter: ");
    scanf ("%c", &letter);
    printf ("You typed the letter %c\n", letter);
    printf ("The ASCII number of this letter is %d\n", letter);

    printf ("Enter an integer: ");
    scanf ("%d", &number);
    printf ("The integer you typed is %d here\n", number);
    printf ("Look at this         : %4d here \n", number);
    printf ("And this             : %-4d here\n", number);
    printf ("The floating point representation is %3.2f\n", (float)number);
    printf ("The exponential representation is %3.2e\n", (float)number);
    }
```

3. Press **Ctrl-F9** to run the program. The "Enter a letter:" message appears on the screen.

4. Type **A** and press **Return**. The program displays the following:

```
Hello, world!
Hello, world!

Enter a letter: A
You typed the letter A
The ASCII number of this letter is 65
Enter an integer:
```

5. Type **89** and press **Return**. Turbo C++ briefly displays the program results on the screen, then returns you back to the Turbo C++ editing window.

Module 47

6. Press **Alt-F5** to view the program results. Notice how the program displays the number 89 differently, depending on the + or – sign of the flag field.

   ```
   Hello, world!
   Hello, world!

   Enter a letter: A
   You typed the letter A
   The ASCII number of this letter is 65
   Enter an integer: 89
   The integer you typed is 89 here
   Look at this           :   89 here
   And this               : 89   here
   The floating point representation is 89.00
   The exponential representation is 8.9e+01
   ```

7. Press **Alt-F5** to return to the Turbo C++ editor.
8. Press **Alt-Spacebar** and type **C** and type **N** to clear the desktop.
9. Turn to Module 21 to continue the learning sequence.

Module 48
REFERENCES

DESCRIPTION

Referencing, unique to C++, creates "references" (sometimes called "aliases") to an existing object. References let you pass arguments to functions by reference instead of value.

The reference operators are:

    &   reference operator
    *   dereference operator

When using the reference and dereference operators, think of them as pointers.

APPLICATIONS

When you want to pass an object to (or from) a function, passing a reference is often the most efficient way of doing it. To declare a reference, simply place the reference operator in front of the variable:

```
int   number = 0;
int   &ref = number;        // Declares a reference

ref = 3;                    // Same effect as number = 3;
```

To pass arguments by reference, use the reference operator within a function parameter list such as:

```
void sqr1 (int i);
void sqr2 (int &i);

number = 4;
sqr1 (number);              // Argument passed by value
sqr2 (number);              // Argument passed by reference
```

The dereference operator (*) dereferences an item. If you have a declaration:

```
char *p;                    // a pointer to a char
char c = 'W';               // a char
```

you can do the following:

```
p = &c;                     // assign the address of c to p
*p = 'E';
                            // the variable pointed to by p will now contain 'E'
```

Module 48

TYPICAL OPERATION

In this program, you experiment with the reference operator. Begin from within Turbo C++ with no windows open.

1. Press **Alt-F** and type **N** to create a new file.
2. Type the following:

```
#include <iostream.h>

void main()
    {
    int number = 0;
    int &ref = number;

    void value_func (int i);
    void ref_func (int &i);

    cout << "Type a number ";
    cin >> number;
    cout << "This is the value of number = " << number <<"\n";
    cout << "This is the value of ref    = " << ref <<"\n";

    ref_func (number);
    value_func (number);
    ref_func (number);

    cout << "This is the value of number = " << number <<"\n";
    cout << "This is the value of ref    = " << ref <<"\n";
    }

void value_func (int i)
    {
    int j;
    j = i;
    i = i * i;
    cout << "\n(Passed by value)\n";
    cout << "The square of " << j << " is " << i << "\n";
    }

void ref_func (int &i)
    {
    int j;
    j = i;
    i = i * i;
    cout << "\n(Passed by reference)\n";
    cout << "The square of " << j << " is " << i << "\n";
    }
```

3. Press **F2**. Turbo C++ displays a Save Editor File dialog box.

4. Type **ref.cpp** and press **Return**.
5. Press **Ctrl-F9** to run the program. The program displays the message "Type a number."
6. Type **3** and press **Return**.
7. Press **Alt-F5** to view the program results.

```
Type a number 3
This is the value of number = 3
This is the value of ref    = 3

(Passed by reference)
The square of 3 is 9

(Passed by value)
The square of 9 is 81

(Passed by reference)
The square of 9 is 81
This is the value of number = 81
This is the value of ref    = 81
```

Notice that the value for the variables "number" and "ref" are the same because "ref" points to the value stored in the "number" variable.

When the program calls the ref_func function, it passes the value of "number" by reference, meaning that the ref_func function changes the value of "number" from 3 to 9.

When the program calls the value_func function, it passes a copy of the value of "number," which means that the value_func function does not change the value of "number."

When the program calls the ref_func function a second time, it changes the value of "number" from 9 to 81.

8. Press **Alt-F5** to return to the Turbo C++ editor.
9. Press **Alt-Spacebar** and type **C** to clear the desktop.
10. Turn to Module 32 to continue the learning sequence.

Module 49
STORAGE CLASS SPECIFIERS

DESCRIPTION

Storage class specifiers let you change the characteristics of a variable within a function. Variables may be local or global and may exist temporarily or permanently for the life of the program.

Turbo C++ provides five types of storage class specifiers:
    auto   register   typedef
    extern   static

APPLICATIONS

auto

The default storage class specifier is auto, which declares a variable as local that exists only while the function runs.

Only functions that declare a local variable can use that variable. For example, consider two functions as follows:

```
void main()
    {
    int i, j;
    void sum (int a, int b);

    printf ("Type two numbers\n");
    scanf ("%d %d", &i, &j);
    sum (i, j);
    }

void sum(int a, int b)
    {
    int    k;

    k = a + b;     /* k = i + j would be illegal */
    printf ("The sum total = %d\n", k);
    }
```

The main( ) function declares two local variables called i and j while the sum(int a, int b) function declares one local variable called k.

The main( ) function cannot use the k variable because the k variable is only declared in the sum(int a, int b) function. Likewise, the sum(int a, int b) function cannot use the variables i and j.

Because function variables automatically default to the auto storage class, you do not need to declare variables with the auto storage class specifier. The following declarations are equal:

```
int  i, j;    (equivalent to ==>)   auto i, j;
char k;       (equivalent to ==>)   auto char k;
```

extern

The extern storage class declares variables that are global. Global variables are available to all functions within a program. Modifying the above program, we can make i and j global variables.

```
int  i, j;

void main()
    {
    void sum ();

    printf ("Type two numbers\n");
    scanf ("%d %d", &i, &j);
    sum ();
    }

void sum()
    {
    int  k;

    k = i + j;
    printf ("The sum total = %d\n", k);
    }
```

The above program simply places the i and j variable declaration outside of all the functions. Notice that you do not need to use the extern keyword.

The only time you need to use the extern specifier is when you want access to a variable that is declared in another file.

register

The register storage class may be used only for local variables (those declared within a function). This storage class tells the compiler to store the variables in a register, making your program faster and smaller.

Turbo C++ lets you select register variable options from the Options menu, choosing the Compiler and Optimizations commands. By checking Automatic in the dialog box, Turbo C++ automatically allocates variables to registers. Thus, specifying the register storage class is rarely necessary.

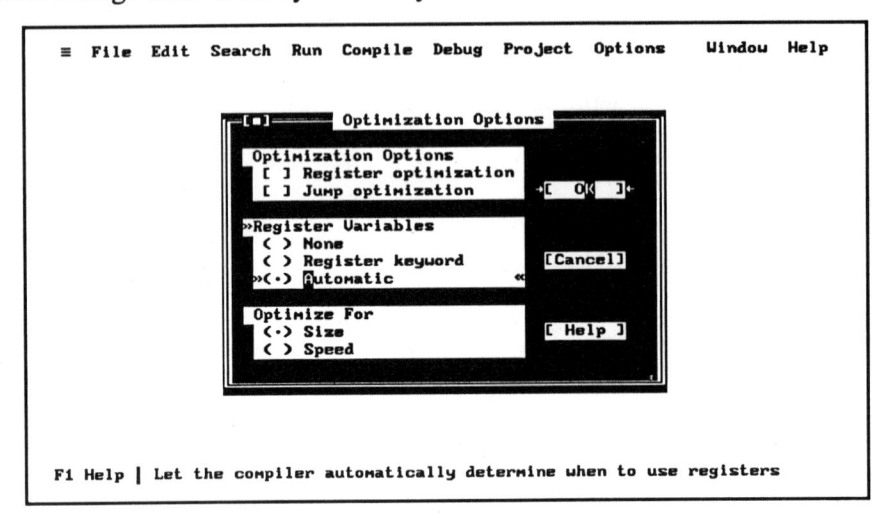

static

The static storage class may be used with global or local variables. A static variable retains its value through repeated function calls. If you declare a global static variable, only functions in that file can use that variable. Functions stored in other files cannot use global static variables.

Modifying the above program, we can create a global static variable:

```
int   i, j;

void main()
    {
    void sum ();

    printf ("Type two numbers\n");
    scanf ("%d %d", &i, &j);
    sum();
    sum();
    }

void sum()
    {
    static int    k;

    k += i + j;
    printf ("The sum total = %d\n", k);
    }
```

This program calls the sum( ) function twice. The first time the sum( ) function is called, the value of k is set to 0 and calculates a new value for k. The second time the sum( ) function is called, it uses the new value of k.

typedef

The typedef specifier lets you associate names with data types. If you're familiar with another programming language, you could rename the int data type to INTEGER such as:

```
typedef  int         INTEGER;
```

Then to declare a variable as a type int, you could do one of the following:

```
int  i, j;
```

or

```
INTEGER i, j;
```

Use the typedef specifier to name your own data types.

TYPICAL OPERATION

In this program, you experiment with using static and global variables. Begin from within Turbo C++ with no windows open.

1. Press **Alt-F** and type **N** to create a new file.
2. Type the following:

    ```
    void main()
        {
        int i, j;
        void sum (int a, int b);

        printf ("Type two numbers\n");
        scanf ("%d %d", &i, &j);
        sum (i, j);
        }

    void sum(int a, int b)
        {
        int  k;

        k = a + b;    /* k = i + j would be illegal */
        printf ("The sum total = %d\n", k);
        }
    ```

3. Press **Ctrl-F9** to run the program. The program displays the message "Type two numbers."
4. Type **2**, press the **Spacebar**, type **3**, and press **Return**.
5. Press **Alt-F5** to view the program results.

Module 49

```
Type two numbers
2 3
The sum total = 5
```

6. Press **Alt-F5** to return to the Turbo C++ editor.
7. Modify the program as follows:

    ```
    int  i, j;

    void main()
         {
         void sum ();

         printf ("Type two numbers\n");
         scanf ("%d %d", &i, &j);
         sum ();
         }

    void sum()
         {
         int   k;

         k = i + j;
         printf ("The sum total = %d\n", k);
         }
    ```

8. Press **Ctrl-F9** to run the program. The program displays the message "Type two numbers."
9. Type **2,** press the **Spacebar**, type **3**, and press **Return**.
10. Press **Alt-F5** to view the program results.

    ```
    Type two numbers
    2 3
    The sum total = 5
    ```

11. Press **Alt-F5** to return to the Turbo C++ editor.
12. Modify the program as follows:

    ```
    int  i, j;

    void main()
         {
         void sum ();

         printf ("Type two numbers\n");
         scanf ("%d %d", &i, &j);
         sum();
         sum();
         }
    ```

```
void sum()
    {
    static int   k;

    k += i + j;
    printf ("The sum total = %d\n", k);
    }
```

13. Press **Ctrl-F9** to run the program. The program displays the message "Type two numbers."
14. Type **2**, press the **Spacebar**, type **3**, and press **Return**.
15. Press **Alt-F5** to view the program results.

    ```
    Type two numbers
    2 3
    The sum total = 5
    The sum total = 10
    ```

16. Press **Alt-F5** to return to the Turbo C++ editor.
17. Press **Alt-Spacebar** and type **C** and type **N** to clear the desktop.
18. Turn to Module 44 to continue the learning sequence.

Module 50
STREAMS

DESCRIPTION

A stream refers to any input source or output destination. Typically, the input source is the keyboard and the output destination is the monitor. For more sophisticated applications, you may need to read and write data to and from a disk file.

Turbo C++ provides three standard streams called:
    stdin   standard input
    stdout   standard output
    stderr   standard error

These streams are always available so you do not have to declare them in your program.

APPLICATIONS

Use streams to give your program input and for storing your program's output.

Redirecting streams

Normally, your Turbo C++ programs assume input will come from the keyboard and output will go to the monitor. To redirect or change the input, use the < symbol when typing the program name from the DOS prompt, such as:

    C:\>program_name <infile.dat

This redirects the input from the keyboard to a file called infile.dat. To redirect the output, use the > symbol when typing the program name from the DOS prompt, such as:

    C:\>program_name <infile.dat >outfile.dat

Opening and closing streams

To open a file to use as a stream, call the fopen function, which has the following declaration:

    FILE *fopen(const char *filename, const char *mode)

The *filename variable represents the name of the file to open, including the drive and/or directory path such as C:\DATA\INFILE.DAT.

The *mode variable represents one of the following parameters:

"r"	open file for reading only
"w"	open file for writing only
"a"	open file for appending
"r+"	open file for reading and writing (starting at beginning)
"w+"	open file for reading and writing (truncate if file already exists)
"a+"	open file for reading and writing (append if file already exists)

To close a file, call the fclose function, which has the following declaration:

```
int fclose (FILE *stream);
```

The fclose function returns a 0 if it successfully closes the file, otherwise it returns EOF.

The following example would open and close a file called "input.dat":

```
#include <stdio.h>

void main()
    {
    FILE *file_pointer;

    file_pointer = fopen ("input.dat", "r+");
    fclose (file_Pointer);
    }
```

Programs can receive the name of a file to open from a string (as in the above example) by using the scanf function to get the filename from the keyboard or from the command line.

For example, to read a filename from the command line:

```
program_name input.dat output.dat
```

your program would look like:

```
void main (int argc, char *argv[])
    {
    }
```

The argc value counts the number of program parameters. (In the above example, the number is 3.)

The argv[] array points to each of the parameters. So argv[0] points to program_name, argv[1] points to input.dat, and argv[2] points to output.dat.

Text and binary streams

Turbo C++ provides two types of streams: text and binary. A text stream consists of ASCII files, such as your Turbo C++ programs. A binary stream consists of data such as an executable (.EXE) file.

Text streams input and output functions

Text stream input functions return EOF if it reaches the end of an input file or if an error occurs. The five text stream input functions are:

fgetc	reads a character from the stream
getc	reads a character from the stream
getchar	reads a character from stdin (equivalent to getc (stdin)
fgets	reads from the stream into an array until it encounters a new-line character
gets	reads from stdin until it encounters a new-line character

The five text stream output functions return EOF if an error occurs, otherwise they return the character that was written:

fputc	writes a character to the stream
putc	writes a character to the stream
putchar	writes a character to stdout (equivalent to putc (c, stdout))
fputs	writes a string to the stream
puts	writes a string to stdout
fprintf	writes a variable number of items to the stream
printf	writes a variable number of items to stdout

Since many of the text stream input and output functions test for an EOF or error, Turbo C++ provides two functions that determine which event occurs.

Detecting EOF and errors

The feof function returns a nonzero value if the end of a stream is reached.

    int feof (FILE *stream)

The ferror function returns a nonzero value if an error occurs during the operation on a stream.

    int ferror (FILE *stream)

Binary stream input and output functions

Turbo C++ provides five binary stream functions:

fread	reads data from a binary file
fwrite	writes data to a binary file
fseek	allows repositioning within a binary file
ftell	returns current file position as a long integer
rewind	positions file to its beginning

Generally you should only use these functions once you understand how your computer stores and retrieves data to a disk file.

TYPICAL OPERATION

In this program, you write a program that checks if a file exists on your hard disk. Begin from within Turbo C++ with no windows open.

1. Press **Alt-F** and type **N** to create a new file.
2. Type the following:

   ```
   #include <stdio.h>
   #include <stdlib.h>

   void main()
     {
     FILE *file_pointer;
     char *filename[11];

     printf ("What filename do you want to check?\n");
     scanf ("%s", &filename);
     if ((file_pointer = fopen (filename, "r")) == NULL)
       printf ("%s does not exist\n", filename);
     else
       printf ("%s exists\n", filename);
     fclose (file_pointer);
     }
   ```

3. Press **Ctrl-F9** to run the program. The program displays the message:

   What filename do you want to check?

   ### NOTE
   The following step assumes you have the file COMMAND.COM installed on drive C:\ of your computer.

4. Type **C:\COMMAND.COM** and press **Return**. The program displays the message C:\COMMAND.COM exists and returns to the editor.
5. Press **Ctrl-F9** to run the program again.
6. Type **C:\NONSENSE.XYZ** and press **Return**. The program displays the message C:\NONSENSE.XYZ does not exist and returns to the editor.
7. Press **Alt-Spacebar,** type **C** and type **N** to clear the desktop.
8. Turn to Module 49 to continue the learning sequence.

Module 51
SWITCH

DESCRIPTION

The switch statement is a more efficient way of representing nested if-else statements that checks a single variable against multiple discrete values. When the switch statement is executed, control passes to the case label which matches the variable's value.

Control continues down through the switch statement until a break is reached or the end of the switch is encountered, at which point the statement following the switch will execute. The statements inside of the switch statement can be any legal C statement—you can even embed switch statements or use if-else statements.

```
switch(variable)
    {
    case value1:    statement1;
                    break;
    case value2:    statement2;
    case value3:    statement3;
                    break;
    default:        statement4;
    }
```

"variable"
The variable is of a basic variable type (char, int, float). It cannot be a structure, union, "string," etc.

"value1, value1, value3"
There must be a case statement for each value that you want to match. You can't use ranges in the value slots.

"statement1, statement2, statement3, statement4"
Any valid statement or block of statements.

APPLICATIONS

Use the switch statement to control execution based on the value of a single variable. If you need to control execution using ranges or multiple variables, you'll need to use if-else statements instead (see Module 40).

When making decisions based on a single data item, the switch statement clarifies the program structure. This could be part of the main control loop of an editor program:

```
if(c == ESC || c == 'Q' || c == 'q')
    end_edit();
else if(c == UP)
    up();
else if(c == DOWN)
    down();
else
    input(c);
```

It is much clearer when it is written using the switch control structure.

```
switch(c)
    {
    case UP:        up();        break;
    case DOWN:      down();      break;
    case ESC:
    case 'Q':
    case 'q':       end_edit(); break;
    default:        input(c);
    }
```

The switch statement is more readable and usually executes faster than the corresponding if-else structure (due to optimization done automatically by the Turbo C++ compiler).

TYPICAL OPERATION

In this program, you use the switch statement to rewrite the program you created in Module 40 with multiple if-else statements. Begin from within Turbo C++ with no windows open.

1. Press **Alt-F** and type **N** to create a new file.
2. Type the following:

```
#include <stdio.h>

#define TAB      '\t'
#define RETURN   '\r'
#define ESC      0x1B

void main()
    {
    int c;

    while((c=getch()) != EOF)
        switch(c)
        {
        case TAB:   printf("You pressed a TAB\n"); break;
```

Module 51

```
            case RETURN: printf("\n"); break;
            case 'A':    printf("\nYou've hit A\n");
            case 'a':    printf("Not another a\n"); break;
            case ESC:    exit(0);
            default:     printf("%c",c);
            }
    }
```

3. Press **Ctrl-F9** to run the program.
4. Press **Tab**. The program prints the following message:

    `You pressed a TAB`

5. Type **a**. The program prints the following message:

    `Not another a`

6. Type **A**. Notice that the program prints two messages because there is not a break statement after the line "case 'A':printf("You've hit A\n");

    ```
    You've hit A
    Not another a
    ```

7. Press **Return**. The program advances the screen display by a line.
8. Press **Esc**. The program returns you to the Turbo C++ editor.
9. Press **Alt-Spacebar** and type **C** and type **N** to clear the desktop.
10. Turn to Module 37 to continue the learning sequence.

Module 52
WHILE

DESCRIPTION

The while-do control structure provides the while loop for C. A while loop always executes body at least once. (This is different from a do-while loop which may never execute even once.)

```
while(condition)
    statement(s);
```

First the program executes the statements, then tests the condition. If condition is true, the statements execute again. If the condition is false, control transfers to the statement immediately following the while loop.

The condition is any expression or relation which can be used in an if-else control structure such as (a < b) or (letter == 'a').

APPLICATIONS

Use the while loop whenever you need to repeat a statement (or block of statements) at least once. This is the most commonly used loop in C++.

Make sure the statements within the while loop change something inside the condition, or your program will go into an endless loop. Beginning programmers often run into this problem.

One trick that is encountered in C++ code is the null-body while.

```
while(body())
    ;
```

This loop executes until some condition makes body() return a 0 (false). Since C++ requires a statement after the condition, you can use a semicolon by itself as a null-statement. Now you can repeat the while loop indefinitely until body() returns a 0.

TYPICAL OPERATION

In this program, you use the while statement to create a loop that prints a message a specific number of times. Begin from within Turbo C++ with no windows open.

1. Press **Alt-F** and type **N** to create a new file.

Module 52

2. Type the following:
```
void main()
    {
    int i, loop;

    i = 0;
    printf ("How many times do you want to loop?\n");
    scanf ("%d", &loop);

    while (i++ < loop)
        printf ("Loop %d\n", i);
    }
```

3. Press **Ctrl-F9** to run the program. The program displays the message:
   ```
   How many times do you want to loop?
   ```

4. Type **5** and press **Return**.

5. Press **Alt-F5** to see the program results on the screen.
   ```
   How many times do you want to loop?
   5
   Loop 1
   Loop 2
   Loop 3
   Loop 4
   Loop 5
   ```

6. Press **Alt-F5** to return to the Turbo C++ editor.

7. Press **Alt-Spacebar** and type **C** and type **N** to clear the desktop.

8. Turn to Module 29 to continue the learning sequence.

Module 53
CLASSIFICATION ROUTINES

DESCRIPTION

Turbo C++ contains twelve character classification macros that identify the following:

Macro	Tests if a character is
isalnum	Alphanumeric. (a-z), (A-Z), or (0-9)
isalpha	Alphabetic. (a-z) or (A-Z)
isascii	In the standard 128-character ASCII set. ASCII characters have values of 0-127 (0x00-0x7F). If you are using any foreign or math characters (values of 128-255 (0x80-0xFF)), they are not considered to be ASCII characters by this routine.
iscntrl	A control character. Control characters are ASCII characters with values of 0-31 (0x00-0x1F) and 127 (0x7F).
isdigit	A digit. (0-9)
isgraph	A printing character, excluding the space character. Printable nonwhitespace characters have values of 33-126 (0x21-0x7E).
islower	A lowercase letter. (a-z)
isprint	A printing character, including the space character. Printable characters have values of 32-126 (0x20-0x7E).
ispunct	A punctuation character. (! " # $ % & ' ( ) * + , - . / : ; < = >? @ [\ ] ^ _ ` {	} ~)
isspace	A space character. Whitespace characters have values 8-13 and 32 (0x08-0x0D and 0x20). (Tab, line feed, vertical feed, form feed, and carriage return)
isupper	An uppercase letter. (A-Z)
isxdigit	A hexadecimal digit. (0-9), (A-F), and (a-f)

Character classification macros identify what type of value is in a character variable. If a character variable is the type being checked, the macro returns a nonzero value (TRUE). If it isn't, the macro returns a zero value (FALSE).

Module 53

APPLICATIONS

You use classification macros to determine what kind of value a character variable contains. You may need to know this to identify certain kinds of characters. For example, if your program asks that the user type a number, but the user types a letter instead, you would want your program to catch this error.

If you want to print a file, you need to make sure the file contains all printable characters. If you want your program to accept control character commands, you need to identify when the user presses a control character.

Anytime you need to identify the type of keys a user presses, you can use one of these twelve character classification macros.

To use these character classification macros, you need to put this include statement in your program:

```
#include    <ctype.h>
```

TYPICAL OPERATION

In this example, you write a program that displays all of the characters from 0 to 256 (0x00-0xFF). The if statement will filter out the ^Z character which is used as an end of file by DOS so you can print out the file.

1. Press **Alt-F** and type **N** to open a new file.
2. Type the following:

```
#include <ctype.h>
#define CTRL_Z   0x1A

main()
    {
    int i;

    printf("         an  al  as  cn  dg  gr  lo  pr  pu  sp  up  xd\n");
    for(i=0x00; i<=0xFF; i++)
    {
        if(i == CTRL_Z)                         // trap ^z
            continue;
        printf("%3.3d:  %2.2s %2.2s %2.2s %2.2s %2.2s %2.2s", i,
            (isalnum(i) ? " *" : "  "),
            (isalpha(i) ? " *" : "  "),
            (isascii(i) ? " *" : "  "),
            (iscntrl(i) ? " *" : "  "),
            (isdigit(i) ? " *" : "  "),
            (isgraph(i) ? " *" : "  "));
        printf(" %2.2s %2.2s %2.2s %2.2s %2.2s %2.2s [%c]\n",
            (islower(i) ? " *" : "  ")),
            (isprint(i) ? " *" : "  "),
```

212

```
            (ispunct(i) ? " *" : "  "),
            (isspace(i) ? " *" : "  "),
            (isupper(i) ? " *" : "  "),
            (isxdigit(i) ? " *" : "  "), i);
    }
    return(0);
}
```

3. Press **Ctrl-F9**. Turbo C++ compiles and runs the program. The program results appear on the screen briefly before Turbo C++ displays the Turbo C++ editor and integrated environment.

4. Press **Alt-F5** to view the program results. The ASCII decimal code appears on the left side of the screen and the corresponding ASCII character appears on the right side.

```
231:                                    [Φ]
232:                                    [θ]
233:                                    [Ω]
234:                                    [δ]
235:                                    [∞]
236:                                    [ø]
237:                                    [∈]
238:                                    [∩]
239:                                    [≡]
240:                                    [±]
241:                                    [≥]
242:                                    [≤]
243:                                    [⌠]
244:                                    [⌡]
245:                                    [+]
246:                                    [≈]
247:                                    [°]
248:                                    [·]
249:                                    [·]
250:                                    [√]
251:                                    [ⁿ]
252:                                    [²]
253:                                    [■]
254:                                    [ ]
255:
```

5. Press **Alt-F5** to return to the Turbo C++ integrated environment.
6. Press **Alt-Spacebar**; type **C** and type **N** to clear the desktop.
7. Turn to Module 54 to continue the learning sequence.

Module 54
CONVERSION ROUTINES

DESCRIPTION

Turbo C++ provides seventeen conversion routines:

Routine	Purpose
atof	Convert a string to a float
atoi	Convert a string to an int
atol	Convert a string to a long
ecvt	Convert float to string
fcvt	Convert float to string
gcvt	Convert float to string
itoa	Convert int to string
ltoa	Convert long to string
strtod	Convert string to double
strtol	Convert string to long
strtoul	Convert string to unsigned long
toascii	Convert characters to ASCII
_tolower	Convert characters to lowercase
tolower	Convert characters to lowercase
_toupper	Convert characters to uppercase
toupper	Convert characters to uppercase
ultoa	Convert unsigned long to a string

APPLICATIONS

atof

```
#include <Math.h>     // prototype in math.h and stdlib.h

double atof(const char *s);
```

The atof( ) function accepts a string s and returns a double. The string must be in the following format:
    Optional whitespace
    Optional sign
    String of digits
    Optional decimal point

Optional trailing string of digits
Optional e or E followed by an optional signed integer

or s can be one of the following special strings:

+INF	positive infinity
−INF	negative infinity
+NAN	not a number
−NAN	not a number

The first unrecognizable character (which includes NULL and '\n') ends the conversion.

You use this function to convert a number, represented as a string, to an actual number.

atoi( )
```
#include <stdlib.h>

int atoi(const char *s);
```

The atoi( ) function takes the string s and returns an integer. The characters must be in the following format:

Optional whitespace
Optional sign
Digits

The first unrecognizable character (which includes NULL and '\n') ends the conversion. If atoi( ) is unable to convert the string, it returns 0.

You use this function to convert an integer, represented as a string, to an actual number.

atol( )
```
#include <stdlib.h>

long atol(const char *s);
```

The atol( ) function takes a string s and returns a long value. The characters must be in the following format:

Optional whitespace
Optional sign
Digits

The first unrecognizable character (which includes NULL and '\n') ends the conversion. If atoi( ) is unable to convert the string, it returns 0.

You use this function to convert a long integer, represented as a string, to an actual number.

ecvt( )

```
#include <stdlib.h>

char *ecvt(double value,int n,int *decimal,int *sign);
```

The ecvt( ) function translates a float to a string. It takes a value and creates a string n digits long. If the value has more digits than n, the low-order digits are truncated. The position of the decimal point is stored in the int pointed to by decimal. The sign of the number is negative if the int pointed to by sign is nonzero. There is no error handling with this function.

ecvt( ) differs from fcvt( ) in the way that they treat significant digits. ecvt( ) is looking at a total number of digits, while fcvt( ) is looking for the number of digits to the right of the decimal point. gcvt( ), the other float-string converter, stores the converted string in a defined buffer and it tries to convert the float to FORTRAN F format (or E format).

The ecvt( ) function is not part of ANSI C. The sprintf( ) function is recommended for portability.

fcvt( )

```
#include <stdlib.h>

char *fcvt(double value, int n,int *decimal,int *sign);
```

The fcvt( ) function translates a float to a string. It takes a value and creates a string n digits long. If the value has more digits than n, the low-order digits are truncated.

The position of the decimal point is stored in the int pointed to by decimal. The sign of the number is negative if the int pointed to by sign is nonzero. There is no error handling with this function.

The fcvt( ) function is not part of ANSI C. The sprintf( ) function is recommended for portability.

gcvt( )

```
#include <stdlib.h>

char *gcvt(double value,int n, char *buf);
```

The gcvt( ) function translates a float to a string. It takes a value and creates a string, buf, with n significant digits. Buf is a number in FORTRAN F format (if possible). If gcvt( ) can't return an F format number, it returns an E format string. There is no error handling with this function. It returns a pointer to the starting address of buf.

The gcvt( ) function is not part of ANSI C. The sprintf( ) function is recommended for portability.

itoa( )

```
#include <stdlib.h>

char *itoa(int x,char *s,int b);
```

The itoa( ) function takes x in base b (a number between 2 and 36 inclusive) and converts it into a string s. There must be enough room in s to hold 17 characters. itoa( ) returns a pointer to s. There is no error handling with this function.

ltoa( )

```
#include <stdlib.h>
char *ltoa(long l,char *s,int b);
```

The ltoa( ) function takes l in base b (a number between 2 and 36 inclusive) and converts l into the string s. There must be enough room in s to hold 33 characters. ltoa( ) returns a pointer to s. There is no error handling with this function.

You use this function to convert a long value to a string.

strtod( )

```
#include <stdlib.h>

double strtod(const char *s,char **p);
```

The strtod( ) function converts a string, s, into a double, which is returned. The pointer p is set to the last character converted. If this character is not 0 (the end of the string), then an error has probably occurred. strtod( ) returns +HUGE_VAL or –HUGE_VAL if an error occurs. The string, s, must be in the following format:

Optional whitespace
Optional sign
Optional digits
Optional decimal point
Optional digits
Option e or E
Optional decimal point
Option digits

The following are also allowed:

+INF	positive infinity
–INF	negative infinity
+NAN	positive not a number
–NAN	negative not a number

Conversion is terminated by the first unrecognizable character. You use this to convert a number, represented as a string, to a double value.

strtol( )

```
#include <stdlib.h>

long strtol(const char *s, char **p,int b);
```

The strtol( ) function converts a string, s, into a long, which is returned. The base b can be between 2 and 36 inclusive. The pointer p is set to the last character converted. If this character is not 0 (the end of the string), then an error has probably occurred. strtol( ) returns a +HUGE_VAL or –HUGE_VAL on overflow, and it returns 0 if there is a problem in the conversion. The string, s, must be in the following format:

- Optional whitespace
- Optional sign
- Optional zero
- Optional x or X
- Optional digits

Conversion is terminated by the first unrecognizable character.

The optional zero is used for octal numbers (standard C notation). The optional zero followed by an x or X is used for hexadecimal numbers (standard C notation). These are used to figure out the base if b is 0.

You use this function to convert a number, represented as a string, to a long value.

strtoul( )

```
#include <stdlib.h>

unsigned long strtoul(const char *s,char **p,int b);
```

The strtoul( ) function converts a string, s, into an unsigned long, which is returned. The base b can be between 2 and 36 inclusive. The pointer p is set to the last character converted. If this character is not 0 (the end of the string), then an error has probably occurred. strtoul( ) returns a +HUGE_VAL or –HUGE_VAL on overflow, and it returns 0 if there is a problem in the conversion. The string, s, must be in the following format:

- Optional whitespace
- Optional sign
- Optional zero
- Optional x or X
- Optional digits

Conversion is terminated by the first unrecognizable character.

The optional zero is used for octal numbers (standard C notation). The optional zero followed by an x or X is used for hexadecimal numbers (standard C notation). These are used to figure out the base if b is 0.

You use this function to convert a number, represented as a string, to an unsigned long value.

toascii( )
```
#include  <ctype.h>

int toascii(int c);
```

The toascii( ) macro converts characters into ASCII (values 0-127). It does this by removing the high bit which is not used in true ASCII (it is used in IBM extended ASCII). This function is not ANSI C compatible and may not be portable.

_tolower( ) and tolower( )
```
#include  <ctype.h>

int _tolower(int c);
int tolower(int c);
```

The _tolower( ) and tolower( ) functions converts characters to lowercase (if it is an uppercase letter). If c is not an uppercase letter, the original character is returned.

For program portability purposes, the _tolower( ) function is only available on UNIX systems. The tolower( ) function is available on UNIX systems and ANSI C. To insure program portability, use the tolower( ) function instead.

_toupper( ) and toupper( )
```
#include  <ctype.h>

int _toupper (int c);
int toupper(int c);
```

The toupper( ) function converts characters to uppercase (if it is a lowercase letter). If c is not a lowercase letter, the original character is returned.

For program portability purposes, the _toupper( ) function is only available on UNIX systems. The toupper( ) function is available on UNIX systems and ANSI C. To insure program portability, use the toupper( ) function instead.

ultoa( )
```
#include <stdlib.h>

char *ultoa(unsigned long u,char *s,int b);
```

The ultoa( ) function takes u in base b (between 2 and 36 inclusive) and converts it into s. It returns a pointer to the beginning of s. The string s must be 33 characters long. There is no error handling with this function.

You use this function to convert an unsigned long value to a string.

Module 54

TYPICAL OPERATION

In this program, you experiment with several of the Turbo C++ conversion routines. Begin from within Turbo C++ with no windows open.

1. Press **Alt-F** and type **N** to create a new file.
2. Type the following:

```
#include <stdlib.h>
#include <stdio.h>
#include <ctype.h>

int main(void)
    {
    float real_number;
    int   whole_number;
    char *string1 = "3.1459";
    char *string2 = "125";
    char string3[20];

    real_number = atof(string1);
    printf ("String = %s  Number = %5.3f\n", string1, real_number);

    whole_number = atoi(string2);
    printf ("String = %s    Number = %d\n", string2, whole_number);

    itoa(whole_number, string3, 10);
    printf ("Number = %d   String = %s\n", whole_number, string3);

    return 0;
    }
```

3. Press **Ctrl-F9** to run the program.
4. Press **Alt-F5** to view the program results.

```
String = 3.1459    Number = 3.146
String = 125       Number = 125
Number = 125       String = 125
```

5. Press **Alt-F5** to return to the Turbo C++ editor.
6. Press **Alt-Spacebar**, type **C** and type **N** to clear the desktop.
7. Turn to Module 56 to continue the learning sequence.

Module 55
DIAGNOSTIC ROUTINES

DESCRIPTION
The diagnostic routines provided with Turbo C++ are:

Function	Purpose
assert	Tests a condition
matherr	User-modifiable math error handler
perror	Print a system error message

APPLICATIONS
assert( )
```
#include <assert.h>    // required
#include <stdio.h>     // recommended
void assert(int test);
```
The assert( ) macro tests a condition. If the condition is false (evaluates to 0), the following message is printed:
```
Assertion failed: test, file filename, line linenum
```
where
> test describes the failed test (the argument to the assert)
> filename is the name of the file being compiled
> linenum is the line number of the assert( ).

To comment out the effect of the assert( ) function, you can include the following statement above #include <assert.h>.
```
#define NDEBUG
```
This will disable all of your assert( ) statements. That way you can test execution by disabling a single line.

matherr( )
```
#include <math.h>      // Prototype here
int matherr(struct exception *e);
```
The non-ANSI matherr( ) function is called whenever an error occurs in one of the math library routines. This routine is what is commonly called a "hook"—it provides a place for the programmer to hang a routine. When you create a function by the name

of matherr( ), it overrides the default behavior of matherr( ) letting you handle special problems that may come up.

Because matherr( ) is not an ANSI function, it may not be available in the future. You should avoid using this function, since future versions of Turbo C++ may not support it.

Matherr( ) uses the exception structure defined as:

```
struct exception
{
    int type;
    char *name;
    double arg1, arg2, retval;
};
```

where

type	is an enum _mexcep (DOMAIN, SING, OVERFLOW, TLOSS).
name	is a pointer to a string holding the name of the function which caused the error
arg1,2	are the argument(s) passed the function name
retval	is the value which matherr( ) will return

The enum _mexcep values are defined as

DOMAIN	argument was not in the function domain
SING	argument results in a singularity
OVERFLOW	argument causes a result > MAXDOUBLE
UNDERFLOW	argument causes a result < MINDOUBLE
TLOSS	argument causes a result with total loss of significant digits

Matherr( ) returns e->retval. The default value of 1 is returned if a UNDERFLOW or TLOSS occurs, otherwise a default value of 0 is returned (a retval of 0 means that matherr( ) didn't know what to do with the result). You can return a value of your own choosing by modifying matherr( ).

When a 0 is returned by matherr( ), Turbo C++ assumes that you were unable to resolve the problem detected by matherr( ). Errno is set to 0 and an error message is printed.

If a nonzero value is returned by matherr( ), Turbo C++ assumes that you were able to resolve the problem detected by matherr( ). Errno is not set to a value and no messages are displayed.

perror( )

```
#include <stdio.h>      // Prototype here
void perror(const char *s);
```

Diagnostic Routines

The perror( ) function outputs the last generated error message to stderr. The variable s is usually set to the filename of the program in order to generate messages which look like:

```
program:  error message
```

perror( ) uses the errno (number of the last system error), sys_errlist (an array of error messages), sys_nerr (the number of error messages in the array) global variables.

TYPICAL OPERATION

In this program, you experiment with the assert( ) and perror( ) functions. Begin from within Turbo C++ with no windows open.

1. Press **Alt-F** and type **N** to create a new file.
2. Type the following:

```
#include <stdio.h>
#include <assert.h>

void main()
    {
    int div;
    FILE *file_ptr;

    file_ptr = fopen ("xyz.xyz", "r");
    if (file_ptr == NULL)
      perror ("File does not exist");

    for (div=5; div > -1; div--)
      {
      assert (div != 0);
      printf ("1/%d = %f\n", div, 1.0/div);
      }
    }
```

3. Press **Ctrl-F9** to run the program.
4. Press **Alt-F5** to view the program results.

```
File does not exist: No such file or directory
1/5 = 0.200000
1/4 = 0.250000
1/3 = 0.333333
1/2 = 0.500000
1/1 = 1.000000
Assertion failed: div !=0, file NONAME00.C, line 15
Abnormal program termination
```

5. Press **Alt-F5** to return to the Turbo C++ editor.

Module 55

6. Add the following line:

    ```
    #include <stdio.h>
    #define NDEBUG
    #include <assert.h>

    void main()
       {
       int div;
       FILE *file_ptr;

       file_ptr = fopen ("xyz.xyz", "r");
       if (file_ptr == NULL)
         perror ("File does not exist");

       for (div=5; div > -1; div--)
         {
         assert (div != 0);
         printf ("1/%d = %f\n", div, 1.0/div);
         }
       }
    ```

7. Press **Ctrl-F9** to run the program.
8. Press **Alt-F5** to view the program results. Notice that the #define NDEBUG statement turns the assert( ) function off.

    ```
    File does not exist: No such file or directory
    1/5 = 0.200000
    1/4 = 0.250000
    1/3 = 0.333333
    1/2 = 0.500000
    1/1 = 1.000000
    Floating point error: Divide by 0.
    Abnormal program termination
    ```

Notice that the program results of the first program tell the exact line and statement where the program fails. In the second program with the #define NDEBUG statement, the results do not tell you where the program failed.

9. Press **Alt-F5** to return to the Turbo C++ editor.
10. Press **Alt-Spacebar** and type **C** and type **N** to clear the desktop.
11. Turn to Module 57 to continue the learning sequence.

Module 56
DIRECTORY CONTROL ROUTINES

DESCRIPTION

Directory control routines let your Turbo C++ programs move, remove, and manipulate file directories. Turbo C++ provides twelve directory control routines:

Function	Purpose
chdir	Change current directory
findfirst	Search a disk directory for a filename
findnext	Continue the findfirst search for a filename
fnmerge	Build a path given the drive, directory, and filename
fnsplit	Split a path into the drive, directory, and filename
getcurdir	Get the current directory for a specific drive
getcwd	Get the current directory
getdisk	Get the current drive number
mkdir	Make a directory
rmdir	Remove a directory
searchpath	Search the DOS path for a filename
setdisk	Return the total number of available disk drives

To use these functions, your Turbo C++ programs must use the <dir.h> include file such as:

        #include <dir.h>

To use the findfirst( ) function, you must also use the <dos.h> include file with the <dir.h> file such as:

        #include <dir.h>
        #include <dos.h>

The *chdir(dir)* function changes the current working directory to the directory specified by the variable "dir." For example, the following changes the directory to "C:\TC"

        chdir ("C:\TC");

The chdir(dir) function works exactly like the CD or CHDIR command provided with MS-DOS. If successful, this routine returns a value of 0. If not successful, it returns a value of −1 to designate an error. When an error occurs, the chdir(dir) routine sets the global variable "errno" to

        ENOENT   Path not found

225

Module 56

The *findfirst(path, ffblk, attrib)* function searches the "path" for the file described by "ffblk" that matches specific file attributes specified by the "attrib" variable.

The "attrib" variable may equal one of six values:

FA_RDONLY	Read-only files
FA_HIDDEN	Hidden files
FA_SYSTEM	System files
FA_LABEL	Volume labels
FA_DIREC	Directories
FA_ARCH	Archive files

Typically, you would specify the "path" and the "attrib" and the findfirst(path, ffblk, attrib) function would return the file in the "ffblk" structure. The ffblk structure is as follows:

```
struct ffblk {
    char ff_reserved[21];    /* used by DOS */
    char ff_attrib;          /* file attribute */
    int ff_ftime;            /* file time */
    int ff_fdate;            /* file date */
    long ff_fsize;           /* file size */
    char ff_name[13];        /* file name */
};
```

The following would find the first hidden file in the C:\TC directory:

```
findfirst ("C:\TC", &filedata, FA_HIDDEN);
```

To retrieve the hidden filename, your program would have to retrieve the ff_name field from the ffblk structure.

The findfirst (path, ffblk, attrib) function returns 0 upon success or –1 when there are no more files to be found or there is an error. On an error, the global variable errno is set to either:

ENOENT	Filename not found
ENMFILE	No more files

The *findnext(ffblk)* function continues a file search first started by the findfirst( ) function. It returns 0 upon success and –1 when an error occurs. On an error, the global variable "errno" is set to either:

ENOENT	Filename not found
NOMFILE	No more files

The *fnmerge(path, drive, dir, name, ext)* function creates a pathname, path, from strings describing the drive, path, filename, and file extension. It has no return value.

The *fnsplit(path, drive, dir, name, ext)* function splits a file path into strings describing the drive, dir, name, and extension. fnsplit( ) returns an integer made of five flags (described in <dir.h>). They are:

EXTENSION
FILENAME
DIRECTORY
DRIVE
WILDCARDS

These flags describe which strings have been filled in by fnsplit( ).

The *getcurdir(drive, dir)* function gets the current working directory on the drive specified by the variable "drive." The variable "drive" specifies a disk drive with an integer according to the following table:

0	Current drive
1	A:
2	B:
3	C:

(and so on)

If "drive" isn't the current drive, then dir won't be the current working directory returned by getcwd( ). It returns a 0 if successful or a −1 if there is an error.

The following would get the current working directory on drive C:

    getcurdir(3, dirname);

The *getcwd(buffer, buflen)* function gets the current working directory. The "buffer" variable stores the full pathname and the "buflen" variable specifies the maximum length of the pathname.

If the pathname is longer than the length specified by "buflen," this function returns an error. The following gets the full pathname from the current working directory, specifying a maximum pathname length of 80:

    getcwd(buffer, 80);

If there is an error, this function sets the global variable "errno" to one of the following:

ENODEV	No such device
ENOMEM	Not enough memory
ERANGE	Pathname exceeds maximum specified pathname length

The *mkdir(path)* function creates a directory described by the variable "path." This works the same as MKDIR or MD command provided by MS-DOS. It returns a 0 if the directory was successfully created or a −1 if there is an error. If an error is encountered, the global variable "errno" is set to either:

| EACCES | Permission denied |
| ENOENT | No such file or directory |

The following creates a directory called C:\SAMPLES:

    mkdir("C:\SAMPLES");

The *rmdir(path)* function removes the directory described by the "path" variable as long as the directory is empty, is not the root directory, and is not the working directory. This is the same as a RMDIR or RD provided by MS-DOS.

It returns a 0 if the directory is successfully removed or a −1 if there is an error. If an error is encountered, the global variable errno is set to either:

    EACCES   Permission denied
    ENOENT   No such file or directory

The following removes an empty directory called C:\SAMPLES:

```
rmdir("C:\SAMPLES");
```

The *searchpath(file)* function searches the DOS PATH environment for the file specified by the "file" variable. It returns a pointer to a full pathname if it finds the file, otherwise it returns a NULL value. This function can be used to look for DOS utilities (like FORMAT) by looking at the PATH.

The *setdisk(drive)* function changes the working drive. The value of "drive" is an integer.

    0   Current drive
    1   A:
    2   B:
    3   C:

(and so on)

The following sets the current drive to drive C:

```
setdisk(3);
```

APPLICATIONS

Directory Control routines let your programs access disk files. These routines can be particularly useful for writing file handling interfaces into your program (like XTree Professional) or for creating installation programs.

Use the chdir, getcurdir, getcwd, mkdir, and rmdir functions to manipulate file directories.

Use the findfirst and findnext routines to search for individual files. Use the fnmerge and fnsplit routines to manipulate the pathname where a file has been found.

Use the getdisk and setdisk routines to get and set the current disk drive (drive A:, B:, C:, etc.).

TYPICAL OPERATION

The following program creates a directory, makes it the current directory, and then lists some statistics. When it is finished, it removes the directory and looks for the

MORE.COM DOS command by searching the PATH environment variable. Begin from within Turbo C++ with no windows open.

1. Press **Alt-F** and type **N** to create a new file.
2. Type the following:

```
#include <stdio.h>            // io info
#include <dir.h>              // directory info
#include <dos.h>              // dos specific info

main()
{
    char path[MAXPATH], s[MAXPATH];
    char drive[MAXDRIVE], dir[MAXDIR], filename[MAXFILE], ext[MAXEXT];
    char *fname;
    char *template = "CXXXXXX";
    char *newdir = "Module60";
    FILE *file;
    int d, disk, flag, numdrives, result;
    struct ffblk ffblk;

    printf("We begin in the \"%s\" directory\n", getcwd(path,MAXPATH));
    result=mkdir(newdir);
    printf("And create the \"%s\" directory\n",newdir);
    if(result == 0)            // make sure we created the directory
    {
        chdir((const char *)newdir);
        printf("Then we CD into it\n");
    }

// The following loop would find all of the files in the current dir
// if it was looking in a dir which had files.  Since this dir is
// empty, neither of the following two messages should print.
        if(findfirst("*.*",&ffblk,0) == 0)
        {
            printf("Then we look for files to display\n");
            do
            {
                flag = fnsplit(path,drive,dir,filename,ext);
                printf("File: \"%s\"", path);
                fnmerge(s,drive,dir,filename,ext);
            } while(findnext(&ffblk) == 0);
        }

// Let's create a table of stats listing the current drive, dir, and
// the number of available drives (according to Turbo C).
        printf("\nLet's print out some statistics.\n");
        printf("\tCurrent drive:  %c:\n",(disk=getdisk()+'A'));
        getcurdir((d=disk-'A'+1), path);
        printf("\tCurrent dir:    %s\n\n",path);
```

Module 56

```
              printf("\tCurrent drives: %d\n\n", setdisk(d));

    // Clean up before concluding by removing the "newdir"
              chdir("..");
              rmdir(newdir);
              printf("Now let's rmdir(\"%s\")\n",newdir);
    // Find the MORE.COM program by searching PATH
              fname = searchpath("MORE.COM");
              printf("\nLet's search PATH for the MORE command\n");
              printf("Path to MORE: %s\n",fname);
        }
        else
    // The following line will print if the directory "Module60" already
    exists
              printf("Couldn't create directory %s\n",newdir);
        return(0);               // Normal termination
    }
```

3. Press **Ctrl-F9** to run the program.

NOTE

The following step assumes you are running Turbo C++ from the C:\TC\BIN directory. If you are running Turbo C++ from a different directory, you may see slightly different results.

4. Press **Alt-F5** to see the following program results on the screen.

```
    We begin in the "C:\TC\BIN directory
    And create the "Module60" directory
    Then we CD into it

    Let's print out some statistics.
            Current drive:  C:
            Current dir:    TC\BIN\MODULE60

            Current drives: 5

    Now let's rundir("Module 60")

    Now let's search PATH for the MORE command
    Path to MORE: C:\DOS\MORE.COM
```

5. Press **Alt-F5** to return to the editor.
6. Press **Alt-Spacebar** and type **C** and type **N** to clear the desktop.
7. Turn to Module 55 to continue the learning sequence.

Module 57
GRAPHICS ROUTINES

DESCRIPTION

The graphics routines work only with IBM computers. These routines let you draw graphics on the screen. Turbo C++ provides eighty-two graphics routines:

Routine	Purpose
arc	Draw arc
bar	Draw 2D bar
bar3d	Draw 3D bar
circle	Draw circle
cleardevice	Clear entire graphics screen
clearviewport	Clear current viewport
closegraph	Close graphics system
detectgraph	Detects driver and mode
drawpoly	Draw polygon
ellipse	Draw ellipse
fillellipse	Draw & fill ellipse
fillpoly	Draw & fill polygon
floodfill	Fill a region
getarccoords	Get last arc( ) coords
getaspectratio	Get current aspect ratio
getbkcolor	Get current background color
getcolor	Get current foreground color
getdefaultpalette	Get default palette
getdrivername	Get the current driver name
getfillpattern	Get the current fill pattern
getfillsettings	Get current fill info
getgraphmode	Get current graphics mode
getimage	Get a screen image
getlinesettings	Get current line info
getmaxcolor	Get max colors in current mode
getmaxmode	Get max mode number for current driver
getmaxx	Get max x coord in current mode
getmaxy	Get max y coord in current mode
getmodename	Get current mode name

getmoderange	Get mode number range
getpalette	Get current palette info
getpalettesize	Get size of current palette
getpixel	Get color of pixel (x,y)
gettextsettings	Get current text info
getviewsettings	Get current viewport info
getx	Get current x coord
gety	Get current y coord
graphdefaults	Reset graphics settings to defaults
grapherrormsg	Get error msg string
_graphfreemem	Graphics dealloc hook
_graphgetmem	Graphics alloc hook
graphresult	Get graphics error status
imagesize	Get size of bitmap in bytes
initgraph	Initialize graphics
installuserdriver	Use your own driver
installuserfont	Use own font
line	Draw line
linerel	Draw line to point relative to CP
lineto	Draw line to (x1,y1) from CP
moverel	Move CP to point rel to CP
moveto	Move CP to (x,y)
outtext	Display string at CP
outtextxy	Display string at (x,y)
pieslice	Draw a pie slice
putimage	Draw bitmap
putpixel	Set pixel (x,y) to a specified point
rectangle	Draw rectangle
registerbgidriver	Register a driver
registerbgifont	Register a font
restorecrtmode	Restore the screen
sector	Draw sector
setactivepage	Set active screen page
setallpalette	Set colors in palette
setaspectratio	Set aspect ratio
setbkcolor	Set background color
setcolor	Set drawing color
_setcursortype	Set cursor appearance
setfillpattern	Set user-defined fillpattern
setfillstyle	Set fillpattern and color
setgraphbufsize	Set graphics buffer size
setgraphmode	Set screen to graphics mode

setlinestyle	Set line style
setpalette	Set color in palette
setrgbpalette	Set 256 color palette
settextjustify	Set graphics text justification
settextstyle	Set text style info
setusercharsize	Set character size
setviewport	Set new viewport
setvisualpage	Set visible screen page
setwritemode	Set image drawing operator
textheight	Pixel height
textwidth	Pixel width

APPLICATIONS

To use these graphics routines, you need to include the <graphics.h> header in your program. Remember that these graphic routines are unique to Turbo C++ and may not work with other C compilers or non-IBM compatible computers.

arc( )

```
void far arc(int x,int y,int start,int end,int radius);
```

The arc( ) function draws an arc centered at (x,y) in the default color and thickness. The arc starts with a starting angle of start and ends at the ending angle of end.

A unit circle can be drawn at (10,10) with:
```
arc(10,10,0,360,1);
```

bar( )

```
#include <conio.h>     // additional header file needed

void far bar(int left,int top,int right,int bottom);
```

The bar( ) function creates a two-dimensional bar using the current fillcolor and fillpattern with an upper left corner of (left,top) and a lower right corner of (right,bottom).

To draw a 2D bar use:
```
bar(left,top,right,bottom);
```

To draw an outline bar use:
```
bar3d(left,top,right,bottom,0,0);
```

where the current fillcolor and fillpattern are set to the background color.

bar3d( )

```
void far bar3d(int left,int top,int right,int bottom,int depth,int tf);
```

Module 57

The bar3d( ) function draws a three-dimensional bar from an upper left corner of (left,top) to a lower right corner of (right,bottom) with a depth of (depth) and an optional top (defined by tf), using the current line color and linestyle, and is filled with the current fillcolor and fillpattern.

The tf (top flag) determines whether to put a top on the bar. If tf is zero, no top is drawn. If tf is nonzero, a top is drawn. The tf=0 option lets you stack bars on top of each other.

A standard 3D bar is drawn with:

```
bar3d(left,top,right,bottom,(left-right)/4,1);
```

A 2D outline bar is drawn with:

```
bar3d(left,top,right,bottom,0,0);
```

where the current fillcolor and fillpattern are set to the background color.

circle( )

```
void far circle(int x,int y,int radius);
```

The circle( ) function draws a circle of radius radius centered at (x,y) in the current line color and thickness.

If the circle isn't as round as you'd like, adjust the aspect ratio to see if you can get it rounder (aspect ratio is set using setaspectratio( )).

cleardevice( )

```
void far cleardevice(void);
```

The cleardevice( ) function clears the graphics screen to the current background color. The current position is also homed (set to (0,0)).

clearviewport( )

```
void far clearviewport(void);
```

The clearviewport( ) function clears the current viewport to the current background color. The current position is homed (set to (0,0)) relative to the viewport. (Viewports are set with the setviewport( ) function.)

closegraph( )

```
void far closegraph(void);
```

The closegraph( ) function cleans up and closes the graphics system (deallocating memory, etc.). To modify the way that the system deallocates memory, you can use the user hook _graphfreemem( )).

detectgraph( )

```
void far detectgraph(int far *d,int far *m);
```

The detectgraph( ) function checks your computer to see what kind of graphics hardware it has if you use DETECT as the driver (then it recommends what it thinks is the highest resolution screen possible for your adapter). You can override what DETECT would provide by specifying any other value for d (the pointer to the driver).

detectgraph( ) uses a far pointer to an int, d, for the driver and a far pointer to an int, m, for the mode

The detectgraph( ) function is automatically called from initgraph( ), so you don't have to call it unless you want to use a mode which is not the default mode.

Driver	Numeric
DETECT	0
CGA	1
MCGA	2
EGA	3
EGA64	4
EGAMONO	5
IBM8514	6
HERCMONO	7
ATT400	8
VGA	9
PC3270	10

Driver	Mode	Numeric	Resolution	Palette	Pages
CGA	CGAC0	0	320x200	C0	1
	CGAC1	1	320x200	C1	1
	CGAC2	2	320x200	C2	1
	CGAC3	3	320x200	C3	1
	CGAHI	4	640x200	2 clr	1
MCGA	MCGAC0	0	320x200	C0	1
	MCGAC1	1	320x200	C1	1
	MCGAC2	2	320x200	C2	1
	MCGAC3	3	320x200	C3	1
	MCGAMED	4	640x200	2 clr	1
	MCGAHI	5	640x480	2 clr	1
EGA	EGALO	0	640x200	16 clr	4
	EGAHI	1	640x350	16 clr	2
EGA64	EGA64LO	0	640x200	16 clr	1
	EGA64HI	1	640x350	4 clr	1
EGAMONO	EGAMONOHI	3	640x350	2 clr	1

(64K)

Module 57

Driver	Mode	Numeric	Resolution	Palette	Pages
	EGAMONOHI	3	640x350	2 clr	1 (256K)
IBM8514	IBM8514LO	0	640x480	256 clr	1
	IBM8514HI	1	640x480	256 clr	1
HERCMONO	HERCMONOHI	0	720x348	2 clr	2
ATT400	ATT400C0	0	320x200	C0	1
	ATT400C1	1	320x200	C1	1
	ATT400C2	2	320x200	C2	1
	ATT400C3	3	320x200	C3	1
	ATT400MED	4	640x200	2 clr	1
	ATT400HI	5	640x400	2 clr	1
VGA	VGALO	0	640x200	16 clr	2
	VGAMED	1	640x350	16 clr	2
	VGAHI	2	640x480	16 clr	1
PC3270	PC3270HI	0	720x350	2 clr	1

drawpoly( )

    void far drawpoly(int v,int far *vlist);

The drawpoly( ) function draws a polygon with v vertices using the points listed in vlist. Vlist has the form: x0,y0,x1,y1,...xn,yn. Remember to end your vlist with the first coordinates if you want a closed polygon.

To draw a triangle, you could use the following vlist:

    vlist[ ]={0,0,0,10,10,10,0,0};
    // the fourth set of points closes the triangle

    drawpoly(3,vlist);

ellipse( )

    void far ellipse(int x,int y,int start,int end,int xrad,int yrad);

The ellipse( ) function draws an ellipse with a center of (x,y), horizontal axis of xrad, vertical axis of yrad, starting angle of start and ending angle of end. If start=0 and end=360, a complete ellipse is drawn.

fillellipse( )

    void far fillellipse(int x,int y,int xrad,int yrad);

The fillellipse( ) function draws an ellipse with a center of (x,y), horizontal axis of xrad, and vertical axis of yrad. It is filled with the current fillcolor and fillpattern.

fillpoly( )

```
void far fillpoly(int vs,int far *vlist);
```

The fillpoly( ) function is used to draw a polygon with v vertices using the points listed in vlist, and then filling that polygon with the current fillcolor and fillpattern. Vlist has the form: x0,y0,x1,y1,...xn,yn. Unlike drawpoly( ), fillpoly( ) does not require you to close your polygon.

To draw a triangle, you could use the following vlist:

```
vlist[]={0,0,0,10,10,10};

fillpoly(3,vlist);
```

floodfill( )

```
void far floodfill(int x,int y,int border);
```

The floodfill( ) function flood fills the area defined by border color (border) and containing point (x,y). Borland requests that you avoid using this function whenever possible, suggesting the fillpoly( ) function as an alternative.

getarccoords( )

```
void far getarccoords(struct arccoordstype far *acs);
```

The getarccoords( ) function returns a pointer to an arccoordstype structure containing the parameters used in the last arc( ) function. The arccoordstype structure looks like:

```
struct arccoordstype
{
    int x,y;
    int xstart,ystart,xend,yend;
};
```

The x and y ints describe point (x,y) (the center point of the arc), while xstart and ystart are the starting point (xstart,ystart) and xend and yend are the ending point (xend,yend).

When creating drawings which require a line to connect with an end of an arc, getarccoords( ) can provide you with the endpoints.

getaspectratio( )

```
void far getaspectratio(int far *x,int far *y);
```

The getaspectratio( ) function returns the current aspect ratio through two pointers to far ints, x and y in terms of a y baseline of 10,000. X is normally less than y except in certain modes of the VGA where the aspect ratio is 1 (x=y).

getbkcolor( )

```
int far getbkcolor(void);
```

The getbkcolor( ) function returns the current background color as an int value. The colors are:

Number	Symbolic Name	Number	Symbolic Name
0	BLACK	8	DARKGRAY
1	BLUE	9	LIGHTBLUE
2	GREEN	10	LIGHTGREEN
3	CYAN	11	LIGHTCYAN
4	RED	12	LIGHTRED
5	MAGENTA	13	LIGHTMAGENTA
6	BROWN	14	YELLOW
7	LIGHTGRAY	15	WHITE

getcolor( )

```
int far getcolor(void);
```

The getcolor( ) function returns an int value representing the current drawing color. The current drawing color can be one of the following:

In CGA Modes:

Palette Number	1	2	3
0	CGA_LIGHTGREEN	CGA_LIGHTRED	CGA_YELLOW
1	CGA_LIGHTCYAN	CGA_LIGHTMAGENTA	CGA_WHITE
2	CGA_GREEN	CGA_RED	CGA_BROWN
3	CGA_CYAN	CGA_MAGENTA	CGA_LIGHTGRAY

In other modes (EGA/VGA):

Number	Symbolic Name	Number	Symbolic Name
0	BLACK	8	DARKGRAY
1	BLUE	9	LIGHTBLUE
2	GREEN	10	LIGHTGREEN
3	CYAN	11	LIGHTCYAN
4	RED	12	LIGHTRED
5	MAGENTA	13	LIGHTMAGENTA
6	BROWN	14	YELLOW
7	LIGHTGRAY	15	WHITE

getdefaultpalette( )

```
struct palettetype *far getdefaultpalette(void);
```

The getdefaultpalette( ) function returns a pointer to a palettetype structure containing a description of the default palette initialized by the driver. The palettetype structure looks like:

```
struct palettetype
{
    unsigned char size;
    signed char colors[MAXCOLORS+1];
};
```

The size describes the size of the palette; colors[] lists the colors available in the current palette.

getdrivername( )

```
char * far getdrivername(void);
```

The getdrivername( ) function returns a pointer to a string containing the name of the current driver.

getfillpattern( )

```
void far getfillpattern(char far *p);
```

The getfillpattern( ) function lets you see the current fillpattern by setting a pointer p to point at the range of eight bytes which describes the fillpattern.

getfillsettings( )

```
void far getfillsettings(struct fillsettingstype far *f);
```

The getfillsettings( ) function sets f to point at a fillsettingstype structure containing information describing the current fillcolor and fillpattern. The fillsettingstype structure looks like:

```
struct fillsettingstype
{
    int pattern;
    int color;
};
```

getgraphmode( )

```
int far getgraphmode(void);
```

The getgraphmode( ) function returns an int describing the current graphics mode. The returned graphics mode is described in detectgraph( ).

getimage( )

```
void far getimage(int l,int t,int r,int b,void far *bm);
```

The getimage( ) function fills bm with a bitmap defined with an upper left corner of (left,top) and a lower right corner of (right,bottom). The first two bytes of bm contain the width and height of the image.

getlinesettings( )

```
void far getlinesettings(struct linesettingstype far *l);
```

The getlinesettings( ) function sets l to point to a linesettingstype structure containing a description of the current line style, thickness, and pattern. The linesettingstype structure looks like:

```
struct linesettingstype
{
     int linestyle;
     unsigned upattern;
     int thickness;
};
```

The linestyle can be:

Number	Name
0	SOLID_LINE
1	DOTTED_LINE
2	CENTER_LINE
3	DASHED_LINE
4	USERBIT_LINE

where USERBIT_LINE is a user-defined linestyle. The upattern is a 16-bit pattern which is used in this mode to describe the bitpattern of the line.

The thickness may be:

Number	Name	Description
0	NORM_WIDTH	1 pixel wide
1	THICK_WIDTH	3 pixels wide

getmaxcolor( )

```
int far getmaxcolor(void);
```

The getmaxcolor( ) function returns the largest number that you can pass to setcolor( ) while in the current graphics mode.

getmaxmode( )

```
int far getmaxmode(void);
```

The getmaxmode( ) function returns the largest mode number available for the current driver. The difference between getmaxmode( ) and getmoderange( ) is getmaxmode( ) gets the number directly from the driver, while getmoderange( ) gets it from the Borland driver.

getmaxx( )

```
int far getmaxx(void);
```

The getmaxx( ) function returns the highest value that x can contain (this point conveniently corresponds with the right edge of the screen).

getmaxy( )

```
int far getmaxy(void);
```

The getmaxy( ) function returns the highest value that y can contain (this point conveniently corresponds with the bottom edge of the screen).

getmodename( )

```
char *far getmodename(int mode);
```

The getmodename( ) function returns a pointer to the name of the current graphics mode.

getmoderange( )

```
void far getmoderange(int d,int far *min,int far *max);
```

The getmoderange( ) function sets min and max to the minimum and maximum ends of the mode number range for the current driver. If there is an error, min and max are both set to –1.

getpalette( )

```
void far getpalette(struct palettetype far *p);
```

The getpalette( ) function sets p to a structure containing information describing the current palette. This function doesn't work with the IBM 8514 driver.

getpalettesize( )

```
int far getpalettesize(void);
```

The getpalettesize( ) function returns the size of the current palette. In EGA modes, this number is typically 16. In CGA modes it can be 4 or 2.

getpixel( )

```
unsigned far getpixel(int x,int y);
```

The getpixel( ) function returns the color of pixel (x,y).

gettextsettings( )

```
void far gettextsettings(struct textsettingstype far *t);
```

The gettextsettings( ) function sets t to a textsettingstype structure describing the current text attributes. The textsettingstype structure looks like:

```
struct textsettingstype
{
    int font;
    int direction;
    int charsize;
    int horiz;
    int vert;
};
```

Font describes the current font. There are two kinds of fonts: bit-mapped (default) and vector (stroked) fonts. Vector fonts are kept in .CHR files and can only be accessed one at a time.

Direction describes the direction in which characters are drawn. There are only two choices (instead of the expected 4): left to right and bottom to top. (You can get the other two directions (right to left and top to bottom) by reversing the string with strrev( ) before writing the string to the screen.)

Number	Name
0	HORIZ_DIR
1	VERT_DIR

Charsize describes the character scaling factor. 1 sets the characters to the original size (8x8 fonts fills 8x8 pixels), while 0 sets the characters to the default size (a scaling factor of 4 or the scaling factor set with setusercharsize( )).

Horiz describes horizontal justification. You usually want to set horiz to LEFT_TEXT. There are three supported values:

Number	Name	Description
0	LEFT_TEXT	text is left-justified
1	CENTER_TEXT	text is centered
2	RIGHT_TEXT	text is right-justified

Vert describes vertical justification. You usually want to set vert to TOP_TEXT. There are three supported values:

Number	Name	Description
0	BOTTOM_TEXT	text is justified from bottom
1	CENTER_TEXT	text is centered
2	TOP_TEXT	text is justified from top

getviewsettings( )

          void far getviewsettings(struct viewporttype far *v);

The getviewsettings( ) function sets v to point to a viewporttype structure containing the current viewport information. The viewporttype structure looks like:

          struct viewporttype
          {
               int left;
               int top;
               int right;
               int bottom;
               int clip;
          };

where left, top, right, and bottom describe a view port with upper left corner (left,top) and lower right corner (right,bottom). Clip determines whether or not the viewport clips images (images are clipped if clip is not equal to zero).

getx( )

          int far getx(void);

The getx( ) function returns the current x coordinate. The coordinate is relative to the upper left corner of the current viewport.

gety( )

          int far gety(void);

The gety( ) function returns the current y coordinate. The coordinate is relative to the upper left corner of the current viewport.

graphdefaults( )

          void far graphdefaults(void);

The graphdefaults( ) function resets the viewport, current position, palette, background color, foreground color, fill style, fill pattern, text font, and text justification to their defaults.

grapherrormsg( )

          char *far grapherrormsg(int err);

The grapherrormsg( ) function returns a pointer to a string describing graphics error err. The err value is generated by graphresult( ).

_graphfreemem( )

```
void far _graphfreemem(void far *p,unsigned s);
```

The _graphfreemem( ) function lets you customize graphics memory deallocation. The default version of _graphfreemem( ) calls free( ) to free the memory. But there are situations where you need to have complete control over what objects are deallocated (you may decide to not deallocate certain items, for example) — _graphfreemem( ) gives you that control.

The closegraph( ) function uses the _graphfreemem( ) function to deallocate memory resources.

_graphgetmem( )

```
void far *far _graphgetmem(unsigned s);
```

The _graphgetmem( ) function lets you customize graphics memory allocation. The default version of _graphgetmem( ) calls malloc( ) to allocate memory. There are situations where you need to have complete control over what objects are allocated (you may decide to realloc( ) certain items, for example) — _graphgetmem( ) gives you that control.

The initgraph( ) function uses the _graphgetmem( ) function to allocate memory resources.

graphresult( )

```
int far graphresult(void);
```

The graphresult( ) function returns the error status of the last used graphics command. The error code returned can be one of the following:

Number	Symbolic Name	Error Message
0	grOk	No error
-1	grNoInitGraph	(BGI) Graphics not installed
-2	grNotDetected	Graphics hardware not detected
-3	grFileNotFound	Device driver file not found
-4	grInvalidDriver	Invalid device driver file
-5	grNoLoadMem	Not enough memory to load driver
-6	grNoScanMem	Out of memory in scan fill
-7	grNoFloodMem	Out of memory in flood fill
-8	grFontNotFound	Font file not found
-9	grNoFontMem	Not enough memory to load font
-10	grInvalidMode	Invalid graphics mode for selected driver
-11	grError	Graphics error
-12	grIOerror	Graphics I/O error
-13	grInvalidFont	Invalid font file

-14	grInvalidFontNum	Invalid font number
-15	grInvalidDeviceNum	Invalid device number
-18	grInvalidVersion	Invalid version number

To access the error message, pass the number returned from graphresult( ) to grapherrormsg( ). Grapherrormsg( ) returns a pointer to the error message string.

imagesize( )

```
unsigned far imagesize(int l,int t,int r,int b);
```

The imagesize( ) function returns the size of a bitmapped image (bounded by an upper left corner (l,t) and a lower right corner (r,b)) in bytes. This can be used to dynamically allocate memory to store an image.

initgraph( )

```
void far initgraph(int far *d,int far *m,char far *p);
```

The initgraph( ) function initializes the BGI graphics package. You can set the driver using d, the mode using m, and you can specify a path to the driver with p. The integer values for the driver and mode are listed in the detectgraph( ) function. The path set by p is a valid DOS path.

installuserdriver( )

```
void far installuserdriver(char far *n,int huge (*d)(void));
```

The installuserdriver( ) accesses third-party (non-Borland) graphics drivers through initgraph( ). The filename of the driver is n which must have a BGI extension, and an optional autodetect function can be linked into the BGI through d.

If you want to use a Sun 1152x900 screen, the driver may be kept in the file SUN.BGI and have an autodetect function of detectsun( ). To install it so that initgraph( ) would recognize it, you could use:

```
installuserdriver("SUN",detectsun);
```

before you use initgraph( ).

installuserfont( )

```
int far installuserfont(char far *n);
```

The installuserfont( ) function lets you install a third-party vector font into the current graphics environment. You pass installuserfont( ) a pointer to a string containing the filename of the font, and it returns a font ID number for you to use with settextstyle( ). You can have up to 20 fonts installed at any given time.

line( )

```
void far line(int x0,int y0,int x1,int y1);
```

The line( ) function draws a line with endpoints (x0,y0) and (x1,y1). The current position is not updated.

linerel( )

```
void far linerel(int x1,int y1);
```

The linerel( ) function draws a line with endpoints at the current position and at a point x1 points horizontal and y1 points vertical from the current position. The current position is moved to the new point.

lineto( )

```
void far lineto(int x1,int y1);
```

The lineto( ) function draws a line from current position to (x1,y1). The current position is moved to the new endpoint.

moverel( )

```
void far moverel(int x,int y);
```

The moverel( ) function lets you move the current position to a point x points horizontal and y points vertical from the current position.

moveto( )

```
void far moveto(int x,int y);
```

The moveto( ) function lets you move the current position to point (x,y).

outtext( )

```
void far outtext(char far *s);
```

The outtext( ) function outputs string s at the current position. The CP is only changed if LEFT_TEXT and HORIZ_DIR are set. If they are, CP changes by textwidth(s).

outtextxy( )

```
void far outtextxy(int x,int y,char far *s);
```

The outtextxy( ) function outputs string s at (x,y).

pieslice( )

```
void far pieslice(int x,int y,int s,int e,int r);
```

The pieslice( ) function lets you draw a slice of a pie graph with a center (x,y), radius r, and a starting angle of s and an ending angle of e. The pie slice is filled using the current fill settings.

putimage( )

```
void far putimage(int l,int t,void far *bm,int o);
```

The putimage( ) function puts the bitmap pointed to by bm onto the screen with the upper left corner being (l,t). The first two bytes of bm must give the width and height of the image (this is automatically set by getimage( )). You can specify how the image is to be put on the screen by using one of the following image drawing operators in o.

Number	Name
0	COPY_PUT
1	XOR_PUT
2	OR_PUT
3	AND_PUT
4	NOT_PUT

The COPY_PUT operator does a straight transfer of bm to the screen. The other four do a Boolean operation to bm first. NOT places an inverse image onto the screen, while the other three operations use the existing section of the screen and bm as the two operands.

putpixel( )

```
void far putpixel(int x,int y,int c);
```

The putpixel( ) function sets pixel (x,y) to color c.

rectangle( )

```
void far rectangle(int l,int t,int r,int b);
```

The rectangle( ) function draws a rectangle with an upper left corner (l,t) and a lower right corner (r,b).

registerbgidriver( )

```
int registerbgidriver(void (*d)(void));
```

The registerbgidriver( ) function loads and registers a driver. This accesses drivers which have been linked into the program. The pointer d points to the graphics driver which was linked to the program. If the driver is valid, a nonnegative integer is returned as the driver number (which must be used in initgraph( ) to initialize the driver). If there is an error, a negative integer is returned.

For example, you've linked the sun( ) driver to your program. To register it for use by initgraph( ), you can use:

    registerbgidriver(sun);

registerbgifont( )

    int registerbgifont(void (*font)(void));

The registerbgifont( ) function loads and registers a font. This accesses fonts which have been linked into the program. The pointer f points to the font which was linked to the program. If the font is valid, a nonnegative integer is returned as the font ID (which can be used by settextstyle( )). If there is an error, a negative integer is returned.

restorecrtmode( )

    void far restorecrtmode(void);

The restorecrtmode( ) function restores the screen mode to the mode that it had before initgraph( ) was called.

sector( )

    void far sector(int x,int y,int s,int e,int xr,int yr);

The sector( ) function draws and fills a sector (between angles s and e) of an ellipse whose center is (x,y) with radii of xr and yr.

setactivepage( )

    void far setactivepage(int page);

The setactivepage( ) function sets the active screen page for drawing. This is useful when page-flipping animated objects. You can setactivepage( ) to the nondisplayed screen, draw on it, and then display it with setvisualpage( ). Only certain modes have multiple pages. See the chart in detectgraph( ).

setallpalette( )

    void far setallpalette(struct palettetype far *p);

The setallpalette( ) function sets the current palette to the values pointed at by p. This can dynamically change all of the colors within a palette. The difference between setallpalette( ) and setpalette( ) is that setpalette( ) lets you change a single color in the palette, while setallpalette( ) lets you change all of the colors in the current palette. The colors used are:

Number	CGA Symbolic Name	VGA/EGA Symbolic Name
0	BLACK	EGA_BLACK
1	BLUE	EGA_BLUE
2	GREEN	EGA_GREEN

3	CYAN	EGA_CYAN
4	RED	EGA_RED
5	MAGENTA	EGA_MAGENTA
6	BROWN	---
7	LIGHTGRAY	EGA_LIGHTGRAY
8	DARKGRAY	---
9	LIGHTBLUE	---
10	LIGHTGREEN	---
11	LIGHTCYAN	---
12	LIGHTRED	---
13	LIGHTMAGENTA	---
14	YELLOW	---
15	WHITE	---
20	---	EGA_BROWN
56	---	EGA_DARKGRAY
57	---	EGA_LIGHTBLUE
58	---	EGA_LIGHTGREEN
59	---	EGA_LIGHTCYAN
60	---	EGA_LIGHTRED
61	---	EGA_LIGHTMAGENTA
62	---	EGA_YELLOW
63	---	EGA_WHITE

The setallpalette( ) function does not work with the IBM 8514 driver. If you wish to set the palette of an IBM 8514 or of a VGA in 256-color mode, use setrgbpalette( ).

setaspectratio( )

    void far setaspectratio(int x,int y);

The setaspectratio( ) function changes the current aspect ratio. If your circles appear elliptical, either your aspect ratio is off, or your monitor needs adjusting. You can fix the circle by changing the aspect ratio.

setbkcolor( )

    void far setbkcolor(int c);

The setbkcolor( ) function sets the background color to the color c as defined in the current palette. The symbolic names of the colors are described in getbkcolor( ).

setcolor( )

    void far setcolor(int c);

The setcolor( ) function sets the drawing color to the color c as defined in the current palette.

_setcursortype( )

```
#include <conio.h>

void _setcursortype(int t);
```

The _setcursortype( ) function sets the cursor's appearance to one of the following:

Symbolic Name	Description
_NOCURSOR	no cursor displayed on the screen
_SOLIDCURSOR	normal block cursor
_NORMALCURSOR	normal underline cursor

setfillpattern( )

```
void far setfillpattern(int *p,int c);
```

The setfillpattern( ) function sets the current fillpattern and fillcolor. The fillpattern is a user-defined array of eight bytes which is pointed to by p. The fillcolor is pointed to by c.

setfillstyle( )

```
void far setfillstyle(int p,int c);
```

The setfillstyle( ) function sets the current fillpattern and fillcolor. The fillpattern, p, is one of the system-provided patterns. The color is a color from the current palette.

setgraphbufsize( )

```
#include <graphics.h>

unsigned far setgraphbufsize(unsigned b);
```

The setgraphbufsize( ) function sets the size of the internal graphics buffer which is used by routines like floodfill( ). This function resets the buffer size to b and return the previous size of the buffer.

setgraphbufsize( ) must be called before initgraph( )—it has no effect until initgraph( ) is called. The default buffer is 4K—if you are having problems using too much memory, you can reduce the size of this buffer, or if you are encountering "Out of flood memory" errors, you can increase the size of the buffer.

setgraphmode( )

```
void far setgraphmode(int m);
```

The setgraphmode( ) function sets the current screen mode. It is usually used along with restorecrtmode( ) to switch between text and graphics modes.

setlinestyle( )

        void far setlinestyle(int s,unsigned p,int t);

The setlinestyle( ) function sets the members of the linesettingstype structure to a line style of s, line pattern of p, and a thickness of t. The pattern is only used if USERBIT_LINE is the style of the line, and it is a 2-byte pattern describing which bits on the line are to be set.

setpalette( )

        void far setpalette(int cn,int c);

The setpalette( ) function sets palette color number cn to actual color c. If you are working in CGA mode you can only change the background color (cn can only be set to 0; anything else is an error). The color values used are described in setallpalette( ).

setpalette( ) cannot be used with the IBM 8514 or VGA in 256 color mode; use setrgbpalette( ) instead.

setrgbpalette( )

        void far setrgbpalette(int cn,int r,int g,int b);

The setrgbpalette( ) function sets color cn to the color made by

combining r (red), g (green), and b (blue). Cn has a range of 0-255, and r,g, and b only use the six most significant bits of the lower byte.

settextjustify( )

        void far settextjustify(int h,int v);

The settextjustify( ) function determines what type of justification is to be used with text that is drawn when in graphics mode. The default values are LEFT_TEXT (for h), and TOP_TEXT (for v). Other justifications available are described in gettextsettings( ).

settextstyle( )

        void far settextstyle(int f,int d,int s);

The settextstyle( ) function sets the font (f), direction (d), and size of text (s). The direction and size are described in gettextsettings( ).

setusercharsize( )

        void far setusercharsize(int mx,int dx,int my,int dy);

The setusercharsize( ) function sets the size of text with finer control than you can get using settextstyle( ). A call to settextstyle( ) must be made before using setusercharsize( ) to set the character size to 0. The default width is then scaled to mx:dx and the default height is scaled to my:dy. For example, if you want to double the height of the character, you want to have a ratio of 2:1.

So you set my to 2 and dy to 1. If you want the character to be one-eighth the default size (which is probably unreadable), you can set it with a ratio of 1:8.

setviewport( )

```
void far setviewport(int l,int t,int r,int b,int cf);
```

The setviewport( ) function sets the viewport dimensions to a rectangle with an upper left corner of (l,t) and a lower right corner of (r,b). The coordinates are absolute coordinates (not relative to the previous viewport).

The cf flag determines whether to clip an image at the viewport (if it is nonzero, the image is clipped).

setvisualpage( )

```
void far setvisualpage(int p);
```

The setvisualpage( ) function will make page p visible. It is used to animate images by "page-flipping" between two graphics pages. Only certain modes have multiple pages; see the chart under detectgraph( ) for more information.

setwritemode( )

```
void far setwritemode(int mode);
```

The setwritemode( ) function sets the image drawing operator which is used to draw lines. The most common two are:

```
COPY_PUT
XOR_PUT
```

where COPY_PUT overwrites any existing image and XOR_PUT lets you restore the background (by doing another XOR_PUT).

textheight( )

```
int far textheight(char far *s);
```

The textheight( ) function returns the height of the current text string in pixels.

textwidth( )

```
int far textwidth(char far *s);
```

The textwidth( ) function returns the width of the current text string in pixels.

TYPICAL OPERATION

In this program, you create a simple drawing. Begin from within Turbo C++ with no windows open.

1. Press **Alt-F** and type **N** to create a new file.
2. Type the following:

```
#include <graphics.h>
#include <stdlib.h>
#include <stdio.h>
#include <conio.h>
#include <dos.h>

void main()
    {
    int gdriver = DETECT, gmode;
    int x,y,radius,x1,y1,x2,y2;

    detectgraph (&gdriver, &gmode);
    initgraph (&gdriver, &gmode, "..\\bgi");

    x = 100;
    y = 50;
    radius = 20;

    ellipse (x,y,0,360,radius,(radius/3)+2);
    ellipse (x,y-4,190,357,radius,(radius/3));
    line (x+7,y-6,x+10,y-12);
    circle (x+10,y-12,2);
    line (x-7,y-6,x-10,y-12);
    circle (x-10,y-12,2);
    setfillstyle (1, getmaxcolor());
    floodfill (x+1,y+4,getcolor());
    x1 = x-(radius+1);
    y1 = y-14;
    x2 = x+(radius+1);
    y2 = y+(radius/3)+3;
    delay (4000);

    closegraph();
    }
```

3. Press **Ctrl-F9** to run the program. The program draws a circular image near the top left corner of your monitor.

Module 57

4. Press **Alt-Spacebar** and type **C** and type **N** to clear the desktop.
5. Turn to Module 58 to continue the learning sequence.

Module 58
INPUT/OUTPUT ROUTINES

DESCRIPTION

The Turbo C++ input/output routines let your programs accept and display data.

Function	Purpose
access	Determine accessibility of a file
cgets	Console get string
_chmod	Change file access mode
chmod	Change file mode
chsize	Change size of file
clearerr	Clear stream error flags
_close	Close a file
close	Close a file
cprintf	Console printf( )
cputs	Console put string
_creat	Create a file
creat	Create a file
creatnew	Create a new file
creattemp	Create a file (DOS 3.3 only)
cscanf	Console formatted input
dup	Duplicate a file handle
dup2	Duplicate a file handle to an existing file handle
eof	Detects EOF (end of file)
fclose	Close a stream
fcloseall	Close all open streams
fdopen	Open stream from handle
feof	Detect EOF for a stream
ferror	Error detect for stream
fflush	Flush stream buffers
fgetc	Get char from stream
fgetchar	Get char from stdin
fgetpos	Get file pointer position
fgets	Get string from stream
filelength	Get file size
fileno	Get file handle

Module 58

flushall	Flush all streams
fopen	Open a stream
fprintf	Write formatted output to stream
fputc	Put a character on a stream
fputchar	Put a character on stdout
fputs	Puts a string on a stream
fread	Read data from a stream
freopen	Associate a new file with an open stream
fscanf	Stream formatted input
fseek	Reposition file pointer
fsetpos	Position file pointer
fstat	Get info on file
ftell	Get current file pointer position
fwrite	Write to stream
getc	Get a character from the stream
getch	Get a character from keyboard with no echo to screen
getchar	Get a character from stdin
getche	Get a character from keyboard with echo to screen
getftime	Get file date & time
getpass	Reads a password
gets	Get a string from stdin
getw	Get next integer from stream
ioctl	Controls an i/o device
isatty	Checks for device type
kbhit	Checks for keystrokes
lock	Lock part of a file
lseek	Positions file pointer
_open	Opens a file
open	Opens a file (ANSI C)
putc	Put a character to a stream
putch	Puts a character to the screen
putchar	Puts a character to stdout
puts	Put string to stdout
putw	Puts an integer on a stream
_read	Read from a file
read	Reads from a file
remove	Deletes a file
rename	Renames a file
rewind	Repositions file pointer to the beginning of a stream
setbuf	Sets buffer to a stream
setftime	Sets file time & date
setmode	Sets file read mode

setvbuf	Sets buffer for a stream
sopen	Open shared file
sprintf	Writes formatted output to a string
sscanf	Read formatted input from a string
stat	Get information on a file
tell	Gets current file pointer position
tmpfile	Creates a temporary file
tmpnam	Creates a temporary filename
ungetc	Puts a character back into the input stream
ungetch	Puts a character back into the keyboard buffer
unlock	Unlocks part of a file
vfprintf	Writes formatted string to a stream
vfscanf	Gets formatted input from a stream
vprintf	Writes formatted to stdout
vsprintf	Writes formatted output to string
vsscanf	Gets formatted input from a stream
_write	Writes to a file
write	Writes to a file

APPLICATIONS

To use these i/o functions, your programs need to include the <stdio.h> header. Some functions may require additional header files such as <conio.h> or <io.h>.

When updating streams, you cannot follow an input with an output or vice versa. You must separate your inputs and outputs with either rewind( ) or fseek( ).

Most functions return 0 on success and –1 on failure. If a function returns –1, errno will be set so you can see what caused the failure. Common errno values are:

>EACCES (permission denied)
>EMFILE (too many open files)
>ENOENT (file not found or unable to find path)

access( )

>   #include <io.h>
>
>   int access(const char *f,int m);

The access( ) function determines the accessibility of file f by looking at the file attribute byte. The integer m can be one of the following:

Num	Description
0	Check for file existence
1	Execute permission (Not DOS)
2	Write permission

4	Read permission
6	Read and Write permission

cgets( )

    #include <conio.h>

    char *cgets(char *s);

The cgets( ) function gets a string from the console. s[0] should contain the maximum length of s. The function will set s[1] to the actual number of characters read. The read string will begin at s[2] (this is the address which will be returned from cgets( )). If a CR/LF (Carriage Return/Line Feed) pair is encountered, they will be replaced with a NULL (end of string terminator).

_chmod( )

    #include <io.h>

    int _chmod(const char *f,int c [, int a]);

The _chmod( ) function gets the current DOS attribute byte (like access( )) when c is set to 0. If c is set to 1, _chmod( ) will change the attribute byte to a. This is unique to DOS and is nonportable.

The portable version of this function is chmod( ). The attribute a can be one of the following:

Sym Val	Description
FA_RDONLY	Read-only
FA_HIDDEN	Hidden
FA_SYSTEM	DOS System file
FA_LABEL	Volume label
FA_DIREC	Directory
FA_ARCH	Archived (Modified)

_chmod( ) returns the current attribute on success.

chmod( )

    int chmod(const char *f,int m);

The chmod( ) function changes the file access mode of file f to m.

The mode m can be one (or both, if ORed) of the following:

Sym Val	Description
S_IWRITE	Write permission
S_IREAD	Read permission

chsize( )

    #include <io.h>

    int chsize(int h,long s);

The chsize( ) function changes the size of the file whose handle is h to size s. If s is smaller than the original file size, the file is truncated and an EOF is placed at the new end of file.

If s is larger than the original file size, the file is extended to the new size by padding the file with NULLs.

clearerr( )

    void clearerr(FILE *f);

The clearerr( ) function clears the error flags for file f. If you hit an EOF or encounter an error on a stream, you will continue to get an error status until you reset the flags using clearerr( ).

_close( )

    #include <io.h>

    int _close(int h);

The _close( ) function closes the file whose handle is h. If you need a ^Z at the end of the file you need to explicitly write it before closing the file. If there is an error, −1 will be returned and errno will be set to EBADF (bad file handle). The FILE * version of close is fclose( ).

close( )

    #include <io.h>

    int close(int h);

The close( ) function closes the file whose handle is h. If you need a ^Z at the end of the file, you need to explicitly write it before closing the file. If there is an error, −1 will be returned and errno will be set to EBADF (bad file handle). The FILE * version of close is fclose( ).

cprintf( )

    #include <conio.h>

    int cprintf(const char *f [,...]);

The cprintf( ) function writes a formatted string to the console and then returns the number of characters written. The main difference between cprintf( ) and printf( ) is

Module 58

that cprintf( ) does not translate '\n' into a CR/LF pair—it translates '\n' into a LF. Besides that, cprintf( ) works just like printf( ).

cputs( )

```
#include <conio.h>

int cputs(const char *s);
```

The cputs( ) function puts a string to the console and then returns the last character written. The main difference between cputs( ) and puts( ) is that cputs( ) does not translate '\n' into a CR/LF pair—it translates '\n' into a LF. Besides that, cputs( ) works just like puts( ).

_creat( )

```
#include <dos.h>
#include <io.h>

int _creat(const char *f,int a);
```

The _creat( ) function creates a file. This function is nonportable and works only with DOS. The created file is opened for read/write in binary mode with an attribute byte of a. If _creat( ) is successful, it returns the new file handle. If the file already exists, its size is set to 0, overwriting the original file. The attribute byte a can be one of the following:

Sym Val	Description
FA_RDONLY	Read only permission
FA_HIDDEN	Hidden file
FA_SYSTEM	System file

creat( )

```
#include <io.h>
#include <sys\stat.h>

int creat(const char *f,int a);
```

The creat( ) function creates a file. This function is portable. The created file is opened for read/write in binary mode with an attribute byte of a. If creat( ) is successful, it returns the new file handle. If the file already exists, its size is set to 0, overwriting the original file. The attribute byte a can be one of the following (or both ORed):

Sym Val	Description
S_IREAD	Read permission
S_IWRITE	Write permission

creatnew( )

    #include <dos.h>
    #include <io.h>

    int creatnew(const char *f,int a);

The creatnew( ) function creates a file. The created file is opened for read/write in binary mode with an attribute byte of a. If creat( ) is successful, it returns the new file handle. If the file already exists, −1 is returned and errno is set to EEXIST (file already exists). The file is not overwritten. The attribute byte a uses the same values as _creat( ).

creattemp( )

    #include <dos.h>
    #include <io.h>

    int creattemp(char *p,int a);

The creattemp( ) function creates a unique temporary file with attribute byte a in the directory described by p. The created file is opened for read/write in _fmode (either O_TEXT or O_BINARY). If creattemp( ) is successful, it returns the new file handle. The attribute byte uses the same values as _creat( ).

You must explicitly delete the file if you don't want it to remain in the directory after program execution. (You can delete it with unlink( ).)

cscanf( )

    #include <conio.h>

    int cscanf(const char *f [,add,...]);

The cscanf( ) function gets formatted input from the console and returns the number of fields scanned, converted, and stored. Fields which were unable to be stored are not included in the return value.

The return value can also be EOF (if an EOF is encountered).

The cscanf( ) functions works just like the scanf( ) command except cscanf( ) receives input from the console instead of the stdin stream. For format field and add format information, see scanf( ).

dup( )

    #include <io.h>

    int dup(int handle);

Module 58

The dup( ) function duplicates a file handle by creating a new file handle which is attached to the same file, file pointer, and access mode. If dup( ) is successful it returns the new file handle.

dup2( )

```
#include <io.h>

int dup2(int oh, int nh);
```

The dup2( ) function duplicates oh to nh returning 0 on success.

eof( )

```
#include <io.h>

int eof(int h);
```

The eof( ) function detects if an EOF has been reached in file h. If EOF was reached, a 1 is returned; a 0 is returned if EOF was not reached. A −1 is returned if there was an error.

fclose( )

```
int fclose(FILE *f);
```

The fclose( ) function flushes associated buffers and then closes file f. Memory resources used by the file are automatically freed except for memory allocated using setbuf( ) and setvbuf( ). To free setvbuf( ) memory, pass a NULL as the buffer pointer and then fclose( ) the file.

The setvbuf( ) memory will be freed. It will return 0 on success, EOF on error.

fcloseall( )

```
int fcloseall(void);
```

The fcloseall( ) function closes all open files except for the five system files (stdin, stdout, stderr, stdprn, and stdaux). It will return the number of closed files.

fdopen( )

```
FILE *fdopen(int h,char *m);
```

The fdopen( ) function creates a stream from an open file handle.

The mode m describes the file's mode—it will be one of the following:

Mode	Description
r	Read only
w	Write only
a	Append
r+	Update an existing file

w+	Create a file (allow update while open)
a+	Append and possibly update
b	Binary mode
t	Text mode

The FILE * of the new file will be returned.

feof( )

```
int feof(FILE *f);
```

The feof( ) macro detects EOF in stream f. If EOF was detected, a nonzero value will be returned. A 0 will be returned if the EOF was not encountered yet. Once EOF is detected, you must rewind( ) or clearerr( ) the file to clear the EOF.

ferror( )

```
int ferror(FILE *f);
```

The ferror( ) macro detects errors in stream f returning nonzero when an error is detected, zero otherwise. Once an error is detected, you must rewind( ) or clearerr( ) the file to clear the error status.

fflush( )

```
int fflush(FILE *f);
```

The fflush( ) function flushes a buffered stream, f, returning 0 on success, EOF on error. If f is an input stream, it is cleared. If f is an output stream, it is written out. fflush( ) has no effect on unbuffered streams.

fgetc( )

```
int fgetc(FILE *f);
```

The fgetc( ) function gets the next char from stream f. It converts the read char into an int (without sign extension). If there is an error, it will return EOF.

fgetchar( )

```
int fgetchar(void);
```

The fgetchar( ) macro returns the next character from the stdin stream. If there is an error, it will return EOF.

fgetpos( )

```
int fgetpos(FILE *f,fpos_t *p);
```

The fgetpos( ) function gets the current file pointer position for stream f and puts it into the variable pointed to by p.

fgets( )

    char *fgets(char *s,int n,FILE *f);

The fgets( ) function gets a string s from stream f of no more than n–1 characters. If a newline is encountered, fgets( ) also terminates. If a newline was encountered, it will be the last character of the read string and a NULL will be appended after it. Otherwise, there is no newline and a NULL is appended at the end of the string.

On success a pointer is returned pointing to the beginning of s. If an error occurs, a NULL is returned.

filelength( )

    #include <io.h>

    long filelength(int h);

The filelength( ) function returns the length of the file whose handle is h in bytes. If there is an error, –1 is returned.

fileno( )

    int fileno(FILE *f);

The fileno( ) macro returns the file handle for an open stream. If there are multiple handles on stream f, the first handle created for the stream is returned.

flushall( )

    #include <stdio.h>

    int flushall(void);

The flushall( ) function flushes all buffers in the way described in fflush( ). The number of open files is returned by flushall( ).

fopen( )

    FILE *fopen(const char *f,const char *m);

The fopen( ) function opens a stream whose pointer is returned. The file f is opened in mode m which can be one of the following:

Mode	Description
r	Read only
w	Write only
a	Append
r+	Update an existing file
w+	Update (delete if existing file, then update)
a+	Update after going to EOF

b	Binary mode
t	Text mode

One of the last two modes can be combined with any of the previous modes. So, for example, to update an existing file in binary mode you'd use "r+b."

The filename, f, can be a variable or a constant.

fopen( ) returns a pointer to the file unless there is an error, in which case it returns NULL.

fprintf( )

```
int fprintf(FILE *file,const char *format[,arg,...]);
```

The fprintf( ) function uses format to define an output string which will be written to file. If a printf( ) format specifier is used, the corresponding arguments follow the format in the same order as specified. The number of bytes output is returned if successful. Otherwise, an EOF is returned.

fputc( )

```
int fputc(int c,FILE *f);
```

The fputc( ) function puts c to file f. If there is an error, EOF is returned; otherwise, the character written is returned.

fputchar( )

```
int fputchar(int c);
```

The fputchar( ) function puts c to the stdout stream. If there is an error, EOF is returned; otherwise, the character written is returned.

fputs( )

```
int fputs(const char *s,FILE *f);
```

The fputs( ) function puts string s to file f. If there is an error, EOF is returned; otherwise, the last character written is returned.

fread( )

```
size_t fread(void *b,size_t s,size_t n,FILE *f);
```

The fread( ) function reads n records of s bytes into the memory pointed to by b from the file f. The return value is the number of items read. If the number of items read is less than the expected number, an error or EOF was encountered.

freopen( )

```
FILE *freopen(const char *f,const char *m,FILE *s);
```

The freopen( ) function will reopen stream s as file f using mode m. The modes used are found in fopen( ). If there is an error, NULL will be returned; otherwise, the new file pointer will be returned.

fscanf( )

```
int fscanf(FILE *F,const char *f[,add,...]);
```

The fscanf( ) function gets formatted input from a named stream, F, and returns the number of fields scanned, converted, and stored. Fields which were unable to be stored are not included in the return value. The return value can also be EOF (if an EOF is encountered).

fscanf( ) works just like the scanf( ) command except fscanf( ) receives input from a named stream instead of the stdin stream. For format field and add format information, see scanf( ).

fseek( )

```
int fseek(FILE *f,long o,int s);
```

The fseek( ) function positions the file pointer of file f. It starts at s and moves o bytes away. The starting position can be one of the following:

Sym Val	Description
SEEK_SET	Beginning of File
SEEK_CUR	Current file position
SEEK_END	End of File

The return value is nonzero when there is an error. If a zero is returned there may be an error (the pointer has been positioned but wasn't verified).

For file pointer positioning using file handles, use lseek( ).

fsetpos( )

```
int fsetpos(FILE *f,const fpos_t *p);
```

The fsetpos( ) function sets the file pointer position to the position where the last fgetpos( ) was called. fsetpos( ) will clear error and EOF flags, and it will clear the last ungetc( ).

fstat( )

```
#include <sys\stat.h>

int fstat(int h,struct stat *b);
```

The fstat( ) function fills the stat structure pointed to by b with the file information of the file whose handle is h. The stat structure looks like:

```
struct    stat
{
short st_dev;    // drive or device number
short st_ino;    // inode number (Not DOS)
short st_mode;   // file mode (see below)
short st_nlink;  // number of links (in DOS this is
                 // always 1)
int   st_uid;    // user id (Not DOS)
int   st_gid;    // group id (Not DOS)
short st_rdev;   // same as st_dev in DOS
long  st_size;   // file size in bytes
long  st_atime;  // last access time
long  st_mtime;  // last modify time (same as st_atime in
                 // DOS)
long  st_ctime;  // creation time (same as st_atime in
                 // DOS)
};
```

The file mode is defined by ORing one of the following symbols:

S_IFCHR	If h is a device (character device)
S_IFREG	If h is a regular file

and at least one of these

S_IWRITE	Write permission
S_IREAD	Read permission

The fstat( ) function will return 0 on success; otherwise, it returns −1.

ftell( )

```
long int ftell(FILE *f);
```

The ftell( ) function tells you what the current file position is in bytes from the beginning of the file. If there is an error −1L will be returned; otherwise, the current file position is returned.

fwrite( )

```
size_t fwrite(const void *b,size_t s,size_t n,FILE *f);
```

The fwrite( ) function writes n records of s bytes from the memory pointed to by b to the file f. The return value is the number of items written. If the number of items written is less than the expected number, an error or EOF occurred.

Module 58

getc( )

    int getc(FILE *f);

The getc( ) macro returns the next character from stream f. The returned character is converted into an int (without sign extension). If there is an error, EOF will be returned.

getch( )

    #include <conio.h>

    int getch(void);

The getch( ) function gets a single character from the keyboard without echoing the character to the screen. To echo the character, use getche( ). The return value is the character read. To read a function key you have to getch( ) twice—the first time you'll receive a 0x00.

getchar( )

    int getchar(void);

The getchar( ) macro returns the next character from the stdin stream. The returned character is converted into an int (without sign extension). If there is an error, EOF is returned.

getche( )

    #include <conio.h>

    int getche(void);

The getche( ) function gets a single character from the keyboard, echoing the character to the screen. If you don't want echoing, use getch( ). To read function keys, getch( ) is recommended (users wonder what a <NULL> is).

getftime( )

    #include <io.h>

    int getftime(int h,struct ftime *f);

The getftime( ) function gets the file date and time (for file f) as described in the ftime structure and puts it into f. The ftime structure looks like:

```
struct ftime
{
unsigned ft_tsec: 5;      // second
unsigned ft_min: 6;       // minute
unsigned ft_hour: 5;      // hour
unsigned ft_day: 5;       // day
```

```
    unsigned ft_month: 4;    // month
    unsigned ft_year: 7;     // year - 1980
};
```

If there is an error, getftime( ) will return a –1. Otherwise the return value will be 0.

getpass( )

```
#include <conio.h>

char *getpass(const char *p);
```

The getpass( ) function gets a password from the user by displaying a prompt, p, disabling echo, and then reading a password of up to eight characters. The returned string can be up to 9 characters in length (when you add the trailing NULL).

gets( )

```
char *gets(char *s);
```

The gets( ) function gets a string from stdin which is terminated by a newline. The area of memory that s points to should be large enough to hold the incoming record. When the newline is read it is converted into an end of string (NULL). If successful, a pointer to s will be returned; otherwise, a NULL will be returned.

getw( )

```
int getw(FILE *f);
```

The getw( ) function will get the next integer (or word—it's two bytes long) from f. If there is an error, EOF will be returned. Using getw( ) with a file opened in text mode is not recommended.

ioctl( )

```
#include <io.h>

int ioctl(int h,int f[,void *dx,int cx]);
```

The ioctl( ) function uses interrupt 0x44 to control I/O devices by using the f system call. Available system calls are:

Number	Description
0	Get device info
1	Set device info (in dx)
2	Read cx bytes into dx
3	Write cx bytes from dx
4	Read cx bytes into dx using h as a drive number
5	Write cx bytes from dx using h as a drive number
6	Input Status
7	Output Status

Module 58

8	Removable media? (DOS 3.x or later)
11	Set share conflict retry (DOS 3.x or later)

If there is an error −1 will be returned. On success, calls 0-1 will return DX, 2-5 will return the number of bytes transferred, 6-7 will return the device status, 8 will return 0 if removable, 1 if fixed, 11 will return 0 on success.

isatty( )

    #include <io.h>

    int isatty(int h);

The isatty( ) function returns a nonzero value if h is a terminal, console, printer, serial port, or other character device. If it isn't, a zero will be returned.

kbhit( )

    #include <conio.h>

    int kbhit(void);

The kbhit( ) function checks the keyboard queue to see if a key's been pressed. If the user has pressed a key, you can retrieve it using getch( ) or getche( ) (if you want to echo it). A 0 is returned if no key presses are waiting mournfully for service in the keyboard queue.

lock( )

    #include <io.h>

    int lock(int h,long o,long l);

The lock( ) function will lock a section of file h starting at offset o for l bytes. A 0 will be returned on success, a −1 on error.

The DOS command SHARE.EXE must be run before lock( ) is invoked since it relies on that program. You must be using DOS 3.00 or later to use this feature.

To unlock a locked file section, use unlock( ).

lseek( )

    #include <io.h>

    long lseek(int h,long o,int s);

The lseek( ) function positions the file pointer of file handle h. It starts at s and moves o bytes away. The starting position can be one of the following:

Sym Val	Description
SEEK_SET	Beginning of File
SEEK_CUR	Current file position
SEEK_END	End of File

The return value is −1L when there is an error. If lseek( ) was successful the new position (measured from the beginning of the file in bytes) is returned. The return value is undefined when you lseek( ) a console, printer, modem, or other device which can't have its file pointer repositioned.

For file pointer positioning using streams, use fseek( ).

_open( )

```
#include <fcntl.h>
#include <io.h>

int _open(const char *f,int o);
```

The _open( ) function opens file f using the following flags as o:

Sym Val	Description
O_RDONLY	Read permission
O_WRONLY	Write permission
O_RDWR	Read/Write permission
O_TEXT	Text mode
O_BINARY	Binary mode
O_NOINHERIT	Do not pass file to child processes
O_DENYALL	Deny shared access to everyone else
O_DENYWRITE	Deny write privilege to shared accesses
O_DENYREAD	Deny read privilege to shared accesses
O_DENYNONE	Deny nothing

open( )

```
#include <fcntl.h>
#include <io.h>

int open(const char *f,int a [,unsigned m]);
```

The open( ) function opens file f with an access a and an optional mode m. The access mode a can be made by ORing the required symbolic values:

Sym Val	Description
O_RDONLY	Read permission
O_WRONLY	Write permission
O_RDWR	Read/Write permission
O_TEXT	Text mode
O_BINARY	Binary mode

Module 58

O_NDELAY	Unix only
O_APPEND	Append to an existing file (used with O_WRONLY or O_RDWR)
O_CREAT	Create file
O_TRUNC	If file exists, truncate it to 0
O_EXCL	If file exists, return error

O_EXCL needs to be used with O_CREAT. Also, files created using O_CREAT must also use the m argument which uses the following (optionally ORed) symbolic values:

S_IWRITE	Write only
S_IREAD	Read only

The return value of open( ) is the handle to the file. If there is an error, –1 is returned.

putc( )

    int putc(int c,FILE *f);

The putc( ) macro puts c to file f. If there is an error, EOF will be returned; otherwise, the character written will be returned.

putch( )

    #include <conio.h>

    int putch(int c);

The putch( ) function puts c to the current text window. It does not translate newline characters into CR/LF pairs. If there is an error, EOF will be returned; otherwise, the character written will be returned.

putchar( )

    int putchar(int c);

The putchar( ) macro puts c to the stdout stream. If there is an error, EOF will be returned; otherwise, the character written will be returned.

puts( )

    int puts(const char *s);

The puts( ) function puts string s to the stdout stream and appends a newline character. If there is an error, EOF will be returned; otherwise, a nonnegative value will be returned.

putw( )

    int putw(int w,FILE *f);

The putw( ) function writes an integer w to f. If there is an error, EOF will be returned; otherwise, the integer written will be returned. If an EOF is returned, you should use ferror( ) or feof( ) to determine if it was a –1 or an EOF.

_read( )

    #include <io.h>

    int _read(int h,void *b,unsigned s);

The _read( ) function reads s bytes from h into b. It returns the number of bytes read unless there is an error, in which case it will return –1. This is a DOS-specific function.

read( )

    #include <io.h>

    int read(int h,void *b,unsigned s);

The read( ) function reads s bytes from h into b. It returns the number of bytes read, except in text mode where it will return the number of bytes read — carriage returns and control Zs. It will return 0 on EOF, and a –1 when an error is encountered. It is ANSI compatible.

remove( )

    int remove(const char *f);

The remove( ) macro deletes file f. It returns 0 on success and –1 if an error occurs.

rename( )

    int rename(const char *on, const char *nn);

The rename( ) function renames file on to nn. It cannot rename files across drives, but it can across directories, moving a file from one directory to another (like the fabled mv UNIX command). It doesn't accept wildcards either. It returns –1 on error, a 0 on success.

rewind( )

    void rewind(FILE *f);

The rewind( ) function will reset the file pointer to the beginning of the file while also clearing the error and EOF flags.

setbuf( )

    `void setbuf(FILE *f,char *b);`

The setbuf( ) function associates buffer b with stream f. If b is NULL then I/O will be unbuffered. You can switch between buffered and unbuffered I/O (if you really want to) but you should assign buffering right after the file is opened (it makes more sense that way).

setftime( )

    `#include <io.h>`

    `int setftime(int h,struct ftime *f);`

The setftime( ) function sets the file date and time to the values in the ftime structure pointed to by f. The ftime structure is described in getftime( ).

setmode( )

    `#include <io.h>`

    `int setmode(int h,int m);`

The setmode( ) function lets you change the mode of open file f between binary and text. The m value can either be O_BINARY (for binary mode) or O_TEXT (for text mode). A return value of 0 is returned if successful; otherwise, a value of –1 is returned.

setvbuf( )

    `int setvbuf(FILE *f,char *b,int t,size_t s);`

The setvbuf( ) function associates buffer b of size s and type t with stream f. The types of buffering that are allowed are:

Sym Val	Description
_IOFBF	Full buffering. Read operations fill the buffer completely. Write operations wait until the buffer is full.
_IOLBF	Line buffering. Read operations fill the buffer completely. Write operations wait until the buffer is full or a newline is encountered before writing.
_IONBF	No buffering. Read operations read directly from the file. Write operations write directly to the file.

If b is NULL, the buffer will be dynamically allocated for you. It will also be automatically freed when you close the file.

setvbuf( ) returns 0 on success. A nonzero value means that an error has occurred.

sopen( )

```
#include <fcntl.h>
#include <io.h>
#include <sys\stat.h>
#include <share.h>

int sopen(char *f,int a,int s,int m);
```

The sopen( ) macro opens a file f with access a, file sharing type s, and mode m. It returns a file handle on success, −1 on error. The access mode can be any of the values used with the open( ) function. The mode m can be one of the following (or both of them ORed):

Sym Val	Description
S_IWRITE	Write only
S_IREAD	Read only

The file sharing type is one of the following:

Sym Val	Description
SH_COMPAT	Compatibility mode
SH_DENYRW	Deny read/write permission
SH_DENYWR	Deny write permission
SH_DENYRD	Deny read permission
SH_DENYNONE	Deny nothing
SH_DENYNO	Deny nothing

sprintf( )

```
int sprintf(char *b,const char *f[,arg,...]);
```

The sprintf( ) function puts a formatted string defined by f into buffer b. It works like the printf( ) command, and the format string f is explained in the printf( ) command section. The return value is the number of bytes written to b, excepting the terminating NULL. If there is an error, an EOF is returned.

sscanf( )

```
int sscanf(const char *b,const char *f[,add,...]);
```

The sscanf( ) function reads buffer b using f as a description format to determine which address to put the contents. It adheres to the rules of scanf( ). If there is an error, EOF will be returned. Otherwise, the number of fields successfully scanned, converted, and stored will be returned.

stat( )

```
#include <sys\stat.h>

int stat(char *f,struct stat *s);
```

Module 58

The stat( ) function fills a stat structure pointed to by s with information on the file, f. The stat structure is described in the fstat( ) function. The main difference between fstat( ) and stat( ) is that stat( ) returns the stats of a file described as a string, and fstat( ) returns the stats of a file described as a file handle. If successful, 0 will be returned; otherwise, –1 will be returned.

tell( )

```
#include <io.h>

long tell(int h);
```

The tell( ) function returns the current file pointer position, by returning the number of bytes from the beginning of the file. If there is an error, a –1 will be returned; otherwise, the position will be returned.

tmpfile( )

```
FILE *tmpfile(void);
```

The tmpfile( ) function will create and open a temporary file, returning a FILE pointer to it. When the file is closed it will automatically be deleted from disk. The file is opened using a mode of "w+b." If there is an error, a –1 will be returned.

tmpnam( )

```
char *tmpnam(char *s);
```

The tmpnam( ) function returns a unique name which can be used as a temporary file. The temporary file created this way must be removed by the programmer after use or it will be left where created.

If s is NULL, then the filename will be internally stored, and a pointer to that string will be returned. Otherwise, the generated name will be stored in the array pointed to by s and a pointer to s will be returned.

ungetc( )

```
int ungetc(int c,FILE *f);
```

The ungetc( ) function will unget (return) a character to stream f. The return value is the character pushed back (converted into an int without sign extension) or EOF if an error occurs. This function is useful in certain parsing conditions where you can't tell if you've completed a token until you've read one character past the token. (You can then return the delimiter in case there is special processing which requires the delimiter.)

ungetch( )

```
int ungetch(int c);
```

The ungetch( ) function will unget (return) a character to the console. It can only return a single character—if you attempt to ungetch( ) multiple characters, only the most recently ungot character will be available for future reads. It will return the last character pushed back unless there is an error, in which case it will return EOF.

unlock( )

```
int unlock(int h,long o,long l);
```

The unlock( ) function will unlock a section of file h (starting at o for a length of l) which has been locked using lock( ). This will make that section available to the next user. If successful, a 0 will be returned; otherwise, −1 will be returned.

vfprintf( )

```
#include <stdarg.h>
#include <stdio.h>

int vfprintf(FILE *F,const char *f,va_list va);
// put formatted string to file
```

The vfprintf( ) function uses f to define an output string which will be written to file F. If a printf( ) format specifier is used, the corresponding arguments will follow in a va_list as returned by va_arg( ) or va_start( ). The number of bytes output will be returned if successful. Otherwise, an EOF will be returned.

vfscanf( )

```
#include <stdarg.h>
#include <stdio.h>

int vfscanf(FILE *F,const char *f,va_list va);
// get formatted str from file
```

The vfscanf( ) function gets formatted input from a named stream, F, and returns the number of fields scanned, converted, and stored. Fields which were unable to be stored are not included in the return value. The return value can also be EOF (if an EOF is encountered).

vfscanf( ) works just like the fscanf( ) command except vfscanf( ) accepts a va_list va which describes the fields to be accepted. For format field information, see scanf( ).

vprintf( )

```
#include <stdarg.h>
#include <stdio.h>
```

Module 58

```
int vprintf(const char *f,va_list va);
// put formatted str to stdout
```

The vprintf( ) function puts formatted output to stdout using a va_list created by va_arg( ) or va_start( ) instead of a variable list of arguments. It returns the number of bytes output unless there is an error, in which case it will return EOF.

vsprintf( )

```
#include <stdarg.h>
#include <stdio.h>

int vsprintf(char *b,const char *f,va_list va);
// put formatted str to b
```

The vsprintf( ) is the va_list version of sprintf( ). It works exactly the same as a sprintf( ) except it requires a va_list created by va_start( ) or va_arg( ). It returns the number of bytes output unless there is an error, in which case it will return EOF.

vsscanf( )

```
#include <stdarg.h>
#include <stdio.h>

int vsscanf(const char *b,const char *f,va_list va);
// get formatted input from b
```

The vsscanf( ) function works just like the sscanf( ) function except it requires a va_list created by va_start( ) or va_arg( ). It returns the number of bytes output unless there is an error, in which case it will return EOF.

_write( )

```
#include <io.h>

int _write(int h,void *b,unsigned l);
// DOS write to file
```

The _write( ) function writes l bytes from b to h. It only works in binary mode, so caution should be used when working with text mode files (this means it doesn't translate LF into CR/LF). The file pointer positioning is also not automatic.

The number of bytes written are returned unless there is an error, in which case EOF will be returned. The return value should be checked since it is possible to write less than the expected amount to h without receiving an error message.

write( )

```
#include <io.h>

int write(int h,void *b,unsigned l);
```

// ANSI write to file

The write( ) function writes 1 byte from b to h. The number of bytes written are returned unless there is an error, in which case EOF will be returned. The return value should be checked since it is possible to write less than the expected amount to h without receiving an error message.

TYPICAL OPERATION

In this program, you write a program that reads a text file and displays it on the screen. Begin from within Turbo C++ with no windows open.

1. Press **Alt-F** and type **N** to create a new file.
2. Type the following:

```
#include <stdio.h>
#include <conio.h>

void main()
   {
   FILE *fp1;
   char oneword[100];
   char c;
   int i;

   fp1 = fopen("a:readtext.c","r");

   do
     {
     c = fscanf(fp1,"%s",oneword);
     printf("%s\n",oneword);
     } while (c != EOF);
   printf ("Press any to continue:");
   while (!kbhit());
   fclose(fp1);
   }
```

3. Press **F2** to save the file. Turbo C++ displays a Save Editor File dialog box. Make sure you have a formatted blank disk in drive A.
4. Type **A:TEXTREAD.C** and press **Return**.
5. Press **Ctrl-F9** to run the program.

   Press any to continue:

6. Press **Return**.
7. Press **Alt-Spacebar** and type **C** to clear the desktop.
8. Turn to Module 59 to continue the learning sequence.

Module 59
INTERFACE ROUTINES

DESCRIPTION

The interface routines provide an interface to BIOS routines.

Function	Purpose
absread	Read absolute sector
abswrite	Write absolute sector
bdos	Access bios call
bdosptr	Access bios call w/pointer
bioscom	Access serial port
biosdisk	Access bios disk calls
biosequip	Check equipment
bioskey	Keyboard bios
biosmemory	Get size of base memory
biosprint	Printer i/o
biostime	Read or set the bios timer
country	Return country information
ctrlbrk	Sets the ctrl-break handler
disable	Disable hardware interrupts
dosexterr	Gets extended DOS error information
enable	Enable hardware interrupts
FP_OFF	Gets far address offset
FP_SEG	Gets far address segment
geninterrupt	Generate a software interrupt
getcbrk	Get ctrl-break setting
getdfree	Get disk free information
getdta	Get disk transfer address
getfat	Get File Allocation Table (FAT) information for a specific drive
getfatd	Get File Allocation Table (FAT) information for default drive
getpsp	Gets the Program Segment Prefix (PSP)
getvect	Gets interrupt vector
getverify	Gets current DOS verify status
harderr	Set hardware interrupt handler
hardresume	Return to DOS on hardware error
hardretn	Return to program on hardware error

inport	Gets a word from a port
inportb	Gets a byte from a port
int86	8086 software interrupt
int86x	8086 software interrupt interface
intdos	DOS interrupt interface
intdosx	DOS interrupt interface
intr	Alternate 8086 software interrupt interface
keep	TSR exit and remain resident function
MK_FP	Make a far pointer
outport	Sends a word to a port
outportb	Sends a byte to a port
parsfnm	Parse a filename
peek	Gets a word at memory specified by the segment and offset
peekb	Gets a byte of memory specified by the segment and offset
poke	Stores an integer at a memory location specified by the segment and offset
pokeb	Stores a byte at a memory location specified by the segment and offset
randbrd	Random block read
randbwr	Random block write
segread	Read segment registers
setcbrk	Set ctrl-brk check flag
setdta	Set disk transfer address
setvect	Set interrupt vector
setverify	Set verify flag
sleep	Suspend process for a specified number of seconds
unlink	Delete a file

APPLICATIONS

The interface routines are for advanced programmers. You should be familiar with C++ programming and how an IBM computer works before you use these routines. If you don't know what you're doing, you could accidentally destroy any data stored on your hard disk.

Most of these functions require the <dos.h> header file. If you are to use a different header file, it will be mentioned.

For those functions that require an unsigned char to describe a drive, the drive numbers are as follows:

Num	Description
0	Default drive
1	A:

2   B:
3   C:
4   D:
5   E:
(and so on....)

absread( )

#include <io.h>

int absread(int d,int n,int s,void *b);

The absread( ) function reads n blocks from drive d starting with block s into the memory pointed to by b. If absread( ) is successful, it will return 0; otherwise, it will return −1. absread( ) uses INT 0x25.

You are limited to 64K of data read per absread( ). To read more than 64K you must call absread( ) for each block of 64K.

abswrite( )

#include <io.h>

int abswrite(int d,int n,int s,void *b);

The abswrite( ) function writes n blocks to drive d starting with block s from the memory pointed to by b. If abswrite( ) is successful, it will return 0; otherwise, it will return −1. abswrite( ) uses INT 0x26.

You are limited to 64K of data written per abswrite( ). To write more than 64K you must call abswrite( ) for each block of 64K.

bdos( )

int bdos(int c,unsigned dx,unsigned al);

The bdos( ) function accesses BIOS interrupts which use integer arguments and then returns the contents of AX. Interrupts which require a pointer use bdosptr( ).

bdosptr( )

int bdosptr(int c,void *a,unsigned al);

The bdosptr( ) function accesses BIOS interrupts which use pointer arguments and then returns the contents of AX (or −1 if there is an error). Interrupts which require integers should use bdos( ).

When used in compact, large, or huge memory models, a points to the DS and DX values to be used in the call. In the other memory models in points to the value of DX.

bioscom( )

    #include <bios.h>

    int bioscom(int c,char p,int port);

The bioscom( ) function will do command c using parameters p through the serial port, returning a status int. The command can be one of the following:

Number	Description
0	Set communications using p
1	Send p through port
2	Receive a char (see return value)
3	Current status of port

You create the parameters, p, by ORing one item out of each of the following categories:

DATA BITS

Number	Description
0x02	7 bits
0x03	8 bits

STOP BITS

Number	Description
0x00	1 Stop bit
0x04	2 Stop bits

PARITY

Number	Description
0x00	No parity
0x80	Odd parity
0x18	Even parity

SPEED

Number	Description
0x00	110 baud
0x20	150 baud
0x40	300 baud
0x60	600 baud
0x80	1200 baud
0xA0	2400 baud
0xC0	4800 baud
0xE0	9600 baud

The value of port is one less than the number of the port. For example, COM1 would be 0, COM3 would be 2, etc.

Module 59

The return int has the following value:

Bit	Description
15	Time out
14	Transmit shift register empty
13	Transmit hold register empty
12	Break detect
11	Frame error
10	Parity error
9	Overrun error
8	Data ready
7	Line signal Detect
6	Ring indicator
5	Data set ready
4	Clear to Send
3	Receive line signal detect change
2	Trailing edge ring detector
1	Data set Ready change
0	Clear to Send change

If you were using command 2, the lower 8 bits would contain the value of the received character and the upper 8 bits would be 0. On an error, the lower byte is undefined and the upper byte is nonzero.

biosdisk( )

```
#include <bios.h>

int biosdisk(int c,int d,int h,int t,int s,int n,void *b);
```

The biosdisk( ) function uses Interrupt 0x13 to issue command c to drive d, head h, track t, sector s, for n sectors, using the memory pointed to by b, and returning an int described below.

The commands available are as follows (the IBM PC only recognizes commands 0-5; all models XT or up recognize the others):

Hex Cmd	Description
0	Drive controller hard reset
1	Last disk operation status
2	Read from disk
3	Write to disk
4	Verify disk
5	Format track
6	Format track, flagging bad sectors
7	Format drive starting at specified track

8	Current Drive parameters
9	Initialize drive-pair characteristics
A	Long read
B	Long write
C	Disk Seek
D	Alternates disk reset
E	Read sector buffer
F	Write sector buffer
10	Test if drive ready
11	Recalibrate drive
12	Controller RAM Diagnostic
13	Drive Diagnostic
14	Controller internal diagnostic

The return values are:

Hex	Description
0x00	Success
0x01	Bad command
0x02	Address mark not found
0x03	Write-protected disk
0x04	Sector not found
0x05	Hard Disk reset failure
0x06	Disk changed since last operation
0x07	Drive parameter activity failed
0x08	DMA Overrun
0x09	DMA Attempt across segment boundary
0x0A	Bad sector detected
0x0B	Bad track detected
0x0C	Unsupported track
0x10	Bad CRC/ECC on read
0x11	CRC/ECC corrected data warning
0x20	Controller failure
0x40	Seek failure
0x80	Attachment response failure
0xAA	Hard disk Drive not Ready
0xBB	Hard Disk Undefined error
0xCC	Write fault
0xE0	Status error
0xFF	Sense failure

Module 59

biosequip( )

    #include <bios.h>

    int biosequip(void);

The biosequip( ) function lists the equipment on the machine running the program by using Interrupt 0x11 and returning the equipment in an int. The return value is:

Bit	Description
15\ 14/	Number of parallel printers (0-3)
13	Serial printer attached flag
12	Game I/O attached flag
11\ 10 \ 9 /	Number of COM ports (0-7)
8	DMA capability flag
7\ 6/	Number of disk drives (1-4)
5\ 4/	Initial video mode (0-3 listed below)
3\ 2/	Motherboard RAM chip size (0-3 listed below)
1	Math Coprocessor flag
0	Boot from disk

INITIAL VIDEO MODE

Num	Description
0	Unused
1	40x25 monochrome with color card
2	80x25 monochrome with color card
3	80x25 monochrome with monochrome card

MOTHERBOARD RAM CHIP SIZE

Num	Description
0	16K
1	32K
2	48K
3	64K

bioskey( )

    #include <bios.h>

    int bioskey(int c);

The bioskey( ) function checks if there is a key waiting, get a keystroke, or get the keyboard status by returning an int with the appropriate values. The command c can be one of the following:

HEX	Description
0	Get next keystroke
1	Character waiting in queue?
2	Get keyboard status

The return value for each command is different.

RETURN VALUE FOR GET NEXT KEYSTROKE (0)

If the low byte is nonzero, the high byte is the ASCII character read. If the low byte is zero, the high byte is the scan code read. A table of scan codes is located in Appendix F, an ASCII Table is in Appendix D.

RETURN VALUE FOR WAITING CHARACTER (1)

If the return value is zero, there is no key waiting in the keyboard queue. If the return value is nonzero, there is a waiting key—use bioskey(0) to get it.

RETURN VALUE FOR KEYBOARD STATUS (2)

The return value is as follows:

Bit	Description
7	Insert on
6	Caps Lock on
5	Num Lock on
4	Scroll Lock on
3	Alt pressed
2	Ctrl pressed
1	Left Shift key pressed
0	Right Shift key pressed

biosmemory( )

    #include <bios.h>

    int biosmemory(void);

The biosmemory( ) function returns the size of base memory (in K) by using Interrupt 0x12.

biosprint( )

    #include <bios.h>

    int biosprint(int c,int i,int port);

The biosprint( ) function does command c, possibly using character i, through the parallel port, returning a printer status. The command can be one of the following:

Module 59

Hex	Description
0	Print char p
1	Initialize port
2	Read printer status

The return value can be:

Bit	Description
7	Not busy
6	ACK
5	Out of paper
4	Printer Selected
3	I/O error
2	unused
1	unused
0	Time out

biostime( )

```
#include <bios.h>

long biostime(int c,long t);
```

The biostime( ) function uses command c on the timer, possibly using t to reset the timer, and returns the current timer value. The command can be:

Hex	Description
0	Return current timer value
1	Set timer to t

country( )

```
struct country *country(int x,struct country *c);
```

The country( ) function will either set the current country to x, or it will fill the country structure c with the current information. It will return a pointer to c unless there is an error, in which case it will return 0. The country structure looks like:

```
struct country
{
int co_date;              // date format
char co_curr[5];          // currency symbol
char co_thsep[2];         // thousands separator
char co_desep[2];         // decimal separator
char co_dtsep[2];         // date separator
char co_tmsep[2];         // time separator
char co_currstyle;        // currency style (see below)
char co_digits;           // currency significant digits
char co_time;             // time format
char co_case;             // case map
```

```
char co_dasep[2];      // data separator
char co_fill[10];      // unused
};
```

Most of these fields are straightforward, but the following two need explanation:

DATE FORMAT

Num	Description
0	MM/DD/YY
1	DD/MM/YY
2	YY/MM/DD

CURRENCY STYLE

Num	Description
0	$xxx.xx
1	xxx.xx$
2	$ xxx.xx
3	xxx.xx $

ctrlbrk( )

```
void ctrlbrk(int (*f)(void));
```

The ctrlbrk( ) function sets f as the interface handler for the control break key. If function f returns 0, the current program will abort; any other value will allow execution to continue.

disable( )

```
void disable(void);
```

The disable( ) macro disables all interrupts except for NMI (nonmaskable interrupt). This lets you process your current interrupt in peace without having to worry about another one breaking in and interrupting everything.

dosexterr( )

```
int dosexterr(struct DOSERROR *e);
```

The dosexterr( ) function returns extended DOS error information into the DOSERROR structure pointed to by e. The DOSERROR structure looks like:

```
struct DOSERROR
{
char de_exterror;
char de_class;
char de_action;
char de_locus;
};
```

The return value will be 0 if the previous DOS call was successful. If there is an error, the return value will be nonzero.

enable( )

    void enable(void);

The enable( ) macro enables all interrupts, resetting disable( ).

FP_OFF( )

    unsigned FP_OFF(void far *p);

The FP_OFF( ) macro returns the offset of p. To set the segment value of p use FP_SEG( ).

FP_SEG( )

    unsigned FP_SEG(void far *p);

The FP_OFF( ) macro returns the offset of p. To set the segment value of p use FP_OFF( ).

geninterrupt( )

    void geninterrupt(int i);

The geninterrupt( ) macro will generate interrupt i (usually written in hexadecimal) using the current settings of the registers (as loaded through _AH, etc). After the interrupt has been generated, the state of the registers can be unpredictable.

getcbrk( )

    int getcbrk(void);

The getcbrk( ) function returns 1 if the control break state is on. If it is off, getcbrk( ) will return 0.

getdfree( )

    void getdfree(unsigned char d,struct dfree *t);

The getdfree( ) function loads the dfree structure pointed to by t with the disk free information from disk d.

The dfree structure looks like:

```
struct dfree
{
unsigned df_avail;      // available clusters
unsigned df_total;      // total clusters
unsigned df_bsec;       // bytes/sector
unsigned df_sclus;      // sectors/cluster
};
```

If there is an error, getdfree( ) will return 0xFF in df_sclus.

getdta( )

    char far *getdta(void);

The getdta( ) function gets the address of the current disk transfer address. In the tiny, small, and medium models, the segment of the dta will be assumed to be the current segment. In the compact, large, and huge models, the complete segment address will be returned.

getfat( )

    void getfat(unsigned char d,struct fatinfo *i);

The getfat( ) function uses the d to select the drive to use to set the members of the fatinfo structure pointed to by i. The fatinfo structure looks like:

    struct fatinfo
    {
    char fi_sclus;   // sectors/cluster
    char fi_fatid;   // FAT id byte
    char fi_nclus;   // number of clusters
    char fi_bysec;   // bytes/sector
    }

getfatd( )

    void getfatd(struct fatinfo *i);

The getfatd( ) function sets the fatinfo structure pointed to by i to the information obtained from the current drive. The fatinfo structure is described in getfat( ).

getpsp( )

    unsigned getpsp(void);

The getpsp( ) function returns the segment address of the current PSP. Since this uses the interrupt call 0x62, which only exists in DOS 3.x, you may want to use the global variable _psp instead.

getvect( )

    void interrupt (*getvect(int i))( );

The getvect( ) function returns a pointer to the interrupt handler for interrupt i. The interrupts range from 0 to 255.

getverify( )

    int getverify(void);

The getverify( ) function returns the status of the verify flag. If the return value is 0, the verify flag is off. Otherwise, it is on.

harderr( )

```
void harderr(int (*f)( ));
```

The harderr( ) function sets a hardware error handler, f( ), to interrupt vector 0x24. The interrupt handler will be called with the following prototype:

```
f(int di, int ax, int bp, int si);
```

where di is the error value, ax points to the erring device, and bp and si point to the device driver of the erring device.

If ax is negative, a device error occurred; if it is nonnegative, a drive error occurred. If a drive error occurs, you can get the drive number by:

```
ax & 0x00FF
```

The device driver address is represented by (bp:si) where bp is the segment and si is the offset. The device driver can be inspected using peek( ) and peekb( ) but cannot be modified using poke( ) and pokeb( ).

Function f( ) is restricted to interrupts 0x01 through 0x0C. Other interrupt calls will corrupt DOS (you can't use any of the standard I/O calls).

Function f( ) must return one of the following values:

Num	Description
0	Ignore
1	Retry
2	Abort

hardresume( )

```
void hardresume(int r);
```

The hardresume( ) function will return to DOS using one of the following return codes:

Num	Description
0	Ignore
1	Retry
2	Abort (uses interrupt 0x23)

hardresume( ) and hardretn( ) are recommended ways of returning from function f( ) defined in harderr( ).

hardretn( )

```
void hardretn(int i);
```

The hardretn( ) function will return to the calling program using one of the following return codes:

Num	Description
0	Ignore
1	Retry
2	Abort (uses interrupt 0x23)

hardresume( ) and hardretn( ) are recommended ways of returning from function f( ) defined in harderr( ).

inport( )

>   int inport(int p);

The inport( ) function will get the next word waiting at port p.

inportb( )

>   unsigned char inportb(int p);

The inportb( ) function will get the next byte waiting at port p.

int86( )

>   int int86(int i,union REGS *I,union REGS *O);

The int86( ) function generates interrupt i using input registers I and output register O. The registers in I and O can be accessed with either the I.x.ax or I.h.al and I.h.ah syntax depending on whether you want to look at a single byte or a word (the x registers are word sized and the h and l registers are byte sized). Unions I and O can be the same union, but they do not have to be.

If you want to generate an interrupt which requires segment registers, use int86x( ).

The int86( ) function returns the contents of AX.

int86x( )

>   int int86x(int i,union REGS *I,union REGS *O,struct SREGS *S);

The int86x( ) function generates interrupt i using segment registers S, input registers I, and output registers O. The registers in I and O can be accessed with either I.x.ax or I.h.al and I.h.ah syntax depending on whether you want to look at a single byte or a word (the x registers are word sized and the h and l registers are byte sized). To access the segment registers you use the S.ds syntax. Unions I and O can be the same union, but they do not have to be.

If you want to generate an interrupt which doesn't require segment registers, use int86( ).

The int86x( ) function returns the contents of AX.

Module 59

intdos( )

    `int intdos(union REGS *I,union REGS *O);`

The intdos( ) function loads the registers with I and then generates an interrupt 0x21. O will contain the contents of the registers after the interrupt. The contents of AX will be returned.

intdosx( )

    `int intdosx(union REGS *I,union REGS *O,struct SREGS *S);`

The intdosx( ) function loads the registers with I and S before generating an interrupt 0x21. O will contain the contents of the registers after the interrupt. The contents of AX will be returned.

intr( )

    `void intr(int i,struct REGPACK *R);`

The intr( ) function is yet another way to generate an interrupt. i contains the value of the desired interrupt and R contains all of the register information. The REGPACK structure looks like:

```
struct REGPACK
{
unsigned r_ax, r_bx, r_cx, r_dx;
unsigned r_bp, r_si, r_di, r_ds, r_es, r_flags;
};
```

The REGPACK structure is used for both input and output registers.

keep( )

    `void keep(unsigned char s,unsigned size);`

The keep( ) function will terminate the current program, returning to DOS with the status in s. Size paragraphs of the program will remain in memory after termination—the rest will be freed.

MK_FP( )

    `void MK_FP(unsigned s,unsigned o);`

The MK_FP( ) macro will create a far pointer using s as the segment and o as the offset (s:o) to create the address for the far pointer.

outport( )

    `void outport(int p,int word);`

The outport( ) function writes word to port p. If you want to write a byte to a port, use outportb( ).

outportb( )
>   void outportb(int p,unsigned char byte);

The outportb( ) function writes byte to port p. If you want to write a word to a port, use outport( ).

parsfnm( )
>   char *parsfnm(const char *n,struct fcb *f,int o);

The parsfnm( ) function uses interrupt 0x29 to parse a string s for a filename. If one is encountered, the fcb structure pointed to by f will be filled with the parsed info passing o to AL to determine which option is to be used.

peek( )
>   int peek(unsigned s,unsigned o);

The peek( ) macro gets the contents of the word at segment s and offset o (s:o).

peekb( )
>   char peekb(unsigned s,unsigned o);

The peekb( ) macro gets the contents of the byte at segment s and offset o (s:o).

poke( )
>   void poke(unsigned s,unsigned o,int word);

The poke( ) macro puts word into segment s, offset o (s:o).

pokeb( )
>   void poke(unsigned s,unsigned o,int byte);

The pokeb( ) macro puts byte into segment s, offset o (s:o).

randbrd( )
>   int randbrd(struct fcb *f,c);

The randbrd( ) function reads c records using the fcb structure pointed to by f. It will return one of the following values:

Num	Description
0	All requested records read
1	EOF encountered, last record complete
2	Allocated buffer too small, the next read would have overwritten part of it
3	EOF encountered, last record incomplete

randbwr( )

```
int randbwr(struct fcb *f,c);
```

The randbwr( ) function writes c records using the fcb structure pointed to by f. It will return one of the following values:

Num	Description
0	All requested records read
1	EOF encountered, last record complete
2	Allocated buffer too small, the next read would have overwritten part of it
3	EOF encountered, last record incomplete

segread( )

```
void segread(struct SREGS *s);
```

The segread( ) function gets the segment registers and puts them into the SREGS structure. The SREGS structure looks like:

```
struct SREGS
{
unsigned cs;
unsigned ds;
unsigned es;
unsigned ss;
};
```

setcbrk( )

```
int setcbrk(int c);
```

The setcbrk( ) function sets the value of the control break checking flag. A 0 will turn control break checking off, allowing checking only during I/O calls. A 1 will turn control break checking on, allowing checking at every system call.

setdta( )

```
void setdta(char far *d);
```

The setdta( ) function sets the address of the current disk transfer address. In the tiny, small, and medium models, the segment of the dta will be assumed to be the current segment. In the compact, large, and huge models, the complete segment address will be assumed.

setvect( )

```
void setvect(int i,void interrupt (*f)( ));
```

The setvect( ) function sets the interrupt handler for vector i to function f. The interrupts range from 0 to 255.

setverify( )

    void setverify(int c);

The setverify( ) function will set the DOS verify flag. A 0 will turn verify off. A 1 will turn verify on.

sleep( )

    void sleep(unsigned s);

The sleep( ) function will suspend the current process s seconds.

unlink( )

    int unlink(const char *f);

The unlink( ) function deletes (removes) the file whose path is described by f. Wildcards are not allowed. A 0 will be returned if unlink( ) is successful; otherwise, a –1 will be returned and errno will be set to either ENOENT (filename not found) or EACCES (permission denied).

TYPICAL OPERATION

In this program, you experiment with using the intdos function to generate a DOS interrupt. Begin from within Turbo C++ with no windows open.

1. Press **Alt-F** and type **N** to create a new file.
2. Type the following:

```
#include <dos.h>

int  year, month, day, dayweek;
char *dayweekname, *monthname;
union REGS regs;

void main ()
    {
    regs.h.ah = 0x2A;
    intdos (&regs, &regs);

    year = regs.x.cx;
    month = regs.h.dh;
    day = regs.h.dl;
    dayweek = regs.h.al;

    switch (month)
        {
        case 1 : monthname = "January"; break;
        case 2 : monthname = "February"; break;
        case 3 : monthname = "March"; break;
```

Module 59

```
            case 4 : monthname = "April"; break;
            case 5 : monthname = "May"; break;
            case 6 : monthname = "June"; break;
            case 7 : monthname = "July"; break;
            case 8 : monthname = "August"; break;
            case 9 : monthname = "September"; break;
            case 10: monthname = "October"; break;
            case 11: monthname = "November"; break;
            case 12: monthname = "December"; break;
         }
      printf ("%s %d, %d\n", monthname, day, year);
      }
```

3. Press **Ctrl-F9** to run the program.
4. Press **Alt-F5** to view the program results. The program displays the current date.

    February 12, 1991

5. Press **Alt-F5** to return to the Turbo C++ editor.
6. Press **Alt-Spacebar** and type **C** and type **N** to clear the desktop.
7. Turn to Module 60 to continue the learning sequence.

Module 60
MANIPULATION ROUTINES

DESCRIPTION

The manipulation routines let you manipulate blocks of memory directly.

Function	Purpose
memccpy	Copy a block of bytes
memchr	Search for a character
memcmp	Compare two block lengths
memcpy	Copy a block of bytes
memicmp	Compares bytes of two character arrays
memmove	Copy a block of bytes
memset	Set a block of bytes
movedata	Copy bytes
movmem	Move a block of bytes
setmem	Set a value to a range of memory

APPLICATIONS

The manipulation routines require the <mem.h> header file to be included in your program. If there are any exceptions, they will list required header files.

Make sure that your memory ranges don't overlap; otherwise, unpredictable errors may result. You should only use these functions if you are an advanced C++ programmer and understand how IBM computers store data in memory.

memccpy( )

```
void *memccpy(void *d,const void *s,int c,size_t n);
```

The memccpy( ) function will copy n bytes from s to d until either n bytes have been copied or c is copied to d. If c was encountered, a pointer to the byte after c will be returned, otherwise NULL will be returned.

memccpy( ) differs from memcpy( ) because memccpy( ) will stop if a certain character is encountered.

memchr( )

```
void *memchr(const void *s,int c,size_t n);
```

The memchr( ) function searches n bytes of s for c. If memchr( ) finds c it will return a pointer to c; otherwise, NULL will be returned.

memcmp( )

```
int memcmp(const void *b1,const void *b2,size_t n);
```

The memcmp( ) function compares n bytes of b1 against n bytes of b2. It will return a value:

    < 0   if b1 < b2
    == 0   if b1 == b2
    > 0   if b1 > b2

memcpy( )

```
void *memcpy(void *d,const void *s,size_t n);
```

The memcpy( ) function will copy n bytes of s to d. It will return a pointer to d.

memccpy( ) differs from memcpy( ) because memccpy( ) will stop if a certain character is encountered.

memicmp( )

```
int memicmp(const void *b1,const void *b2,size_t n);
```

The memicmp( ) function will compare b1 to b2 for n bytes without case sensitivity. The return values are the same as memcmp( ).

memmove( )

```
void *memmove(const void *d,const void *s,size_t n);
```

The memmove( ) function will move n bytes of s to d. Overlapping regions don't bother this function.

memset( )

```
void *memset(void *b,int c,size_t n);
```

The memset( ) function sets n bytes of b to c and returns a pointer to b.

movedata( )

```
void movedata(unsigned ss,unsigned so,unsigned ds,unsigned do,size_t n);
```

The movedata( ) function will move n bytes from ss:so to ds:do, where ss is the source segment, so is the source offset, ds is the destination segment, do is the destination offset, and n is the number of bytes to be moved. This provides a memory model independent method of transferring memory ranges to any part of the computer.

movmem( )

```
void movmem(void *s,void *d,unsigned n);
```

The movmem( ) function will move n bytes from s to d. Overlapping regions don't bother this function.

setmem( )

```
void setmem(void *b,unsigned n,char c);
```

The setmem( ) function sets n bytes of b to c.

TYPICAL OPERATION

In this program, you manipulate strings stored in memory. Begin from within Turbo C++ with no windows open.

1. Press **Alt-F** and type **N** to create a new file.
2. Type the following:

```c
#include <mem.h>
#include <stdio.h>

void main()
    {
    char b1[] = "Hello world";
    char b2[] = "Hello world";

    printf("\tb1 [%s]\n",b1);
    printf("\tb2 [%s]\n",b2);

    if(memcmp(b1,b2,3) == 0)
        printf("\tb1 and b2 are the same\n");
    else
        printf("\tb1 and b2 are not the same\n");

    memset(b1,'A',3);
    printf("After being set\n");
    printf("\tb1 [%s]\n",b1);

    if(memcmp(b1,b2,3) == 0)
        printf("\tb1 and b2 are the same\n");
    else
        printf("\tb1 and b2 are not the same\n");

    printf("Final contents\n");
    printf("\tb1 [%s]\n",b1);
    printf("\tb2 [%s]\n",b2);
    }
```

3. Press **Ctrl-F9** to run the program.
4. Press **Alt-F5** to view the program results.

   ```
         b1 [Hello world]
         b2 [Hello world]
         b1 and b2 are the same
   After being set
         b1 [AAAlo world]
         b1 and b2 are not the same
   Final contents
         b1 [AAAlo world]
         b2 [Hello world]
   ```

5. Press **Alt-F5** to return to the Turbo C++ editor.
6. Press **Alt-Spacebar** and type **C** and type **N** to clear the desktop.
7. Turn to Module 61 to continue the learning sequence.

Module 61
MATH ROUTINES

DESCRIPTION
The math routines provide many standard math functions:

Function	Purpose
abs	Absolute value of an integer value
acos	Arc cosine
arg	Complex plane number
asin	Arc sine
atan	Arc tangent
atan2	Arc tangent y/x
cabs	Absolute value of a complex value
ceil	Round a value up to the next integer
_clear87	Clear math coprocessor
complex	Create complex number
conj	Complex conjugate
_control87	Control math coprocessor
cos	Cosine
cosh	Hyperbolic cosine
div	Integer division with div_t result
exp	e to the x
fabs	Absolute value of a double value
floor	Round a value down to the next integer
fmod	x % y (x modulo y)
_fpreset	Reset math coprocessor
frexp	Split a double into mantissa and exponent
hypot	Hypotenuse of right triangle
imag	Imaginary part of complex number
labs	Absolute value of a long value
ldexp	Mantissa times 2 to the exponent
ldiv	x/y (division of longs)
log	Natural logarithm
log10	Logarithm
lrotl	Rotate an unsigned long integer left by a specific number of bits
_lrotr	Rotate an unsigned long integer right by a specific number of bit

modf	Split a value to an integer and fractional part
norm	Magnitude of a complex number
polar	Create complex number from polar
poly	Generate polynomial from args
pow	Computes value of x to the y power
pow10	Computes 10 to the x power
rand	Random number generator between 0 and 32,767
random	Random number generator between 0 and a specified number
randomize	Initialize random number generator from current time
real	Real part of a complex number
_rotl	Rotate an unsigned integer left by a specific number of bits
_rotr	Rotate an unsigned integer right by a specific number of bits
sin	Sine
sinh	Hyperbolic sine
sqrt	Square root of a value
srand	Initialize the random number generator with a specific value
_status87	Math coprocessor status
tan	Tangent
tanh	Hyperbolic tangent

APPLICATIONS

These functions implement many of the common math functions. There are also complex number versions of many of these routines (you can find out which ones by looking at complex.h). These are not explicitly mentioned in this table but are mentioned elsewhere. They are used similarly to these functions.

If you pass a value which is out of the range of a function, the function will return NAN (Not a Number) and set errno to EDOM (Domain error).

If a function returns a value which overflows, the value +HUGE_VAL or –HUGE_VAL will be returned as appropriate. The global variable errno will also be set to ERANGE (range error).

abs( )

```
#include <math.h>        // the function version of abs()
#include <stdlib.h>      // the macro version of abs()

int abs(int x);          // ANSI version
```

The abs( ) function returns the absolute value of an integer. There is a bug in the int version of abs( ): it returns –32,768 when –32,768 is passed to it (+32,768 should be returned, but the number exceeds the range of an int).

If you want the absolute value of a float (or double) you should use fabs( ). If you want the absolute value of a long you should use labs( ). There is also cabs( ) which provides the absolute value of a complex number (not the abs( ) which is overloaded for complex class—the cabs( ) complex is a structure).

acos( )

```
#include <math.h>

double acos(double x);
```

The acos( ) function returns the arc cosine of x. The acos( ) function can only accept numbers in the range of 1 to −1 and will return a value between 0 and pi.

arg( )

```
#include <complex.h>

double arg(complex x);
```

The arg( ) function returns the angle (in radians) of a number in the complex plane. In the complex plane, the positive real axis has an angle of 0 radians, while the imaginary axis has an angle of pi/2 radians. Complex 0 has an angle of 0 radians.

asin( )

```
#include <math.h>

double asin(double x);
```

The asin( ) function returns the arc sine of x. The asin( ) function can only accept numbers in the range of 1 to −1 and will return a value between −pi/2 and pi/2.

atan( )

```
#include <math.h>

double atan(double x);
```

The atan( ) function returns the arc tangent of x. The atan( ) function can only accept numbers in the range of 1 to −1 and will return a value between −pi/2 and pi/2.

atan2( )

```
#include <math.h>

double atan2(double y,double x);
```

The atan2( ) function returns the arc tangent of y/x. The atan2( ) function cannot accept both arguments being 0 (atan2(0,0)) (it will return NAN and set errno to EDOM). atan2( ) will otherwise return a value between −pi and pi.

cabs( )

#include <math.h>

double cabs(struct complex x);

The cabs( ) function takes the complex number x and returns the absolute value of it as a double.

ceil( )

#include <math.h>

double ceil(double x);

The ceil( ) function takes x and returns the next integer up (it rounds x up to the next nearest integer).

_clear87( )

#include <float.h>

unsigned int _clear87(void);

The _clear87( ) function clears the floating point status word (clearing the status of the math coprocessor). The return value is the status before it was cleared. The previous status can be computed by using the following constants:

8087/80287 Status Word format

```
SW_INVALID       0x0001     // Invalid operation
SW_DENORMAL      0x0002     // Denormalized operand
SW_ZERODIVIDE    0x0004     // Division by Zero
SW_OVERFLOW      0x0008     // Overflow
SW_UNDERFLOW     0x0010     // Underflow
SW_INEXACT       0x0020     // Inexact result (Precision Error)
```

8087/80287 Control Word format

```
MCW_EM           0x003f     // Interrupt Exception Masks
EM_INVALID       0x0001     //    Invalid operation
EM_DENORMAL      0x0002     //    Denormalized operand
EM_ZERODIVIDE    0x0004     //    Division by zero
EM_OVERFLOW      0x0008     //    Overflow
EM_UNDERFLOW     0x0010     //    Underflow
EM_INEXACT       0x0020     //    Inexact Result (Precision Error)

MCW_IC           0x1000     // Infinity Control
IC_AFFINE        0x1000     //    Affine
IC_PROJECTIVE    0x0000     //    Projective

MCW_RC           0x0c00     // Rounding Control
```

```
RC_CHOP        0x0c00    //  Chop
RC_UP          0x0800    //  Up
RC_DOWN        0x0400    //  Down
RC_NEAR        0x0000    //  Near

MCW_PC         0x0300    //  Precision Control
PC_24          0x0000    //     24 Bit Precision
PC_53          0x0200    //     53 Bit Precision
PC_64          0x0300    //     64 Bit Precision
```

complex( )

#include <complex.h>

complex complex(double r,double i);

The complex( ) function takes two double arguments and creates a complex class variable from them (using r for the real part of the complex number and i for the imaginary part of the complex number). complex( ) will only work with C++ (since it works with classes), so it is not portable.

conj( )

#include <complex.h>

double conj(complex x);

The conj( ) function takes the complex class variable x and returns the complex conjugate as a double. Like the other functions described in complex.h, it is a C++ function and is not portable.

_control87( )

#include <float.h>

unsigned int _control87(unsigned int new, unsigned int mask);

The _control87( ) function takes a new unsigned int and a mask unsigned and uses them to set certain modes of the math coprocessor to mask (or unmask) floating point exception errors. _control87( ) will then return the new floating point control word. For a summary of the values, see _clear87( ) above.

If you want to change a bit you'll have to make sure that both the mask AND the new value have a one in that bit (the mask will be ANDed to the new value).

cos( )

#include <math.h>

double cos(double x);

Module 61

The cos( ) function takes a double x and returns the cosine of x. The argument is specified in radians and the return value is in the range of −1 to 1.

cosh( )

```
#include <math.h>

double cosh(double x);
```

The cosh( ) function takes a double x and returns the hyperbolic cosine of x. The argument is specified in radians.

div( )

```
#include <stdlib.h>

div_t div(int x,int y);
```

The div( ) function divides x by y and returns the result in a div_t typedefined structure which is defined as:

```
typedef struct
{
int quot;        /* quotient */
int rem;         /* remainder */
} div_t;
```

This function lets you get both a quotient and a remainder simultaneously (as opposed to the / operator which limits you to the quotient and the % operator which limits you to the remainder).

exp( )

```
#include <math.h>

double exp(double x)
```

The exp( ) function takes the double x and returns the exponential of it (e to the x). If exp( ) underflows, it will return 0.0 and errno will not be set.

fabs( )

```
#include <math.h>

double fabs(double x);
```

The fabs( ) function returns the absolute value of x.

floor( )

```
#include <math.h>

double floor(double x);
```

The floor( ) function takes x and returns the next integer down (it rounds x down to the next nearest integer).

fmod( )

```
#include <math.h>

double fmod(double x,double y);
```

The fmod( ) function modulos x and y (x%y). Modulo is the remainder of a division.

_fpreset( )

```
#include <float.h>

void _fpreset(void);
```

The _fpreset( ) function resets the floating point package and should be used after system( ), exec*( ), or spawn*( ) function calls on machines with math coprocessors. As an additional precaution, you should make sure that all math coprocessor execution has concluded before using system( ), exec*( ), and spawn*( ).

frexp( )

```
#include <math.h>

double frexp(double x,int *exp);
```

The frexp( ) function splits a double x into its mantissa (which is returned) and its exponent (which is directly modified).

hypot( )

```
#include <math.h>

double hypot(double x,double y);
```

The hypot( ) function returns the length of a hypotenuse given the sides x and y on a right triangle.

imag( )

```
#include <complex.h>

double imag(complex x);
```

The imag( ) function takes a complex number, x, and returns the imaginary part as a double. The imag( ) function requires C++ and is not portable.

Module 61

labs( )

    #include <math.h>   // also in stdlib.h

    long labs(long x);

The labs( ) function returns the absolute value of argument x. If there is an error, there will be no error return value.

ldexp( )

    #include <math.h>

    double ldexp(double x,int exp);

The ldexp( ) function returns x times 2 to the exp where x is a double and exp is an integer.

ldiv( )

    #include <stdlib.h>

    ldiv_t ldiv(long x,long y);

The ldiv( ) function divides x by y (x/y) and returns a ldiv_t structure:

```
typedef struct
{
long quot;        /* quotient */
long rem;         /* remainder */
} ldiv_t;
```

This function lets you get both a quotient and a remainder simultaneously (as opposed to the / operator which limits you to the quotient and the % operator which limits you to the remainder).

log( )

    #include <math.h>

    double log(double x);

The log( ) function returns the natural logarithm (ln( )) of x. The argument x must be greater than 0.

log10( )

    #include <math.h>

    double log10(double x);

The log10( ) function returns the base 10 logarithm (log( )) of x. The argument x must be greater than 0.

_lrotl( )

#include <stdlib.h>

unsigned long _lrotl(unsigned long x,int count);

The _lrotl( ) function will return x rotated count bits to the left.

_lrotr( )

#include <stdlib.h>

unsigned long _lrotr(unsigned long x,int count);

The _lrotr( ) function will return x rotated count bits to the right.

modf( )

#include <math.h>

double modf(double x,double *intpart);

The modf( ) function will split the argument x, returning the fractional part and putting the integer part of x into the variable pointed at by intpart.

norm( )

#include <complex.h>

double norm(complex x);

The norm( ) function returns the magnitude (square of the absolute value) of x. It requires C++ and is not portable.

polar( )

#include <complex.h>

complex polar(double magnitude, double angle);

poly( )

#include <math.h>

double poly(double x,int degree,double coeffs[ ]);

The poly( ) function generates a polynomial in x at degree using the coefficients in coeff.

pow( )

#include <math.h>

double pow(double x, double y);

Module 61

The pow( ) function returns x to the y power. If x is less than zero and y is not a whole number, errno will be set to EDOM (Domain error).

pow10( )

```
#include <math.h>

double pow10(int x);
```

The pow10( ) function returns 10 to the x power.

rand( )

```
#include <stdlib.h>

int rand(void);
```

The rand( ) function returns a pseudorandom number generated in the range of 0 to RAND_MAX. It will repeat the pseudorandom number sequence every 2 to the 32 numbers. To initialize the pseudorandom number generator, use randomize( ). To get a number in the range of 0 to (n-1), use random( ). (You can get a number in the range of 1-100 by adding 1 to the result of random(100).)

random( )

```
#include <stdlib.h>

int random(int x);
```

The random( ) macro returns a pseudorandom number generated in the range of 0 to x-1. Since random( ) uses rand( ), it will repeat every 2 to the 32 numbers. To initialize the pseudorandom number generator use randomize( ). You can get a number in the range of 1-100 by using random(100)+1. You can get a number in the range of 0-99 by using random(100).

randomize( )

```
#include <time.h>
#include <stdlib.h>

void randomize(void);
```

The randomize( ) macro initializes ("seeds") the pseudorandom number generator by using the current time. You should seed the pseudorandom number generator to lessen the probability of having the same numerical sequence from occurring again. For example, video games which rely on random numbers will often begin with the same "pattern." This is because the pseudorandom number generator was not properly initialized to allow different initial patterns.

real( )

    #include <complex.h>

    double real(complex x);

The real( ) function returns the real part of the complex number x. It is a C++ function and is not portable.

The real( ) function can also convert BCD numbers into float, double, or long double types.

_rotl( )

    #include <stdlib.h>

    unsigned _rotl(unsigned x,int c);

The _rotl( ) function rotates the value x c bits to the left. It is similar to a left shift (<<) except the high bit is rotated to the low bit position.

_rotr( )

    #include <stdlib.h>

    unsigned _rotr(unsigned x,int c);

The _rotr( ) function rotates the value x c bits to the right. It is similar to a right shift (>>) except the low bit is rotated to the high bit position.

sin( )

    #include <math.h>

    double sin(double x);

The sin( ) function returns the sine of x (assumed to be in radians).

sinh( )

    #include <math.h>

    double sinh(double x);

The sinh( ) function returns the hyperbolic sine of x (assumed to be in radians).

sqrt( )

    #include <math.h>

    double sqrt(double x);

The sqrt( ) function returns the positive square root of x. Negative numbers generate an EDOM (Domain error).

srand( )

```
#include <stdlib.h>

void srand(unsigned x);
```

The srand( ) function initializes the pseudorandom number generator with the value x. If x is 1, the pseudorandom number generator will be reinitialized. If a specific value is to be used to seed the pseudorandom number generator, it can be passed instead. This lets you test a program which relies on pseudorandom numbers by having the same range of numbers repeat.

_status87( )

```
#include <float.h>

unsigned _status87(void);
```

The _status87( ) function returns the math coprocessor status word. The bit flags used by _status87( ) are described in _clear87( ).

tan( )

```
#include <math.h>

double tan(double x);
```

The tan( ) function returns the tangent of x (assumed to be in radians).

tanh( )

```
#include <math.h>

double tanh(double x);
```

The tanh( ) function returns the hyperbolic tangent of x (assumed to be in radians).

TYPICAL OPERATION

In this program, you use the sin, cos, and tan functions. Begin from within Turbo C++ with no windows open.

1. Press **Alt-F** and type **N** to create a new file.
2. Type the following:

```
#include <math.h>
#define PI    3.14159
#define MAX   50

void main()
    {
    double  radians, sine, cosine, tangent;
```

```
int     degrees;

degrees = 44;
printf ("Degrees    Radians    Sine    Cosine    Tangent\n");
while (degrees++ < MAX)
  {
  radians = (double) ((degrees * PI) / 180);
  sine = sin(radians);
  cosine = cos(radians);
  tangent = tan(radians);
  printf ("  %d         %2.2lf", degrees, radians);
  printf ("        %1.3lf     %1.3lf      %1.3lf\n", sine,cosine,tangent);
  }
}
```

3. Press **Ctrl-F9** to run the program.
4. Press **Alt-F5** to view the program results.

Degrees	Radians	Sine	Cosine	Tangent
45	0.79	0.707	0.707	1.000
46	0.80	0.719	0.695	1.036
47	0.82	0.731	0.682	1.072
48	0.84	0.743	0.669	1.111
49	0.86	0.755	0.656	1.150
50	0.87	0.766	0.643	1.192

5. Press **Alt-F5** to return to the Turbo C++ editor.
6. Press **Alt-Spacebar** and type **C** and type **N** to clear the desktop.
7. Turn to Module 62 to continue the learning sequence.

Module 62
MEMORY ALLOCATION AND CHECKING ROUTINES

DESCRIPTION

Function	Purpose
allocmem	Allocate a dos segment
brk	Set a new break value
calloc	Clear and allocate memory
coreleft	Available memory
farcalloc	Clear and allocate far memory
farcoreleft	Available memory
farfree	Frees a far memory block
farheapcheck	Check the far heap
farheapcheckfree	Check free blocks in far heap
farheapchecknode	Check block n in far heap
farheapfillfree	Fill free blocks in far heap
farheapwalk	Walk the far heap
farmalloc	Allocate far memory
farrealloc	Reallocate far memory
free	Frees a near memory block
freemem	Frees a dos segment
heapcheck	Check the heap
heapcheckfree	Check free blocks in heap
heapchecknode	Check block n in heap
heapfillfree	Fill free blocks in heap
heapwalk	Walk the heap
malloc	Allocate memory
realloc	Reallocate memory
sbrk	Set new break value
setblock	Realloc dos seg

APPLICATIONS

The memory allocation routines require #include <alloc.h>. Exceptions will have the required header files listed.

allocmem( )

```
#include <dos.h>

int allocmem(unsigned s,unsigned *seg);
```

The allocmem( ) function sets seg to point to an allocated segment of memory s paragraphs (16 bytes=1 paragraph) long. If successful, allocmem( ) will return −1, if there is an error (not enough memory), allocmem( ) will return the number of available blocks.

brk( )

```
int brk(void *a);
```

The brk( ) function lets you reassign the break value to a, extending the program's data segment to a. If this extension is successful, brk( ) will return 0; otherwise, it will return −1.

calloc( )

```
#include <stdlib.h>

void *calloc(size_t n,size_t s);
```

The calloc( ) function allocates n s-sized pieces of memory and clears them to 0. A pointer to the beginning of allocated memory is returned if calloc( ) is successful; otherwise, NULL is returned.

In small, tiny, and medium memory models, calloc( ) will only use memory from the current data segment. To get more memory than that you must use farcalloc( ).

coreleft( )

```
unsigned coreleft(void);         // in small, tiny, and medium models
unsigned long coreleft(void);    // in other memory models
```

The coreleft( ) function returns the amount of unallocated memory. If your program is a small, tiny, or medium model program, coreleft( ) will only report on the amount of memory available in the current data segment. The farcoreleft( ) will tell you how much memory is really available in your machine.

farcalloc( )

```
void far *farcalloc(unsigned long n,unsigned long s);
```

The farcalloc( ) function allocates n s-sized pieces of memory and clears them to 0. A pointer to the beginning of the allocated memory is returned if farcalloc( ) is successful; otherwise, NULL is returned.

Module 62

In huge, compact, and large models, calloc( ) acts like farcalloc( ), except farcalloc( ) requires unsigned long arguments while calloc( ) uses unsigned arguments. If you plan on creating a .COM file, you can't use farcalloc( ) in that program.

farcoreleft( )

    unsigned long farcoreleft(void);

The farcoreleft( ) function returns the amount of memory available — not only in the current data segment but in all of RAM. The coreleft( ) function will do the same thing if you are in the compact, large, or huge model. If you plan on creating a .COM file, you can't use a farcalloc( ) in that program.

farfree( )

    void farfree(void far *b);

The farfree( ) function will deallocate (free) the memory pointed to by b. If you are writing a small or medium model program, farfree( ) can only free memory allocated by farmalloc( ) family of functions; free( ) frees memory allocated by malloc( ). If you plan on creating a .COM file, you can't use farfree( ) in that program.

farheapcheck( )

    int farheapcheck(void);

The farheapcheck( ) function will examine the far heap for any inconsistencies. It will return a positive value if the heap is consistent; otherwise, it will return a negative value. Return values are typically:

Symbolic Name	Description
_HEAPEMPTY	There is no heap in use
_HEAPOK	The heap is consistent — no errors
_HEAPCORRUPT	The heap is inconsistent — there are errors.

farheapcheckfree( )

    int farheapcheckfree(unsigned f);

The farheapcheckfree( ) function will examine the free blocks in the far heap to see if they contain f. If the free blocks contain some value other than f, _BADVALUE will be returned. farheapcheckfree( ) may also return _HEAPEMPTY, _HEAPOK, and _HEAPCORRUPT, as described in farheapcheck( ).

farheapchecknode( )

    int farheapchecknode(void *n);

The farheapchecknode( ) function will check a single node (block of memory) for inconsistencies. It can return the following:

Symbolic Name	Description
_HEAPEMPTY	There is no heap in use
_HEAPCORRUPT	The heap is inconsistent — there are errors.
_BADNODE	Unable to find node n
_FREEENTRY	The node is free
_USEDENTRY	The node is currently in use

farheapfillfree( )

```
int farheapfillfree(unsigned f);
```

The farheapfillfree( ) function will fill _FREEENTRYs with f. The return values are the same as farheapcheck( ).

farheapwalk( )

```
int farheapwalk(struct farheapinfo *i);
```

The farheapwalk( ) function walks the far heap, returning information concerning the current node. Successive calls will return information on succeeding nodes until the end of far heap is reached. The far heap must have been previously checked using farheapcheck( ) to prevent errors. If you try to farheapwalk( ) an empty far heap, _HEAPEMPTY will be returned. If a valid node is encountered, _HEAPOK will be returned. When the end of the far heap is encountered, _HEAPEND will be returned.

Before the first call to farheapwalk, the farheapinfo structure members need to be set properly. i.ptr should be set to NULL. After the first successful call, it will point to the current node.

i.size is the number of bytes used by the current node. i.in_use tells whether or not the block is free or in use (it will be nonzero if it is in use).

farmalloc( )

```
void far *farmalloc(unsigned long n);
```

The farmalloc( ) function allocates n bytes of far memory. If it is successful, it will return the address of the block; otherwise, it will return NULL. Blocks that are allocated with farmalloc( ) should be freed using farfree( ). If you plan on creating a .COM file, you can't use farmalloc( ) in that program.

farrealloc( )

```
void far *farrealloc(void far *b,unsigned long n);
```

The farrealloc( ) function is used to reallocate (adjust the size of) a block of memory, b, which has already been allocated to a length of n bytes. If farrealloc( ) was successful, it will return a pointer to the new block of memory (which might not be at the same address as your original farmalloc( )). If there is an error, NULL will be returned. If you plan on creating a .COM file, you can't use farrealloc( ) in that program.

free( )

    void free(void far *b);

The free( ) function will deallocate (free) the memory pointed to by b. If you are writing a small or medium model program, free( ) can only free memory allocated by the malloc( ) family of functions; farfree( ) frees memory allocated by farmalloc( ) in that program.

freemem( )

    int freemem(unsigned seg);

The freemem( ) function will deallocate (free) seg which was allocated using allocmem( ). If freemem( ) was successful, 0 will be returned. If there was an error, −1 will be returned.

heapcheck( )

    int heapcheck(void);

The heapcheck( ) function will examine the heap for any inconsistencies. It will return a positive value if the heap is consistent; otherwise, it will return a negative value. Return values are typically:

Symbolic Name	Description
_HEAPEMPTY	There is no heap in use
_HEAPOK	The heap is consistent — no errors
_HEAPCORRUPT	The heap is inconsistent — there are errors.

In compact, large, and huge memory models, heapcheck( ) is the same as farheapcheck( ).

heapcheckfree( )

    int heapcheckfree(unsigned f);

The heapcheckfree( ) function will examine the free blocks in the heap to see if they contain f. If the free blocks contain some value other than f, _BADVALUE will be returned. heapcheckfree( ) may also return _HEAPEMPTY, _HEAPOK, and _HEAPCORRUPT, as described in heapcheck( ). In compact, large, and huge memory models, heapcheckfree( ) is the same as farheapcheckfree( ).

heapchecknode( )

    int heapchecknode(void *n);

The heapchecknode( ) function will check a single node (block of memory) for inconsistencies. It can return the following:

Symbolic Name	Description
_HEAPEMPTY	There is no heap in use
_HEAPCORRUPT	The heap is inconsistent — there are errors.
_BADNODE	Unable to find node n
_FREEENTRY	The node is free
_USEDENTRY	The node is currently in use

In compact, large, and huge memory models, heapchecknode( ) is the same as farheapchecknode( ).

heapfillfree( )

    int heapfillfree(unsigned f);

The heapfillfree( ) function will fill _FREEENTRYs with f. The return values are the same as heapcheck( ). In compact, large, and huge memory models, heapfillfree( ) is the same as farheapfillfree( ).

heapwalk( )

    int heapwalk(struct heapinfo *i);

The heapwalk( ) function walks the heap, returning information concerning the current node. Successive calls will return information on succeeding nodes until the end of heap is reached. The heap must have been previously checked using heapcheck( ) to prevent errors. If you try to heapwalk( ) an empty heap, _HEAPEMPTY will be returned. If a valid node is encountered, _HEAPOK will be returned. When the end of the heap is encountered, _HEAPEND will be returned.

Before the first call to heapwalk, the heapinfo structure members need to be set properly. i.ptr should be set to NULL. After the first successful call, it will point to the current node.

i.size is the number of bytes used by the current node. i.in_use tells whether or not the block is free or in use (it will be nonzero if it is in use). In compact, large, and huge memory models, heapwalk( ) is the same as farheapwalk( ).

malloc( )

    void *malloc(size_t n);

The malloc( ) function allocates n bytes of memory. If it is successful, it will return the address of the block; otherwise, it will return NULL. Blocks that are allocated with

Module 62

malloc( ) should be freed using free( ). In compact, large, and huge memory model programs, malloc( ) is the same as farmalloc( ).

realloc( )

```
void *realloc(void *b,unsigned n);
```

The realloc( ) function is used to reallocate (adjust the size of) a block of memory, b, which has already been allocated, to a length of n bytes. If realloc( ) was successful, it will return a pointer to the new block of memory (which might not be at the same address as your original malloc( )). If there is an error, NULL will be returned.

sbrk( )

```
int sbrk(int n);
```

The sbrk( ) function lets you reassign the break value by n bytes, changing the program's data segment by n bytes. If this modification is successful, sbrk( ) will return the old break value; otherwise, it will return −1.

setblock( )

```
int setblock(unsigned seg,unsigned n);
```

The setblock( ) function is used to reallocate (adjust the size of) a dos segment, seg, which has already been allocated with the allocmem( ) function, to a length of n paragraphs. If setblock( ) was successful, it will return −1. If there is an error, it will return the size of the largest block of available memory in paragraphs.

TYPICAL OPERATION

In this program, you use memory allocation routines to see how they affect your computer's available memory. Begin from within Turbo C++ with no windows open.

1. Press **Alt-F** and type **N** to create a new file.
2. Type the following:

```
#include <alloc.h>
#include <stdlib.h>
#include <stdio.h>

void dispmem(void);
void error(const char *);

void error(const char *s)
{
    printf("%s\n",s);
    exit(1);
}
```

```c
void dispmem()
{
    unsigned unear;
    unsigned long ufar;

    unear=coreleft();
    ufar=farcoreleft();

    printf("%u bytes free in segment\n",unear);
    printf("%ul bytes free in far\n\n",ufar);
}

main()
{
    char *b1, *b2;
    char far *f1;

    printf("Before memory allocations\n");
    dispmem();
    if((b1=(char *)malloc(sizeof(char) * 4)) == NULL)
        error("Unable to allocate malloc 1\n");
    if((b2=(char *)calloc(4,sizeof(char))) == NULL)
        error("Unable to allocate calloc 1\n");
    printf("\nAfter malloc and calloc\n");
    printf("malloced memory: [%x%x%x%x]\n",b1[0],b1[1],b1[2],b1[3]);
    printf("calloced memory: [%x%x%x%x]\n",b2[0],b2[1],b2[2],b2[3]);
    dispmem();

    if((f1=(char far *)farmalloc(sizeof(char) * 4)) == NULL)
        error("Unable to allocate farmalloc 1\n");
    printf("\nChange after farmalloc\n");
    dispmem();

    farfree(f1);
    free(b2);
    free(b1);
    printf("\nChange after frees\n");
    dispmem();
}
```

3. Press **Ctrl-F9** to run the program.

NOTE
The following program results may look different, depending on the amount of memory your computer has.

4. Press **Alt-F5** to view the program results.

```
Before memory allocations
63328 bytes free in segment
```

Module 62

```
554881 bytes free in far


After malloc and calloc
malloced memory: [74686973]
calloced memory: [0000]
63312 bytes free in segment
554721 bytes free in far


Change after farmalloc
63312 bytes free in segment
554721 bytes free in far


Change after frees
63328 bytes free in segment
55488 bytes free in far
```

5. Press **Alt-F5** to return to the Turbo C++ editor.
6. Press **Alt-Spacebar** and type **C** and type **N** to clear the desktop.
7. Turn to Module 63 to continue the learning sequence.

Module 63
MISCELLANEOUS ROUTINES

DESCRIPTION

Function	Purpose
delay	Wait for t milliseconds
localeconv	Get locale information
longjmp	Jump to a designated point
nosound	Turn off speaker
setjmp	Create a longjmp( ) label
setlocale	Select a locale
sound	Turn on speaker

APPLICATIONS

delay( )

```
#include <dos.h>

void delay(unsigned t);
```

The delay( ) function halts program execution for t milliseconds.

localeconv( )

```
#include <locale.h>

struct lconv *localeconv(void);
```

The localeconv( ) function returns information on the current locale using a pointer to an lconv structure. The lconv structure looks like:

```
struct lconv
{
char *decimal_point;
char *thousands_sep;
char *grouping;
char *int_curr_symbol;
char *currency_symbol;
char *mon_decimal_point;
char *mon_thousands_sep;
char *mon_grouping;
char *positive_sign;
```

Module 63

```
    char *negative_sign;
    char int_frac_digits;
    char frac_digits;
    char p_cs_precedes;
    char p_sep_by_space;
    char n_cs_precedes;
    char n_sep_by_space;
    char p_sign_posn;
    char n_sign_posn;
};
```

longjmp( )

#include <setjmp.h>

void longjmp(jmp_buf j,int ret);

The longjmp( ) function returns to the setjmp( ) described by j, causing setjmp( ) to return the value ret (which can be any value except 0).

You must use setjmp( ) before using longjmp( ) (which you can think of as a "super goto"). You can't longjmp( ) to a location which has been set by setjmp( ) if the function containing the setjmp( ) has completed execution.

You also need to be careful of using longjmp( ) with overlays, since the overlay manager may not keep proper track of the stack (which will cause unpredictable errors).

nosound( )

#include <dos.h>

void nosound(void);

The nosound( ) function turns the speaker off. It is used to stop the note created by a sound( ) call. You can set the length of the note by using delay( ).

setjmp( )

#include <setjmp.h>

int setjmp(jmp_buf j);

The setjmp( ) function saves a return location for longjmp( ). It will return 0 when initially set and will return a nonzero when longjmp( ) returns to that location.

You must use setjmp( ) before using longjmp( ) (which you can think of as a "super goto"). You can't longjmp( ) to a location which has been set by setjmp( ) if the function containing the setjmp( ) has completed execution. You also need to be careful of using setjmp( ) with overlays, since the overlay manager may not keep proper track of the stack (which will cause all sorts of weird errors).

setlocale( )

    #include <locale.h>

    char *setlocale(int c,char *locale);

The setlocale( ) function is supposed to select a locale and return the name of the previous locale. Turbo C++ only supports the "C" locale at this time, so this function doesn't really have any effect — it was included for ANSI compatibility (it really works in most ANSI Cs).

sound( )

    #include <dos.h>

    void sound(unsigned hz);

The sound( ) function turns the speaker on, causing a note of hz Hz to come out (if your speaker can generate that frequency). Once you start the note, you have to stop it using the nosound( ) function. You can set the length of the note by using delay( ).

TYPICAL OPERATION

In this program, you use the setjmp and longjmp functions along with the sound, nosound, and delay functions. Begin from within Turbo C++ with no windows open.

1. Press **Alt-F** and type **N** to create a new file.
2. Type the following:

```
#include <stdio.h>
#include <setjmp.h>
#include <dos.h>

#define HIGHER 20

void testme();
jmp_buf error_env;

void main()
    {
    int frequency;

    if (setjmp(error_env) != 0)
      {
      printf ("Arrived here from longjmp call\n");
      abort();
      }
    for (frequency = 440; frequency <= 900; frequency += HIGHER)
      {
      sound (frequency);
```

Module 63

```
            delay (100);
            nosound();
            delay (100);
            }
        testme();
        printf ("End of main program\n");
        }

    void testme()
        {
        printf ("Calling longjmp function\n");
        longjmp (error_env, 1);
        }
```

3. Press **Ctrl-F9** to run the program. The program makes several noises before returning you to the Turbo C++ editor.

4. Press **Alt-F5** to view the program results.

        Calling longjmp function
        Arrived here from longjmp call
        Abnormal program termination

Notice that the program never reaches the last statement in the main function, printf ("End of main program\n"), because the abort( ) function is reached first.

5. Press **Alt-F5** to return to the Turbo C++ editor.
6. Press **Alt-Spacebar** and type **C** and type **N** to clear the desktop.
7. Turn to Module 64 to continue the learning sequence.

Module 64
PROCESS CONTROL ROUTINES

DESCRIPTION

The process routines let you control processes (programs which are running) from Turbo C++.

Function	Purpose
abort	Abort program execution
execl	Execute a program by overlaying the parent process
execle	
execlp	
execlpe	
execv	
execve	
execvp	
execvpe	
_exit	Terminate current process without cleanup
exit	Terminate current process with cleanup
getpid	Get the current process ID
raise	Send signal to the current process
signal	Implement signal handler
spawnl	Execute a program by creating a new process and running the program
spawnle	
spawnlp	
spawnlpe	
spawnv	
spawnve	
spawnvp	
spawnvpe	

APPLICATIONS

abort( )

```
#include <process.h>

void abort(void);
```

The abort( ) function will terminate execution of the current program, returning a value of 3 to the calling program or operating system. It will also print the message
```
Abnormal program termination
```
to stderr. It aborts by calling the _exit( ) function described below.

The exec*( ) family of functions

The exec*( ) family of functions will load another program into memory, possibly overlaying the current (or parent) process, and then start execution of that program. It may be used to run programs that are too large to run in memory in parts, or it can be used to transfer control to other programs. The suffixes to exec describe the following features:

p	When looking for program, start in the current directory, and if program is not found there, look down the DOS PATH variable.
l	Pass a fixed number of arguments to program.
v	Pass a variable number of arguments to program.
e	Pass e, a pointer to an environment, to the child process. If you do not pass an environment, the child process will inherit the environment from the parent process.

The exec*( ) family of functions needs to have at least one argument passed (regardless of whether you're using fixed or variable arguments). The first argument (arg0) should be the name of the program (the same value as program). You should terminate variable arguments with a null (argv[n+1] should be NULL). The combined length of the arguments cannot exceed 128 bytes.

The env variable should be an array of character pointers. The strings which the pointers reference should be of the form:
```
var = value
```
Where var is an environment value (like PROMPT or PATH) and value is the value to which the environment value should be set. The last element of env should be NULL. If you pass a NULL env, the child process will inherit the parent's environment.

The exec*( ) family of functions will return nothing if the exec was successful. If there is an error, exec*( ) will return –1 and errno will be set to one of the following:

E2BIG	The argument list was too big
EACCES	Permission denied
EMFILE	Too many open files
ENOENT	Path or filename not found
ENOEXEC	Exec format error
ENOMEM	Not enough memory

execl( )

#include <process.h>

int execl(char *program,char *arg0,*arg1,...,*argn,NULL);

The execl( ) function executes program (found in the current directory) using a fixed number of arguments which are terminated by a NULL as the last argument.

execle( )

#include <process.h>

int execle(char *program,char *arg0,*arg1,...,*argn,char **env);

The execle( ) function executes the program (found in the current directory) using a fixed number of arguments, passing an environment as the final argument.

execlp( )

#include <process.h>

int execlp(char *program,char *arg0,*arg1,...,*argn,NULL);

The execlp( ) function executes the program (either in the current directory or in a directory on the PATH environment variable) using a fixed number of arguments which are terminated by a NULL as the last argument.

execlpe( )

#include <process.h>

int execlpe(char *program,char *arg0,*arg1,...,*argn,char **env);

The execlpe( ) function executes the program (either in the current directory or in a directory on the PATH environment variable) using a fixed number of arguments which are terminated by a NULL as the last argument.

execv( )

#include <process.h>

int execv(char *program, char *argv[]);

The execv( ) function executes the program (found in the current directory) using a variable number of arguments which are in the array of character pointers, argv. The last element of argv must be NULL.

execve( )

#include <process.h>

int execve(char *program, char *argv[],char **env);

The execve( ) function executes the program (found in the current directory) using a variable number of arguments which are in the array of character pointers, argv. The last element of argv must be NULL. The final argument is an environment.

execvp( )

#include <process.h>

int execvp(char *program, char *argv[]);

The execv( ) function executes the program (either in the current directory or in a directory in the PATH environment variable) using a variable number of arguments which are in the array of character pointers, argv. The last element of argv must be NULL.

execvpe( )

#include <process.h>

int execvpe(char *program, char *argv[],char **env);

The execvpe( ) function executes the program (either in the current directory or in a directory in the PATH environment variable) using a variable number of arguments which are in the array of character pointers, argv. The last element of argv must be NULL. The final argument is an environment.

_exit( )

#include <process.h>   // or <stdlib.h>

void _exit(int status);

The _exit( ) function terminates the current process without doing any housekeeping (like closing files). _exit( ) will return status as the current process's exit status. Programs normally have a status of 0 if they terminate correctly; a nonzero value implies an error.

exit( )

#include <process.h>   // or <stdlib.h>

void exit(int status);

The exit( ) function terminates the current process after doing housekeeping (like closing files). It will also execute any exit functions which have been set up by atexit( ). exit( ) will return status as the current process's exit status. Programs normally have a status of 0 if they terminate correctly; a nonzero value implies an error.

getpid( )

```
#include <process.h>

unsigned getpid(void);
```

The getpid( ) function was originally designed to return the unique process ID (PID) that was used by each process in UNIX. Since DOS isn't multitasking, it doesn't use PIDs to identify each process. But the PSP of each process is unique, so getpid( ) has been modified to return the PSP of the current process instead of returning the PID.

raise( )

```
#include <signal.h>

int raise(int signal);
```

The raise( ) function sends signal to the current process. If the current process has an active signal handler, it will be invoked; otherwise, the default action for that specific interrupt will be executed.

The signals that are recognized are:

SIGABRT	Abort Execution	(not DOS)
SIGFPE	Floating Point Error	
SIGILL	Illegal Instruction	(186 up)
SIGINT	Control-Break Interrupt	
SIGSEGV	Segment Violation	(186 up)
SIGTERM	Process termination request	(not DOS)

(not DOS)   not normally generated by DOS or Turbo C++. Must be explicitly generated by program.

(186 up)   Not available on 8086, 8088, and compatible chips. Available on 186, 286, 386, (etc.), and compatible chips.

The raise( ) function returns 0 if successful; otherwise, it will return a nonzero result.

signal( )

```
#include <signal.h>

void (*signal(int sig, void (*func)(int sig[,int code])))(int);
```

Module 64

The signal( ) function is used to create signal handlers. The recognized signals are:

SIGABRT	Abort Execution	(not DOS)
SIGFPE	Floating Point Error	
SIGILL	Illegal Instruction	(186 up)
SIGINT	Control-Break Interrupt	
SIGSEGV	Segment Violation	(186 up)
SIGTERM	Process termination request	(not DOS)

(not DOS)   not normally generated by DOS or Turbo C++. Must be explicitly generated by program.

(186 up)   not available on 8086, 8088, and compatible chips. Available on 186, 286, 386, (etc.), and compatible chips.

The default (provided) signal handling functions are:

SIG_DFL	Default signal	Terminate program
SIG_IGN	Ignore signal	Ignores signal
SIG_ERR	Error signal	Return an error status

You can specify a signal handler by passing signal the signal that you want to handle and the name of the function which should handle the signal. For example, if you want to handle SIGINT with conclude( ), you could do so with the following call:

```
signal(SIGINT,conclude);
```

If signal is successful in replacing the default signal handler with the new handler, it will return a pointer to the previous signal handler; otherwise, it will return SIG_ERR and errno will be set to EINVAL.

The signal( ) function is used to prevent users from exiting programs without cleaning up after themselves. If you're using graphics, for example, you don't want the user to hit Ctrl-C and be left stranded in a high resolution graphics mode. By using signal, you can write a call like:

```
signal(SIGINT,clean_up_graphics);
```

and when the user presses Ctrl-C, your program will expertly clean up the screen and restore it to text mode.

The spawn*( ) family of functions

The spawn*( ) family of functions will load another program into memory, preserving the current (or parent) process, and then start execution of that program. It is used to temporarily run another program while leaving the current program in memory. The suffixes to spawn describe the following features:

p   When looking for program, start in the current directory, and if program is not found there, look down the DOS PATH variable.

l   Pass a fixed number of arguments to program.

v   Pass a variable number of arguments to program.
e   Pass e, a pointer to an environment, to the child process. If you do not pass an environment, the child process will inherit the environment from the parent process.

The spawn*( ) family of functions needs to have at least one argument passed (regardless of whether you're using fixed or variable arguments). The first argument (arg0) should be the name of the program (the same value as program). You should terminate variable arguments with a null (argv[n+1] should be NULL). The combined length of the arguments cannot exceed 128 bytes.

The mode describes what the parent process should do once the child process is created:

P_WAIT   The parent should wait until the child process finishes
P_NOWAIT   The parent should continue while child process runs
P_OVERLAY   The child will overlay the parent (same as exec*( ) family of functions).

Although P_NOWAIT is available, it will not work in Turbo C++ (since the operating system would need to be multitasking for it to work).

The env variable should be an array of character pointers. The strings which the pointers reference should be of the form:

    var = value

Where var is an environment value (like PROMPT or PATH) and value is the value to which the environment value should be set. The last element of env should be NULL. If you pass a NULL env, the child process will inherit the parent's environment.

The spawn*( ) family of functions will return nothing if the spawn was successful. If there is an error, spawn*( ) will return −1 and errno will be set to one of the following:

E2BIG   Argument list too big
EACCES   Permission denied
EMFILE   Too many open files
ENOENT   Path or filename not found
ENOEXEC   Exec format error
ENOMEM   Not enough memory

spawnl( )

    #include <process.h>

    int spawnl(int mode, char *program, char *arg0,*arg1,...,*argn,NULL);

The spawnl( ) function spawns a program (found in the current directory) using a fixed number of arguments which are terminated by a NULL as the last argument.

335

spawnle( )

    #include <process.h>

    int spawnle(int mode, char *program, char
    *arg0,*arg1,...,*argn,NULL,char**env);

The spawnle( ) function spawns the program (found in the current directory) using a fixed number of arguments, passing an environment as the final argument.

spawnlp( )

    #include <process.h>
    int spawnlp(int mode, char *program, char *arg0,*arg1,...,*argn,NULL);

The spawnlp( ) function spawns the program (either in the current directory or in a directory on the PATH environment variable) using a fixed number of arguments which are terminated by a NULL as the last argument.

spawnlpe( )

    #include <process.h>

    int spawnlpe(int mode,char *program,char *arg0,*arg1,...,*argn,NULL,char
    **env);

The spawnlpe( ) function spawns the program (either in the current directory or in a directory on the PATH environment variable) using a fixed number of arguments which are terminated by a NULL as the last argument.

spawnv( )

    #include <process.h>

    int spawnv(int mode,char *program,char *argv[]);

The spawnv( ) function spawns the program (found in the current directory) using a variable number of arguments which are in the array of character pointers, argv. The last element of argv must be NULL.

spawnve( )

    #include <process.h>

    int spawnve(int mode,char *program,char *argv[],char **env);

The spawnve( ) function spawns the program (found in the current directory) using a variable number of arguments which are in the array of character pointers, argv. The last element of argv must be NULL. The final argument is an environment.

spawnvp( )

```
#include <process.h>

int spawnvp(int mode,char *program,char *argv[]);
```

The spawnvp( ) function spawns the program (either in the current directory or in a directory in the PATH environment variable) using a variable number of arguments which are in the array of character pointers, argv. The last element of argv must be NULL.

spawnvpe( )

```
#include <process.h>

int spawnvpe(int mode,char *program,char *argv[],char **env);
```

The spawnvpe( ) function spawns the program (either in the current directory or in a directory in the PATH environment variable) using a variable number of arguments which are in the array of character pointers, argv. The last element of argv must be NULL. The final argument is an environment.

TYPICAL OPERATION

In this program, you experiment with both the exec and spawn functions. Begin from within Turbo C++ with no windows open.

1. Press **Alt-F** and type **N** to create a new file.
2. Type the following:
   ```
   void main( )
        {
        printf ("Hello, world!\n");
        }
   ```
3. Press **F2**. Turbo C++ displays a Save Editor File dialog box.
4. Type **HELLO** and press **Return**.
5. Press **Alt-C** and type **M** to create a HELLO.EXE file.
6. Press **Return**.
7. Press **Alt-F** and type **N** to create a new file.
8. Type the following:
   ```
   #include <process.h>
   #include <signal.h>
   #include <stdio.h>

   void conclude(void)
   {
       printf("That's all!\n");
   ```

```
}

int main(int argc,char **argv)
{
    signal(SIGABRT,conclude);
    if(argc > 3)
        abort();
    else if(argc > 2)
        raise(SIGABRT);
    printf("PID: [%p]\n",getpid());
    if(strcmp(argv[1],"exec") == 0)
        execlp("hello.exe","tree",NULL);
    else if(strcmp(argv[1],"spawn") == 0)
    {
        spawnlp(P_WAIT,"hello.exe","tree",NULL);
        printf("Thanks for waiting around for me...\n");
    }
    else
        exit(3);
    return(0);
}
```

9. Press **F2**. Turbo C++ displays a Save Editor File dialog box.
10. Type **PROCESS** and press **Return**.
11. Press **Alt-C**, type **M**, and press **Return** to create a PROCESS.EXE file.
12. Press **Alt-F** and type **D** to open the DOS shell. The DOS prompt appears.
13. Type **PROCESS EXEC** and press **Return**. The program displays results similar to the following:

    ```
    PID: [3E52]
        Hello, world!
    ```

14. Type **PROCESS SPAWN** and press **Return**. The program displays results similar to the following:

    ```
    PID: [3E52]
    Hello, world!
        Thanks for waiting around for me
    ```

15. Type **EXIT** and press **Return** to return to the Turbo C++ editor.
16. Press **Alt-Spacebar** and type **C** to clear the desktop.
17. Turn to Module 65 to continue the learning sequence.

Module 65
STANDARD ROUTINES

DESCRIPTION

Function	Purpose
atexit	Call a function on exit
bsearch	Binary search
getenv	Get an environment variable
lfind	Linear search
lsearch	Linear search
putenv	Put an environment variable
qsort	Quick sort
swab	Copy bytes with swap
system	Execute command from DOS

APPLICATIONS

atexit( )

```
#include <stdlib.h>

int atexit(atexit_t func);
```

The atexit( ) function attaches a function to the exit( ) function, ensuring that some action is done at the end of the program. Up to 32 functions can be set using the atexit( ) function—they will execute in last set-first executed order. If atexit( ) is unable to attach the function, it will return a nonzero value.

bsearch( )

```
#include <stdlib.h>

void *bsearch(const void *k,const void *b,size_t n,size_t w,int
(*f)(const void *,const void *));
```

The bsearch( ) function will do a binary search of sorted array b with n elements w wide for k using the f function to compare. Binary search is one of the fastest ways to find an item (although it can be a bit confusing for beginning programmers). bsearch( ) will return a pointer to the needed item or 0 if it can't find it.

Let's create a function which takes a table of nonclassical CDs and looks for a certain title. First we need a structure.

```
struct cd
{
char artist[31];
char title[31];
char import;
};
```

We'll need to create an array of them:

```
struct cd cdlist[10];     // create an array of 10 cds
```

and then we need to fill them in (this is done in the Typical Operation part of this module). Now let's write the code to find the "Who Man Four Says" album (this is the "key"—what we're searching for). We need a compare function (I called mine cdcomp( )—the code for it is also in Typical Operations). Now we get to the important part—an actual bsearch( ) call.

```
record = bsearch(&key,cdlist,numrecs,recwidth,cdcomp);
```

The address of the record containing our CD will be returned. Now reset the key to "Porcelin" by Julia Fordham. We don't have that in the table, so 0 is returned.

getenv( )

```
#include <stdlib.h>

char *getenv(char *s);
```

The getenv( ) function gets the value of an environment variable. There are a lot more environment variables in UNIX than in DOS, but you can modify the behavior of your program by having the user set an environment variable to a certain value.

To use getenv( ) you pass it the name of the environment variable (s) that you're looking for. If getenv( ) finds the string, it will return a pointer to a string containing the value of the environment variable. If it doesn't find the environment variable, getenv( ) will return a NULL string.

lfind( )

```
#include <stdlib.h>

void *lfind(const void *k,const void *a,size_t *n,size_t width, int
(*f)(const void *,const void *));
```

The lfind( ) function searches a linearly for k. The array a is defined as containing n items width wide. The function f is used to compare the key against the current item from the array. Unlike bsearch( ), the array a does not have to be sorted for lfind( ). lfind( ) returns a pointer to the first item in the array that matches key. If key does not exist in the array, 0 is returned. Function f is defined in the same way as the compare function in bsearch( ).

The difference between lfind( ) and lsearch( ) is that lsearch( ) will append a record to the end of the array with a value of key if that record was not found in the array.

lsearch( )

```
#include <stdlib.h>

void *lsearch(const void *k,const void *a,size_t *n,size_t w,
int (*f)(const void *,const void *));
```

The lsearch( ) function searches a linearly for k. The array a is defined as containing n items w wide. The function f is used to compare the key against the current item from the array. Unlike bsearch( ), the array a does not have to be sorted for lsearch( ). lsearch( ) returns a pointer to the first item in the array that matches key. If key does not exist in the array, 0 is returned and a record is appended to the array with a value of k. Function f is defined in the same way as the compare function in bsearch( ).

The difference between lsearch( ) and lfind( ) is that lsearch( ) will append a record to the end of the array with a value of key if that record was not found in the array.

putenv( )

```
#include <stdlib.h>

int putenv(const char *n);
```

The putenv( ) function will add the global or static string n to the environment of the current program (it will vanish after the current program finishes running).

The string n must adhere to the rules used by the DOS SET command and it must be global or static—strange things happen when you putenv( ) a dynamic string.

Environment variables can be 'deleted' by setting them to nothing (LIB=). Environment variables can also be modified by using an existing name and changing the associated value. putenv( ) will return −1 if there is an error; otherwise, it will return 0.

qsort( )

```
#include <stdlib.h>

void qsort(void *a,size_t n,size_t w,int (*f)(const void *,const void *));
```

The qsort( ) function will sort the contents of array a using the f function to determine the sort sequence. Array a is defined as having n items and being w chars wide.

swab( )

```
#include <stdlib.h>

void swab(char *s1,char *s2,int n);
```

The swab( ) function copies n (n must be even) bytes from s1 to s2 swapping each pair of bytes. This is necessary if you want to transfer int or float data between an Intel chip and a chip by any other manufacturer in the world (leave it to Intel to do things differently).

system( )

```
#include <stdlib.h>

int system(const char *command);
```

The system( ) command lets you issue a command to the operating system without leaving your C program. You can get the same effect by using one of the spawn*( ) family of functions. The command that you execute must be in the current directory or on one of the directories contained in your PATH environment variable. The operating system shell used in DOS is specified by COMSPEC—this is the shell that will be invoked by system( ).

system( ) will return −1 if there is an error, a 0 if everything goes OK.

TYPICAL OPERATION

In this program, you use the system function to run three DOS directory commands. Begin from within Turbo C++ with no windows open.

1. Press **Alt-F** and type **N** to create a new file.
2. Type the following:

```
#include <stdio.h>
#include <stdlib.h>
#include <string.h>
#include <conio.h>

void main()
    {
    char command[80];
    char *DOS[] = {"DIR /W",
                "DIR /P",
                "DIR"};
    int i;

    for (i = 0; i < 3; i++)
      {
      strcpy (command, DOS[i]);
```

```
            system (command);
            printf ("Now running the DOS %s command\n", DOS[i]);
            printf ("(Press the RETURN key to continue)\n");
            while (!kbhit());
         }
      }
```

3. Press **Ctrl-F9** to run the program. The program displays a wide view of the current directory using the DIR /W command.
4. Press **Return**. The program now displays the current directory using the DIR /P command. Depending on the number of files displayed on the screen, you might have to press **Return** several times until you see the message "Now running the DOS /P command."
5. Press **Return**. The program displays the current directory using the DIR command. Then it returns you to the Turbo C++ editor.
6. Press **Alt-Spacebar** and type **C** and type **N** to clear the desktop.
7. Turn to Module 66 to continue the learning sequence.

Module 66
STRING ROUTINES

DESCRIPTION

The string routines let you manipulate strings. The string routines are:

Function	Purpose
strcat	Concatenate one string to another
strchr	Find first occurrence of a character in a string
strcmp	Compare two strings
strcmpi	Compare two strings (case insensitive)
strcoll	Compare two strings (same as strcmp)
strcpy	Copy one string to another string
strcspn	Length of initial segment of a string not containing a given set of characters
strdup	Duplicate a string to another string
strerror	Return a string message for errno
stricmp	Function version of strcmpi( )
strlen	Length of a string
strlwr	Convert a string to lowercase
strncat	Concatenate a given number of characters to a string
strncmp	Compare part of one string to part of another string
strncmpi	Compare part of one string to part of another string (case insensitive)
strncpy	Copy a specific number of characters from one string to another
strnicmp	Function version of strncmpi( )
strnset	Sets a specified number of characters in a string to a given character
strpbrk	Find first occurrence of a character in a string
strrchr	Find last occurrence of a character in a string
strrev	Reverse the characters in a string
strset	Sets all characters in a string to a given character
strspn	Length of initial segment of a string with specific characters
strstr	Find first occurrence of a substring within a string
strtok	Find tokens
strupr	Convert a string to uppercase
strxfrm	Transform part of a string

APPLICATIONS

strcat( )

```
#include <string.h>     // prototype here

char *strcat(char *b, const char *a);
```

This function concatenates (appends) b to the end of a and returns the concatenated string.

```
char *first="M.F.K. Fisher's ";
char *second="Serve It Forth";
char result[31];

result = strcat(second,first);
printf("%s\n",result);
```

strchr( )

```
#include <string.h>     // prototype here

char *strchr(const char *s,int c);
```

strchr( ) finds the first occurrence of c in s and returns a pointer to the first occurrence of c in s. If c does not appear in s, a NULL is returned.

```
char *s = "Vigil in a Wilderness of Mirrors";
char c = 'V';
char *p;

if(p=strchr(s,c))
  printf("%c was found at %p in \"%s\"\n",c,p,s);
```

strcmp( )

```
#include <string.h>     // prototype here

int strcmp(const char *a,const char *b);
```

Compare a against b and return an int:

```
>0 if a > b
=0 if a == b
<0 if a < b
```

```
char *a="Xenophon";
char *b="Lucretius";
int result;

if((result=strcmp(a,b)) < 0)
   cout << a << " is less than " << b << "\n";
else if(result == 0)
```

345

Module 66

```
        cout << a << " is the same as " << b << "\n";
    else
        cout << a << "is greater than " << b << "\n";
```

strcmpi( )

```
    #include <string.h>        // Macro declaration here

    int strcmpi(const char *a,const char *b);
```

The strcmpi( ) macro compares a against b without case sensitivity (it doesn't differentiate uppercase and lowercase letters) and returns an int:

```
<0 if a < b
=0 if a == b
>0 if a > b

    char *a = "Lucretius";
    char *b = "LUCRETIUS";

    if(strcmp(a,b) != 0)
    {
    cout << "strcmp( ) can tell the difference between \"" << a;
    cout << "\" and \"" << b << "\"\n";
    }
    if(strcmpi(a,b) == 0)
       cout << "but strcmpi( ) can't!\n";
```

strcoll( )

```
    #include <string.h>        // Prototype here

    int strcoll(const char *a,const char *b);
```

strcoll( ) compares a against b. It's the same as strcmp( ). Same arguments, same return value, same example (just replace strcmp( ) with strcoll( )).

strcpy( )

```
    #include <string.h>        // Prototype here

    char *strcpy(char *b,const char *a);
```

strcpy( ) copies a to b and returns b. Most programmers ignore the returned string, but you may need it for some special purpose.

```
    char *a="James Joyce";
    char b[12];

    strcpy(b,a);
    cout << b << '\n';
```

String Routines

strcspn( )

```
#include <string.h>       // Prototype here
size_t strcspn(const char *a,const char *b);
```

strcspn( ) returns the length of the initial substring of a that doesn't contain characters in b.

```
char filename[MAXPATH]="USR\TXT\MISC\CALENDAR";
char filedelims[]=":\\/";
size_t delim_point;

delim_point = strcspn(filename,filedelims);
cout << "the first file delimiter was encountered at " << delim_point;
```

strdup( )

```
#include <string.h>       // Prototype here

char *strdup(const char *s);
```

strdup( ) duplicates a string into a section of memory which it automatically mallocs (as opposed to strcpy( ) which needs to have the destination already allocated). It returns a pointer to the destination string s. Remember to free( ) the memory when you're finished with it.

```
char *poet = "Dante";
char *author_divine_comedy;

author_divine_comedy = strdup(poet);
cout << "The author of the Divine Comedy is " <<
author_divine_comedy << "\n";
free(author_divine_comedy);
```

strerror( )

```
#include <string.h>       // Prototype here or in <stdio.h>
#include <errno.h>        // System errno numbers defined here

char *strerror(int errno);
```

strerror( ) takes an int and returns a pointer to the associated error message. This is often used to display system error messages using the numbers defined in errno.h.

```
cout << strerror(ECURDIR) << "\n";      // display the ECURDIR err msg
```

stricmp( )

```
#include <string.h>       // Prototype here

int stricmp(const char *a,const char *b);
```

347

stricmp( ) is a case insensitive version of strcmp( ). It is the same as strcmpi( ), although the manual says that this is a function version and strcmpi( ) is a macro version. (Your version may be different; you can check string.h for strcmpi( ) and see if there is any source code.)

If there is, you've got a macro version of strcmpi( ). The syntax, example, return value, etc., are the same as strcmpi( ).

strlen( )
```
#include <string.h>     // Prototype here

size_t strlen(const char *a);
```
strlen( ) returns the length of string a. It doesn't count the trailing NULL, so if you're using strlen( ) to figure out how much space to allocate, remember to add 1 to the value returned by strlen( ).
```
size_t length;

length = strlen("Principles of Neural Science");
```

strlwr( )
```
#include <string.h>     // Prototype here

char *strlwr(const char *s);
```
strlwr( ) converts the string s into lowercase and returns a pointer to the converted string.
```
cout << strlwr("This HAS MiXeD case IN it") << '\n';
```

strncat( )
```
#include <string.h>     // Prototype here

char *strncat(char *b,const char *a,size_t n);
```
strncat( ) concatenates n characters of b to a and returns the concatenated string. If b is greater than n characters in length, strncat( ) will truncate the string to a length of n. Otherwise, strncat( ) will concatenate the complete string.
```
char *a = "Lasciate ogne speranza ";
char *b = "voi ch'intrata";

cout << strncat(a,b,3) << '\n';
cout << strcat(a,b) << '\n';
```

strncmp( )
```
#include <string.h>     // Prototype here
```

```
int strncmp(const char *a,const char *b,size_t n);
```

strncmp( ) compares only the first n characters of a and b and returns an int with a value:

    <0   if a<b
    =0   if a==b
    >0   if a>b

```
char *a="Orlando Furioso";
char *b="Orlando Innamorato";

if((strncmp(a,b,7)) == 0)
  cout << "Both of these strings start with \"Orlando\"\n";
else
  cout << "These strings do not start with \"Orlando\"\n";
```

strncmpi( )

```
#include <string.h>      // Macro Definition here

int strncmpi(const char *a,const char *b,size_t n);
```

strncmpi( ) compares n chars of the strings with case insensitivity and returns an int with a value:

    <0 if a<b
    =0 if a==b
    >0 if a>b

This is actually the same as strnicmp( ) although it is supposed to be the macro version of strnicmp( ).

```
char *a="Orlando";
char *b="orlando furioso";
char *c="Roland";

if(strncmpi(a,b,7) == 0)
  cout << "Both strings start with the same 7 chars\n";
if(strncmp(a,b) != 0)
  cout << "strncmp() thinks they are different\n";
if(strncmpi(a,c,2) != 0)
  cout << "strncmpi() can tell that a and c are different\n";
```

strncpy( )

```
#include <string.h>      // Prototype here

char *strncpy(char *b,const char *a,size_t n);
copy n characters of a to b
```

strncpy( ) copies the first n characters of a to b and returns a pointer to b. If there are more than n characters in a, a will be truncated to n characters and it will not be terminated with a NULL.

If there are less than n characters in a, a will be padded to n characters using NULLs.

```
char *a="Orlando Furioso";
char b[20];

strncpy(b,a,7);
cout << b << '\n';       // You'll get garbage after 'Orlando' because
                         // it isn't NULL terminated
strncpy(b,a,20);         // You'll only get 'Orlando Furioso' because
                         // b is NULL-padded.
cout << b << '\n';
```

strnicmp( )

```
#include <string.h>     // Prototype here

int strnicmp(const char *a,const char *b,size_t n);
```

strnicmp( ) is the function version of strnicmp( ). It will compare the first n characters of a and b with case insensitivity. See strncmp( ) for examples of how to use strnicmp( ).

strnset( )

```
#include <string.h>     // Prototype here

char *strnset(char *s,int c,size_t n);
```

strnset( ) lets you set n chars in s to c. This can be used to initialize a string with spaces or with some other character. It returns a pointer to the string s.

```
char *s = "She loves me not";

cout << s << '\n';
cout << strset(strchr(s,'n'),' ',3) << '\n';
```

strpbrk( )

```
#include <string.h>     // Prototype here

char *strpbrk(const char *a,const char *b);
```

strpbrk( ) is used to find the first occurrence of a character from a set in a string. It returns a pointer to the first occurrence of the character. If the character doesn't exist, it returns NULL.

```
char *s="April L. Allgaier";
char *p;
```

```
p = strpbrk(s,"Ll");
cout << p << '\n';        // outputs:  " L. Allgaier"
```

strrchr( )

```
#include <string.h>      // Prototype here

char *strrchr(const char *s,int c);
```

strrchr( ) finds the last occurrence of c in s. It returns a pointer to the last occurrence of c or a NULL if c is not in s.

```
char *filename="c:/usr/txt/book/chapter1.txt";

cout << (strrchr(filename,'/')+1) << '\n';
```

strrev( )

```
#include <string.h>      // Prototype here

char *strrev(char *s);
```

strrev( ) reverses the characters in string s. It returns a pointer to the reversed string.

```
char *s="Agenbite of Inwit"

cout << strrev(s) << '\n';
```

strset( )

```
#include <string.h>      // Prototype here

char *strset(char *s,int c);
```

strset( ) will set all of the characters in string s to the value of c. It returns a pointer to the initialized string, s. This can be used to initialize data entry fields to spaces, although strnset( ) is a better choice.

```
char *s="Offend me still. Speak on."

strset(s,' ');
```

strspn( )

```
#include <string.h>      // Prototype here

size_t strspn(const char *a,const char *b);
```

strspn( ) returns the length of the initial span of a which contains only the characters in b.

```
char *s="The Darkest Road";
char *d = "Tadehrt";

cout << "There are " << strspn(s,d) << " chars in the initial span\n";
```

strstr( )

  #include <string.h> // Prototype here

  char *strstr(const char *a,const char *b);

strstr( ) finds a substring b in string a. It returns a pointer to the location of b (if it finds it) or NULL (if it doesn't).

  char *s="One of his favorite author's was Primo Levi";
  char *a="Primo Levi";

  cout << "The substring " << a << " is found at " << strstr(s,a) << '\n';

strtok( )

  #include <string.h> // Prototype here

  char *strtok(const char *a,const char *d);

strtok( ) breaks a string up into tokens using a list of delimiters. It returns a pointer to the current token and a NULL when the end of the string is reached.

  char *s="He preferred Mahler to Brahms";
  char *d=" ,.?!";

  cout << strtok(s,d) << '\n';
  while(cout << strtok(NULL,d) << '\n')
   ;

strupr( )

  #include <string.h> // Prototype here

  char *strupr(char *s);

strupr( ) converts s into uppercase and returns a pointer to the converted string.

strxfrm( )

  #include <string.h> // Prototype here

  size_t strxfrm(char *a,char *b,size_t n);

strxfrm( ) transforms b into a for no more than n characters. This is functionally the same as strncpy( ). It returns the number of characters copied.

  char *a="The time has come, the walrus said";
  char *b="The space has gone, the kid sordid";

  cout << strxfrm(a,b,18) << '\n';

TYPICAL OPERATION

In this program, you manipulate strings using a variety of the string routines. Begin from within Turbo C++ with no windows open.

1. Press **Alt-F** and type **N** to create a new file.
2. Type the following:

```
#include <alloc.h>
#include <dir.h>
#include <iostream.h>
#include <stdio.h>
#include <string.h>
#include <errno.h>

void main()
    {
    char *a="Xenophon";
    char *b1 = "LUCRETIUS";
    char *b="Lucretius";
    char *first="M.F.K. Fisher's ";
    char *j="James Joyce";
    char *p;
    char *s = "Vigil in a Wilderness of Mirrors";
    char *second="Serve It Forth";
    char c = 'V';
    char filedelims[]=":\\/";
    char filename2[MAXPATH]="USR\TXT\MISC\CALENDAR";
    char j1[12];
    char result[31];
    int retint;
    size_t delim_point;

    p = result;
    p = strcat(first,(const char *)second);
    printf("%s\n",p);
    if((p=strchr(s,c)) != 0)
      printf("%c was found at %p in \"%s\"\n",c,p,s);

    if((retint=strcmp(a,b)) < 0)
      cout << a << " is less than " << b << "\n";
    else if(retint == 0)
      cout << a << " is the same as " << b << "\n";
    else
      cout << a << "is greater than " << b << "\n";

    if(strcmp(b,b1) != 0)
      {
    cout << "strcmp() can tell the difference between \"" << a;
      cout << "\" and \"" << b << "\"\n";
```

353

```
            }
        if(strcmpi(a,b) == 0)
           cout << "but strcmpi() can't!\n";
        if(strcoll(a,b) != 0)
           {
   cout << "strcmp() can tell the difference between \"" << a;
           cout << "\" and \"" << b << "\"\n";
           }
        strcpy(j1,j);
        cout << b << '\n';

        delim_point = strcspn(filename2,filedelims);
        cout << "the first file delimiter was encountered at " <<
delim_point << "\n";

        cout << strerror(ECURDIR) << "\n";      // display the ECURDIR err msg
        }
```

3. Press **F2** to save the file on disk. Turbo C++ displays a Save Editor File dialog box.
4. Type **STRINGS.CPP** and press **Return**.
5. Press **Ctrl-F9** to run the program.
6. Press **Alt-F5** to view the program results.

```
M.F.K. Fisher's Serve It Forth
Xenophon is greater than Lucretius
strcmp() can tell the difference between "Xenophon" and "Lucretius"
strcmp() can tell the difference between "Xenophon" and "Lucretius"
Lucretius
the first file delimiter was encountered at 1
Attempted to remove current directory
```

7. Press **Alt-F5** to return to the Turbo C++ editor.
8. Press **Alt-Spacebar** and type **C** to clear the desktop.
9. Turn to Module 67 to continue the learning sequence.

Module 67
TEXT WINDOW DISPLAY ROUTINES

DESCRIPTION

The text window display routines let you define coordinates of a text window on screen and manipulate text.

Function	Purpose
clreol	Clear to eol in current window
clrscr	Clear current window
delline	Delete current line in window
gettext	Get text from screen
gettextinfo	Get mode information
gotoxy	Move cursor to (x,y)
highvideo	Set high intensity on
insline	Insert line in window
lowvideo	Set low intensity on
movetext	Move text in window
normvideo	Set normal intensity on
puttext	Put text in rectangle
textattr	Set text attribute
textbackground	Set background color
textcolor	Set foreground color
textmode	Set text mode
wherex	Get x coordinate
wherey	Get y coordinate
window	Create a window

APPLICATIONS

The text window functions are all prototyped in the <conio.h> header file, which must be included in programs that use these functions.

clreol( )

```
void clreol(void);
```

The clreol( ) function clears the current line from the current cursor position to the edge of the current window. The cursor position is not moved.

Module 67

clrscr( )
> void clrscr(void);

The clrscr( ) function clears the current window and puts the cursor in the home position (1,1).

delline( )
> void delline(void);

The delline( ) function deletes the current line in the current window and moves the remaining lines up to fill in its place. Text outside of the current window is not affected.

gettext( )
> int gettext(int l,int t,int r,int b,void *d);

The gettext( ) function reads the text characters within the rectangle bounded by (l,t) and (r,b) and puts them into the memory area pointed to by d. gettext( ) will return 0 if there is an error, a nonzero results if it is successful.

The memory pointed to by d will contain the contents of the bounding rectangle read left to right top to bottom, with 2 bytes for each character location (the first byte will be the character, the second the character's attribute).

gettextinfo( )
> void gettextinfo(struct text_info *r);

The gettextinfo( ) function will set r to a text_info structure containing information describing the current text mode. The text_info structure looks like:

```
struct text_info
{
unsigned char winleft;
unsigned char wintop;
unsigned char winright;
unsigned char winbottom;
unsigned char attribute;
unsigned char normattr;
unsigned char currmode;
unsigned char screenheight;
unsigned char screenwidth;
unsigned char curx;
unsigned char cury;
};
```

The upper left corner of the current window is described by (winleft,wintop). The lower right corner of the current window is described by (winright,winbottom). The current text attribute is set to attribute, the normal attribute is set to normattr. The current mode can be one of the following:

Symbolic Name	Description
BW40	monochrome 40 columns
BW80	monochrome 80 columns
CO40	color 40 columns
CO80	color 80 columns

The height and width of the window are described by screenheight and screenwidth. The current cursor position is described by (curx,cury).

gotoxy( )

    void gotoxy(int x,int y);

The gotoxy( ) function moves the cursor to (x,y). If an error occurs, the cursor will not be moved.

highvideo( )

    void highvideo(void);

The highvideo( ) function sets high-intensity characters on. Output continues in high intensity until a lowvideo( ) or normvideo( ) is encountered. To reset text output to normal, use normvideo( ).

insline( )

    void insline(void);

The insline( ) function inserts a line at the current cursor position and moves all following lines of text down one line in the current window.

lowvideo( )

    void lowvideo(void);

The lowvideo( ) function sets low-intensity characters on. Output continues in low intensity until a highvideo( ) or normvideo( ) is encountered. To reset text output to normal, use normvideo( ).

movetext( )

    int movetext(int l,int t,int r,int b,int dl,int dt);

The movetext( ) function moves the text bounded by (l,t) and (r,b) to (dl,dt). ((l,t) moves to (dl,dt).) If there is an error, 0 will be returned; otherwise, a nonzero value will be returned.

Module 67

normvideo( )
    void normvideo(void);

The normvideo( ) function sets normal intensity characters on. This is the default intensity of text. Text intensity can be modified with highvideo( ) and lowvideo( ).

puttext( )
    int puttext(int l,int t,int r,int b,void *s);

The puttext( ) function puts the text pointed to by s into the area bounded by (l,t) and (r,b). Puttext( ) uses absolute coordinates, not relative coordinates. A 0 will be returned if there is an error, a nonzero result means success.

textattr( )
    void textattr(int a);

The textattr( ) function sets the text attribute to a. A is of the following format:

    B   Blink bit
    b   three-bit background attribute (0x00-0x07)
    f   four-bit foreground attribute (0x00-0x0F)

The background attribute is set by:

    a = COLOR << 4;

The blink bit can be set by adding BLINK to a.

    a += BLINK;

The foreground color is set by adding the foreground color:

    a += COLOR;

The colors are defined as:

Number	Color	Foreground Only?
0	BLACK	
1	BLUE	
2	GREEN	
3	CYAN	
4	RED	
5	MAGENTA	
6	BROWN	
7	LIGHTGRAY	
8	DARKGRAY	Y
9	LIGHTBLUE	Y
10	LIGHTGREEN	Y
11	LIGHTCYAN	Y
12	LIGHTRED	Y

13	LIGHTMAGENTA	Y
14	YELLOW	Y
15	WHITE	Y

textbackground( )

```
void textbackground(int a);
```

The textbackground( ) function sets the background color to a. A can have a value between 0 and 7 as defined in the table for textattr( ).

textcolor( )

```
void textcolor(int a);
```

The textcolor( ) function sets the foreground color to a. A can have a value between 0 and 15 as defined in the table for textattr( ).

textmode( )

```
void textmode(int m);
```

The textmode( ) function sets the current text mode to m. Valid values of m are:

Number	Symbolic Name	Description
−1	LASTMODE	last text mode
0	BW40	monochrome 40 columns
1	CO40	color 40 columns
2	BW80	monochrome 80 columns
3	CO80	color 80 columns
7	MONO	monochrome 80 columns
64	C4350	EGA 43 line or VGA 50 line mode

textmode( ) should only be used from one text mode to go into another. It should be used cautiously since it clears the screen when it resets (destroying any windows that may have been open).

wherex( )

```
int wherex(void);
```

The wherex( ) function returns the x coordinate of the cursor.

wherey( )

```
int wherey(void);
```

The wherey( ) function returns the y coordinate of the cursor.

window( )

```
void window(int l,int t,int r,int b);
```

Module 67

The window( ) function creates a window bounded by (l,t) and (r,b). The new window becomes the current window. Minimum window size is 1x1.

TYPICAL OPERATION

In this program, you create two windows and write text in one of them. Begin from within Turbo C++ with no windows open.

1. Press **Alt-F** and type **N** to create a new file.
2. Type the following:

```
#include <stdio.h>
#include <conio.h>

#define LEFT_TOP   0xDA
#define RIGHT_TOP  0xBF
#define HORIZ      0xC4
#define VERT       0xB3
#define LEFT_BOT   0xC0
#define RIGHT_BOT  0xD9

#define x1  1
#define x2  77
#define y1  1
#define y2  9

void main()
    {
    int i, j, y;

    clrscr();
    textcolor (BLUE);
    textbackground (WHITE);
    /* Draw the top of the window */
    window (x1, y1, x2, y2);
    putchar (LEFT_TOP);
    for (i = x1; i < x2; i++)
      putchar (HORIZ);
    putchar (RIGHT_TOP);

    y = y1;
    /* Draw the middle of the window */
    for (j = y1; j < y2; j++)
      {
      y++;
      gotoxy (x1,y);
      putchar (VERT);
      for (i = x1; i < x2; i++)
        putchar (' ');
```

360

```
        putchar (VERT);
        }

    /* Draw the bottom */
    gotoxy (x1,y2);
    putchar (LEFT_BOT);
    for (i = x1; i < x2; i++)
        putchar (HORIZ);
    putchar (RIGHT_BOT);
    putchar ('\n');

    window (10, 10, 40, 15);
    cprintf ("Press any key to continue\r\n");
    while (!kbhit());
    gotoxy (1,1);
    delline();
    cprintf ("Program aborting");
    delay (1000);
    }
```

3. Press **Ctrl-F9** to run the program.

          Press any key to continue

4. Press **Return**. The program displays a new message:

          Program aborting

5. Press **Alt-Spacebar** and type **C** and type **N** to clear the desktop.
6. Turn to Module 68 to continue the learning sequence.

Module 68
TIME AND DATE ROUTINES

DESCRIPTION

Function	Purpose
asctime	Convert date and time to ASCII string
ctime	Convert date and time to string
difftime	Difference between two times
dostounix	Convert DOS date and time to UNIX format
ftime	Gets time in timeb struct
getdate	Get date
gettime	Get time
gmtime	Convert date and time to Greenwich mean time (GMT)
localtime	Convert date and time to a structure
mktime	Convert time to calendar format
setdate	Set the system date
settime	Set the system time
stime	Set system time and date
strftime	Format time for output
time	Get time and date
tzset	Set timezone
unixtodos	Convert UNIX date and time to DOS format

APPLICATIONS

asctime( )

```
#include <time.h>

char *asctime(const struct tm *tm);
```

The asctime( ) function takes a pointer to a tm structure and returns a 26-character string:

```
Sun Sep 09 01:00:00 1990\n\0
```

ctime( )

```
#include <time.h>

char *ctime(const time_t *time);
```

The ctime( ) function takes a pointer to a time_t value and returns a 26-character string:

```
Fri Dec 08 07:23:00 1967\n\0
```

difftime( )

```
#include <time.h>

double difftime(time_t t2, time_t t1);
```

The difftime( ) function takes two time_t variables and returns the difference between them in seconds.

dostounix( )

```
#include <dos.h>

long dostounix(struct date *d,struct time *t);
```

The dostounix( ) function takes DOS date and time structures and converts them into UNIX format.

ftime( )

```
#include <sys\timeb.h>

void ftime(struct timeb *b);
```

The ftime( ) function fills in the timeb structure pointed to by b with the current time. The timeb structure is:

```
struct timeb
{
long time;
short millitm;
short timezone;
short dstflag;
};
```

time is the time in seconds since Midnight, January 1, 1970, GMT.

millitm is the millisecond time.

timezone is the difference between the current time zone and GMT in minutes.

dstflag is 0 if daylight savings time is not in effect, and nonzero if daylight savings time is in effect.

getdate( )

```
#include <dos.h>

void getdate(struct date *d);
```

Module 68

The getdate( ) function gets the system date and uses it to fill in a DOS date structure:
```
struct date
{
int da_year;
char da_day;
char da_mon;
};
```

da_year is the current year.

da_day is the current day.

da_mon is the current month (a number between 1 and 12 inclusive).

gettime( )
```
#include <dos.h>

void gettime(struct dostime *t);
```

The gettime( ) function gets the system time and returns it in a dostime structure:
```
struct dostime
{
unsigned char ti_min;
unsigned char ti_hour;
unsigned char ti_hund;
unsigned char ti_sec;
};
```

ti_min is the minutes

ti_hour is the hour

ti_hund is the hundredths of seconds

ti_sec is the seconds

gmtime( )
```
#include <time.h>

struct tm *gmtime(const time_t *t);
```

The gmtime( ) function takes a time_t and returns a pointer to a struct tm containing a time converted to GMT (Greenwich Mean Time). The tm structure is:
```
struct tm
{
int tm_sec;     // 0-59
int tm_min;     // 0-59
int tm_hour;    // 0-23
int tm_mday;    // 1-31
int tm_mon;     // 0-11
int tm_year;    // 00-99
```

```
            int tm_wday;        // 0-6
            int tm_yday;        // 0-365
            int tm_isdst;       // 0 or nonzero (is daylight savings
                                // time)
        };
```

localtime( )

```
        #include <time.h>

        struct tm *localtime(const time_t *t);
```

The localtime( ) function takes a pointer to a time_t variable and returns a pointer to a tm structure, adjusting the time and date for the time zone and daylight savings time (they can be set using the tzset( ) function). The tm structure is described in gmtime( ) above.

mktime( )

```
        #include <time.h>

        time_t mktime(struct tm *t);
```

The mktime( ) function takes a pointer to a tm structure and returns a time_t variable. The tm structure is described above in gmtime( ).

setdate( )

```
        #include <dos.h>

        void setdate(struct date *d);
```

The setdate( ) function sets the system date to the date in the date structure.

settime( )

```
        #include <dos.h>

        void settime(struct dostime *t);
```

The settime( ) function sets the system time to the time in the dostime structure.

stime( )

```
        #include <time.h>

        int stime(time_t *t);
```

The stime( ) function sets the system time and date to the value pointed to by t.

strftime( )

    #include <time.h>

    size_t _cdecl strftime(char *s,size_t n,const char *f,const struct tm);

The strftime( ) function converts a pointer to a tm structure to a string, s (with a maximum length of n), using f to format the string. The format is similar to the format of a printf( ), except the following characters are used.

%%	a percent sign (%)
%a	weekday abbreviation
%A	weekday
%b	month name abbreviation
%B	month name
%c	date and time
%d	day of month (two-digit format)
%H	hour (two-digit format, 24-hour clock)
%I	hour (two-digit format, 12-hour clock)
%j	Julian date (day of the year)
%m	month (two-digit format)
%M	minute (two-digit format)
%p	AM/PM
%S	second (two-digit format)
%U	week number, Sunday as start of week (0 to 52)
%w	weekday (0-6,0=Sunday)
%W	week number, Monday as start of week (0 to 52)
%x	date
%X	time
%y	year (two-digit format)
%Y	year (four-digit format)
%Z	time zone name (blank if time zone is undefined)

time( )

    #include <time.h>

    time_t time(time_t *t);

The time( ) function returns the system time in a time_t. The time is based on the number of seconds since midnight January 1, 1970 GMT.

tzset( )

    #include <time.h>

    void tzset(void);

The tzset( ) function uses the environment variable TZ to set the tzname, timezone, and daylight. TZ has the following format:

    TZ="PST8PDT"

Where PST is a three-character tzname (time zone name), 8 is an optionally signed number describing the time offset from GMT (Greenwich Mean Time), and PDT is an optional three-character daylight savings description (if there aren't any characters here, daylight savings is assumed to not exist in your time zone).

The variable tzname[0] will be your timezone name and tzname[1] will be your daylight savings description; timezone is the difference between your time zone and GMT in seconds, and daylight is nonzero if a daylight savings time description is included.

unixtodos( )

    #include <dos.h>

    void unixtodos(long time,struct date *date,struct dostime *dtime);

The unixtodos( ) function converts the UNIX date and time into DOS format. DOS date and time will be returned in the structures pointed to by date and dtime.

unixtodos( ) is not portable.

TYPICAL OPERATION

In this program, you retrieve the current date and time from your computer and display it on the screen. Begin from within Turbo C++ with no windows open.

1. Press **Alt-F** and type **N** to create a new file.
2. Type the following:

```
#include <dos.h>
#include <stdio.h>

void main()
    {
    void finddate();
    void findtime();

    printf ("The time is: ");
    findtime();
    printf ("The date is: ");
    finddate();
    }

void findtime()
    {
    char *noon, *dayweekname;
```

Module 68

```c
        struct time ttime;

    gettime (&ttime);

    noon = "am";
    if (ttime.ti_hour >= 12)
      if (ttime.ti_hour > 12)
        ttime.ti_hour = ttime.ti_hour - 12;
      noon = "pm";
    printf ("%d:", ttime.ti_hour);

    if (ttime.ti_min < 10)
      printf ("0%d", ttime.ti_min);
    else
      printf ("%d", ttime.ti_min);

    if (ttime.ti_sec < 10)
      printf (":0%d", ttime.ti_sec);
    else
      printf (":%d", ttime.ti_sec);

    printf (" %s\n", noon);
    }

void finddate()
    {
    char *monthname;
    struct date ddate;

    getdate (&ddate);

    switch (ddate.da_mon)
        {
        case 1 : monthname = "January"; break;
        case 2 : monthname = "February"; break;
        case 3 : monthname = "March"; break;
        case 4 : monthname = "April"; break;
        case 5 : monthname = "May"; break;
        case 6 : monthname = "June"; break;
        case 7 : monthname = "July"; break;
        case 8 : monthname = "August"; break;
        case 9 : monthname = "September"; break;
        case 10: monthname = "October"; break;
        case 11: monthname = "November"; break;
        case 12: monthname = "December"; break;
        }

    printf ("%s %d, %d\n", monthname, ddate.da_day, ddate.da_year);
    }
```

Time and Date Routines

3. Press **Ctrl-F9** to run the program.
4. Press **Alt-F5** to view the program results. You see a display similar to the following but with different time and dates:

   ```
   The time is: 4:30:13 pm
   The date is: October 24, 1990
   ```

5. Press **Alt-F5** to return to the Turbo C++ editor.
6. Press **Alt-Spacebar** and type **C** and type **N** to clear the desktop.
7. Turn to Module 69 to continue the learning sequence.

Module 69
VARIABLE ARGUMENT LIST ROUTINES

DESCRIPTION

The variable argument list routines let you create functions with a variable number of arguments. The variable argument list routines are:

Function	Purpose
va_start	Start variable list processing
va_arg	Get next variable argument
va_end	End variable list processing

APPLICATIONS

The three variable argument list macros provide an interface to functions with variable argument lists. They all require the following header file:

```
#include <stdarg.h>
```

and they are used together to implement the variable argument interface.

va_start( )

```
void va_start(va_list ap, last_fixed_arg);
```

The va_start( ) macro points ap at the first argument in the argument list (after the last_fixed_arg). If we wanted to be able to read a variable list of ints, we would declare the variable as:

```
int sum(int first,...) {...}
```

so that the first argument is set up properly. The va_start( ) for this example would be:

```
va_list ap;
va_start(ap,first);
```

Some variable argument routines use a first argument of a different type (printf( ) is a good example). These functions would be declared as:

```
int printf(char *format,...) {...}
```

The va_start( ) for this example would be:

```
va_list ap;
va_start(ap,format);
```

va_arg( )

    type va_arg(va_list ap,type);

The va_arg( ) macro returns the current argument in the argument list and then increments to point to the next argument in the list. When the end of the list is reached, va_arg( ) will return 0. An example (continuing the sum( ) function described earlier) would be:

```
total = first;
while((x=va_arg(ap,int)))
    total += x;
```

First we set the initial total to the value of the first argument (as described under "va_start( )"). Then we read the current argument into a and see if it is 0 (remember, va_arg( ) returns 0 when it reaches the end of the list). Once we've read the number and it's good, add it to the total.

va_end( )

    void va_end(va_list ap);

The va_end( ) macro closes the reading of the variable argument list and sets things up so the calling function can return a value (if it needs to). You invoke it with:

    va_end(ap);

TYPICAL OPERATION

1. Press **Alt-F** and type **N** to create a new file.
2. Type the following:

```
#include <stdio.h>
#include <stdarg.h>

int sum(int first,...)
{
    int total=0,x=0;
    va_list va;

    va_start(va,first);
    total = first;
    while((x=va_arg(va,int)) != 0)
        total += x;
    va_end(va);
    return(total);
}

void err(char *s,...)
{
    va_list va;
```

```
        va_start(va,s);
        vfprintf(stderr,s,va);
        va_end(va);
        exit(2);
}

#pragma argsused
int main(int argc,char **argv)
{
        if(argc > 1)
                err("usage:  vararg\n");
        printf("The sum of 1+2+3+4+5+6 is %d\n",sum(1,2,3,4,5,6,0));
        err("The sum of 1+3+5 is %d\n",sum(1,3,5,0));
        return(0);
}
```

3. Press **Ctrl-F9** to run the program.
4. Press **Alt-F5** to view the program results.

```
The sum of 1+2+3+4+5+6 is 21
The sum of 1+3+5 is 9
```

5. Press **Alt-F5** to return to the Turbo C++ editor.
6. Press **Alt-Spacebar,** type **C** and type **N** to clear the desktop.
7. Turn to Module 43 to continue the learning sequence.

Appendix A
TURBO C++ FUNCTION KEY COMMANDS

Function Key	Action
F1	Help
F2	Save (File menu)
F3	Open (File menu)
F4	Go to cursor (Run menu)
F5	Zoom (Window menu)
F6	Next (Window menu)
F7	Trace into (Run menu)
F8	Step over (Run menu)
F9	Make
F10	Menu
Ctrl-F1	Topic search (Help menu)
Ctrl-F2	Program reset
Ctrl-F3	Call stack (Debug menu)
Ctrl-F4	Evaluate and Modify
Ctrl-F5	Size/Move (Window menu)
Ctrl-F6	
Ctrl-F7	Add watch (Debug menu)
Ctrl-F8	Toggle breakpoint (Debug menu)
Ctrl-F9	Run
Ctrl-F10	
Shift-F1	Index (Help menu)
Shift-F2	GREP
Shift-F3	Turbo Assembler
Shift-F4	Turbo Debugger
Shift-F5	
Shift-F6	
Shift-F7	
Shift-F8	
Shift-F9	
Shift-F10	

Appendix A

Function Key	*Action*
Alt-F1	Previous topic (Help menu)
Alt-F2	
Alt-F3	Close (Window menu)
Alt-F4	Inspect (Debug menu)
Alt-F5	User screen
Alt-F6	
Alt-F7	Previous error (Search menu)
Alt-F8	Next error (Search menu)
Alt-F9	Compile to .OBJ
Alt-F10	
Alt-X	Quit
Alt-0	List (Window menu)
Alt-Spacebar	System menu
Shift-Del	Cut
Shift-Ins	Paste
Ctrl-Ins	Copy
Ctrl-Del	Clear

Appendix B
USING THE TURBO C++ COMMAND-LINE COMPILER

Turbo C++ provides you with two versions of the Turbo C++ compiler. The first version, called the Integrated Development Environment (IDE), provides an editor, compiler, and debugger.

The second version only includes the Turbo C++ compiler, called the command-line compiler. To use the command-line compiler, you need a separate editor and debugger, such as Turbo Debugger.

The integrated development environment is usually best for developing and testing your programs, but if you already have a favorite editor or debugger, then use the Turbo C++ command-line compiler instead.

You may also want to use the Turbo C++ command-line compiler if you are creating large C++ programs. Sometimes your programs may require so much memory to compile that you cannot use the Turbo C++ integrated development environment without getting an Out of Memory message.

Choosing Options with the Command-line Compiler

With the integrated development environment, you choose compiler options through menus. With the command-line compiler, you must specify the compiler options you want to use.

For example, consider compiling one Turbo C program that will use 80287 math coprocessor instructions and a second program to work without a math coprocessor.

To compile these programs using the Turbo C integrated environment, you would go through four separate steps.

1. Change the compiler options, using the Turbo C++ pull-down menus, to use 80287 math coprocessor instructions.
2. Compile the first program.
3. Change the compiler option to compile a program to run on a computer without a math coprocessor.
4. Compile the second program.

To compile these same programs using the Turbo C++ command-line compiler only requires two steps.

Appendix B

1. Compile the first program using the -f287 command-line option such as: **TCC -f287 PROGRAM1.C**.
2. Compile the second program using the -f command-line option such as: **TCC -f PROGRAM2.C**.

By letting you specify compiler options for each program, the Turbo C++ command-line compiler lets you quickly compile programs that use different options.

Running the Turbo C++ Command-Line Compiler

To run the Turbo C++ command-line compiler, type TCC (instead of TC to run the integrated development environment) followed by a set of command-line arguments and the program name you want to compile.

Turbo C++ command-line options let you control the following:

- Memory models
- Macro definitions
- Code generation options
- Optimization options
- Source code options
- Error-reporting options
- Segment-naming control options
- Compilation control options
- EMS and extended memory options

If you are not sure how to specify a compiler option with the Turbo C++ command-line compiler, just type TCC and press Return. Turbo C++ will display a help screen.

The TURBOC.CFG File

To prevent specifying a long list of compiler options each time you use the Turbo C++ command-line compiler, you can store your most frequently used options in a configuration file called TURBOC.CFG.

NOTE

The Turbo C command-line compiler, TCC.EXE, uses the TURBOC.CFG configuration file. The Turbo C integrated development environment, TC.EXE, uses the TCCONFIG.TC configuration file. Thus you can define two different compiler options, one for the command-line compiler and one for the integrated development environment.

You can create the TURBOC.CFG file using any word processor or editor, including the Turbo C editor. If you use a word processor, the TURBOC.CFG file must be saved as an ASCII or text file.

For example, to define a tiny memory model (-mt), 8087 emulation (-f), and maximum optimization (-O), your TURBOC.CFG file would contain the following line:

    -mt -f -O

When you run the command-line compiler, Turbo C++ will use the options specified in the TCCONFIG.TC file unless you override them.

Overriding the TURBOC.CFG File Options

To override an option defined in the TURBOC.CFG file, simply type the option followed by a dash. For example, if you specified the **-a** option in the TURBOC.CFG file, you would override that option by typing **-a-** such as:

    TCC -a- PROGRAM.C

Using an Alternate Configuration File

Sometimes you may want to use more than one set of predefined compiler options. To do this, Turbo C++ lets you use alternate configuration files.

Simply save the compiler options in an ASCII or text file using a word processor or the Turbo C editor, and give the file any name you choose, such as ALT.CFG or TCC2.CFG.

To read the compiler options stored in a file other than the TURBOC.CFG file, type + followed by the file path and name. If you wanted to use the compiler options stored in a file called ALT.CFG stored on the C:\TC directory, you would type:

    TCC +C:\TC\ALT.CFG

If you wanted to specify compiler options in addition to those stored in the ALT.CFG file, you would type the command options after the alternate configuration file such as:

    TCC +C:\TC\ALT.CFG -f -O

Converting Configuration Files

You can create one configuration file for the Turbo C++ integrated development environment (TCCONFIG.CFG) and a second configuration file for the Turbo C++ command-line compiler (TURBO.CFG).

If you are using the Turbo C++ command-line compiler but want to convert the settings stored in the Turbo C++ IDE TCCONFIG.CFG file, you need to use the TCCNVT.EXE program.

To use the TCCNVT.EXE program, you would type TCCONFIG followed by the file you want to convert. Optionally, you can also specify the filename to store the settings.

Appendix B

For example, if you wanted to convert the TCCONFIG.CFG file for use with the Turbo C command-line compiler, you would type the following:

```
TCCNVT TCCONFIG.CFG
```

The above command will convert the TCCONFIG.CFG file to the TURBO.CFG file. If you want to save the TCCONFIG.CFG settings in a different filename, type the above command followed by the filename such as:

```
TCCNVT TCCONFIG.CFG NEW.CFG
```

The above command saves the TCCONFIG.CFG file in a file called NEW.CFG. If you do not specify a filename, the TCCNVT.EXE program automatically stores the settings in the TCCONFIG.CFG or TURBO.CFG file.

Thus, if you are converting the TCCONFIG.CFG file, the TCCNVT.EXE program will save the settings to the TURBO.CFG file. If you are converting the TCCONFIG.CFG file, the TCCNVT.EXE program will save the settings to the TCCONFIG.CFG file.

Appendix C
CUSTOMIZING TURBO C++

You can customize the Turbo C++ integrated development environment (IDE) by running the TCINST.EXE program. When you run the TCINST program, a menu appears.

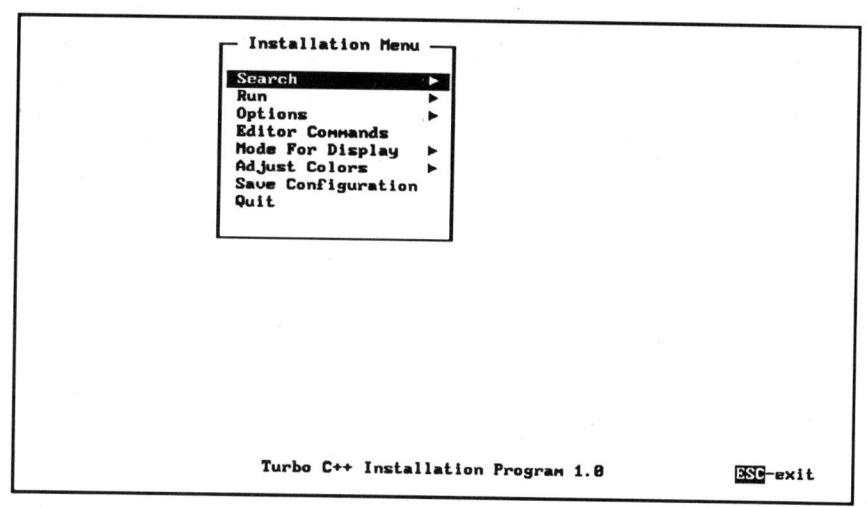

```
┌─ Installation Menu ─┐
│ Search            ▶ │
│ Run               ▶ │
│ Options           ▶ │
│ Editor Commands     │
│ Mode For Display  ▶ │
│ Adjust Colors     ▶ │
│ Save Configuration  │
│ Quit                │
└─────────────────────┘

Turbo C++ Installation Program 1.0         ESC-exit
```

Search

The search option lets you change the way the Turbo C++ editor searches for strings when you use the Search menu. The settings include:

Direction (Forward/Backward): Searches forward or backward, depending on the Scope (see below).

Scope (From cursor/Entire scope): Searches from the cursor forward or backward, depending on the direction (see above). Or searches the entire file regardless of the cursor location or Direction setting.

Origin (Global/Selected text): Searches the entire file or only a highlighted block of text.

Case sensitive (On/Off): Distinguishes between uppercase and lowercase letters.

Whole words only (On/Off): Searches for whole words or words that may be part of another word. Searching for "the" with this option off might find the words "theater," "thesis," or "bathe."

Appendix C

Regular expression (On/Off): Searches for words using GREP-like wildcards (^, $, ., *, +, [ ], and \). This is an advanced feature.

Prompt on replace (On/OFF): Used with the search and replace feature of the editor. When turned on, it will prompt you before replacing a word. When turned off, it will replace a word without prompting you for verification.

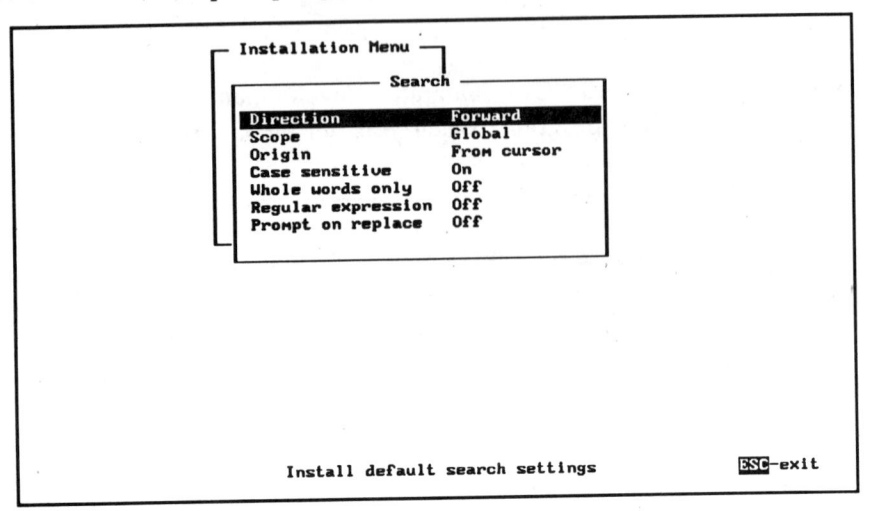

```
┌─ Installation Menu ─┐
    ┌─ Search ──────────────────┐
    │ Direction         Forward │
    │ Scope             Global  │
    │ Origin            From cursor │
    │ Case sensitive    On      │
    │ Whole words only  Off     │
    │ Regular expression Off    │
    │ Prompt on replace Off     │
    └───────────────────────────┘

    Install default search settings    ESC-exit
```

Run

Many programs let you enter command-line arguments when you load a program. Command-line arguments let you load a program and a command right from the DOS prompt.

While writing your Turbo C++ programs using the integrated development environment, the Run option lets you specify the command-line arguments to use. Without setting the arguments with this option, you cannot test command-line arguments from within the integrated development environment.

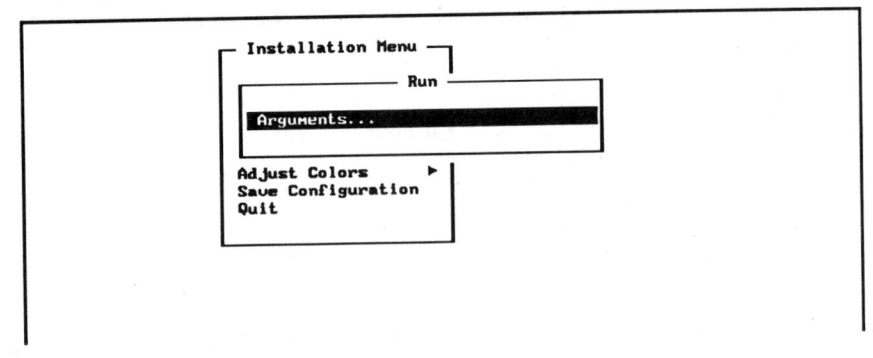

```
┌─ Installation Menu ─┐
       ┌─ Run ─────────────────┐
       │ Arguments...          │
       │                       │
       │ Adjust Colors       ► │
       │ Save Configuration    │
       │ Quit                  │
       └───────────────────────┘
```

380

Options

This feature lets you change the more technical specifications of Turbo C, such as the memory model, degree and type of optimization, and code generation. Unless you are an experienced Turbo C++ programmer, you should use the default settings.

The only features that beginners may wish to change are the directory and environment settings. The directory settings let you specify in which directory you have stored the Include and Library files.

The environment settings let you change the editor commands or modify the left and right mouse buttons to perform different functions.

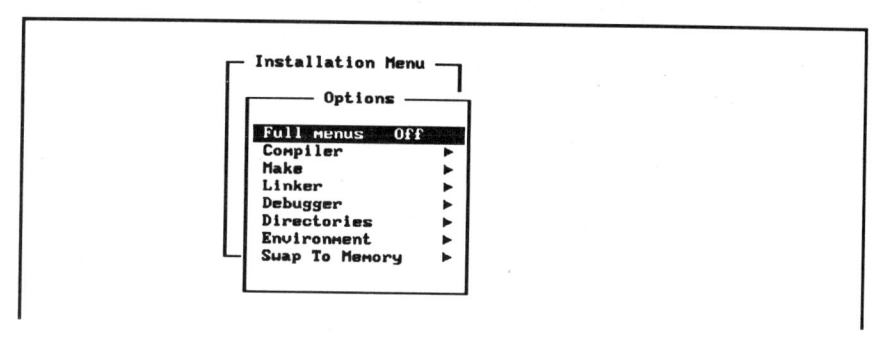

```
┌─ Installation Menu ─┐
  ┌─ Options ─┐
  │ Full menus   Off  │
  │ Compiler        ► │
  │ Make            ► │
  │ Linker          ► │
  │ Debugger        ► │
  │ Directories     ► │
  │ Environment     ► │
  │ Swap To Memory  ► │
  └───────────────────┘
```

Editor Commands

This lets you redefine the keys you use for moving the cursor within the Turbo C editor. The default values are similar to WordStar commands.

```
                        Install Editor
Command name         Primary              Secondary
Cursor Left        · <CtrlS>            · <Lft>
Cursor Right       · <CtrlD>            · <Rgt>
Word Left          · <CtrlA>            · <CtrlLft>
Word Right         · <CtrlF>            · <CtrlRgt>
Cursor Up          · <CtrlE>            · <Up>
Cursor Down        · <CtrlX>            · <Dn>
Scroll Up          · <CtrlW>            ·
Scroll Down        · <CtrlZ>            ·
Page Up            · <CtrlR>            · <PgUp>
Page Down          · <CtrlC>            · <PgDn>
Left of Line       × <CtrlQ>S           · <Home>
Right of Line      × <CtrlQ>D           · <End>
Top of Screen      × <CtrlQ>E           · <CtrlHome>
Bottom of Screen   × <CtrlQ>X           · <CtrlEnd>
Top of File        × <CtrlQ>R           · <CtrlPgUp>
Bottom of File     × <CtrlQ>C           · <CtrlPgDn>
Move to Block Begin × <CtrlQ>B          ·
Move to Block End  × <CtrlQ>K           ·
Move to Previous Pos × <CtrlQ>P         ·

←↑↓→-select  PgUp-PgDn-page  ↵-modify  R-restore factory defaults  ESC-exit
F4-Key modes:  (×)-WordStar-like  (■)-Ignore case  (·)-Verbatim
```

Appendix C

Mode for Display

This lets you define the type of screen your computer uses. If you are using Turbo C with a computer that uses an LCD screen or VGA monitor, you may wish to change this option.

For EGA and VGA monitors, you can adjust the number of lines displayed from the default of 25 to 43 lines (EGA) or 50 lines (VGA).

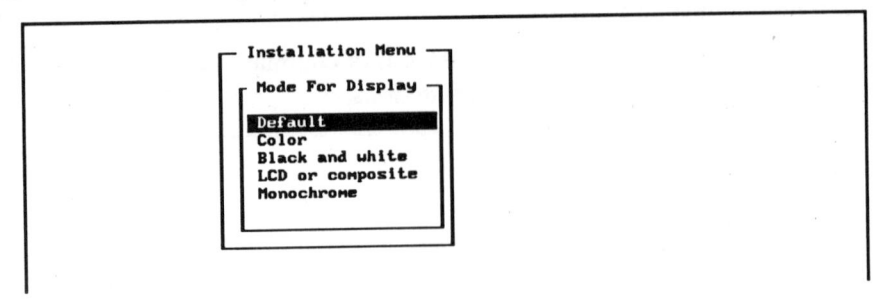

```
┌─ Installation Menu ─┐
│ ┌─ Mode For Display ─┐ │
│ │ Default            │ │
│ │ Color              │ │
│ │ Black and white    │ │
│ │ LCD or composite   │ │
│ │ Monochrome         │ │
│ └────────────────────┘ │
└────────────────────────┘
```

Adjust Colors

You can change the colors of the integrated development environment, including the menus, windows, and dialog boxes. You use this option to adjust the colors so they are easiest for you to see.

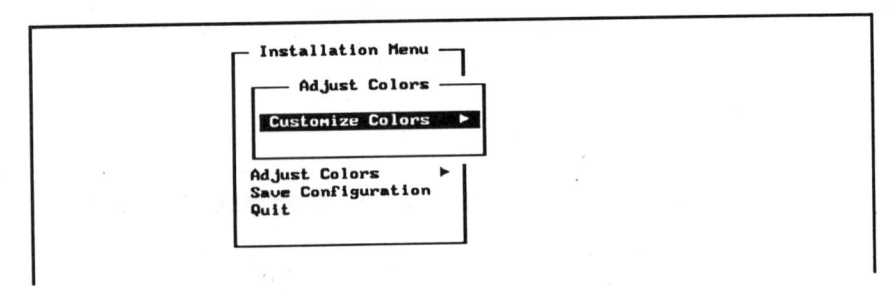

```
┌─ Installation Menu ─┐
│ ┌─ Adjust Colors ─┐  │
│ │ Customize Colors ▶│ │
│ └──────────────────┘ │
│  Adjust Colors    ▶  │
│  Save Configuration  │
│  Quit                │
└──────────────────────┘
```

Save Configuration

Any changes you made using the above options will not be saved unless you choose this option last.

Quit

This exits the Turbo C installation menu. If you have not used the Save configuration option (see above) first, any changes you made will be lost.

WHY CUSTOMIZE TURBO C++?

You may want to customize Turbo C++ for personal reasons or to make Turbo C++ work properly with your computer system.

Using EGA with a CGA Monitor

If you have a CGA monitor with an EGA video display card, Turbo C++ will not run properly. To modify Turbo C++ so it will work on your computer, you must perform the following steps:

1. Type **TCINST** and type **Enter**. The Turbo C++ installation menu appears.
2. Type **M** to choose Mode for display.
3. Press **Esc** to return to the main TCINST menu.
4. Type **O** to choose Options.
5. Type **E** to choose Environment.

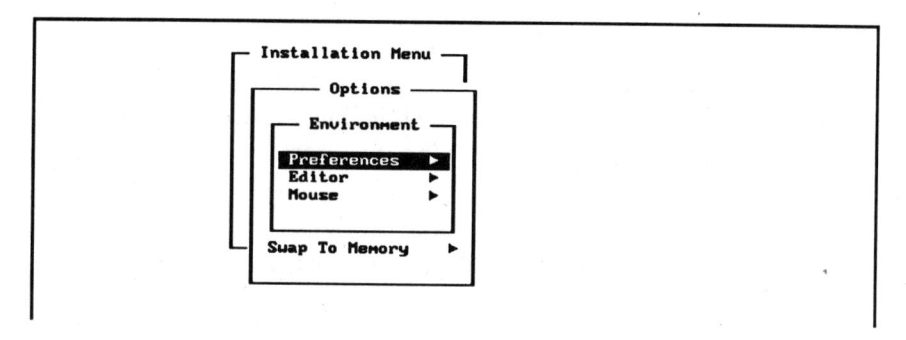

```
┌─ Installation Menu ──────────┐
│   ┌─ Options ────────────┐   │
│   │  ┌─ Environment ──┐  │   │
│   │  │ Preferences  ▶ │  │   │
│   │  │ Editor       ▶ │  │   │
│   │  │ Mouse        ▶ │  │   │
│   │  └────────────────┘  │   │
│   │  Swap To Memory   ▶  │   │
│   └──────────────────────┘   │
└──────────────────────────────┘
```

6. Type **P** to choose Preferences.

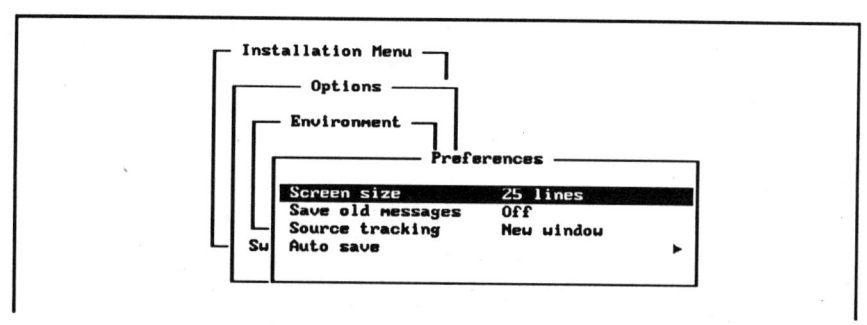

```
┌─ Installation Menu ──────────────────┐
│  ┌─ Options ────────────────────┐    │
│  │  ┌─ Environment ──────────┐  │    │
│  │  │       ┌─ Preferences ──────────┐
│  │  │       │ Screen size     25 lines │
│  │  │       │ Save old messages  Off   │
│  │  │       │ Source tracking  New window │
│  │  Su     │ Auto save               ▶ │
└──┴──┴──────┴──────────────────────────┘
```

7. Type **S** to choose Screen Size.

Appendix C

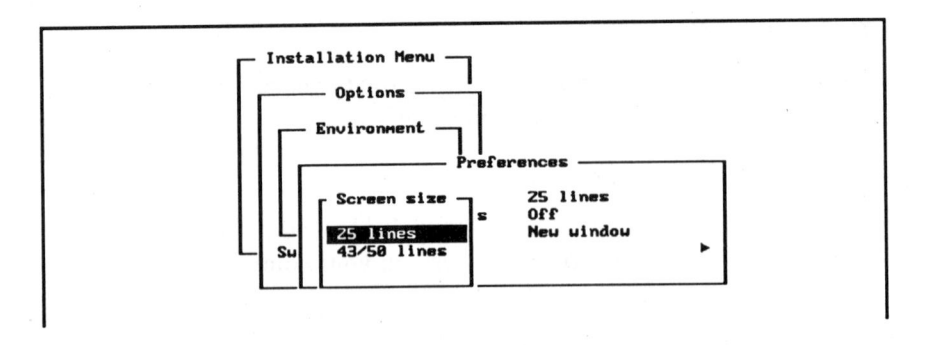

```
┌─────────────────────────────────────────────────────────┐
│           ┌─ Installation Menu ─┐                       │
│         ┌─── Options ───┐                               │
│       ┌─── Environment ──┐                              │
│                ┌──── Preferences ────┐                  │
│       ┌─ Screen size ─┐   25 lines                      │
│                       │s  Off                           │
│       │  25 lines  │      New window                    │
│       │ 43/50 lines│                           ▶        │
│    Su └───────────┘                                     │
│                                                         │
└─────────────────────────────────────────────────────────┘
```

8. Press **Up** and **Down** arrow to select 43/50 Line Display and press **Return**.
9. Press **Esc** three times to return to the main installation menu.
10. Type **A** to save your configuration.
11. Type **Q** to quit the Turbo C++ installation.

Personalizing Turbo C++

A second reason why you might want to change the Turbo C++ environment is to make the program easier to use. This might include choosing different colors, displaying more lines on the screen, or defining the directories where you store your files.

In general, the more familiar you become with Turbo C++, the more likely you will want to customize it to suit your needs. If you are just learning Turbo C++, use the default values until you feel experienced enough to change these values.

Appendix D
ASCII TABLE

^@	0	00		NUL	Null	^]	29	1D	↔	GS	Group Separator
^A	1	01	☺	SOH	Start of Header	^^	30	1E	▲	RS	Record Separator
^B	2	02	☻	STX	Start of Text	^_	31	1F	▼	US	Unit Separator
^C	3	03	♥	ETX	End of Text		32	20			Space
^D	4	04	♦	EOT	End of Transmission	!	33	21	!		Exclamation Point
^E	5	05	♣	ENQ	Enquiry	"	34	22	"		Double Quote
^F	6	06	♠	ACK	Acknowledge	#	35	23	#		Number Sign
^G	7	07	●	BEL	Bell	$	36	24	$		Dollar Sign
^H	8	08	◘	BS	Backspace	%	37	25	%		Percent Sign
^I	9	09	○	HT	Horizontal Tab	&	38	26	&		Ampersand
^J	10	0A	◙	LF	Line Feed	'	39	27	'		Single Quote
^K	11	0B	♂	VT	Vertical Tab	(	40	28	(		Left Parenthesis
^L	12	0C	♀	FF	Form Feed	)	41	29	)		Right Parenthesis
^M	13	0D	♪	CR	Carriage Return	*	42	2A	*		Asterisk
^N	14	0E	♫	SO	Shift Out	+	43	2B	+		Plus
^O	15	0F	✻	SI	Shift In	,	44	2C	,		Comma
^P	16	10	▶	DLE	Data Link Escape	-	45	2D	-		Hyphen
^Q	17	11	◀	DC1	Device Control 1	.	46	2E	.		Period
^R	18	12	↕	DC2	Device Control 2	/	47	2F	/		Slash
^S	19	13	‼	DC3	Device Control 3	0	48	30	0		Zero
^T	20	14	¶	DC4	Device Control 4	1	49	31	1		One
^U	21	15	§	NAK	Neg. Acknowldege	2	50	32	2		Two
^V	22	16	▬	SYN	Synch Idle	3	51	33	3		Three
^W	23	17	↕	ETB	End of Text Block	4	52	34	4		Four
^X	24	18	↑	CAN	Cancel	5	53	35	5		Five
^Y	25	19	↓	EM	End of Medium	6	54	36	6		Six
^Z	26	1A	→	SUB	Substitute	7	55	37	7		Seven
^[	27	1B	←	ESC	Escape	8	56	38	8		Eight
^\	28	1C	∟	FS	File Separator	9	57	39	9		Nine

Appendix D

:	58	3A	:	Colon	^	94	5E	^	Circumflex
;	59	3B	;	Semicolon	_	95	5F	_	Underline
<	60	3C	<	Less Than	`	96	60	`	Acute Accent
=	61	3D	=	Equal Sign	a	97	61	a	a
>	62	3E	>	Greater Than	b	98	62	b	b
?	63	3F	?	Question Mark	c	99	63	c	c
@	64	40	1	At Sign	d	100	64	d	d
B	66	42	B	B	e	101	65	e	e
C	67	43	C	C	f	102	66	f	f
D	68	44	D	D	g	103	67	g	g
E	69	45	E	E	h	104	68	h	h
F	70	46	F	F	i	105	69	i	i
G	71	47	G	G	j	106	6A	j	j
H	72	48	H	H	k	107	6B	k	k
I	73	49	I	I	l	108	6C	l	l
J	74	4A	J	J	m	109	6D	m	m
K	75	4B	K	K	n	110	6E	n	n
L	76	4C	L	L	o	111	6F	o	o
M	77	4D	M	M	p	112	70	p	p
N	78	4E	N	N	q	113	71	q	q
O	79	4F	O	O	r	114	72	r	r
P	80	50	P	P	s	115	73	s	s
Q	81	51	Q	Q	t	116	74	t	t
R	82	52	R	R	u	117	75	u	u
S	83	53	S	S	v	118	76	v	v
T	84	54	T	T	w	119	77	w	w
U	85	55	U	U	x	120	78	x	x
V	86	56	V	V	y	121	79	y	y
W	87	57	W	W	z	122	7A	z	z
X	88	58	X	X	{	123	7B	{	Left Brace
Y	89	59	Y	Y	|	124	7C	|	Vertical Bar
Z	90	5A	Z	Z	}	125	7D	}	Right Brace
[	91	5B	[	Left Bracket	~	126	7E	~	Tilde
\	92	5C	\	Backslash	↑	127	7F	DEL	Delete
]	93	5D	]	Right Bracket		128	80	Ç	C Cedilla

ASCII Table

129	81	ü	u Dieresis		164	A4	ñ	n Tilde
130	82	é	e Acute		165	A5	Ñ	N Tilde
131	83	â	a Circumflex		166	A6	ª	Ord Feminine
132	84	ä	a Dieresis		167	A7	º	Ord Masculine
133	85	à	a Grave		168	A8	¿	Question Down
134	86	å	a Ring		169	A9	⌐	
135	87	ç	c Cedilla		170	AA	¬	Logical Not
136	88	ê	e Circumflex		171	AB	½	Half
137	89	ë	e Dieresis		172	AC	¼	Quarter
138	8A	è	e Grave		173	AD	¡	Exclaim Down
139	8B	ï	i Dieresis		174	AE	«	Guillemot Left
140	8C	î	i Circumflex		175	AF	»	Guillemot Right
141	8D	ì	i Grave		176	B0		
142	8E	Ä	A Dieresis		177	B1	▒	
143	8F	Å	A Ring		178	B2	■	
144	90	É	E Acute		179	B3	│	
145	91	æ	æ		180	B4	┤	
146	92	Æ	Æ		181	B5	╡	
147	93	ô	o Circumflex		182	B6	╢	
148	94	ö	o Dieresis		183	B7	╖	
149	95	ò	o Grave		184	B8	╕	
150	96	û	u Circumflex		185	B9	╣	
151	97	ù	u Grave		186	BA	║	
152	98	ÿ	y Dieresis		187	BB	╗	
153	99	Ö	O Dieresis		188	BC	╝	
154	9A	Ü	U Dieresis		189	BD	╜	
155	9B	¢	Cent		190	BE	╛	
156	9C	£	Pound		191	BF	┐	
157	9D	¥	Yen		192	C0	└	
158	9E	Pt			193	C1	┴	
159	9F	*f*	Florin		194	C2	┬	
160	A0	á	a Acute		195	C3	├	
161	A1	í	i Acute		196	C4	─	
162	A2	ó	o Acute		197	C5	┼	
163	A3	ú	u Acute		198	C6	╞	

Appendix D

199	C7	⊩		228	E4	Σ		Sigma
200	C8	▪		229	E5	σ		sigma
201	C9	⊩		230	E6	μ		mu
202	CA	⊥		231	E7	γ		gamma
203	CB	⊤		232	E8	φ		phi
204	CC	⊩		233	E9	Θ		theta
205	CD	=		234	EA	Ω		Omega
206	CE	✚		235	EB	δ		delta
207	CF	⊥		236	EC	∞		Infinity
208	D0	⊥		237	ED	⌀		Not Infinite
209	D1	⊤		238	EE	∈		Element of
210	D2	π		239	EF	∩		Intersection
211	D3	⊔		240	F0	≡		Equivalence
212	D4	⊢		241	F1	±		Plus/Minus
213	D5	⊢		242	F2	≥		Greater Than
214	D6	π		243	F3	≤		Less Than
215	D7	⊩		244	F4	⌠		Integral Top
216	D8	≠		245	F5	⌡		Integral Bottom
217	D9	⌐		246	F6	÷		Division
218	DA	⌐		247	F7	~		Approximate
219	DB	■	Full Box	248	F8	°		Degree
220	DC	▬	Bottom Box	249	F9	•		Bullet
221	DD	▮	Left Box	250	FA	·		Centered Period
222	DE	▮	Right Box	251	FB	√		Radical
223	DF	▬	Top Box	252	FC	ⁿ		Superscript n
224	E0	α	alpha	253	FD	²		Superscript 2
225	E1	β	beta	254	FE	■		Box
226	E2	Γ	Gamma	255	FF			
227	E3	π	pi					

Appendix E
OPERATOR PRECEDENCE TABLE

Operator	Level	Evaluation Direction	Function
::	1	Right	global scope
::	1	Left	class scope
->	2	Left	member selection
.	2	Left	member selection
[]	2	Left	indexing
( )	2	Left	function call
( )	2	Left	type constructor
sizeof( )	2	Left	object size
++	3	Right	increment
--	3	Right	decrement
~	3	Right	bitwise NOT
!	3	Right	logical NOT
+	3	Right	unary plus
-	3	Right	unary minus
*	3	Right	dereference
&	3	Right	address of
( )	3	Right	type cast
new	3	Right	object constructor
delete	3	Right	object destructor
->*	4	Left	member pointer selection
.*	4	Left	member pointer selection
*	5	Left	multiplication
/	5	Left	division
%	5	Left	modulus
+	6	Left	addition
-	6	Left	subtraction
<<	7	Left	left shift
>>	7	Left	right shift
<	8	Left	less than
<=	8	Left	less than or equal
>	8	Left	greater than

Appendix E

Operator	Level	Evaluation Direction	Function
>=	8	Left	greater than or equal
==	9	Left	equal (relational)
!=	9	Left	not equal
&	10	Left	bitwise AND
^	11	Left	bitwise XOR
|	12	Left	bitwise OR
&&	13	Left	logical AND
||	14	Left	logical OR
?:	15	Left	conditional evaluation
=	16	Right	basic assignment
*=	16	Right	multiplication assignment
/=	16	Right	division assignment
%=	16	Right	modulo assignment
+=	16	Right	addition assignment
-=	16	Right	subtraction assignment
<<=	16	Right	left shift assignment
>>=	16	Right	right shift assignment
&=	16	Right	bitwise AND assignment
^=	16	Right	bitwise XOR assignment
|=	16	Right	bitwise OR assignment
,	17	Right	sequential operator

Appendix F
KEYBOARD SCAN CODE TABLE

Key	Scan code (hex)	Scan code (decimal)	Key	Scan code (hex)	Scan code (decimal)
Esc	01	1	F	21	33
!1	02	2	G	22	34
@2	03	3	H	23	35
#3	04	4	J	24	36
$4	05	5	K	25	37
%5	06	6	L	26	38
^6	07	7	:;	27	39
&7	08	8	"'	28	40
*8	09	9	~	29	41
(9	0A	10	←Shift	2A	42
)0	0B	11	| \	2B	43
_-	0C	12	Z	2C	44
+=	0D	13	X	2D	45
Backspace	0E	14	C	2E	46
←/→	0F	15	V	2F	47
Q	10	16	B	30	48
W	11	17	N	31	49
E	12	18	M	32	50
R	13	19	<,	33	51
T	14	20	>.	34	52
Y	15	21	/?	35	53
U	16	22	→Shift	36	54
I	17	23	PrtSc*	37	55
O	18	24	Alt	38	56
P	19	25	Spacebar	39	57
{[	1A	26	Caps lock	3A	58
}]	1B	27	F1	3B	59
Return	1C	28	F2	3C	60
Ctrl	1D	29	F3	3D	61
A	1E	30	F4	3E	62
S	1F	31	F5	3F	63
D	20	32	F6	40	64

Appendix F

Key	Scan code (hex)	Scan code (decimal)	Key	Scan code (hex)	Scan code (decimal)
F7	41	65	Minus sign	4A	74
F8	42	66	4 ←	4B	75
F9	43	67	5	4C	76
F10	44	68	6 →	4D	77
F11	D9	217	+	4E	78
F12	DA	218	1 End	4F	79
Num lock	45	69	2 ↓	50	80
Scroll lock	46	70	3 PgDn	51	81
7 Home	47	71	0 Ins	52	82
8 ↑	48	72	Del	53	83
9 PgUp	49	73			

Appendix G
EXTENDED KEY CODE TABLE

ASCII Characters = ASCII Code

Special Keys = NULL+Code (The following Code)

Code	Key	Code	Key
3	Null	61	F3
15	Reverse Tab	62	F4
16	Alt Q	63	F5
17	Alt W	64	F6
18	Alt E	65	F7
19	Alt R	66	F8
20	Alt T	67	F9
21	Alt Y	68	F10
22	Alt U	71	Home
23	Alt I	72	Up Arrow
24	Alt O	73	PgUp
25	Alt P	75	Left Arrow
30	Alt A	77	Right Arrow
31	Alt S	79	End
32	Alt D	80	Down Arrow
33	Alt F	81	PgDn
34	Alt G	82	Insert
35	Alt H	83	Delete
36	Alt J	84	Shift F1
37	Alt K	85	Shift F2
38	Alt L	86	Shift F3
44	Alt Z	87	Shift F4
45	Alt X	88	Shift F5
46	Alt C	89	Shift F6
47	Alt V	90	Shift F7
48	Alt B	91	Shift F8
49	Alt N	92	Shift F9
50	Alt M	93	Shift F10
59	F1	94	Ctrl F1
60	F2	95	Ctrl F2

Appendix G

Code	Key	Code	Key
96	Ctrl F3	119	Ctrl Home
97	Ctrl F4	120	Alt 1
98	Ctrl F5	121	Alt 2
99	Ctrl F6	122	Alt 3
100	Ctrl F7	123	Alt 4
101	Ctrl F8	124	Alt 5
102	Ctrl F9	125	Alt 6
103	Ctrl F10	126	Alt 7
104	Alt F1	127	Alt 8
105	Alt F2	128	Alt 9
106	Alt F3	129	Alt 0
107	Alt F4	130	Alt -
108	Alt F5	131	Alt =
109	Alt F6	132	Ctrl PgUp
110	Alt F7	133	F11
111	Alt F8	134	F12
112	Alt F9	135	Shift-F11
113	Alt F10	136	Shift-F12
114	Ctrl PrtSc	137	Ctrl-F11
115	Ctrl Left Arrow	138	Ctrl-F12
116	Ctrl Right Arrow	139	Alt-F11
117	Ctrl End	140	Alt-F12
118	Ctrl PgDn		

Appendix H
TURBO C++ EXERCISES

1. About This Book
    a. Explain the advantages of the C++ language over other languages like BASIC or Pascal.
    b. Describe two features of object-oriented programming.
    c. What are the minimum hardware requirements for running Turbo C++?
    d. List three personal reasons why you want to learn to program in C++. The more specific your reasons, the more you can learn from this book.
2. Program Overview
    a. List three features of Turbo C++.
    b. Name three ways to display the Turbo C++ pull-down menus.
    c. How can you use the Turbo C++ hypertext help system?
    d. Why would you want to hide the more advanced features of Turbo C++ from the menus?
    e. Explain how the Turbo C++ debugger can help you write programs that work correctly.
3. A Sample Session with Turbo C++
    a. Explain "debugging."
    b. What are "functions"?
    c. What is the name of the one function every Turbo C++ program must have?
    d. Which function key will save your file?
4. Compile menu
    a. What is a "project" and why would you use one?
    b. How can you use .OBJ files with other languages?
    c. List three ways to display the Compile menu.
5. Debug menu
    a. What does the Inspect command do and why would you use it?
    b. Explain how you can use the Evaluate/Modify command to debug your programs.
    c. Why would you want to use the Watches command?
    d. What are breakpoints and how can you use them?
6. Edit menu
    a. How can you select text in a window using the keyboard? Using the mouse?
    b. What does the Copy Example command do?
    c. What is the difference between the Cut and Clear commands?
    d. What does the Restore Line command do? What are its limitations?

Appendix H

7. File menu
   a. Which command lets you save a file under a different name?
   b. List three ways to display the File menu.
   c. What type of information does the Get Info command show?
   d. How can you print only a portion of a file?
   e. What is the difference between the DOS Shell and the Quit command?
   f. Which keys can you press to choose the Quit command without displaying the File menu?

8. Help menu
   a. What type of information does the Contents command give? The Index command? The Topic Search command? The Help on Help command?
   b. Which command would you use to find help on a specific topic or Turbo C++ command?
   c. Which command would you use to display help on the C++ language?
   d. List four ways to display the Help menu.

9. Options menu
   a. What does the Options menu let you do?
   b. What does turning on the Full Menus command do?
   c. Which command lets you change the appearance of the Turbo C++ integrated environment?
   d. How can you change the way Turbo C++ optimizes your programs? When should you change these values?

10. Project menu
    a. What makes up a project?
    b. List three ways to display the Project menu.
    c. How can you change the options that Turbo C++ uses to work with project files?

11. Run menu
    a. What is the difference between the Run command and the Trace command?
    b. Give two reasons for using the Go to cursor command.
    c. What is the difference between the Trace and the Step over commands?
    d. What does the Arguments command do and why would you want to use it?

12. Search menu
    a. Name the six different search criteria.
    b. How can you use the Locate Function command when debugging your programs?
    c. Which window needs to appear on the screen to use the Previous Error and Next Error commands?
    d. How can you tell Turbo C++ to automatically replace text when using the Replace command?

13. System menu
    a. List three ways to display the System menu.
    b. Describe where the System menu appears on the Turbo C++ menu bar at the top of the screen.

c. What is the difference between the Clear Desktop and Repaint Desktop commands?
  d. How can you use the System menu to run and install other programs like Turbo Assembler or Turbo Debugger?

14. Window menu
    a. List three ways to display the Window menu.
    b. What is the difference between the Tile and Cascade commands?
    c. Which function key can you press to quickly resize a window to fill the entire screen?
    d. What does the User Screen display do and why would you use it?
    e. Why would you use the Project Notes command?
    f. What does the List command do?
    g. What does the Register command do?

15. # stringizing operator
    a. Give one use for the # stringizing operator.
    b. Why would you want to store a complicated, but frequently needed, statement as a preprocessor macro name?

16. ## token pasting operator
    a. What does the ## token pasting operator do?
    b. How can you use the ## token pasting operator to create multiple variables?
    c. If you didn't use the ## token pasting operator, how else could you create multiple variables with similar names?

17. #define and #undef
    a. What is a macro?
    b. Name two advantages to using the #define command to define a macro.
    c. Why would you want to use the #define command to define macro names for program statements?
    d. How can you only compile certain parts of your program using the #define, #ifdef, or #ifndef commands?

18. #error
    a. What does the #error directive do and why would you want to use it?
    b. How can you use the #error directive to display messages to the user?

19. #if, #elif, #else, #endif
    a. List three ways you can use the #if, #elif, #else, and #endif preprocessor commands.
    b. Why would you want to use logical operators with the #if preprocessor?

20. #ifdef and #ifndef
    a. What is conditional compilation and why would you want to use it?
    b. Write down the correct syntax for using the #ifdef and #ifndef commands with #endif, #elif, and #else.
    c. How can you use the #ifdef and #ifndef commands for writing C++ programs to run on different operating systems?

Appendix H

21. #include
    a. What is structured programming and why would you want to use it?
    b. What is modular programming and how does it differ from structured programming?
    c. Write down the two ways to list header files with the #include directive.
    d. What are header files?

22. #line
    a. What does the #line directive do?
    b. What is the primary use for the #line directive?

23. #pragma
    a. What does the #pragma command do and how does it relate to specific compilers like Turbo C++?
    b. List the seven pragmas that Turbo C++ supports.
    c. Which pragma should you use to set up certain conditions before program execution?

24. Advanced Data Types
    a. List five advanced data types.
    b. Which data type lets you define sets?
    c. What is the difference between structures and unions?
    d. How can you use typedef data types to make your programs easier to read and understand?

25. Arithmetic Operators
    a. What is the difference between unary and binary operators?
    b. What is the difference between prefix and postfix when used with the increment and decrement operators?
    c. List the precedence of arithmetic operators.
    d. What happens if you mix data types, such as integers with float, while using arithmetic operators?
    e. Why should you use the increment and decrement operators instead of adding or subtracting 1 from a value?

26. Assembly Language
    a. List the two ways you can embed assembly language instructions in a Turbo C++ program.
    b. Why would you want to use assembly language in your Turbo C++ programs?
    c. What other programs may you need to use to mix assembly language programs with Turbo C++?

27. Assignment Operators
    a. What does the simple assignment operator do?
    b. What are the four items you can assign a variable to using the simple assignment operator?
    c. How can compound assignment operators save space?
    d. What is a disadvantage to using compound assignment operators?

28. Basic Data Types
    a. List the four basic data types in Turbo C++.
    b. List the five different varieties of integer types. Include their ranges and how much memory (in bytes) each data type uses.
    c. Why can you represent characters in C++ as integers?
    d. Why do you need to assign variables to data types?
    e. What is casting and why would you want to use it?
    f. How can you use data types to make your programs more efficient?

29. Break
    a. What does the break statement do inside a do-while, for, switch, or while statement?
    b. What happens if you omit the break statement inside a switch statement?

30. Byte Operators
    a. What do the byte operators do?
    b. Would you use byte operators as a beginning Turbo C++ programmer?
    c. Which byte operators can you use to perform faster multiplication and division?

31. Class Operators
    a. List the three class operators.
    b. What does the new constructor operator do?
    c. When would you need to use the :: scope access operator?

32. Classes
    a. What are classes and how do they differ from ordinary data structures like arrays or structures?
    b. List the three levels of accessibility with classes.
    c. List the three ways to define a class.
    d. What is the default level of accessibility for creating a class with the struct keyword? For the union keyword? For the Class keyword?
    e. What is the difference between data members and member functions?

33. Comments
    a. Describe three ways to include comments in your program.
    b. Give two reasons for using comments.
    c. What are the two ways to comment out multiple lines of code? To comment out a single line of code?

34. Continue
    a. How does the continue statement differ from the break statement?
    b. What does the continue statement do?

35. Do-while
    a. List two other ways to create a loop in turbo C++.
    b. At the very least, how many times will a do-while loop run?
    c. How can you avoid an endless loop?
    d. How can you replace a do-while loop with a while loop?

Appendix H

36. For
    a. Write down the syntax for a while loop.
    b. how can you avoid an endless loop?
    c. Explain how the for loop differs from a do-while loop.

37. Function Definition
    a. How many functions can a C++ program contain?
    b. What are function prototypes and how can they help you write error-free programs?
    c. Why should you use functions at all?

38. Goto
    a. What does the goto statement do?
    b. What are two alternatives to using the goto statement?
    c. What is a label and why do you need one when using a goto statement?

39. Identifiers
    a. What must be the first character of an identifier?
    b. How many characters can you use in an identifier? How many are "significant"?
    c. What does an identifier represent?
    d. What is meant by case sensitive? How does this affect the way Turbo C++ treats identifiers?
    e. How can you use identifiers to make your programs easier to read and understand?

40. If-else
    a. List at least three variants of the if-else statement.
    b. When would you need to use the if-else statement?
    c. Besides Boolean values (true or false), what else can you use to check a condition in an if-else statement?

41. Inheritance
    a. Explain what inheritance does and its advantages.
    b. Can you use inheritance with other data types besides classes?
    c. What is multiple inheritance?

42. Logic Operators
    a. What do logic operators do?
    b. List the four types of logic operators.
    c. List the four types of relational operators.
    d. List the two types of equality operators.
    e. List the three types of logic operators.
    f. Write down the syntax for the condition operator.

43. Memory Models
    a. How do memory models affect the way your program works?
    b. List the six different memory models and explain the uses for each.
    c. Describe two ways to change memory models before compiling your programs.
    d. What do pointer modifiers do?

44. Miscellaneous Operators
    a. What is the proper syntax for using the type cast operator for converting integer data types to float?
    b. How can you find the size of an object measured in bytes?
    c. What is the difference between the structure member reference operator and the structure member selector?
    d. Why would you want to use the scope access operator?
45. Overloading
    a. How can overloading function names make your programs easier to understand?
    b. Give an example of a built-in overloaded operator and explain how it works.
    c. List five operators you cannot overload.
46. Pointer Operators
    a. Explain the difference between variables and pointers.
    b. Which operator lets you retrieve the address of a variable?
    c. What is the syntax for creating multidimensional arrays?
    d. What is the difference between explicit and implicit arrays?
    e. How can you define a string with an array?
47. Printf( ) and scanf( )
    a. Write down the syntax for the printf( ) function and explain the purpose of part.
    b. What is the suppression character and how does it work?
    c. What is the character escape and why would you use it?
48. References
    a. Which is more efficient, passing arguments to a function by reference or by value?
    b. List the reference and dereference operators.
    c. Explain why you would need to dereference an item.
49. Storage Class Specifiers
    a. List the five types of storage class specifiers.
    b. Which of the five types is the default storage class specifier?
    c. Why is the register storage class rarely necessary?
    d. How can you declare a global variable that is declared in a separate file?
    e. How does the static storage class affect the value of a variable through repeated function calls?
50. Streams
    a. Explain what a stream is and how it works.
    b. What are the three standard streams provided by Turbo C++?
    c. Why would you ever need to redirect a stream?
    d. How can you open a file as a stream?
    e. What is the difference between text and binary streams?
51. Switch
    a. What is an alternative to using the switch statement?
    b. If you need to control execution using ranges or multiple variables, should you use the if-else or the switch statement?
    c. Which is faster, the if-else statement or the switch statement?

Appendix H

52. While
    a. At the very least, how many times will a while loop execute?
    b. What is a null-body while loop and why would you want to use it?
    c. How can you prevent an endless loop in the while statement?

53. Classification Routines
    a. List all twelve classification routines and explain what each one does.
    b. What is the difference between the iaslnum and the isalpha classification routines?
    c. What is the range for foreign language or math characters?
    d. What is the range for whitespace characters such as tab, line feed, and form feed?

54. Conversion Routines
    a. How could you convert a number (represented as a string) into an actual number?
    b. What is the main difference between the ecvt( ) function and the fcvt( ) function?
    c. Name three functions that convert strings to numbers.
    d. Name five functions that convert numbers to strings.

55. Diagnostic Routines
    a. Name the three diagnostic routines and explain what they do.
    b. Why should you avoid using the matherr( ) function?
    c. How can you comment out multiple assert( ) statements?

56. Directory Control Routines
    a. Which header file must you include to use directory control routines?
    b. Why would you want to control directories from within your programs?
    c. Which two routines search for individual file names?
    d. Why would you need to know the current disk drive to manipulate directories?

57. Graphics Routines
    a. Are the Turbo C++ graphic routines common in all C compilers or specific to Turbo C++?
    b. Which header file must you include to use these graphic routines?
    c. What is the difference between the cleardevice( ) and the clearviewport( ) routines?
    d. Which routine will check to see what type of graphics hardware is installed in the computer?
    e. How would you fill a defined area with a specific color or pattern?
    f. List the fifteen background colors available.
    g. List the five types of lines Turbo C++ can draw.
    h. Which function will restore graphic specifications to the default values?

58. Input/output Routines
    a. What must you do to update streams?
    b. List the three common errno values.
    c. List six file attributes that the _chmod( ) function retrieves.
    d. What is the difference between the scanf( ), cscanf( ), and fscanf( ) functions?
    e. Which functions detect an EOF in a stream?

59. Interface Routines
    a. List six functions that let you access interrupts.
    b. Why shouldn't beginners use interface routines?
    c. Which header file must you include to use these interface routines?
    d. Name the two functions that get the File Allocation Table information (FAT).

60. Manipulation Routines
    a. Which header file must you include to use these manipulation routines?
    b. What is the difference between the memcpy, memccpy, movedata, and the memmove routines?
    c. What is the difference between the memcmp and the memicmp routines?

61. Math Routines
    a. List all the functions that return the absolute value of a number.
    b. What is the difference between the atan and the atan2 functions?
    c. What do the randomize and srand functions do and why might you use them prior to using the rand or random functions?
    d. How can you convert radians to degrees and vice versa?
    e. Which header file must you include to use these math routines?

62. Memory Allocation And Checking Routines
    a. Which functions depend on the type of memory model used?
    b. What is the difference between the malloc( ) and the farmalloc( ) functions?
    c. Which header file must you include to use these memory allocation and checking routines?

63. Miscellaneous Routines
    a. How does the longjmp( ) routine work and why would you use it?
    b. How can you use the sound( ), delay( ), and nosound( ) functions to create music?
    c. Why is the setlocale( ) function used in Turbo C++?

64. Process Control Routines
    a. Explain the difference between the exec and the spawn routines.
    b. What is the difference between the abort, _exit, and exit routines?
    c. Which header file must you include to use these process control routines?

65. Standard Routines
    a. How do the bsearch and the qsort functions work?
    b. What is the difference between the atexit and the system functions?
    c. Besides using the system( ) function, how else could you temporarily exit a program to return to DOS?
    d. Which header file must you include to use these standard routines?

66. String Routines
    a. Explain the difference between the strcmp, strcmpi, and the strcoll functions.
    b. Which header file must you include to use these string routines?
    c. How does the strcpy function differ from the strdup function?
    d. Why would you want to use stricmp, the function version of strcmpi( )?

Appendix H

67. Text Window Display Routines
   a. Give two reasons why you would want to display text in a window on the screen.
   b. Which header file must you include to use these text window display routines?
   c. What is the difference between the clreol( ) and the clrscr( ) functions?
   d. What type of information does the gettextinfo( ) function return and what could you use it for?
   e. How does highvideo differ from normvideo and lowvideo?

68. Time And Date Routines
   a. What is the difference between the asctime( ) and the ctime( ) functions?
   b. What is the structure of timeb and why would you need to use this information?
   c. How can you retrieve the current date and time?
   d. Which header file must you include to use most of these time and date routines?

69. Variable Argument List Routines
   a. Which header file must you include to use these variable argument list routines?
   b. Explain the differences between the va_start( ), va_arg( ), and va_end( ) functions.
   c. In what order would you use these variable argument list routines?

Index

stringizing operator, 67, 179
token pasting operator, 69, 179
#define, 71
#else, 75
#elsif, 75
#endif, 75, 131
#error, 75
#if, 77
#ifdef, 72, 73, 81, 131
#ifndef, 73, 81
#include, 84
#line, 88
#pragma, 90
#undef, 71

A
abort, 329
About Turbo C++, 58
abs, 304
absread, 282
abswrite, 282
access, 257
acos, 305
Add item, 45
Add watch, 21, 373
Adjust colors, 382
allocmem, 317
arc, 233
arg, 305
Arguments, 51
Arithmetic operators, 102
ASCII table, 385
asctime, 362
asin, 305
Assembly language, 106
assert, 221
Assignment operators, 108
atan, 305
atan2, 305
atexit, 339
atof, 214
atoi, 215
atol, 215

B
bar, 233
bar3d, 233
bdos, 282
bdosptr, 282
Binary operators, 102
bioscom, 283
biosdisk, 284
biosequip, 286
bioskey, 286
biosmemory, 287
biosprint, 287
biostime, 288
Boolean, 111
Boolean operators, 158
Boolean relations, 158
break, 116
Breakpoints, 21
brk, 317
bsearch, 339
Build all, 17
Byte operators, 119

C
cabs, 306
Call stack, 20, 373
calloc, 317
Cascade, 61
ceil, 306
cgets, 258
Change dir, 33
chdir, 225
chmod and _chmod, 258
chsize, 259
circle, 234
class, 98, 127
Class operators, 123
Classes, 126
Classification routines, 211
Clear, 28, 374
Clear desktop, 58
cleardevice, 234
clearerr, 259
clearviewport, 234
Close, 61, 374

close and _close, 259
Close project, 45
closegraph, 234
clreol, 355
clrscr, 356
Command-line compiler, 375
Comments, 131
Compile menu, 16
Compile to OBJ, 17, 374
Compiler, 41
complex, 307
Condition operator, 164
Conditional compilation, 72, 75, 77
conj, 307
Contents, 36
continue, 135
Conversion routines, 214
Conversion, data type, 175, 214
Copy, 28, 374
Copy example, 28
coreleft, 317
cos, 307
cosh, 308
country, 288
cprintf, 259
cputs, 260
creat and _creat, 260
creatnew, 261
creattemp, 261
cscanf, 261
ctime, 362
ctrlbrk, 289
Cut, 28, 374
_clear87, 306
_control87, 307

D
Data type conversion, 175
Debug menu, 20
Debugger, 41
Defining macros, 71
delay, 325

405

Index

Delete item, 45
Delete watch, 21
delline, 356
detectgraph, 235
Diagnostic routines, 221
difftime, 363
Directories, 41
Directory control routines, 225
disable, 289
div, 308
do-while, 138
DOS shell, 33
dosexterr, 289
dostounix, 363
drawpoly, 236
dup, 261
dup2, 262

E
ecvt, 216
Edit menu, 27
Edit watch, 21
Editor commands, 381
ellipse, 236
enable, 290
enum, 96
Environment, 41
eof, 262
Equality operators, 164
Evaluate/Modify, 20, 373
execl, 331
execle, 331
execlp, 331
execlpe, 331
execv, 331
execve, 332
execvp, 332
execvpe, 332
exit and _exit, 332
Exiting a loop, 116, 135, 149
exp, 308
Extended key code table, 393

F
fabs, 308
farcalloc, 317
farcoreleft, 318

farfree, 318
farheapcheckfree, 318
farheapchecknode, 318
farheapcheck, 318
farheapfillfree, 319
farheapwalk, 319
farmalloc, 319
farrealloc, 319
fclose, 262
fcloseall, 262
fcvt, 216
fdopen, 262
feof, 263
ferror, 263
fflush, 263
fgetc, 263
fgetchar, 263
fgetpos, 263
fgets, 264
File menu, 32
filelength, 264
fileno, 264
fillellipse, 236
fillpoly, 236
Find, 53
findfirst, 226
findnext, 225
floodfill, 237
floor, 308
flushall, 264
fmod, 309
fnmerge, 226
fnsplit, 226
fopen, 264
for, 140
fprintf, 265
fputc, 265
fputchar, 265
fputs, 265
FP_OFF, 290
FP_SEG, 290
fread, 265
free, 320
freemem, 320
freopen, 266
frexp, 309
fscanf, 266
fseek, 266

fsetpos, 266
fstat, 266
ftell, 267
ftime, 363
Full menus, 41
Function definition, 11, 143
fwrite, 267
_fpreset, 309

G
gcvt, 216
geninterrupt, 290
Get info, 33
getarccoords, 237
getaspectratio, 237
getbkcolor, 237
getc, 268
getcbrk, 290
getch, 268
getchar, 268
getche, 268
getcolor, 238
getcurdir, 227
getcwd, 227
getdate, 363
getdefaultpalette, 239
getdfree, 290
getdrivername, 239
getdta, 291
getenv, 340
getfat, 291
getfatd, 291
getfillpattern, 239
getfillsettings, 239
getftime, 268
getgraphmode, 240
getimage, 240
getlinesettings, 240
getmaxcolor, 240
getmaxmode, 241
getmaxx, 241
getmaxy, 241
getmodename, 241
getmoderange, 241
getpalette, 241
getpalettesize, 241
getpass, 269
getpid, 333

Index

getpixel, 242
getpsp, 291
gets, 269
gettext, 356
gettextinfo, 356
gettextsettings, 242
gettime, 364
getvect, 291
getverify, 291
getviewsettings, 243
getw, 269
getx, 243
gety, 243
gmtime, 364
Go to cursor, 51, 373
Go to line number, 54
goto, 149
gotoxy, 357
graphdefaults, 243
grapherrormsg, 243
Graphics routines, 231
graphresult, 244
GREP, 373
_graphfreemem, 244
_graphgetmem, 244

H

harderr, 292
hardresume, 292
hardretn, 292
Header file, 84
heapcheck, 320
heapcheckfree, 320
heapcheckmode, 321
heapfillfree, 321
heapwalk, 321
Help, 373
Help menu, 36
Help on help, 37
highvideo, 357
hypot, 309

I

Identifiers, 154
if-else, 157
imag, 309
imagesize, 245
Include files, 46
Index, 36, 373

Inheritance, 160
initgraph, 245
inport, 293
inportb, 293
Input/output routines, 255
insline, 357
Inspect, 20, 374
installuserfont, 245
installuserdriver, 245
int86, 293
int86x, 293
intdos, 294
intdosx, 294
Interface routines, 280
intr, 294
ioctl, 269
isalnum, 211
isalpha, 211
isascii, 211
isatty, 270
iscntrl, 211
isdigit, 211
isgraph, 211
islower, 211
isprint, 211
ispunct, 211
isspace, 211
isupper, 211
isxdigit, 211
itoa, 217

K

kbhit, 270
keep, 294
Keyboard scan code table, 391

L

labs, 310
ldexp, 310
ldiv, 310
lfind, 340
line, 246
linerel, 246
lineto, 246
Link EXE file, 17
Linker, 41
List, 62, 374
Local options, 46

localeconv, 325
localtime, 365
Locate function, 54
lock, 270
log, 310
log10, 310
Logic operators, 163
longjmp, 326
lowvideo, 357
lsearch, 341
lseek, 270
ltoa, 217
_lrotl, 311
_lrotr, 311

M

Make, 41, 373
Make EXE file, 17
malloc, 321
Manipulation routines, 299
Math routines, 303
matherr, 221
Member functions, 127
memccpy, 299
memchr, 299
memcmp, 300
memcpy, 300
memicmp, 300
memmove, 300
Memory allocation and checking routines
Memory models, 169
memset, 300
Menu, 373
Message, 61
Miscellaneous routines, 325
Miscellaneous operators, 174
mkdir, 227
mktime, 365
MK_FP, 294
Mode for display, 382
modf, 311
Modular programming, 84
movedata, 300
moverel, 246
movetext, 357
moveto, 246

407

Index

movmem, 301

N
New, 33
Next error, 54, 374
Next, 61, 373
norm, 311
normvideo, 358
nosound, 326

O
Open, 33, 373
open and _open, 271
Open project, 45
Operator precedence, 103, 389
Operators
    Arithmetic, 102
    Assignment, 108
    Boolean, 158
    Byte, 119
    Class, 123
    Condition, 164
    Equality, 164
    Logic, 163
    Miscellaneous, 174
    Pointer, 182
    Precedence, 103, 389
    Relational, 163
Options menu, 40
outport, 294
outportb, 295
Output, 61
outtext, 246
outtextxy, 246
Overloading, 179

P
parsfnm, 295
Paste, 28, 374
peek, 295
peekb, 295
perror, 222
pieslice, 247
Pointer operators, 182
Pointers, 171
poke, 295
pokeb, 295
polar, 311

poly, 311
pow, 311
pow10, 312
Previous error, 54, 374
Previous topic, 37, 374
Print, 33
printf, 187
Process control routines, 329
Program reset, 50, 373
Project, 62
Project menu, 45
Project notes, 62
putc, 272
putchar, 272
putenv, 341
putimage, 247
putpixel, 247
puts, 272
puttext, 358
putw, 273

Q
qsort, 341
Quit, 33, 374, 382

R
raise, 333
rand, 312
randbrd, 295
randbwr, 296
random, 312
randomize, 312
read and _read, 273
real, 313
realloc, 322
rectangle, 247
References, 193
Register, 62
registerbgidriver, 247
registerbgifont, 248
Relational operators, 163
remove, 273
Remove all watches, 21
Remove messages, 17
rename, 273
Repaint desktop, 58
Replace, 54
Reserved words, 154
Restore line, 28

restorecrtmode, 248
rewind, 273
rmdir, 228
Run menu, 50
Run, 50, 373, 380
_rotl, 313
_rotr, 313

S
Save, 33, 41, 373
Save all, 33
Save configuration, 382
sbrk, 322
scanf, 187
Search, 379
Search again, 54
Search menu, 53
searchpath, 228
sector, 248
segread, 296
setactivepage, 248
setallpalette, 248
setaspectratio, 249
setbkcolor, 249
setblock, 322
setbuf, 274
setcbrk, 296
setcolor, 249
setdate, 365
setdisk, 228
setdta, 296
setfillpattern, 250
setfillstyle, 250
setftime, 274
setgraphbufsize, 250
setgraphmode, 250
setjmp, 326
setlinestyle, 251
setlocale, 327
setmem, 301
setmode, 274
setpalette, 251
setrgbpalette, 251
settextjustify, 251
settextstyle, 251
settime, 365
setusercharsize, 251
setvbuf, 274

408

Index

setvect, 296
setverify, 297
setviewport, 252
setvisualpage, 252
setwritemode, 252
Show clipboard, 28
signal, 333
sin, 313
sinh, 313
Size/move, 61, 373
sleep, 297
sopen, 275
sound, 327
spawnl, 335
spawnle, 336
spawnlp, 336
spawnlpe, 336
spawnnv, 336
spawnv, 336
spawnve, 336
spawnvp, 337
spawnvpe, 337
sprintf, 275
sqrt, 313
srand, 314
sscanf, 275
Standard routines, 339
stat, 275
Step over, 51, 373
stime, 365
Storage class specifier, 196
strcat, 345
strchr, 345
strcmp, 345
strcmpi, 346
strcoll, 346
strcpy, 346
strcspn, 347
strdup, 347
Streams, 202
strerror, 347
strftime, 366
stricmp, 347
String routines, 344
Strings, 184
strlen, 348

strlwr, 348
strncat, 348
strncmp, 348
strncmpi, 349
strncpy, 349
strnicmp, 350
strnset, 350
strpbrk, 350
strrchr, 351
strrev, 351
strset, 351
strspn, 351
strstr, 352
strtod, 217
strtok, 352
strtol, 218
strtoul, 218
struct, 97, 126, 184
strupr, 352
strxfrm, 352
swab, 342
switch, 206
system, 342
System menu, 58, 374
   textheight, 252
   textwidth, 252
_setcursortype, 250
_status87, 314

T

tan, 314
tanh, 314
tell, 276
Text window display
   routines, 355
textattr, 358
textbackground, 359
textcolor, 359
textmode, 359
Tile, 61
time, 366
Time and date routines, 362
tmpfile, 276
tmpnam, 276
toascii, 214
Toggle breakpoint, 21, 373
tolower and _tolower, 219

Topic search, 36, 373
toupper and _toupper, 219
Trace, 51, 373
Transfer, 41
Turbo Assembler, 58, 107,
   373
Turbo Debugger, 58, 373
Turbo Linker, 107
typedef, 98
tzset, 366

U

ultoa, 219
Unary operators, 102
ungetc, 276
ungetch, 277
union, 98, 127
unixtodos, 367
unlink, 297
unlock, 277
User screen, 62, 374

V

Variable argument list
   routines, 370
va_arg, 371
va_end, 371
va_start, 370
vfprintf, 277
vprintf, 277
VROOMM, 6
vscanf, 277
vsprintf, 278
vsscanf, 278

W

Watch, 62
Watches, 21
wherex, 359
wherey, 359
while, 209
window, 359
Window menu, 60
write and _write, 278

Z

Zoom, 61, 373

Other Books from Wordware Publishing, Inc.

Business-Professional Books
Business Emotions
The Business Side of Writing
Confessions of a Banker
Consulting Handbook for the High-Tech Professional
Hawks Do, Buzzards Don't
How to Win Pageants
Innovation, Inc.
Investor Beware
MegaTraits
Occupying the Summit
Steps to Strategic Management
To Be or Not to Be an S.O.B

Computer Aided Drafting
Illustrated AutoCAD (Release 9)
Illustrated AutoCAD (Release 10)
Illustrated AutoCAD (Release 11)
Illustrated AutoLISP
Illustrated AutoSketch 1.04
Illustrated AutoSketch 2.0
Illustrated GenericCADD Level 3

Database Management
The DataFlex Developer's Handbook
Illustrated dBASE III Plus
Illustrated dBASE IV
Illustrated dBASE IV 1.1
Illustrated FoxPro
Illustrated Paradox 3.0 Volume II (2nd Ed.)

Desktop Publishing
Achieving Graphic Impact with Ventura 2.0
Desktop Publisher's Dictionary
Handbook of Desktop Publishing
Illustrated PFS:First Publisher 2.0 & 3.0
Illustrated PageMaker 3.0
Illustrated Ready, Set, Go! 4.5 (Macintosh)
Illustrated Ventura 2.0
Illustrated Ventura 3.0 (Windows Ed.)
Illustrated Ventura 3.0 (DOS/GEM Ed.)
The Desktop Studio: Solutions for Multimedia with the Amiga
Ventura Troubleshooting Guide

General Advanced Topics
Illustrated Dac Easy Accounting 3.0
Illustrated Dac Easy Accounting 4.1
Illustrated Harvard Graphics 2.3
Illustrated Novell NetWare 2.15 (2nd Ed.)
Novell NetWare: Adv. Tech. and Applications
Understanding 3COM Networks

Integrated
Illustrated Enable/OA
Illustrated Framework III
Illustrated Microsoft Works 2.0
Illustrated Q & A 3.0 (2nd Ed.)

Programming Languages
Illustrated C Programming (ANSI) (2nd Ed.)
Illustrated Clipper 5.0
The DataFlex Developer's Handbook

Programming Languages (cont.)
The FOCUS Developer's Handbook
Graphic Programming with Turbo Pascal
Illustrated Turbo C++
Illustrated Turbo Pascal 5.5
Illustrated Turbo Pascal 6.0

Spreadsheet
Illustrated Lotus 1-2-3 2.01
Illustrated Lotus 1-2-3 Rel. 3.0
Illustrated Lotus 1-2-3 Rel. 2.2
Illustrated Microsoft Excel 2.10 (IBM)
Illustrated Microsoft Excel 1.5 (Macintosh)
Illustrated Quattro
Illustrated SuperCalc 5

Systems and Operating Guides
Illustrated Microsoft Windows 2.0
Illustrated Microsoft Windows 3.0
Illustrated MS/PC DOS 3.3
Illustrated MS/PC DOS 4.0 (6th Ed.)
Illustrated MS/PC DOS 5.0
Illustrated UNIX

Word Processing
Illustrated DisplayWrite 4
Illustrated Microsoft Word 5.0
Illustrated Microsoft Word for the Mac
Illustrated WordPerfect 1.0 (Macintosh)
Illustrated WordPerfect 5.0
Illustrated WordPerfect 5.1
Illustrated WordStar 3.3
Illustrated WordStar 6.0
Illustrated WordStar Professional (Rel. 5)
WordPerfect: Advanced Applications Handbook
WordPerfect Wizardry Adv. Tech. and Applications

Popular Applications Series
Creating Newsletters with Ventura
Desktop Publishing with WordPerfect
Learn DOS in a Day
Learn Microsoft Works in a Day
Learn Quattro Pro in a Day
Learn WordPerfect in a Day
Mailing Lists using dBASE
Object Oriented Programming with Turbo C++
Presentations with Harvard Graphics
WordPerfect Macros

Regional
Exploring the Alamo Legends
Forget the Alamo
The Great Texas Airship Mystery
100 Days in Texas: The Alamo Letters
Rainy Days in Texas Funbook
Texas Highway Humor
Texas Wit and Wisdom
That Cat Won't Flush
They Don't Have to Die
This Dog'll Hunt
Unsolved Texas Mysteries

Call Wordware Publishing, Inc. for names of the bookstores in your area
(214) 423-0090